THE CATHOLIC RECEPTION OF CONTINENTAL PHILOSOPHY IN NORTH AMERICA

The Catholic Reception of Continental Philosophy in North America

EDITED BY GREGORY P. FLOYD
AND STEPHANIE RUMPZA

UNIVERSITY OF TORONTO PRESS
Toronto Buffalo London

Toronto Buffalo London
utorontopress.com

ISBN 978-1-4875-0649-0 (cloth)
ISBN 978-1-4875-3429-5 (EPUB)
ISBN 978-1-4875-3428-8 (PDF)

Library and Archives Canada Cataloguing in Publication

Title: The Catholic reception of continental philosophy in North America / edited by Gregory P. Floyd and Stephanie Rumpza.
Names: Floyd, Gregory P., 1984–, editor. | Rumpza, Stephanie, 1986–, editor.
Description: Includes bibliographical references and index.
Identifiers: Canadiana (print) 20190206470 | Canadiana (ebook) 20190206535 | ISBN 9781487506490 (cloth) | ISBN 9781487534288 (PDF) | ISBN 9781487534295 (EPUB)
Subjects: LCSH: Catholic Church and philosophy – United States. | LCSH: Catholic Church and philosophy – Canada. | LCSH: Continental philosophy – United States. | LCSH: Continental philosophy – Canada.
Classification: LCC BX1795.P47 C38 2020 | DDC 261.5/1 – dc23

University of Toronto Press acknowledges the financial assistance to its publishing program of the Canada Council for the Arts and the Ontario Arts Council, an agency of the Government of Ontario.

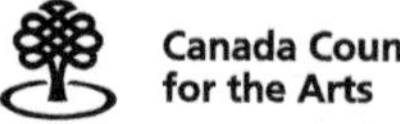

Conseil des Arts
du Canada

Funded by the Government of Canada | Financé par le gouvernement du Canada | Canada

Dedicated in loving memory to Rev. William Richardson, S.J.

He who seeks shall find;
He who knocks shall have the door opened (Mt. 7:7)

My wish for your work – for which you alone bear the responsibility – is this: May it help set in motion the manifold thinking of the simple business of thought, which, by reason of its very simplicity, abounds in hidden plenitude.

M. Heidegger to W. Richardson, April 1962

Contents

Acknowledgments

The idea for this volume originated at a conference, sponsored by the Marquette Lonergan Project, directed by Fr. Robert Doran, S.J., and designed by Jonathon Heaps. We first of all would like to thank them for calling attention to the questions that set the agenda for the work pursued in this volume. We would also like to thank Patrick Byrne and Jeffrey Bloechl for their wisdom and guidance in navigating the perils of collaborative scholarship and academic publishing.

A special thank you to those who have supported our work, first of all Dermot Moran and the Philosophy Department at Boston College, as well as Candace Hetzner and the Morrissey Graduate School of Arts and Sciences. We are also grateful for the support of the Lonergan Institute, particularly Kerry Cronin, and Msgr. Richard Liddy and the Center for Catholic Studies at Seton Hall University.

Finally, thank you to the editorial team at University of Toronto Press, guided expertly by Stephen Shapiro, for helping us tell the best version of a fascinating story.

THE CATHOLIC RECEPTION OF CONTINENTAL PHILOSOPHY IN NORTH AMERICA

Introduction: Catholics and Continental Thought – a Curious Allegiance

STEPHANIE RUMPZA

What has Freiburg to do with Rome? Or perhaps better, what has Freiburg to do with Washington, D.C.? Simon Critchley may have overstated his case by claiming that Continental programs in the United States are "mostly" found in Catholic universities "with some notable exceptions."[1] Yet it remains a fact that one out of every four of people who teach Continental philosophy do so within a Catholic program, and on the many lists of the top Continental programs in the United States, one finds a number of Catholic universities: Boston College, DePaul, Duquesne, Fordham, Loyola Chicago, and Villanova.[2] It remains the case today that there is a link here. But it is not much explored or studied.

Whatever else may be true, we can observe that in the history of North America, Continental philosophy and Catholicism share this commonality: they have been, for the most part in most places, marginal to their larger cultural and intellectual context. Excepting the earliest Anglo-Catholic settlers and the larger Franco-Catholic population of Canada, the vast majority of North American Catholics can trace their spiritual lineage back to the working-class immigrants who fought hard for recognition in the mostly Protestant New World. Similarly, "Continental" philosophy was transplanted across the sea first largely by European refugees fleeing the Second World War, into an intellectual and cultural context that was not very receptive to it. The term "Continental" itself is, of course, notoriously vague.[3] In the absence of a better one, this volume will focus on what we take to be the core of the "Continental" school proper: the philosophical traditions emerging in the wake of Husserl and Heidegger, including most notably phenomenology, existentialism, hermeneutics, deconstruction, and (to some extent) critical theory. Admittedly, the list might be enumerated differently by other people and at other moments in its development. But it is the most significant one for our purposes, for Catholics have historically supported these central branches of Continental philosophy, albeit with varying degrees of enthusiasm.

What prompted so many North American Catholics to support this school of thought? What spurred the flourishing of Continental philosophy on another continent, in the face of a philosophical environment that seemed often eager to stamp it out? Why do so many Catholics continue to find Continental philosophy attractive, and why do many Continental philosophers continue to work in Catholic departments? This volume aims to raise this question by presenting the basic reception history of the major strains of Continental philosophy up through the present day, while considering how and why this intellectual tradition is of interest to Catholic thinkers.

To understand this curious alliance, we must first know something about the historical, institutional, and intellectual background of the North American continent on which these intellectual traditions developed.

A Brief History of North American Philosophy

America has always been influenced by its religious roots. Prior to the Civil War, American philosophy was taught mainly by thinkers practising religion or at least friendly to it. Primary traditions included scholastic Puritanism, Deism, American transcendentalism, idealism, and pragmatism. Almost every significant intellectual was also religious in some way,[4] and most were deeply concerned with moral and personal development. Heading into the twentieth century, however, things began to change. Industrial development, a population boom, and 14 million new European immigrants rapidly increased American prosperity, and cultural attention was seduced toward materialism. Against the dominant force of idealism arose various movements of "naturalism," which entailed a denial of anything transcending nature, whether that be God or ideas. It was thus a force necessarily hostile to traditional religion. This stream of thought included the crude reductionism of empiricism, as well as the more refined process thought begun by Alfred North Whitehead and further permutations of pragmatism. Coming into full force in the 1930s, naturalism was the perfect preparation for American philosophy to welcome the exiled Vienna Circle with open arms. Reigning from their strategic footholds at Harvard, the University of Chicago, UCLA, and Iowa, these European logical positivists found their work adopted almost instantly as their elite students spread to premier institutions throughout the United States. Idealism managed to survive for a time under new forms in the American personalism movement, most notably through the work of Edgar Brightman and Borden Parker Brown at Boston University. However, philosophy during this time was under pressure to move beyond its idealist past, to abandon metaphysics, and to settle for a more sceptical, scientific approach, such as the one offered by logical positivism.

At the same time, there was some dissatisfaction about the state of philosophy among the broader public. With science seeming to have robbed religion of its prior force, many people believed that philosophy needed to step in as the voice of morality. It was generally understood that the task of philosophy was to advocate for the education of the whole human person, as we see from a 1945 conference that surveyed major cities and universities in the United States and Canada.[5] In a world that had just suffered through the Second World War, popular sentiment demanded a greater source of life's meaning than naturalism seemed able to provide.

Around this time, what we today call "Continental philosophy" began to take root. Several North Americans had studied with Husserl before the 1930s, but the great boost came with the influx of European scholars during the war. The institutions that welcomed them were often less prestigious than those hosting the logical positivists, and their influence on the field was slower to take hold; nevertheless, these programs would become important Continental havens in the following years. Fordham became home to Dietrich von Hildebrand in 1943 and Balduin Schwarz in 1947; while the New School of Social Research hosted Aron Gurwitsch, Alfred Schütz, and Hannah Arendt, in addition to Dorion Cairns, an American student of Husserl's. Duquesne University hosted a succession of visiting scholars from Europe through the 1940s, and Northwestern and Yale became increasingly friendly to the Continental tradition.[6]

During these years, that tradition was not yet firmly established on American soil. While phenomenologists were teaching, none of these programs were developed enough to form a cohort of graduate students in their tradition. The future American phenomenologists were receiving their training in Europe, particularly at the Husserl Archives at the Catholic University of Leuven, which had been established in 1939, when Franciscan priest and scholar Herman Leo van Breda brought Husserl's manuscripts there to save them from destruction at the hands of the Nazis. The work these North Americans would produce on returning to their native country was not primarily creative, but focused first on transposing European ideas into the context, language, and temperament of American culture – a particularly difficult task.[7] James Edie observed that the Husserlian transcendental ego was "clearly repugnant to post-Jamesian American philosophical temper," which in its practical and populist roots had an innate distaste for scholarly elitism and a strong interest in relating philosophy to lived experience.[8] At the end of the 1950s, Hebert Spiegelberg judged that the Husserlian phenomenological movement in America had begun to lose its momentum.[9]

That might have been the end of phenomenology in America if not for a second wave of Continental thought: existentialism. Existential phenomenology had been spreading through literature and theatre brought back by returning GIs; now it began to both awaken and answer the thirst for reflection on the meaning of life after the war and in the face of rapid scientific development.[10] Thanks to the presence of phenomenologists, this literary tradition was able to move into philosophy departments, bringing with it an interest in Merleau-Ponty and Heidegger. The new emphasis on the *Lebenswelt* was an important element in phenomenology's growth during this time, and it was this that drew the interest of John Wild. He had been unimpressed by his encounter with Husserl in the 1930s; however, his studies in France two decades later led him to discover Merleau-Ponty and the phenomenological life-world. Upon his return to Harvard in 1957, he insisted that his students set aside their Aristotle and begin to translate this new existentialist phenomenology.[11] Wild also joined a number of scholars in an attempt to bring phenomenology into conversation with the American intellectual heritage, renewing the prior efforts of Alfred Schütz.[12] As a result of these efforts to connect with American culture, existential phenomenology began to blossom through the late 1950s and into the 1960s.

The newer, French-inspired scholars, led by Wild, with their existential phenomenological interests, and the older, German-inspired scholars, led by Aron Gurwitsch, with their more classical phenomenological interests, came together in 1962 to found an alternative to the Anglo-American-dominated APA (American Philosophical Association): SPEP, the Society for Phenomenology and Existentialist Philosophy.[13] By the end of the 1960s, American phenomenologists were sharpening their scholarly rigour and training their own graduate students; meanwhile, more schools were hiring in phenomenology, translations were becoming available, and specialized scholarly societies were being founded, including the Husserl, Heidegger, and Merleau-Ponty Circles. The university presses of Duquesne and Northwestern began publishing significant lists in Continental thought. Penn State, Vanderbilt, Boston College, and Tulane soon joined the ranks of Continental schools, followed by Stony Brook.[14]

Interest in Heidegger was at its height during this decade, spurred by the popularity of Paul Tillich's Heideggerian-influenced theology in Protestant circles in the 1950s. The year 1962 saw the release of the much-anticipated translation of *Being and Time* by American philosopher Edward Robinson and Scottish theologian John Macquarrie. This was followed by New York Jesuit William Richardson's masterful 1963 work *Heidegger: Through Phenomenology to Thought*, the first English study of Heidegger from his early to his late period, which provided a scholarly foundation for confronting the still living giant.[15] Interestingly enough, Heidegger was adopted first and most strongly in America by theologians – he was a special favourite among Catholics. They felt a natural affinity with him, as they could sense in *Being and Time* his religious roots, however much he had attempted to cover them over. Moreover, they found in Heidegger a critique of Cartesianism and ontotheology, seeing in his work a long overdue corrections to the errors of the day.[16] Some of this enthusiasm for Heidegger was significantly dampened by Hans Jonas's highly critical keynote address at Drew University's conference on Heidegger and theology; other scholars, though, rallied around Richardson, who continued to defend Heidegger's importance as a thinker despite his notorious collaboration with Nazism.[17]

Thus we can see that even before the more obvious contemporary waves of phenomenology interested in religion, Catholics were from the beginning an important part of the tradition's reception. Some of the earliest programs in phenomenology were at Duquesne and Fordham, both Catholic institutions, and by the 1960s more Catholic universities had joined their ranks as leading Continental departments. As Caputo points out, some of the most significant scholars to promote phenomenology, especially in the 1960s, were Catholic or had been strongly influenced by theology.[18] Support for Continental philosophy did not come solely from Catholics, but it remains incontestable that Catholic thinkers and Catholic institutions have been strong supporters of Continental philosophy from its earliest days on the continent.

A Brief History of North American Catholicism

What influenced so many Catholics to champion Continental philosophy in America? To answer this question, we must first return to the late nineteenth century, a time when Catholics had largely withdrawn from contemporary intellectual life. Unwelcome at many secular and Protestant universities and uninterested in the atheist rationalisms of the day, most of them took refuge in fideism instead of confronting the modern world.[19] The First Vatican Council met to discuss these issues in 1879, and Pope Leo XIII, himself trained as a philosopher, issued the encyclical *Aeterni Patris* a decade later. Both insisted that the Catholic response to the problematic anti-religious modern philosophy was lacking and that intellectual error must be met with intellectual correction. As modern *philosophies* were the problem to be confronted, Catholics needed to look elsewhere for an intellectual system that would sustain their counteroffensive. Thomas Aquinas was put forward as the champion to help them face the errors of the day – in particular, a scepticism that one could know truth – and scholars began to take up his philosophy and theology with renewed vigour.[20]

This Thomism insisted that the task of philosophy is to study the first principles, the ultimate causes, to prepare us for our final end as human beings, that is, the beatific vision of God. It must do this by the light of human reason, which beginning from experience can truly reach an absolute and unchanging truth beyond it, unaided by the higher level of supernatural revelation, and untainted by the particularities of history, experience, or culture.[21] Against the excesses of extreme scepticism and extreme rationalism, philosophy ought to shun errors of "evolutionism," "psychologism," and "phenomenalism," which demoted being, respectively, to becoming, to the ego, or to mere appearance. Instead, it must have a measured confidence in reason's genuine achievements – for example, that the human person can be demonstrated to be a non-dualistic unity of matter and immortal spirit, with free will and innate knowledge of moral laws, and that the human being is made for an end beyond our natural capacities. Reason also leads us to know the existence of a free, personal, all-powerful God, who created the universe. Yet because God so transcends creation, reason also admits its limited capacity to know this God by its own power. In a traditional Neoscholastic model, philosophy is thus the "handmaid" for theology, demonstrating as far as it can, but open about the fact that reason alone fails to come to ultimate truth by its own means. In Catholic education, theology, with its supernatural gift of Revelation, is essential, for it explains that the person is in fact made for the final end of beatitude with God – made to perfect these efforts of human reason with a gift far beyond our native abilities and joyfully surpassing our wildest imagination. Philosophy is thus a *preparation* for theology, which is not weakness on the part of philosophy but simply the full dignity of the task laid out for it. In fact, such a relationship is important for theology as well, because theology needs a rational clarification of its concepts, questions, and methods. Because there is only one truth, neither theology nor philosophy should be threatened by this relationship, nor should natural science, for that matter. A genuine accomplishment in one field is a genuine accomplishment for all of human knowledge. To doubt the capacity of reason or the unity of truth is to bring about the disintegration of reality and the fragmentation of the individual.[22]

The force of this Neoscholastic school breathed new vigour into Catholic intellectual life and encouraged the study of sources, which in turn gave us the critical Leonine editions of Aquinas's works that are highly valued today. Yet the flaws of Neoscholasticism were also recognized by philosophers of the day. It lacked a basic historical and evolutionary sophistication, and worst of all, it was enforced. This muzzling of the spirit of philosophical inquiry often did not lead to authentic philosophy or even to Aquinas himself, but rather to "a closed, safe, and sterile Thomism, imposed by legislated authority," that aimed to vanquish its enemies rather than pursue the truth.[23] Where the rest of Western philosophical education emphasized original sources, Catholics distilled their Neoscholasticism into a flood of third-rate textbooks, which held sway especially in seminaries.[24] Many of the brightest minds of the twentieth century found this authoritarian Neoscholastic atmosphere stifling. Instead of meeting Cartesian rationalism and German idealism on an equal intellectual field, Catholics were often expected to meet them with textbook Thomism fideistically declared to be rational. Moreover, that fideism did not do justice to the original spirit of Thomas, having become infected along the way by the very non-Catholic modern philosophy it had originally been resurrected to defeat.[25] Some, including Chenu, Congar, Schillebeeckx, and de Lubac, tried to revive Aquinas by challenging dominant interpretations, by unearthing his historical influences, by revealing his relation to the biblical and patristic tradition, by putting forward traditional conversation partners as equally valid starting points, and by developing new and creative ways to expand on Thomistic ideas in conversations with contemporaries. Others, including Rahner, Lonergan, and Balthasar, drew from contemporary (and even secular) philosophical sources of inspiration outside of Aquinas, including idealism, phenomenology, hermeneutics, existentialism, and historicism.[26] The response of the Neoscholastics was predictably oppositional: most of these scholars were called to Rome to be questioned, and many had their teaching authority revoked.[27] Pius XII reinforced the Thomistic tradition in 1950 with *Humani Generis*. As Weisheipl observes, such a response only turned the ire of the scholars from Neoscholasticism to the teaching authority of the Church.[28]

It is important to note that Bernard Lonergan was the only North American at the forefront of these theological and philosophical movements. Many other Americans had been trained in Europe, but it took time for any of these ideas to be taken up in their native universities, and time for their universities to develop to a comparable level. For many years, Catholics were rarely among the social, intellectual, or economic elite on the mostly Protestant continent. While Catholics were a clear majority in French Canada, they were too often under the authority of the Anglo-Protestants (reflecting at times the obeisance of Catholic leaders), and this would eventually prompt a radical rejection of religion during the Quiet Revolution. In English-speaking North America, Catholics were found among the immigrant working classes of diverse nationalities, and by the time they began to gain a coherent cultural prominence they were often accused of anti-intellectualism and fascism.[29] Early Catholic universities were tasked not only with perpetuating Catholic tradition and culture but also with filling a significant education gap for their underprivileged students. Robert Hassenger went so far as to claim in 1967 that largely due to the struggle with this social and economic imbalance, "there is no real Catholic intellectual tradition in the United States."[30]

This began to change somewhat during the Catholic Renaissance of the middle decades of the twentieth century, which had been spurred by the embrace of the powerfully systematic Neoscholasticism, but it took time for the Catholic universities to win an established place among the country's top institutions. This was in part because Catholic universities very often emphasized tradition and apologetics over scholarship – a stance reinforced by flaws in institutional organization and by a clerical control that held deep reservations about the laity's competence.[31] Then again, the goal of a Catholic education was never simply to advance specialization or intellectual ability; rather, it was to facilitate the integral development of the whole person. Philosophy and theology were thus particularly important, for they helped a student understand and pursue his or her proper end as a human being; in its extreme form, philosophy was meant to impart a Catholic culture and way of life, even at the graduate level. Reflecting the early influence of the European model of education, philosophy was an essential requirement of Catholic colleges and universities, for seminarians as well as for lay undergraduates, most of whom took between twelve and eighteen credit hours.[32] For these reasons, despite their almost tribal loyalties, Catholics professed immediate support for the secular educational reforms of Abraham Flexner, Robert Hutchins, and Mortimer Adler, who praised Aquinas and Aristotle and tried to fight the fragmentation of overspecialization by reintroducing general education requirements in undergraduate programs in the 1930s.[33]

Even if Catholic universities did not have the elite history of a Harvard or Yale, trends in Catholic education had a strong statistical impact on American philosophy as a whole. While it is true that Catholics were isolated from other philosophical traditions by their own Thomistic language, their great emphasis on philosophy sealed their significance through sheer numbers: almost 30 per cent of all philosophy jobs in the United States during the 1960s were at Catholic programs, and of the swiftly increasing number of PhDs in philosophy awarded to Americans, one quarter were granted by Catholic institutions, particularly by the prominent graduate programs of Duquesne, Fordham, Georgetown, Marquette, St John's New York, St Louis, Notre Dame, Laval, Montreal, Ottawa, and the Medieval Institute of Toronto. The newly formed graduate programs at Boston College and DePaul were soon to join their ranks.[34]

Thomism continued to hold sway in America through the middle of the century. The ACPA (American Catholic Philosophical Association) during this time could very well have been called the American Thomistic Society, apart from the inclusion of a few token Franciscans.[35] Its strongest centres were in the middle of the continent: the Medieval Institute at the University of Toronto, which had been founded during the war by Jacques Maritain and Étienne Gilson, followed by the Catholic University of America, Notre Dame, St Louis University, and Marquette; French speakers would find themselves at the Neoscholastic departments of Laval, Ottawa, and Montreal. Because of their linguistic plurality and cultural ties to Europe, the great Catholic universities of Quebec were early to host top Continental thinkers, albeit first as easy foils for the "superior" Neoscholastic positions. But it was not long before Continental thinking began to have an appeal in its own right.[36]

By the early 1960s, even as the Neoscholastic bulwark of the Midwest continued to hold, European developments were beginning to trickle into North American universities, in large part because one out of every four Catholic academics had been trained abroad, primarily at Leuven, Fribourg, and the Gregorian in Rome.[37] Having taken root on the east coast, notably at Fordham, Duquesne, and Montreal, a new philosophy was being carried back into the classrooms by younger Catholic scholars – the trio (mentioned in one breath by writers of the 1960s) of phenomenology, existentialism, and personalism. This was due not to a refutation of Thomism, or to critical dialogue with it, but to a lack of interest entirely, particularly in the time and effort required to gain proficiency with its technical framework.[38] The brilliance of Gilson and Maritain was not enough to balance the flood of mediocre Neoscholastic philosophy, and the dusty world of textbook Aquinas and his schoolmen seemed impossibly out of touch with the concerns of the contemporary culture. The younger generation was rejecting the "complacent answers" of the Thomist manuals and looking for "something more restless, personal, existential, and psychologically meaningful."[39] The barriers separating Catholics from non-believers were no longer so culturally and intellectually entrenched. Quebec was vehemently rejecting its religious roots, and while the situation was not so drastic in anglophone North America, religion was beginning to detach itself from the institutions that had traditionally harboured it.[40] One could no longer assume that practising religion was a priority in students' lives, or that Catholicism's chosen philosophical spokesmen resonated with them. Alongside this weakening in religious traditions came the loss of a shared world made meaningful by God – yet this did not entail a loss of interest in religion altogether. Indeed, the growth of atheism injected a new urgency and vitality into the question of religion, leading to the famous 1966 *Time* article "Is God Dead?"[41] Meanwhile, alongside great economic and cultural growth in the Western world and the rise of globalism came an increasing sense of individual alienation. Education was becoming more fragmented as universities became increasingly specialized. The rise of technology and the growth of bureaucracy, both "material incarnation[s] of rationalism,"[42] had unseated the focus on human subjectivity. Horror still lingered over the Nazi atrocities that had arisen in a supposedly enlightened Europe.[43] The "disturbing paradox" was that "at the very time when man must unite as a race, he is disintegrating as a person."[44]

In the midst of this crossroads of identity, Pope John XXIII called for a new council that would address the role of the Church in the modern world. The Second Vatican Council first met in 1962, the same year SPEP was founded and *Being and Time* was released in English. North American Catholics, a large number of whom were already straining at the bit, were encouraged to enter more deeply into dialogue with the modern world and take up more openly the intellectual achievements of the age, without thereby discarding their tradition.

Navigating Traditions Then: Catholics and Continental Thought in the 1960s

In response to this invitation, scholars began to openly discuss alternatives to Neoscholasticism and future strategies for Catholic philosophy. The most obvious step was to return to the sources themselves, setting aside the textbook sedimentation and exploring Aquinas as a living and dynamic thinker, as was already being done by many European scholars, including, importantly, Gilson at Toronto. These changes were already being integrated into the North American academy and would continue into the future. But there was more to be done. If the intellectual context was no longer limited to the narrow rationalism of the late nineteenth century, the Catholic response would have to be re-evaluated.

We can catch a particularly interesting glimpse of the struggle to engage the other mid-century philosophical schools through a series of conferences held during the 1960s – including several held at the sole pontifical school in the United States, the Catholic University of America, as well as the flagship elite Catholic university, Notre Dame – to discuss the role of philosophical education in higher education in North America.[45] The papers presented at these gatherings represented a range of opinions and traditions, from the Heideggerian William Richardson, Husserlian-trained Dietrich von Hildebrand, and existentialist Wilfrid Desan, to Neoscholastics such as George Klubertanz and James Weisheipl and Thomistic-trained yet forward-looking Thomas Langan and Norris Clarke, not to mention those inspired by Analytic philosophy, process thought, and historicism. Despite their multitude of perspectives, these authors expressed many of the same interests and concerns, and although they were shaped by the intellectual climate of the time, it is evident how relevant many of their questions remain today. How, they asked, could Catholic philosophers go beyond the currently formative tradition of Neoscholasticism? At the very least, most were clear about *this*: one must avoid at all costs the extremes of scepticism and overconfidence, both of which undermine the philosophical spirit, either by denying the possibility of truth or entrenching one in stubborn denial of the pressing questions faced by the age. Yet, given this, what contemporary school of philosophy could be true to the aims of Catholic education? As we have said, the world of American philosophy had always been marked by pluralism, more so than the European centres, which had clearly centralized institutions of education.[46] These Catholics thus had a number of movements to consider when facing the philosophical world around them.

Exhausted by a century dominated by the overconfidence of idealism, Americans were largely taking the opposite course: a suspicion of transcendence altogether, and of course religion along with it.[47] As we have seen above, the largest family of American philosophy during this time fell under the reductive materialism of "naturalism," embracing schools of crude scientific empiricism, logical positivism, and the "analytic" thought that was heir to positivism's achievements.[48] Even if most Catholics, in their proud realism, shared this school's repugnance for idealism, they clearly had nothing in common with such a narrow understanding of truth and rationality.[49] Naturalistic philosophies were too immediately hostile to Catholic thinking to even be considered as a fitting vehicle for Catholic questions.[50]

Ordinary language philosophy, by contrast, was less evidently oppositional. Inspired by Wittgenstein's *Philosophical Investigations*, and developed in the work of Gilbert Ryle and J.L. Austin, this family of philosophers fought to "cure" philosophers of the desire for a grand system and a univocal language. Such systems may seem to do real work, but they are inevitably illusory, for they remove words from their only grounding in a meaningful form of life. While this school of thought was very uncomfortable for those deeply entrenched in the Neoscholastic system, it was not necessarily opposed to religion in all its forms, as the empirical philosophical schools were, even (or perhaps especially) where it urged a philosophical silence on the ineffable God. Some Catholics argued that its more moderate forms could be brought into productive conversation with interpretations of Aquinas and Aristotle, particularly a linguistic analysis of analogy.[51] Others valued its analytic clarity and rigour during this time of change and confusion.[52] Its insistence on bringing back philosophy to forms of life seemed to have a natural affiliation with religious practice. Pragmatists, too, shared this interest in resisting empty theorizing and bringing attention back to life.[53] As one of the few philosophies that was American in origin, its openness to religion developed in part out of its shared historical roots. The first pragmatist, William James, was after all the son of the religious philosopher Henry James. At the same time, many Catholics worried that American pragmatists and ordinary language philosophers were shying away from a sufficiently rich account of truth or meaning. Many viewed them as overly sceptical and limited to the surface, as reducing truth to a set of activities and ethical norms to mere convention or brute utility.[54] Even if it was less closed to Catholic thinking than naturalism, some questioned whether this branch of philosophy could do justice to the spiritual quest of the human person, the richness of truth, and the goodness and intelligibility of the created universe.

As for phenomenology, existentialism, and personalism, there was a similarly broad range of reactions. Most Catholic scholars of the time continued to be sceptical of Husserl, fearing a new Cartesianism and intellectual abstraction similar to logical positivism; some also found in phenomenology a descriptive, surface-level method of mere "appearance" and not essential reality, yet another form of relativism and subjectivism.[55] Yet, defenders argued, a phenomenology rooted in the lifeworld could avoid the worst of this abstraction and gather up the experience of the whole person. Such an existential phenomenology proclaimed the end of metaphysics, rejected logical systems aiming to present a unified truth, and often bracketed questions of God – yet it kept open a quest for meaning. Some felt a greater affinity with this existential search, interpreting it as an interior openness or desire for the transcendent God.[56] Others saw this more personal approach as a complement to the objective system of Thomism, a way of updating Neoscholasticism for the contemporary era. Unlike Neoscholasticism, it resonated deeply with the spirit of the age, because it sought to rescue the person from a society ruled by technology and to free truth from systems ruled by logical technicality or practical technique. Some Catholics believed that a philosophy that could integrate the person had the potential to integrate the overly specialized university, a role philosophy had first been given in medieval times and that was needed more than ever amid the fragmentation of modern education.[57] Others worried that the phenomenological method was powerless as an ethical system, for it did not sufficiently move to an evaluative stance, remaining too trapped in subjective experience and was thus too open-ended to discern good from evil. At the very least, however, the lived character of existential philosophy and its call for authenticity promised a greater openness of the person to the call of truth.[58]

Thus, while these Catholic philosophers considered all primary traditions of contemporary philosophy, there was a reason most preferred Continental thought; of the options given, an existentialist, personalist phenomenology seemed by many the most ready to meet the concerns of Catholic philosophy. By the end of the decade, Catholic philosophy departments, while still dominated by neo-Thomists, were opening up to other schools of thought. Philosophers who were pursuing traditions of empiricism, ordinary language philosophy, and pragmatism at Catholic universities made up only 9 per cent altogether, while over 20 per cent of philosophers teaching in Catholic departments identified themselves as phenomenologists, existentialists, or personalists.[59]

Thus, through the records left by these 1960s conferences, we can catch a glimpse of why many leading Catholic philosophers decided to offer a qualified welcome to Continental thinking. Yet perhaps we ought not to take this thinking at face value. After all, by what criteria were these philosophers judging what makes a good Catholic philosophy? Underpinning their evaluation was a particular set of assumptions that remained largely unquestioned. Many of them seemed to be only prepared to accept, as Catholics, a philosophy that served as a unifying system of truth, one that maintained the integrity of the person and upheld the proper degree of confidence in reason. That is, they had already decided in advance what philosophy must be, based on Neoscholastic principles. But if Neoscholasticism had been found wanting, and philosophy itself was in question, was it really so straightforward to recognize what a Catholic philosophy must or must not be? Perhaps they had not faced up to the truly radical nature of the questioning that was being demanded. At stake was not simply a series of different philosophical problems, or a change in philosophical tools, but a whole change in vision. As Leo XIII recognized, to resolve the nineteenth-century philosophical debates, Catholicism required a new frame, a development of its understanding of the nature of truth,[60] or as Lonergan describes it: one had to put the new wine into new wineskins.[61] Could twentieth-century concerns be answered in the same way? It is easy to limit oneself to the range of answers anticipated by an old philosophical framework, but this closes off answers that might come out of new philosophical thinking, that might address the central concerns of Catholic philosophy by an as yet uncharted path. At the same time, how can one take on a new frame without jettisoning the tradition of Catholic thinking that is so deeply bound with the Church's identity? Catholicism carries with it the weight of millennia of self-reflection. One cannot abandon this tradition and begin from nothing, for what remained would no longer be anything like Catholicism.

Surely we are not limited to these two extremes: *either* hollowing out contemporary philosophical traditions as a vehicle for Neoscholastic aims, *or* dissipating Catholic tradition and identity to fit whatever the contemporary schools are currently saying. But then who says which philosophy can fit with the Catholic tradition, and which cannot? Without plunging into the many intricate permutations of the twentieth-century debate over the coherence of the term "Christian philosophy," we can admit there is at least some initial tension in a tradition that claims at the same time the dignity of human reason and the necessity of a divinely given revelation that exceeds it. If faith and dogma give answers in advance, can Catholics really be open to truly rational thought? Neoscholasticism had argued its way to some harmony between philosophy and theology: philosophy prepares for revelation, and theology begins from the data of revelation, using philosophy's achievements to clarify its thinking. But to what extent can an originally non-Catholic philosophical tradition be a preparation for this divine revelation or an aid for structuring theological thinking? Of course, nothing binds us to Neoscholasticism's configuration of philosophy and theology, nor must we believe this relation is configured in precisely one way to begin with. Might there be still other ways of seeing the relationship of reason and revelation that would provide paths out of this dilemma? Without answering these questions, we can see clearly that the identity and nature of theology is bound up with that of philosophy for Catholic thinking.

Another question also arises: if the traditional philosophical framework of Catholicism vanishes, will the coherence of Catholic thought and Catholic institutions vanish along with it? Ernan McMullin goes so far as to argue that the fate of the Catholic university is bound up with its philosophy department, and should philosophy melt into secular thinking, it will dissolve the Catholic identity, following the fate of many traditionally Protestant universities.[62] As Philip Gleason argues, Neoscholasticism had given the "theoretical rationality for the existence of Catholic colleges and universities as a distinctive element in American higher education."[63] Without it, there was no clear sense of mission and purpose. This identity crisis of the Catholic university, caused by the identity crisis of philosophy, was waged in full force throughout the 1960s, and although the conversation has quieted, the problem has not been clearly solved today.[64]

Navigating Traditions Today

The challenges of philosophy, as we have begun to see, open onto a series of ever deepening questions that are intimately tied to the identity of Catholicism, of the university, and of the human person. Those questions have yet to find clear answers – indeed, sometimes they have yet to be posed clearly. But perhaps this is not a cause for despair. If we have learned anything from our "postmodern" philosophy (and here we must admit Continental as well as Analytic), it is that the desire for the security of ultimate answers and grand overarching systems is an "idolatrous" one.[65] Truth is compromised not by our failure to grasp it at once but rather by our arrogance in thinking we have definitively arrived at it. The philosopher must once again take up with tireless humility the Socratic quest, knowing that the love of wisdom is not yet the possession of it.

As Continental philosophy has pressed on since the 1960s, we have seen it spin out in directions both much more and much less hospitable to Catholic thought. Continental thinking in North America today has embraced new developments in phenomenology and existentialism so that its influence now extends from hermeneutics and deconstructionism to critical theory, psychoanalysis, and radical political theory. North America has played a critical role as host for original thinking across traditional institutional boundaries – particularly so regarding the connection between Continental philosophy and religion in the wake of the "theological turn" in French phenomenology.[66] But Continental thinking is not just for departments of philosophy and theology; it is also for departments of English, French, German, sociology, political science, communications, and rhetoric, and many Catholics have found themselves on this terrain.

If we have learned anything from developments in Continental thinking, it is that Catholic thinkers cannot live under the illusion that tradition means passing down truths as if they were dusty family heirlooms. Nor can they hide behind old names and old explanations. They must carry the past forward by continuing to think through its questions in a new context, in Aquinas as much as Heidegger, in Augustine as much as Wittgenstein – and yes, even in the Neoscholastics, who, in our contemporary haste to overthrow the old, have perhaps not always been given the generous attention they deserve.[67] Today, it seems, Catholics must learn to live with a plurality of philosophical paths, and whether this is the healthy plurality of a living tradition or the incoherent plurality of disintegration can be discovered only by entering the fray.

Our contributors to this volume take up precisely this work. The many dimensions of Continental thought offer fruitful insights as well as challenges for Catholic thinking, an interplay that extends well beyond what a single volume could fully present. Our task here is but to make a start, by exploring in dialogue some of the foundational questions concerning the relationship between Catholicism and Continental philosophy today. Our contributors here are thus philosophers and theologians working in North America who focus on the Continental movements that have been most influential for Catholics. They raise again the questions of how this alliance came to be and why, and they propose new ways Catholics might respond to this alliance in the future. They describe the intellectual, institutional, systematic, and historical conditions that shed light on our present situation, and they anticipate future challenges to it. They test ways these traditions can be configured in alliance, recognizing both the powerful advantages as well as the significant dangers to the identity of each tradition. By taking a stance on this evolving relationship between Catholics and Continental philosophy, many of them serve as living demonstrations that this productive reception is far from over.

In chapter 1, Daniel Dahlstrom follows the top Catholic philosophy departments as they engaged with phenomenology during the critical phases of its development, from 1950 to 1980. Focusing primarily on the German tradition, especially Husserl and Heidegger, he provides concrete information about leading scholars, institutional origins, and graduate dissertations. He then reflects on this data, examining the differences between the Catholic and the secular engagement with these traditions, why the Catholics were attracted to the phenomenological tradition, and where they continued to maintain reservations.

In chapter 2, Gregory P. Floyd examines in detail the meeting of Neoscholasticism and Continental philosophy in the twentieth century. Floyd uses Bernard Lonergan as a test case of the Catholic relationship to Continental thought, from suspicion to appreciation. Lonergan recognized in particular a shared desire for authenticity and a robust understanding of the "world mediated by meaning." Nevertheless, he also maintained important points of tension with Continental philosophy in his critical realism and insistence on continuing to rethink metaphysics.

John D. Caputo has been a leading figure in the reception of Continental thought in North America, so it is only fitting that his chapter 3, in bridging past and present, should turn at times to personal memories. He recounts the early days of Continental philosophy that led to the first meeting of the SPEP, which he attended, as well as the context in which it was it was embraced by Catholics as well as Protestants and Jews. Given this latent religious interest among its adherents, Caputo argues that a "theological turn" was almost inevitable for Catholics and non-Catholics alike. Caputo highlights in particular the critical importance of the hermeneutic tradition for Catholics, particularly in the wake of Vatican II, and considers the challenges an American Continental philosophy will face as it moves forward.

In chapter 4, Patrick H. Byrne provides a case study of one Catholic institution's decision to open a doctoral program along the lines of Continental philosophy at a key moment in the 1960s. Beginning with the goal of a Neoscholastic education at Boston College and with a demonstrated failure to achieve it, Byrne recounts the philosophy department's attempt to remedy this problem by turning to phenomenology. He supports his analysis with his experience as a student and later as a professor and chair of philosophy. The possibility for this shift to Continental philosophy, Byrne argues, can be found in its openness to meaning, which resonates with many of the institutional and intellectual values constituent of Catholic higher education.

Jean Grondin recounts in chapter 5 the development of Continental thought in key parts of French Canada and its complicated relationship with Catholicism. The embrace of Continental thought occurred at the same time as the radical backlash against francophone universities' deeply Catholic heritage. Today, most French-speaking Canadian Continental philosophers shun religion entirely. Grondin suggests that this anti-religious sentiment has been a weak point in their philosophical tradition, and he encourages philosophers to enrich their thinking by opening themselves to dialogue with Catholicism once again.

Christina M. Gschwandtner focuses her chapter 6 on the "theological turn" in French phenomenology, a movement led largely by Catholics. She reflects critically on why this alliance of Catholics and phenomenology developed and how the cultural, institutional, and religious context of France has profoundly shaped its development. After giving an account of how this intellectual tradition has been appropriated across the Atlantic, Gschwandtner suggests ways in which the very different cultural, institutional, and religious context of North America, particularly its pluralism, was able to challenge and develop one of the most important contemporary philosophical traditions for many Catholic philosophers and theologians.

Andrew Prevot shows in chapter 7 how critical theory can be used for theology, unveiling hidden prejudices that irrationally privilege certain norms, often to the detriment of others. However, he also cautions that a truly Catholic critical philosophy must hold fast to doxological Christocentric hope instead of falling into nihilistic despair. He contextualizes the work of contributors O'Regan and Desmond as ways of bringing together the postmodern critique of metaphysics with critical theory for future theological work. Ultimately, Prevot argues for a plurality of philosophies for theological use, rather than one single system or one unified conversation. This does not, however, condemn Catholicism to incoherence. For it is not philosophy that unites Catholic thinkers, he claims, but their doxological Christocentric hope.

In chapter 8, Anne M. Carpenter provides a case study in how contemporary hermeneutics and phenomenology can help Catholic thought navigate a concern particular to North America: the role of science in theological thinking. In her discussion of how philosophy mediates access to scientific studies of memory and tradition, Carpenter proves it is possible to preserve the traditional role of philosophy in theological thinking without forcing philosophy to become a Neoscholastic rational system. Rather, harmony is reached precisely when each field allows the other its proper manner of arriving at meaning. While different in methods, they share this harmonious spirit: neither closes off meaning in advance; both remain open to further meaning.

Bruce Ellis Benson speaks about the reception of deconstruction and its importance for religion in chapter 9. He argues that Derrida was critical in opening up non-religious American Continental thinkers to a deeper engagement with religious questions. Benson recounts his role in founding the Society of Continental Philosophy and Theology in 1997, which united phenomenology, existentialism, deconstructionism, and critical theory with a genuine concern for theological thinking. Benson ends with a call to deepen the conversation – to move beyond textual analysis toward creative engagement, to expand the canon of authorities, and even to enter mutual engagement with Analytic philosophy of religion.

In chapter 10, Jeffrey Bloechl calls to our attention how phenomenology reveals very clearly the essential conflict of identities at stake in this encounter: the relation between Christianity and secular modernity. While the temptation has always been to shut out one side or the other, Bloechl seeks to preserve this tension between the two, thereby allowing a genuinely open dialogue of mutual critique between the two conversation partners. While interpretations will inevitably differ and consensus will not be reached, the particularity of shared experience gives us common ground. He argues that the Catholic university is an ideal place for this dialogue.

Chapter 11 finds William Desmond turning to one of the most pressing issues for a conversation between the Catholic tradition and Continental philosophy: the status of metaphysics. Continental thinking seems to offer a more faithful account of our historical and cultural condition than the rationalistic metaphysics of the Neoscholastics. In light of this Continental critique, Desmond insists that metaphysics must be chastened, though it need not be defeated altogether. By returning to the challenge of Hegel, he seeks to re-establish a transformed "metaxological" metaphysics, one that eschews the ultimate answers of rationalism to remain in the "in between": of totalization and scepticism, of poverty and plenty, of self and other, of possession and longing. Enriching our understanding of truth as fourfold, based on the fourfold plurivocity of being, helps us preserve a traditional sense of the intelligibility of being even while remaining at home in the mystery of its overdetermination.

Cyril O'Regan's chapter 12 reminds us that if Catholics have been enriched by the Continental tradition, many Continental thinkers have in turn been enriched by their engagement with Catholicism. He explores newer waves of Continental thinking that have been strongly influenced by the Christian idea of apocalypse, namely Alain Badiou, Giorgio Agamben, and especially Slavoj Žižek. The suspicions harboured by many Catholics toward these thinkers support, albeit for different reasons, an interpretation of their status as a new "modernism" of the day – just like the earliest waves of phenomenology half a century ago. O'Regan's chapter on such controversial figures serves as a model for critical dialogue between Catholics and other contemporary Continental schools that may have genuine insights to offer, without passing over the inevitability of irreconcilable differences.

That there has been and continues to be a certain alliance between the values of Catholicism and those of Continental philosophy is genuinely interesting and worth exploring for its own sake. But there is more at stake than this. In his recent book *God, Philosophy, Universities*, Alasdair MacIntyre states:

> Traditions are defined retrospectively. It is only on looking back that the unity of a project to which over considerable stretches of time there have been many different contributors, each with their own goals and concerns, becomes apparent. When it does, it is sometimes because of some challenge to a tradition from outside it, a challenge that awakens in those whose lives and work are informed by that tradition a new awareness, both of their shared inheritance and of the issues and problems that they now have to address, if they are to sustain their tradition in the future.[68]

That is, a sense of one's tradition often comes through looking back in the face of a challenge that must be answered in order for the tradition to remain vital. Or, to put it differently, no living tradition is without threats to its existence. The key to continued vitality is not to limit oneself to the safety of one's echo chamber, but rather to pass through the crucible of these challenges. As we have begun to see, these two intellectual traditions of Catholicism and Continental thought can serve as the source of a productive mutual challenge. This interrogation by these two intellectual traditions will grant each of them greater insight into the past as well as future paths of development.

Today it is also critical that we re-evaluate the challenges that face both these traditions, which find themselves in a measure of allegiance. It is common knowledge that Continental philosophy finds itself increasingly under pressure, competing for shrinking academic resources against the dominance of Analytic philosophy, as it has from the beginning. The real threat, however, is far deeper: more than a battle of individual traditions, philosophy itself is in danger in a culture that fails to see its point, as well as the point of all other arts and humanities, and religion along with them. The forces of materialism, reductionism, and scientism are threatening to absorb thinking into neuroscience and subvert spiritual hunger into consumerism. The contemporary obsession with narrow scientific rationality, technological development, and wealth stifle the deeper questions of life and propel society toward the extremes of ideology and cynicism. Yet after looking back over our brief historical sketch, we can also admit that this situation is not entirely new. This has been the dominant paradigm of North American discourse since the early twentieth century. It was their shared rejection of this paradigm that first led to the alliance of Catholic and Continental traditions, and it is what continues to draw them together even while setting them apart. This is as true today as it was in the 1960s, when McMullin observed, perhaps with exasperation, as Catholics were leaving their Neoscholasticism for Continental philosophy: "the Catholic group is moving away from one position that cut them off from their secular counterparts to another which will cut them off almost as much."[69] While Continental thought has indeed made significant inroads into American universities since then, its position remains insecure, and while Catholics are nowhere near as stigmatized as they were in the past, a broad anti-religious sentiment continues to grow.

The alliance in concert with mutual interrogation of these two traditions has strengthened their stand against many powerful contrary currents in contemporary thought and culture. Ultimately, this continued conversation will lay out a path to a better understanding of their unique identities and possibilities in the North American context. It is our hope that this volume will spur on such thinking and prepare both parties for alliances with other contemporary traditions that have opened up in the face of the same threats. We encourage our readers to keep all these challenges in mind as they engage with our contributors. Whatever dialogue it may spark, it is only the rigour of continued questioning that keeps the flame of philosophy alive.

NOTES

1 Simon Critchley, "What Is Continental Philosophy?" *International Journal of Philosophical Studies* 5, no. 3 (1997), 349.

2 Statistics on "top programs" are often subjective and difficult to measure, but the internet today has a wealth of information to aid the prospective graduate student, and lists of these schools are available on most such websites. For statistics on teaching in Catholic universities, see www.philosophynews.com/post/2013/11/29/Graduate-School-Placements-in-Philosophy-Continental-Programs-Job-Type-Placements.aspx. One finds

a less dramatic percentage of Catholic Continental universities in Canada, in part due to different national, political, and institutional organization. Yet Catholics remain conspicuously present in the Canadian reception history. For our purposes here, "North America" will be a shortcut to speak of these two countries.

3 Critiques of the term are numerous. To name just three: Critchley, "What Is Continental Philosophy?," 347–63; Jean Grondin, "Continental or Hermeneutic Philosophy: The Tragedies of Understanding the Analytic and Continental Perspectives," in *Interrogating the Tradition: Hermeneutics and the History of Philosophy*, ed. Charles E. Scott and John Sallis (Albany: SUNY Press, 2000), 75–83; and James Conant, "The Emergence of the Concept of the Analytic Tradition as a Form of Philosophical Self-Consciousness," in *Beyond the Analytic–Continental Divide: Pluralist Philosophy in the Twenty-First Century*, ed. Jeffrey A. Bell, Andrew Cutrofello, and Paul M. Livingston (London: Routledge, 2016), 17–58. Conant argues that the term "Analytic" is just as bad, as is the general opposition of Analytic–Continental which he likens to an opposition of vegetarians and Romanians.

4 W.H. Werkmeister, *A History of Philosophical Ideas in America* (New York: Ronald Press, 1949), 575; see also Donald Gallagher, "Theories of Truth in Contemporary American Philosophy," in *Philosophy and the Integration of Catholic Education*, ed. George F. McLean (Washington, D.C.: Catholic University of America Press, 1962), 87–93.

5 Brand Blanshard, Curt J. Ducasse, Max C. Otto, Arthur E. Murphy, and Charles W. Hendel, *Philosophy in American Education: Its Tasks and Opportunities* (New York: Harper & Brothers, 1945), 13–18, 106–7. See also Philip Gleason, *Contending with Modernity: Catholic Higher Education in the Twentieth Century* (Oxford: Oxford University Press, 1995), 250–1.

6 Anna-Teresa Tymieniecka, "The Theme: The History of American Phenomenology-in-Process," and James M. Edie, "John Wild and Phenomenology," both in *American Phenomenology: Origins and Developments*, ed. E.F. Kaelin and Calvin Schrag, *Analecta Husserliana*, vol. 26 (Dordrecht: Kluwer Academic, 1989), xix–xv, 86; Don Idhe, *Consequences of Phenomenology* (Albany: SUNY Press, 1986), 16; Robert Sweeney, "Phenomenology in North America and 'Continental' Philosophy," in *Phenomenology Worldwide: Analecta Husserliana*, vol. 80 (Dordrecht: Kluwer Academic, 2002), 285.

7 Idhe, *Consequences of Phenomenology*, 9–10, 20–3. Idhe writes at length here of the interaction between disseminating scholarship and original research in the history of phenomenology.

8 James Edie, "Recent Work in Phenomenology," *American Philosophical Quarterly* 1, no. 2 (1964), 115.

9 Herbert Spiegelberg, *The Phenomenological Movement*, vol. 2 (The Hague: Martinus Nijhoff, 1960), 626–7.
10 Tymieniecka, "The Theme," xvi; Edie, "John Wild and Phenomenology," 90–1; Idhe, *Consequences of Phenomenology*, 5.
11 See William McBride, "John Wild, Phenomenology in America, and the Origins of SPEP," *Continental Philosophy Review* 44 (2011), 281–4; Edie, "John Wild and Phenomenology," 85–98; Tymieniecka, "The Theme," xxi.
12 Helmut R. Wagner, "The Place of Alfred Schütz, in *American Phenomenology*, 66–8.
13 James M. Edie, "Introduction," in *An Invitation to Phenomenology: Studies in the Philosophy of Experience*, ed. James M. Edie (Chicago: Quadrangle Press, 1965), 8.
14 See chapter 1 of this volume by Daniel O. Dahlstrom, as well as Idhe, *Consequences of Phenomenology*, 17–18.
15 For more on this reception, see Martin Woessner, "Nihilism, Nothingness, and God: Heidegger and American Theology," in *Heidegger in America* (New York: Cambridge University Press, 2010), 92–131.
16 See chapter 3 in this volume by John D. Caputo, as well as Caputo's "Commentary on Ken Schmitz: 'Postmodernism and the Catholic Tradition,'" *American Catholic Philosophical Quarterly* 73, no. 2 (1999): 253–9.
17 Woessner, *Heidegger in America*, 118–19.
18 See Caputo's chapter 3; see also McBride, "John Wild, Phenomenology in America," 281–4; Edie, "John Wild and Phenomenology," 85–98; and Tymieniecka, "The Theme," xxi.
19 Alasdair MacIntyre, *God, Philosophy, Universities: A Selective History of the Catholic Philosophical Tradition* (Langham: Rowman and Littlefield, 2011), 133–4.
20 Ibid., 152–4; Avery Dulles, SJ "From Vatican I to John Paul II," in *The Two Wings of Catholic Thought: Essays on Fides et Ratio*, ed. David Ruel Foster and Joseph W. Koterski (Washington, D.C.: Catholic University of America Press, 2002), 194.
21 Fergus Kerr, *Twentieth-Century Catholic Theologians* (Malden: Wiley-Blackwell, 2006), 2–3, 11–13.
22 This tradition was never as monolithic as its detractors might make it, yet this broad overview will be sufficient for my purposes here, as will the equation of Neoscholasticism and Neo-Thomism.
23 James A. Weisheipl, "Revival of Thomism as a Christian Philosophy," in *New Themes in Catholic Philosophy*, ed. Ralph MacInerny (Notre Dame: University of Notre Dame Press, 1968), 184.
24 UNESCO, *Teaching Philosophy: International Inquiry* (Paris: Imprimerie Berger-Levrault, 1953).

25 James A. Weisheipl discusses this in some detail, particularly on page 185 in "Revival of Thomism."
26 See chapter 2 in this volume by Gregory P. Floyd for further discussion of Lonergan and the North American negotiation with Neoscholasticism.
27 Fergus Kerr recounts the main lines of these conflicts in *Twentieth-Century Catholic Theologians*.
28 Weisheipl, "Revival of Thomism," 182.
29 Gleason, *Contending with Modernity*, 261–2; Laurence K. Shook, *Catholic Post-Secondary Education in English-Speaking Canada: A History* (Toronto: University of Toronto Press, 1971), 427.
30 See Robert Hassenger's preface to his edited volume, *The Shape of Catholic Education* (Chicago: University of Chicago Press, 1967), 4.
31 Philip Gleason, "American Catholic Education, a Historical Perspective," in *The Shape of Catholic Education*, ed. Hassenger, 30.
32 See Gleason, *Contending with Modernity*, 4, who notes that contrary to popular belief, it was not that Catholic universities derived their educational structure from the seminary, but that both the seminary and the university derived their educational structure from European models; for more detailed statistics, see Ernan McMullin, "Philosophy in the United States Catholic College," in McInerny, 390.
33 Gleason, "American Catholic Education," 47–8. See also a Neoscholastic comparison between the Catholic vision of education and a secular, materialist one in Geoffrey O'Connell, "Catholic Education and Non-Catholic Philosophies," in *Vital Problems of Catholic Education in the United States* (Washington, D.C.: Catholic University of America Press, 1939), 1–23.
34 For facts and statistics, see McMullin's "Philosophy in the United States Catholic College," in McInerny, 372–409; for a survey of how top Catholic Continental programs were developing through and beyond this period, see Dahlstrom's chapter 1 in this volume; and for more focused attention on how one particular institution made the choice to trade a Neoscholastic tradition for a Continental one, see Patrick Byrne's case study of Boston College in chapter 4 of this volume.
35 W. Norris Clarke, "The Future of Thomism," in McInerny, 191.
36 See chapter 5 of this volume by Jean Grondin for more on the reception history of Continental thought in French Canada.
37 McMullin, "Philosophy in the United States Catholic College," 373; W. Norris Clarke, "Current Views on the Intrinsic Nature of Philosophy," in *Christian Wisdom and Christian Formation: Philosophy, Theology, and the Catholic College Student*, ed. J. Barry McGannon, SJ, Bernard J. Cooke, SJ, and George P. Klubertanz, SJ (New York: Sheed and Ward, 1964), 143.

38 Weisheipl, "Revival of Thomism"; and Clarke, "The Future of Thomism," in McInerny, ed., 192, 198.
39 Weisheipl, "Revival of Thomism," 164.
40 Woessner, *Heidegger in America*, 100–1.
41 John E. Smith, "Radical Theology and the Theological Enterprise," in McInerny, 214. See also Robert O. Johann, "Modern Atheism," in McInerny, 348. Caputo discusses some of the "Death of God" philosophies in chapter 3 of this volume.
42 William Barrett, *Irrational Man: A Study in Existential Philosophy* (New York: Anchor Books, 1962), 239.
43 See also ibid., 18–20; Benedict Ashley, "Theology and Philosophy as Disciplines" in *Christian Philosophy in the College and Seminary*, ed. George McLean OMI (Washington, D.C.: Catholic University of America Press, 1966), 8; and Woessner, *Heidegger in America*, 107.
44 George McLean, "The Unity of Truth: Context of an Integrated Catholic Education," in *Philosophy and the Integration of Contemporary Catholic Education*, ed. George McLean (Washington, D.C.: The Catholic University of America Press, 1962), 3.
45 For example, George F. McLean, ed., *Philosophy and the Integration of Contemporary Catholic Education* (1962); J. Barry McGannon, Bernard J. Cooke, and George P. Klubertanz, eds., *Christian Wisdom and Christian Formation* (1964); George McLean, ed., *Christian Philosophy and Religious Renewal* (Washington, D.C.: Catholic University of America Press, 1964); George F. McLean, ed., *Christian Philosophy in the College and Seminary* (1966); Robert Hassenger, ed., *The Shape of Catholic Education* (Chicago: University of Chicago Press, 1967); Ralph MacInerny, *New Themes in Christian Philosophy* (1968).
46 See for example the UNESCO report on the United States, *The Teaching of Philosophy: International Inquiry* (Paris: 1953), 149–82. Renowned Spanish philosopher José Ferrater Mora, fascinated by the pluralism he observed on the American continent, catalogues at least fifteen different primary living philosophical traditions in American discourse: idealism, personalism, realism, naturalism, historicism, immanentism (in which he includes evolutionism, emergentism, pragmatism, to name a few), intuitionism, philosophers of life, philosophical analysis, existentialism, logical positivism, philosophical analysis, linguistic analysis, Neoscholasticism, and dialectical materialism. Ferrater Mora, *Philosophy Today: Conflicting Tendencies in Contemporary Thought* (New York: Columbia University Press, 1960).
47 Werkmeister, *A History*, 577–8.
48 Ferrater Mora, *Philosophy Today*, 18–20.

49 Dietrich von Hildebrand, "Dangers in Constructing a Contemporary Christian Philosophy," in *Christian Philosophy in College and Seminary*, 14.
50 Clarke dismisses them without further comment in "Current Views," 159.
51 Ibid., 155–6; Clarke, "Analytic Philosophy and Language About God" in McLean, ed. (1964), p. 39–50. Although Ordinary Language Philosophy was often attributed to Wittgenstein (perhaps unfairly, despite his undeniable proximity to it), it is important to note that several of his most prominent students, including Elizabeth Anscombe, Peter Geach, and Michael Dummet, were Catholic. This began an important tradition of philosophers and theologians bringing Wittgenstein into dialogue with the Catholic tradition, a school of thought found primarily in England and continuing today through thinkers like Fergus Kerr. Here is one example of how Catholics can find other fruitful philosophical directions besides Continental ones.
52 Reflecting in particular upon confusion of theology of this era, Ernan McMullin declares: "I am inclined to think that every Department of Theology ought to employ an analytic philosopher as its official conscience!" In "Presidential Address: Who Are We?," *Proceedings of the American Catholic Philosophical Association* 61 (1967), 13.
53 Gallagher, "Theories of Truth in Contemporary American Philosophy," in McLean, ed., *A Philosophy*, 92.
54 John K. Ryan, "Systems of Truth," in McLean, ed., *Philosophy and the Integration of Conetmporary Cahtolic Edication*, 77.
55 MacIntyre, *God, Philosophy, Universities*, 158; Benedict Ashley, W.T. Magee, George Klubertanz, "Impact of Contemporary Trends," *Christian Philosophy in College and Seminary*, 122–3.
56 Kenneth Gallagher, "Contemporary Philosophies and the Religious Question," in *Christian Philosophy in College and Seminary*.
57 Ashley, Magee, Klubertanz, "Impact of Contemporary Trends," 120–5; McLean, "The Unity of Truth: The Context of an Integrated Catholic Education" in McLean, ed., *Philosophy and the Integration of Contemporary Catholic Education*, 3–5.
58 Benedict Ashley, "A Phenomenological Approach to Christian Philosophy," *Christian Philosophy in College and Seminary*, 12.
59 This was second only to Thomism, which still made up more than half of the average Catholic philosophy department, no doubt including many senior scholars hired during the heyday of Neoscholasticism. McMullin, "Philosophy in the United States Catholic College," in McInerny, 372.
60 Kerr, *Twentieth-Century Catholic Theologians*, 3.
61 Bernard Lonergan, "Theology in its New Context," in *A Second Collection*, ed. William F.J. Ryan and Bernard J. Tyrrell (Toronto: University of Toronto Press, 1996), 63.

62 McMullin, "Philosophy in the United States Catholic College," in McInerny, 409.
63 Gleason, *Contending with Modernity*, 322.
64 Jeffrey Bloechl gives some thought to this issue in the course of his chapter 10 in this volume.
65 See especially chapter 7 in this volume by Andrew Prevot for the significance of philosophies of critique.
66 Christina M. Gschwandtner discusses in chapter 6 in this volume how the "French Turn" has been transformed in its transposition to the North American context, and Bruce Ellis Benson discusses in chapter 9 how deconstruction was able to advance in openness to religion in the New World in ways that had been closed to it in France.
67 Thus in this volume for example we find such diverse approaches as Cyril O'Regan in chapter 12 giving Žižek a fair hearing, and William Desmond in chapter 11 insisting that we revive a metaphysics that has absorbed the Continental critique. And while Anne M. Carpenter is far from Neoscholasticism, her chapter 8 demonstrates that not all Continental thought is so foreign to Catholic theology, that we can still negotiate a balance between contemporary philosophy and theology in service of the unified truth.
68 Alasdair MacIntyre, *God, Philosophy, Universities*, 165.
69 McMullin, "Philosophy in the United States Catholic College," 372.

1 The Reception of Phenomenology and Existentialism by American Catholic Philosophers: Some Facts and Some Reasons

DANIEL O. DAHLSTROM

Ἐγώ εἰμι ἡ ὁδὸς καὶ ἡ ἀλήθεια
καὶ ἡ ζωή (John 14:6)

In the first half of the twentieth century, as phenomenology and existentialism took root in European philosophy, Catholic philosophers played a significant role in its development and transmission.[1] Given the large contingent of American Catholics, many of them clerics, doing graduate work in Europe, the study of phenomenology and existentialism (hereafter "P&E") quickly gained a foothold in Catholic universities in the United States as well. The purpose of this chapter is twofold: to show *that* P&E, from the 1950s through the 1970s, increasingly became a staple of course offerings and research by graduate students and professors in departments of philosophy in American Catholic PhD-granting universities – and to show *why*.

I

The evidence for the receptiveness of departments of philosophy in American Catholic PhD-granting universities to P&E during this period is fairly robust.[2] Documenting this receptiveness is not always straightforward, however, since it is often more dependent on memories than on records, particularly for the 1950s. At times my discussion will necessarily be anecdotal and impressionistic, reflecting my memories as well as others' memories of attitudes toward Continental European philosophy exhibited by our teachers and recorded in writings in the decades after the Second World War.[3] With the help of a research assistant, however, I have solicited from departments some data on course offerings, specializations, publications, conferences, and topics of dissertations of doctorates conferred during the period.[4] The data, like my memory, are woefully incomplete and certainly fallible, although I have tried to avoid omissions of important figures and works. I apologize in advance for the inevitable oversight or insufficient weight given to certain figures or institutions.[5]

The European Influence and the Prominence of Catholic Philosophers in the Development of P&E in the United States

One important factor in the reception of P&E has already been noted: the sheer number of professors in departments of philosophy at American Catholic universities at the time who did their graduate work at Paris, Rome, and various sites in Germany. Above all, Université catholique de Louvain in Belgium, the site of the largest holdings of Husserl's manuscripts, simultaneously produced a long list of American experts in contemporary phenomenological thinking. The list includes such luminaries as Bernard Boelen (Duquesne, DePaul), Richard Cobb-Stevens (Boston College),[6] Charles De Koninck (Laval), James Edie (Northwestern), Louis Dupré (Georgetown), Alden Fisher (St Louis), Patrick Heelan (Fordham), Joseph Kockelmans (Duquesne, visiting professor), Alphonso Lingis (Duquesne, Penn State), Thomas Munson (DePaul), Adriaan Pepperzak (Loyola), William Richardson (Fordham, Boston College), Robert Sokolowski (Catholic University of America), and Andrew Tallon (Marquette).[7]

Perhaps the most patent evidence of the strength of the reception of Continental philosophy by American Catholic philosophers during this time is the fact that three priests who began their careers as professors at Catholic universities in the 1960s – Robert Sokolowski, Bill Richardson, and Thomas Flynn – developed well-deserved reputations as America's leading experts on the three foremost European phenomenologists: Husserl, Heidegger, and Sartre respectively. Notably, of the twelve philosophers who convened the first organizational meeting of the Heidegger Circle in 1967, hosted by DePaul, half of them hailed from Catholic universities at the time: Boelen, Frings, Kisiel, Langan, Richardson, and Toussaint.[8]

P&E in Catholic Philosophy Departments, 1950–80

A survey of professors working on P&E in American Catholic graduate schools at the time confirms a remarkable openness to this movement. This openness is particularly evident in the case of the sole pontifical university in the United States, **The Catholic University of America**. The leading figure there was Monsignor Robert Sokolowski. A student at CUA in the 1950s, Sokolowski returned from Belgium to the campus in 1963, where he began an illustrious career as a philosopher, teacher, and writer. His publications during the period in question included *The Formation of Husserl's Concept of Constitution* (1964), *Husserlian Meditations* (1974), and *Presence and Absence* (1978).[9] Already on the faculty was Thomas Prufer, a Virginia native who received his PhD in 1959 from Munich with a dissertation on *Sein und Wort nach Thomas von Aquin*. A master interpreter of ancient, medieval, and modern philosophical texts, Prufer regularly gave seminars on Heidegger's *Being and Time*, complementing Sokolowski's offerings on Husserl. Prufer and Sokolowski became fast philosophical friends, enriching each other's thinking, while introducing legions of students to phenomenological and existential themes.

Across town, pursuing graduate studies at **Georgetown**, but often attending Sokolowski's seminars, was John Brough, who received his PhD at Georgetown in 1970 with the dissertation "A Study of the Logic and Evolution of Edmund Husserl's Theory of the Constitution of Time-Consciousness, 1893–1917." Brough would subsequently produce masterful translations of Husserl and distinguish himself as an expert on Husserl's thought. During Brough's undergraduate studies at Georgetown, its department was also home to two Belgian professors, Wilfrid Desan and Louis Dupré, both of whom regularly taught courses and held graduate seminars on figures in P&E. Desan arrived in Georgetown in 1957; his 1954 work, *The Tragic Finale: The Philosophy of Jean-Paul Sartre*, published three years earlier, was among the first of its sort by a North American philosopher (another work on Sartre would follow in 1965). Also in 1954, Thomas P. McTighe, with a recent doctorate from St Louis University, arrived as the department's first lay faculty member. P&E figured prominently in the wide range of courses offered by McTighe. (John Rose, an influential teacher of P&E at Goucher College, in 1984 wrote a dissertation on Plotinus and Heidegger – the last dissertation directed by McTighe.) From the late 1950s until the early 1970s (before departing for Yale), Louis Dupré taught and published extensively, not only on the thought of Marx and Kierkegaard but also on Husserl's phenomenology, not least in terms of its significance for understanding religious experience. Under John Brough's direction, another leading phenomenologist at a Catholic university, John Drummond (Fordham), completed his graduate studies with a dissertation on "Presenting and Kinesthetic Sensations in Husserl's Phenomenology of Perception."[10]

In the 1950s, the faculty at **Fordham** included Dietrich von Hildebrand (a student of Husserl, Scheler, and Reinach, no less) as well as von Hildebrand's own student from the late 1920s in Munich, Balduin Schwarz. The positive reception of P&E within the faculty was further strengthened in 1954 with the addition of Quentin Lauer, who had just completed his studies at the Sorbonne and had produced two monographs in French on Husserl. As Dominic Balestra notes, Lauer's "continental studies, combined with his earlier training in scholastic philosophy, enabled Fr. Lauer to expand the department at Fordham into a leading graduate program for the study of Continental philosophy."[11] Although Lauer would move away from Husserl to the study of French Marxism and Hegel over the following decades, *The Triumph of Subjectivity* (with an introduction by Aron Gurwitsch) in 1958 and *Edmund Husserl: Phenomenology and the Crisis of Philosophy* in 1965 were among the first important contributions by professors at Catholic universities to phenomenological studies. In the 1960s, another Catholic expert on Continental philosophy graced the Fordham department: William Richardson, author of the monumental work *Heidegger: Through Phenomenology to Thought* (1963). Besides regularly teaching courses on Heidegger, Richardson directed the doctoral work of Thomas Sheehan, who would become his friendly rival as the premier American interpreter of Heidegger's thought (not least by offering an alternative reading of what Heidegger was up to). Further contributing to the studies of Continental philosophers at Fordham were Patrick Heelan, a renowned hermeneutical philosopher of science, and Kenneth Gallagher, author of *The Philosophy of Gabriel Marcel* (1962), who also taught courses on Husserl's thought. Also important for the reception of P&E at Fordham, particularly by way of contemporary European currents in theology (transcendental Thomism, Rahner, Marechal, Rousselot), was the Flemish Jesuit, Joseph Donceel, a member of the department from 1950 to 1972.[12]

In the late 1950s, Thomas J. Owens (Fordham PhD, 1952), a Heidegger expert and author of *Phenomenology and Intersubjectivity: Contemporary Interpretations of the Interpersonal Situation* (1970), joined the faculty at **Boston College**. He was joined in the 1960s by Oliva Blanchette, Richard Murphy, and David Rasmussen, who brought expertise in a variety of Continental thinkers and traditions, largely at the intersection of ethical and political reflections (e.g., Blondel's theory of action, Ricoeur's hermeneutics, Schütz's social phenomenology, and the critical theory of Horkheimer, Adorno, and Habermas). Murphy was a Husserl specialist, the author of *Hume and Husserl* (1980). In the 1970s, Rasmussen was editor-in-chief of *Cultural Hermeneutics* and *Philosophy and Social Criticism*. In the early 1970s, Richard Cobb-Stevens began an eminent career as a leading interpreter of Husserl's philosophy, with special attention to its relation to James's pragmatism and to Frege's legacy in Analytic philosophy.[13]

Henry J. Koren, the Dutch chair of the **Duquesne** philosophy and theology departments since 1949, who had received his PhD from CUA, made it a point to bring phenomenologists to campus, including such figures as H.L. van Breda, Stephan Strasser, Jean Ladrière, Louis van Haecht, Joseph J. Kockelmans, and the Dutch priests William Luijpen and Remy Kwant, the former the author of *Existential Phenomenology* (1960), *Phenomenology and Atheism* (1968), and (with Henry J. Koren) *A First Introduction to Existential Phenomenology* (1969), the latter the author of *The Phenomenological Philosophy of Merleau-Ponty* (1963) and *Phenomenology of Social Existence* – all published by Duquesne University Press. Not surprisingly, noted Heidegger scholar Ted Kisel, a graduate student from 1958 to 1962 (Kockelmans was one of his readers), describes Duquesne at the time as "a veritable 'little Louvain.'" The sentiment is shared by Robert Sweeney, who began teaching at Duquesne for eight years in 1956, after completing a doctoral dissertation on Scheler's philosophy of value at Fordham. In the 1960s, Alphonso Lingis, renowned translator of Merleau-Ponty and Levinas and a philosopher in his own right, taught at Duquesne, and another prominent scholar, David Ferrell Krell (more on him below), received his PhD there. Other members of the faculty particularly notable for their contributions to the study of P&E include the Franciscan André Schuwer (one-time chair and noted scholar and translator of Husserl and Heidegger himself), John Sallis (one of the foremost American interpreters of Heidegger's phenomenology and its reception, who graced the department for almost two decades, beginning in the mid-1960s), and Lester Embree (the redoubtable expert on the phenomenological tradition, who arrived in 1974). Alone among North American Catholic universities, Duquesne houses an official branch of the Husserl Archives of Leuven, reflecting its long tradition of affiliation with the Belgian university and P&E. The archives' current home, the Simon Silverman Phenomenology Center, also houses other extensive collections of works by phenomenologists.

For the 1950s, **Notre Dame** does not list any dissertations on figures in P&E, though Yves Simon did direct George Hollenhorst's dissertation on consciousness and A. Robert Caponigri (an expert in Italian thought) directed a dissertation on *Presence and Subjectivity* by Frederick Crosson. Crosson, whose studies included a stint at the University of Paris, would be one of the P&E specialists in the department over the next four decades. But the number of dissertations on P&E in the 1960s suggests a growing interest: Vincent Smith directed Sister Mary Catherine Baseheart's dissertation *The Encounter of Husserl's Phenomenology and the Philosophy of St Thomas in Selected Writings of Edith Stein*; Harry Nielsen directed dissertations on Kierkegaard, Sartre, and Freud; Ralph McInerny on Ortega y Gassett, Blondel, Kierkegaard, and Marcel; and Ernan McMullin on Husserl. Noteworthy in this connection is Ronald Bruzina, a leading American scholar of Husserl's thought, who wrote his dissertation on Husserl and Merleau-Ponty at Notre Dame in 1966 under Crosson. In the 1970s, McInerny directed four dissertations on Kierkegaard and another on Nietzsche and Pascal; David Burrell also directed a dissertation on Kierkegaard, while Ernan McMullin and Cornelius Delaney directed dissertations on Husserl and Rudolf Gerber directed a dissertation on Sartre. This flurry of dissertations and course offerings during these decades (1950s–70s) demonstrates a robust engagement with P&E, even though there was no major scholar of Continental thought with the stature of Lauer, Sokolowski, or Richardson.

Catholic universities in Chicago have provided important contributors to the study of Continental philosophy. **DePaul** became a leading centre of P&E studies in the mid-1960s, particularly with the arrival of Professors Bernard Boelen and Manfred Frings from Duquesne. Boelen was the author of *Existential Thinking: A Philosophical Orientation* (1968) and *Personal Maturity: The Existential Dimension* (1978). Born in Cologne, Frings was chosen by Heidegger to be one of the first editors of his Collected Works (*Gesamtausgabe*). His editing of Heidegger's lectures on Parmenides and Heraclitus from the early 1940s is perhaps overshadowed by the leading role he played in making known the thought of Max Scheler, once dubbed "the Catholic phenomenologist," whose influence on German phenomenologists (perhaps not least Edith Stein and Martin Heidegger) can scarcely be underestimated. Also paramount in putting DePaul on the map for P&E studies is the masterful work of David Krell. In addition to the prodigious feat of translating Heidegger's extensive lectures on Nietzsche with much-needed commentary, Krell edited the widely used Heidegger's *Basic Writings* (1977), again with helpful annotation, while also producing several influential studies of Heidegger, Nietzsche, and German idealism.

In the 1970s, another prominent force in the study of Heidegger emerged on Chicago's North Side, this time at **Loyola**, with the arrival of Thomas Sheehan, whose importance to contemporary studies of Heidegger has already been noted. Also at Loyola during this time was Suzanne Cunningham, author of *Language and the Phenomenological Reductions of Edmund Husserl* (1976), and Hans Seigfried, a German philosopher (Bonn PhD) who had arrived in 1968, bringing with him a unique philosophical outlook based upon critical studies of Kant, Nietzsche, and Heidegger. The end of the 1970s brought the arrival of Adriaan Pepperzak, a former Dutch cleric who completed his doctoral work on *Le jeune Hegel* under Paul Ricoeur in Paris. A recent recipient of the American Catholic Philosophical Association's Aquinas Medal, Pepperzak brought with him an enormous scope of research in P&E, from Hegel to Levinas, but with an abiding concern for the Catholic tradition of spirituality.

The philosophy department at **Marquette** had its doctoral program restored in 1957, under the chairmanship of Gerard Smith (a medievalist and expert on the theology of fellow Jesuit, Henri du Lubac). The ensuing decades witnessed a robust openness to P&E, but also to German Idealist traditions. During 1963–4, a visiting professor from Louvain, Frans Vandenbussche, SJ, addressed, among other things, the question of Christian existentialism. Thomas C. Anderson (Marquette PhD), an expert on Kierkegaard and Sartre, and Howard Kainz (Duquesne PhD), an expert on Hegel, both became members of the department in 1967. Joseph O'Malley and Keith Algozin, specializing in Marx and his relation to Hegel's political philosophy, were also on the faculty during these years (as was Kenneth Schmitz in the early 1960s). An expert on the thought of Karl Rahner, Andrew Tallon (a recent Louvain PhD) joined them two years later. Denis Savage, a student and translator (with this wife) of Ricoeur, was also on the faculty during the 1960s, and noted Schelling expert Michael Vater joined the faculty in 1971. During the 1960s and 1970s, the department offered several graduate courses on P&E: "Phenomenology" (taught by Vandenbussche, Savage), "Existentialism" (taught by Vandenbussche, Boileau), "Nineteenth-Century Existentialism" (taught by Anderson, Collingwood), "Existentialist Ethics" (taught by Anderson), "Twentieth-Century French Phenomenology-Existentialism" (taught by Anderson and Tallon), and "Twentieth-Century German Phenomenology-Existentialism" (taught by Algozin, Stohrer,[14] and Vater). In addition, at the end of the 1960s, the noted medieval scholar Anton Pegis offered courses on knowledge in Aquinas and Husserl, on perception in Aquinas and Merleau-Ponty, and on the nature of being in Aquinas and Heidegger.

The early presence of P&E at **St Louis University** during these years can be traced to two figures: James Collins and Alden Fisher. As early as January, 1946, Collins addressed the "philosophy of existence" in a *Modern Schoolman* entry, but his more celebrated contributions were his books, *The Existentialists* in 1952 and, a year later, *The Mind of Kierkegaard* (the former going through eight, the latter six editions). While pursuing monumental research on the history of modern philosophy, he continued to engage the tradition of P&E.[15] In 1962 he published *Three Paths in Philosophy*, reissued in 1969 as *Crossroads in Philosophy: Existentialism, Naturalism, Theistic Realism.* A synopsis of five existentialist themes in the conclusion to *The Existentialists* is critical (frequently in the name of "perennial philosophy"), but it also makes the case that existentialism is eminently worthy of study by Catholic thinkers.[16] Despite the impact of Collins's forays into existentialism, his research centred on the history of philosophy, not P&E. By contrast, Alden L. Fisher, a student of de Waelhens at Louvain, devoted his energies principally to P&E. In 1963, he translated Merleau-Ponty's *La structure du comportement*, and six years later, he edited *The Essential Writings of Merleau-Ponty.* Following Fisher's untimely death, another eminent specialist in P&E, James L. Marsh, a Northwestern PhD (with strong interests in Lonergan and critical theory as well), joined the department in the 1970s. One additional aspect of the St Louis experience in this connection deserves mention. Graduate students at St Louis had fairly easy access to courses offered at Washington University. As a result, some students availed themselves of the golden opportunity to participate in workshops on phenomenology, conducted at Washington University (several in the 1960s, one in the early 1970s) by Herbert Spiegelberg, a Munich PhD and author of a landmark history of phenomenology.[17]

Other Factors: Gadamer, Theology and Vatican II, the Cold War

Missing in the foregoing gloss on places and people involved in the reception of P&E at this time are three elements, three pieces of the puzzle that should not go without mention. One concerns the influence of a particular personality on the reception, another concerns the reception's relationship to theology, and the third concerns its relationship to the politics of the academy, particularly the Catholic academy, during this time.

1. In 1969 Gadamer was a Visiting Professor at Catholic University of America (perfecting his English at the Theological College for Basselin seminarians). After some other guest professorships, he became a professor at Boston College in 1974, where he remained for more than a decade. Gadamer's presence at these Catholic

universities and others served as an important catalyst for the study of Husserl and Heidegger. There are several reasons for his tremendous influence. He brought with him original interpretations of the history of philosophy (especially Plato and Hegel) and a renowned program of hermeneutics, both erected on a deep foundation in phenomenology. With their emphasis on the history of philosophy, Catholic departments of philosophy welcomed his interpretations of past philosophers. So, too, Catholic philosophers and theologians alike grappled with the nature and implications of his universal hermeneutics. Nor can his first-hand experience of developments in German philosophy in the early twentieth century be underestimated. What made Gadamer such an important figure was, above all, the example of philosophical practice that he set with his generosity and openness to dialogue.

2. A second factor that paved the way for creating a positive reception of P&E in Catholic philosophy departments was the strong impact that phenomenology in particular had on Catholic theology in Europe in the years before and after the Second World War.[18] Phenomenological investigations – by Scheler as well as by Husserl and Heidegger – left an indelible mark on such theologians as Karol Wojtyla, Karl Rahner, Joseph Ratzinger, Edward Schillebeeckx, and Romano Guardini. It became incumbent upon students of their theologies to develop the same facility with phenomenology's methods and concepts that they found in their works.[19] The influence of these Northern European theologians and others upon Vatican II has been widely documented, even if the details remain controversial.[20] The result, particularly evident in the mid-1960s, was the development of an increasingly invigorating synergy between departments of philosophy and theology, many of which shared responsibility for teaching seminarians.
3. The reception of P&E in Catholic philosophy departments during the decades in question coincided with the Cold War, and the Vietnam War was fought through the middle of the period. After the Second World War, the GI Bill and the postwar baby boom (population growth from 152 million in 1950 to 180 million in 1960) helped bring about an unprecedented level of prosperity in the United States (from a GNP of $300 billion in 1950 to over $500 billion in 1960 alone, despite two recessions). With potentially competing economies still reeling from the war's debilitating effects on their infrastructures and productive capacities, a period of political and economic dominance – *Pax Americana* – became the new normal. Most Americans benefited from this prosperity, which contributed

> to a high degree of confidence and a corresponding expansion in higher education. The threat of nuclear annihilation acted, to be sure, as a constant, sobering check on this mood of optimism. Particularly in the 1960s, the Cuban Missile Crisis (which demonstrated that the threat of annihilation was all too concrete), assassinations of leaders (including the first Catholic president and his brother), and two nationally divisive issues at home and abroad (the conflicts over civil rights and the war in Vietnam) cast a pall over American self-assurance.

The experience of Catholics during these times, not least Catholics studying philosophy, could not help but reflect their position within this larger development. Catholics were increasingly upwardly mobile; they were moving away from ethnic enclaves and fragmenting extended families as they assimilated into the all-too-silent majority, the homogenous middle-class – all in the name of doing right by their children. These movements and assimilations represented an unmistakable threat to Catholic ethnicity, if not Catholic identity. At the same time, Catholics were forced to respond to new American versions of old ethical questions of human equality and war. To be sure, while social changes and political positions challenged American Catholics' practice of their beliefs, they also presented them with an opportunity to draw upon the long tradition of sagacious consideration of cognate issues and questions by the Church's past philosophers.

Even from this tortuously attenuated gloss, it would be presumptuous to venture a portrait of certain shared motivations, both explicit and implicit, on the part of Catholics studying philosophy during these years that contributed to the attractiveness of P&E. Still, it is not idle to speculate, particularly given the hegemony enjoyed by the dominant philosophical approaches within American private and public universities during this same period. While increasingly eschewing straightforwardly positivist pretensions, these approaches continued to identify philosophy largely with the analysis of objectively identifiable languages, ordinary or scientific, and with the construction of formal apparatuses capable of capturing their basic structures (and allegedly *capturing*, too, anything falling under them). Many of these loosely labelled "Analytic philosophies" were having, it seemed, a positivist hangover, one that lasted for decades.[21]

Critics of this approach remonstrated that it increasingly removed philosophy from the *agora*, rendering it not simply arcane but politically innocuous, just as a certain senator from Wisconsin would have it.[22] Was the positive reception of P&E a sign of resistance to these developments? Or was the reception simply more of the same (as the proponents of critical theory, another transplanted European tradition, would have it)? The disjunction implied by these questions is overly simplistic, to be sure, particularly if we consider how little difficulty the likes of Sartre and Merleau-Ponty had combining P&E with leftist politics. Of course, the same cannot be said for Husserl or Heidegger. Much more extensive considerations, not least of the particular versions of P&E, are required to address the relation of its appeal for Catholic thinkers to their stance as citizens toward public policies adopted during the decades in question. In any case, however, the engagement in P&E by Catholic philosophers and philosophy departments moved them unmistakably out of the mainstream of American philosophy during these decades.[23]

II

This second part of my reflections presents reasons why Catholic philosophers were receptive to P&E, against the backdrop of, among other things, traditional approaches to philosophy in Catholic universities. For the sake of economy, I limit my considerations to the thinking of Husserl and the early Heidegger.[24] The reception of their phenomenological perspectives was by no means frictionless, and it could hardly be so. Husserl stresses the need to bracket the existence of God as part of the transcendental reduction, while Heidegger insists on the need to think "a-theistically," without relying upon God or belief in God in any sense.[25] The presuppositionlessness of Husserl's phenomenology demands, among other things, that matters of belief be held at arm's length; Heidegger takes his bearings from the temporal character of human existence, its worldliness and mortality. Insisting, moreover, on the primacy of thoughtful description and intuition over demonstrations and explanations,[26] phenomenologists depart – at least *prima facie* – from the time-honoured search for the "first principles and causes of things" that led Aristotle himself to something called "theology."

When philosophy departments in American Catholic universities during the 1950s began to develop interest in P&E, they had the advantage of doing so against the backdrop of a tradition of Thomistic thought, a tradition established by the papacy itself and strongly buttressed ever since. In *Aeterni Patris* (1879), Leo XIII called for the restitution and propagation, as far as possible, of "St. Thomas' golden wisdom."[27] Citing and endorsing this call in his 1907 encyclical against modernism, *Pascendi dominici gregis*, Pius X mandated that "scholastic philosophy be considered the foundation of sacred sciences," a philosophy consisting in "what St. Thomas has bequeathed to us."[28] The restitution prescribed by these Pontiffs began to take hold in North American universities in earnest from the 1920s through the 1940s, not least through the efforts of Jacques Maritain, Étienne Gilson, Yves Simon, and Charles De Koninck. North American versions of this approach (sometimes called "Thomism" or "Neoscholasticism") provided the immediate setting in the following decades for the reception, both positive and negative, of the works of Husserl and Heidegger.[29]

Why Husserl?

Husserl's conception of phenomenology arises in no small part from his attempts to come to grips with the nature of consciousness and experience. Not coincidentally, he shared with his teacher, Franz Brentano, an understanding of the intentional character of experience, the fact that being about something is typically – for Brentano, invariably – built into the structure of consciousness. While Husserl was not himself trained in Scholastic thought, Brentano was.[30] In his *Psychology from an Empirical Point of View* (1874), Brentano states that every mental phenomenon is characterized by what the Scholastics in the Middle Ages would have called "the intentional … inexistence of an object."[31] In an accompanying footnote, he adds that Aristotle, Augustine (*verbum mentis*), and Aquinas speak of intentionality in this sense (indeed, with important consequences for the latter's doctrine of the Trinity). Thus, as Brentano saw quite clearly, an understanding of the intentional structure of consciousness – what would become arguably the fundamental concept of Husserl's phenomenology – continues a tradition of interpretation of mental experiences in the long line of Aristotle and Aquinas. Catholic philosophers, trained in Neoscholastic thought in America and elsewhere, also could not fail to see the connection.[32]

Through critical engagement with Brentano's thinking, Husserl initially made his breakthrough to phenomenology as part of an effort to demonstrate the integrity of logic and mathematics. This demonstration was a response to attempts, at the turn of the last century, to reduce logic and mathematics to psychology ("psychologism"). In this regard, Husserl affirms the ideality of logical and mathematical forms: they are not reducible to intra-mental contents of psychological acts or to physical objects/events ("naturalism"), yet they can be intuited categorically on the basis of sensory intuitions and straightforward perceptions. A sensation of white and the perception of a piece of paper before me are alike necessary but insufficient, he argues, for the perception that, for example, the piece of paper before me is white, that it exists, that white is a colour, that "white" and "colour" are universals, and so on. Husserl's analysis has some stark parallels to a Thomistic understanding of universals, logic, and even a concept like "being" insofar as it spans the realms of real beings and beings of reason.[33] In regard to universals, for example, Aquinas would have it that, while "Socrates is a human being" is true because humanity exists in Socrates, humanity can be considered in abstraction from him, insofar as it exists in others as well. The apprehension of humanity "without its individuating conditions," as Aquinas puts it, corresponds to what Husserl dubs the categorial intuition of a universal.[34]

In 1910–11, "guided by the thought that the highest interests of human culture demand the elaboration of a rigorously scientific philosophy," Husserl undertook a radical criticism of naturalism's pretensions to fulfil this demand and historicism's attempt to abandon it in favour of elaborating a worldview (*Weltanschauung*).[35] These points were bound to strike a chord with the Thomistic and Aristotelian proclivities of Catholic philosophers. But no less important than this two-pronged critique and its grounding in a commitment to a "rigorously scientific philosophy" were the steps Husserl took toward realizing that commitment. Perhaps most responsible for the tremendous appeal of Husserl's phenomenology was the example he set for developing philosophy as a rigorous science. As Prufer and Sokolowski stress, Husserl's phenomenology recovers the distinctiveness of philosophy as a way of thinking, and as such it stands in sharp contrast to the sort of thinking characteristic of particular sciences and worldviews. Herein lies the meaning of the phenomenological reduction, the "step back" (as Heidegger would later put it) from theoretical and practical engagements with particular parts of the world, the withdrawal (*epoche*) that allows us to look at things as a whole. As Sokolowski points out, this effort is continuous with Aristotle's conception of philosophy, indeed, with his characterization of metaphysics as "first philosophy," the title of Husserl's 1923–4 lectures.[36]

Phenomenology, taking its cues from Husserl's intentional analyses and method of reduction, also holds considerable promise for understanding religious experience, a promise recognized by American Catholic philosophers no less than by their European counterparts. To be sure, that promise comes with the challenge that Husserl's method singularly presents to understanding that experience. To see the challenge, consider that after the phenomenological suspension of the world, the pure ego is left with only a "sui generis transcendence," that is, transcendence in immanence.[37] This sui generis transcendence gives rise to a sui generis challenge for a phenomenology of religion, namely, that of coming to terms with the experience of what is transcendently given, what is revealed. There are two sides to the challenge here. In presenting itself with its own meaning rather than receiving it from the believer, the object of faith supersedes any and all active projections of its meaning by the believer; the object of belief is irreducibly given. Yet at the same time, the experience does not take place without the believer's projection, that is, without outward expressions (religious symbols, institutions, interpretations) of her inner intention. Precisely because of its recourse to the reduction and its analyses of forms of active and passive intentionality, a phenomenology of religion is in a privileged position to recognize and grapple with the challenge of articulating this experience.[38]

Why Heidegger?

One obvious reason for the attractiveness of Heidegger's early work is the main Catholic tradition's embrace of metaphysics, based principally upon Scholastic Aristotelian studies of being and beings. At a time when logical positivists were rejecting metaphysics wholesale (as in Carnap's "Overturning of Metaphysics" or Nagel's *Logic without Metaphysics*), or simply eschewing it on purely pragmatic grounds in favour of "the whole of science" (as Quine put it), the strength of Heidegger's analyses and his unabashed, innovative foray into metaphysics had an encouraging effect (even if Heidegger himself subsequently dropped the pursuit of metaphysics or fundamental ontology as such).[39] For followers of Thomas Aquinas, Heidegger's contention that philosophy has progressively forgotten the question of being rings only too true. If metaphysics was in retreat, it was in no small part because a particular conception of being – we might, again, label it "naturalism" – had become unassailable, having been buttressed by the ever-increasing sweep and effectiveness of the scientific method and new technologies. Adhering exclusively to a method of observation, measurement, and experimentation for the sake of determining the most likely combinations of the phenomena at hand provided each science with the greatest assurance of practical successes, while dispensing with arcane metaphysical questions that could not be resolved by straightforward observation, measurement, and/or experimentation. The growth of the separate sciences, with this predetermined promise of achievement, overwhelmed universities and philosophers, shrinking not only the place of philosophy in the academy but also the self-confidence of philosophers that their thinking remained trenchant or viable. Philosophy, once the handmaid of theology, had become the handmaid of science, albeit with the awareness that science increasingly had no need of it.

Thoughtful Catholics, not least those trained in the Thomistic tradition, could appreciate Heidegger's identification of this development and its culmination in an understanding of being that, in the end, equated being with being something humanly manageable (or, indeed, even something capable of being humanly produced).[40] So, too, if one accepts the two notions that being is always the being of something and that it is said analogously of different "things," then it is imperative to begin the analysis of what it means to be not with just any being and certainly not with merely physical or biological beings, but precisely with the sort of being that has an understanding of being. Beginning the investigation of what it means to be with beings who have a mind or soul provides a necessary check on reductionist tendencies. To underscore this point, Heidegger himself invokes the authority of both Aristotle and Aquinas, that is, Aristotle's claim that the soul is in a way all things (*De Anima* III, 8: 431b21) and Aquinas's claim that the soul is what is suited to come together with every being (*De Veritate*, q 1, alc).

This starting point has obvious implications for metaphysical and systematic theological considerations of both humans and God. We have far less purchase on what it means to say that both God and God's creation (including humans) "exist" if, taking our bearings from the existence of inanimate objects, we attempt to attribute existence, understood along those lines, to ourselves, let alone to God. To the extent that traditional metaphysics repeatedly succumbed to the temptation to be "meta-physics" – in the sense of a kind of super-physics, as Heidegger would later put it[41] – his approach tapped into thoughtful believers' long-standing problem with the assimilation of the mystery of faith to such a wooden metaphysics.

The appeal of Heidegger's *Being and Time* (1927) to Catholics, as it was to the larger population, is of course also due in large measure to his ability to describe concrete experiences (both the "everyday" variety and the exceptional) that were typically passed over by philosophers concentrating on epistemology or on explanations (behaviouristic, biological, etc.) of those experiences. But the appeal was due not simply to his descriptions of these experiences, but also to his insistence on placing them in a philosophical, indeed, a metaphysical context, that is, on relating them to the question of the meaning of "being." In the process, Heidegger appropriated not only many religious themes, but also their treatments by Kierkegaard and other Protestant theologians (treatments of themes such as the crowd, fallenness, angst, death, conscience, resoluteness). By bracketing the theological backdrop of these treatments and offering phenomenological analyses of these experiences on their own terms, Heidegger introduced Catholic thinkers to denominationally neutral approaches to these experiences. To take one glaring example, Heidegger made it not merely philosophically respectable but philosophically imperative to address a phenomenon such as angst – something that both positivists and more pragmatically minded naturalists at the time relegated to matters of nonsense or pseudo-questions. Heidegger took pains to ensure that philosophy never wandered too far from concrete experiences, even if, as phenomenology, its task was to bring to light what is operative but hidden or obscured in those experiences. Accordingly, because it refused to indulge an exclusive disjunction of theory and practice, it could present a refreshing alternative to a philosophical tradition residing only *intra mures ecclesiae*, that is, the way that Scholastic thought increasingly appeared to so many students and seminarians at the time.

There is a further reason why Heidegger's writings spoke to so many Catholic philosophers at this time. Heidegger deemed it essential to conduct philosophy in dialogue with the history of philosophy, invariably with a view to unearthing the lasting legacy (or, better, the approaching culmination) of previous interpretations of existence. For all their novelty, tendentiousness, and unorthodoxy, Heidegger's interpretations of the history of philosophy in terms of its ongoing relevance breathed new life into the study of it generally. And this renewal was perhaps felt especially in American Catholic philosophy departments, where, in contrast to most of their secular counterparts, the history of philosophy remained the centre of gravity. Even as debates often raged about the extent to which the dominance of Thomism or Scholasticism should give way to other (analytic, philosophy of science, pragmatic) traditions in these departments, they continued to champion the study of the history of philosophy and by no means medieval philosophy alone. Catholic scholars of the Presocratics and Plato, Augustine and Aquinas, Descartes and Leibniz, Kant and Hegel, Schelling and Nietzsche all found themselves wrestling with Heidegger's ingenious takes on prominent positions adopted by these philosophers.

There was a further aspect of Heidegger's early thinking, closely related to his call to engage with past philosophers and his examples of doing so, that served as a particularly powerful undertow for those who had grown up within the Catholic philosophical tradition. That undertow came from the fact that Heidegger – no less than Aquinas, Scotus, and contemporaries inspired by them – thought by way of commentary on Aristotle's writings. This preoccupation with Aristotle was no doubt traceable in part to his study of medieval philosophy in Freiburg, culminating in his 1915 habilitation, *Duns Scotus' Doctrine of Categories and Meaning*. Heidegger was tireless in his attention to

Aristotle in the 1920s – indeed, *Being and Time* grew out of an attempt to determine the appropriate categories for interpreting Aristotle's texts. In this regard, too, his thinking resonated with Catholic thinkers, who had been weaned on Aristotle.[42]

But perhaps the overriding attractiveness of Heidegger's existential analysis was its identification of the awful freedom indicated by the numbing experience of anxiety. Kierkegaard had already driven home the fundamental relationship between anxiety and freedom – namely, that we are anxious precisely because of our freedom – and Sartre showed how it repeatedly surfaced in concrete, mundane experiences. But Heidegger alone made the crucial point that we are authentically ourselves only in response to this anxiety, when we feely embrace it.

Why Husserl and Heidegger?

In addition to the considerable overlap in the areas reviewed above (e.g., intentionality and being-in-the-world, *epoche* as first philosophy and fundamental ontology), Husserl's and Heidegger's phenomenologies converge in three respects that found a welcome response among American Catholic philosophers. In their phenomenologies, they affirmed the embodied character of human experience, they undertook their analyses of experience from a realist point of view, and they recognized the fundamental nature of truth.

Aquinas's Aristotelian philosophy, by underscoring the embodied character of human existence, presents a more plausible approach to considering the Incarnation than gnostic or dualistic versions of reality. Yet hylomorphism leaves Aristotelians with a difficulty in accounting for the lived experience of the body, particularly if the body is regarded merely as material or instrumental for the soul. Through its analyses of the embodied character of human experience, twentieth-century phenomenology makes a crucial, complementary contribution to traditional Thomistic and Aristotelian thinking. Merleau-Ponty is rightly considered of paramount importance in this regard, but his work builds on *Ideas II*, in which Husserl introduces a conception of the body as it is experienced (*Leib*), in contrast to the body (*Körper*) conceived as an anatomical and/or physiological object. But Merleau-Ponty's work is no less influenced by his adoption of Heidegger's model of being-in-the-world as *le-corps-au-monde* and by its distinctive, directional spacing (as a person navigates among the things within her world), in contrast to Cartesian space.[43]

Given their affinities with Aristotle's philosophical instincts, it is perhaps not surprising that both Husserl and Heidegger engaged in their philosophical analyses from a realist point of view. This realistic bent of their analyses struck yet a further chord with the traditional approaches of Catholic philosophers. However, since both thinkers paid due homage to the insights underlying certain idealist impulses,[44] this claim about their realist perspective requires some explaining. In the 1860s, in the face of the dismal prospects for German idealism in the wake of scientific advances, the slogan "back to Kant" became the watchword, understood as a renewed focus on determining the conditions of the possibility of the sciences. It is against this Neo-Kantian backdrop that Husserl's own slogan "Back to the matters themselves" is to be understood. There were two complementary sides to its import. Husserl was urging philosophers to shift their attention from a previous philosopher's standpoint (with the accompanying emphasis on analysis of the philosopher's writings) to the matters themselves. (Science had outgrown Kant's transcendental principles just as it had Hegel's *Enzyklopädie*.) But, more importantly, he was urging us to understand the matters themselves on their own terms as a condition for further scientific investigation and explanation (on the assumption that if you can't describe it, you can't explain it). Categorial intuitions into states of the matter (*Sachverhalte*) were now to take precedence over considerations of what matters must be like for the sake of a particular theory and its explanations. Despite occasional annoyance with the self-congratulatory tone of Husserl's slogan, Heidegger embraced its basic thrust.[45] Phenomenology, for Husserl as for Heidegger, was to take its bearings, first and last, from how things manifested themselves to us. In this way, they would not only capture and complement realist intuitions but also demonstrate how they could be appropriately and rigorously shaped through phenomenological analysis.

In their different ways, both Husserl and Heidegger expounded a conception of truth that was more basic than the truth of propositions or judgments.[46] Their phenomenologies overcome the logical prejudice of confining truth to a property of propositions or judgments alone – and all the attendant difficulties of such a conception of truth. In this way, they expand or, better, they recognize the scope of truth and its analysis beyond the sciences (which are generally intent on formulating a system of propositions along with their derivations from one another) in ordinary, pre-scientific and pre-theoretical experiences. Heidegger in particular conceives truth in this basic sense along lines closely akin to Aquinas's conception of truth as a transcendental.[47] This phenomenological approach accordingly opens a space for the experience of the truth in faith as well as the consideration of the divine personification of truth ("I am the Way, the Truth, and the Life").

Appendix

Overview of P&E dissertations in American Catholic philosophy departments

School	Heidegger	Husserl	Kierkegaard	Marcel	Merleau-Ponty	Nietzsche	Sartre	Scheler	Other*
Boston College	’71, ’74, ’77	’77†	’79	’68, ’73	’76	’74 (3), ’76†, ’77	’70, ’75†, ’77†	’70, ’77†	’50, ’74, ’75†, ’75, ’76†, ’77
Catholic University of America		’74, ’80	’73	’60†, ’70 (2)	’66, ’69, ’70		’60†, ’70	’51	’63, ’68
DePaul University	’71, ’72, ’73, ’80	’73, ’77	’79		’76, ’80	’76			’72, ’74, ’76 (2), ’77
Duquesne University	’70, ’71†, ’72†, ’72†, ’78 (2), ’80†	’73 (2)		’64, ’73	’68, ’75 (2)	’71†, ’74, ’77	’68, ’77	’68	’63, ’65, ’70, ’71, ’72†, ’72†, ’76, ’77 (2), ’80†, ’80 (2)
Fordham University		’63†, ’75	’59, ’64, ’67	’58, ’60, ’70, ’75	’63†, ’73, ’74 (3), ’75	’57, ’76,	’63†	’62, ’73, ’74, ’76	’56 (2), ’65, ’68, ’71 (2), ’74, ’75, ’76, ’79
Georgetown University	’67†, ’70, ’76	’70, ’75 (2), ’78					’65, ’75		’50, ’56, ’67†, ’76
Loyola University			’72			’75			’75
Marquette University				’70	’67, ’71	’75	’73, ’76†		’63, ’67, ’68, ’72, ’74, ’76†
University of Notre Dame		’60, ’68, ’75	’65, ’72, ’73, ’75 (2)	’62, ’68		’76	’66, ’70		’69, ’78
St Louis University					’71, ’72, ’73		’72	’64	’65, ’66, ’70 (2), ’72 (2), ’73, ’74, ’77, ’78, ’79

* "Other" includes dissertations on Beauvoir (part of a dissertation also on Sartre), Bergson, Blondel, Breton, Buber, Chardin, Derrida, Dilthey, Dumery, Freud (parts of dissertations on Heidegger, Nietzsche, and Sartre), Habermas, Hartmann, Hölderlin (parts of two dissertations also on Heidegger), Jaspers, Le Senne, Levinas, Loewith (part of a dissertation also on Jaspers), Marcuse, Mounier, Rahner (part of a dissertation also on Heidegger), Ricoeur, Schütz, Tillich (part of a dissertation also on Ricoeur), a dissertation on Gilde, Camus, and Dostoyevsky, as well as thematic dissertations.

†: When following two entries of the same year, for the same school, this indicates a single dissertation written on multiple thinkers. So, e.g., "60†" appears in the Catholic University of America row under both Marcel and Sartre, indicating a dissertation on both Marcel and Sartre.

(n): When a number in parentheses follows a year, this indicates multiple dissertations on that thinker for that year. Note, however, that this number will not include any dissertations cross-listed to another thinker (indicated by "†"), and which are given separate entries.

NOTES

1 The following report by Herbert Spiegelberg is telling: "One of the most important events for the introduction of phenomenology into the French-speaking world was the study session of the *Societé Thomiste* on Thomism and German contemporary phenomenology at Juvisy in September 1932. Jacques Maritain and Msgr. Noël presided. Father Daniel Fueling of the University of Salzburg gave an informed report on Husserl and Heidegger, and Father René Kremer of the University of Louvain compared the Thomist with the phenomenological position. In the momentous discussion, not only Msgr. Noël and Étienne Gilson but also old phenomenologists like Alexandre Koyré and Edith Stein took a leading part, trying to play down the idealist character of phenomenology and to stress the differences between Husserl and Heidegger. The spirit of the discussion suggested the possibility of an assimilation of the phenomenological approach by Catholic philosophers without commitment to Husserl's or Heidegger's conclusions." See Herbert Spiegelberg, *The Phenomenological Movement: A Historical Introduction*, 3rd rev. ed. (The Hague: Nijhoff, 1982), 433.

2 The universities are Boston College, Catholic University of America, DePaul, Duquesne, Fordham, Georgetown, Loyola (Chicago), Marquette, Notre Dame, and St Louis. Philadelphia did not have a PhD-conferring Catholic university during these years, but Thomas Busch (a Marquette PhD) and Jack Doody (a Notre Dame PhD) regularly taught courses on Merleau-Ponty and Kierkegaard respectively at Villanova. John Caputo arrived in 1968, and his early and still highly influential studies of Heidegger – *The Mystical Element in Heidegger's Thought* (1978) and (admittedly two years beyond this paper's self-imposed constraints) *Heidegger and Aquinas* (1982) – put Villanova on the map of major destinations for Catholic students with an interest in Heidegger.

3 Special thanks to James Bernauer, John Brough, Jack Caputo, Richard Cobb-Stevens, Gary Gutting, Patrick Murray, Ted Kisiel, John Rose, Tom Sheehan, Robert Sokolowski, and Ted Vitali for reminiscing with me about the reception of P&E in Catholic universities during these years (though, to be sure, none of them is responsible for the characterization of the reception on these pages).

4 See the appendix for a chart identifying dissertations on P&E written in departments of philosophy in American Catholic universities from 1950 to 1980. For his help with gathering information and drafting the appendix, and for his careful reading of a preliminary draft of the paper, I am grateful to Joseph Gamache.

5 Limiting considerations to American Catholic graduate schools specifies this review in three important respects. First, it omits the scope of philosophers at non-Catholic universities who, nonetheless, exercised an influence on the reception of P&E in Catholic universities (e.g., John Wild, Hannah Arendt, Hans Jonas, James Edie, William Earle). Second, it does not engage the importance of Canadian Catholic universities (Collège Dominicain, Laval, St Michael's) and individual scholars of Continental philosophy who moved freely between them and their American counterparts (e.g., Thomas Langan, author of *The Meaning of Heidegger: A Critical Study of Existentialist Phenomenology* [1959], who moved from St Louis University to Indiana University to Paris to St Michael's College; and his fellow Canadian, Kenneth Schmitz, who moved from Loyola University in Los Angeles to Marquette to Indiana [recruited by Langan] to Catholic University of America [before Langan, now in Toronto, again recruited his fellow Canadian, this time back to the north shores of Lake Ontario]). Third, it overlooks the abiding interest in phenomenology and existentialism within undergraduate Catholic colleges and universities at the time. Again, anecdotally, several of my undergraduate philosophy teachers at Divine Word College (Epworth, Iowa) – John Donaghey, William Fitzgibbon, Luis Manuel Rodriguez, and Bernard Wrocklage – studied at the Gregorian in Rome. Professor Wrocklage in particular offered extremely popular, year-long courses on existentialist themes; I also remember that Marcel's *Creative Fidelity* and Scheler's *Man's Place in Nature* were among the required readings during the final year for majors. In the department of philosophy at Xavier (Cincinnati) I remember courses in personalism offered by Bernard Gendreau that were replete with existentialist themes (at odds, apparently, with aspects of the Quebec Thomism propounded at Laval). In both undergraduate institutions, this exposure to phenomenology and existentialism, while by no means discouraged, was situated in a much more thorough study of Scholastic thought (sometimes pejoratively labelled "textbook Thomism").

6 Richard Cobb-Stevens only received his *licentiate* from Louvain, where he wrote a thesis on the work of Paul Ricoeur. Working in the chaplain's office at Yale University, Richard was talking to John Wild, the current chair of the philosophy department and a major proponent of P&E. In the course of their conversation, Wild asked Cobb-Stevens if he would like to come to a dinner he was having for a visiting professor from Paris. The visitor was Paul Ricoeur! At dinner, Ricoeur invited Richard to come to Paris to study with him and, with Wild's encouragement, Richard completed his doctorate, under Ricoeur's direction, from Université de Paris in 1971. Roughly a decade earlier, Adriaan Pepperzak had followed a similar route, moving from the *licentiate* at Louvain to doctoral work under Ricoeur in Paris.

7 Ernan McMullin (Notre Dame) might also be mentioned since he directed a dissertation on Husserl at Notre Dame; famed Aquinas scholars John Wippel (CUA) and Norris Clarke (Fordham) also completed their doctoral studies at Louvain, as did the long-time chair of the philosophy department of Loyola (New Orleans), David A. Boileau. The following also received their doctorates from European universities: Thomas Langan (St Michael's, Toronto) from Institut Catholique in Paris, Parvis Emad (DePaul) from Vienna, Manfred Frings (Duquesne, DePaul) from Cologne, Robert Lechtner (DePaul) from Fribourg.

8 In this group's first gathering, Richardson defended Heidegger's thought from Hans Jonas's charge that it was "profoundly pagan [in] character." For a more definitive version, see William J. Richardson, SJ, "Heidegger and God – and Professor Jonas," *Thought* 40 (1965), 18–40.

9 Sokolowski is widely recognized today as one of the world's leading phenomenologists, not only for the works mentioned but also for work he produced in the ensuing years. He has put his own formidable philosophical stamp on such themes as the nature of moral action and the human person, while also producing acclaimed studies of Christian theology's foundations and the Eucharistic presence.

10 In the 1970s at Georgetown, Kathleen Uhler (1975) and Francis Kelly (1978) also wrote dissertations on Husserl's thought, while George Sefler (1970) and Francis Kane (1976) wrote dissertations on Heidegger's thought (and linguistic analysis). A decade earlier Joseph Mihalich (1965) completed a dissertation on Sartre, and in the 1950s there were dissertations on existential philosophy and Blondel.

11 Dominic Balestra, "Quentin Lauer, in memoriam," *Proceedings*, American Philosophical Association, 1998, 150.

12 Thomas J. Shelley, *Fordham, A History of the Jesuit University of New York: 1841–2003* (New York: Fordham University Press, 2016), 356–8.

13 Two noted contemporary thinkers, Quentin Smith and Dennis Schmidt, completed their graduate studies with dissertations (in 1977 and 1980 respectively) on themes from P&E at Boston College.

14 See note 19 below.

15 Helping him to his car one day in the early 1970s after a seminar on Hegel, Collins showed me that he was working through a copy of Heidegger's *Erläuterungen zu Hölderlins Dichtung*.

16 The five themes may be summarized as follows: (1) philosophizing that closes the gap between intelligence and life; (2) a renewal of metaphysics, taking its bearings from the questioning self and its situation; (3) the worldliness of the human being (being-in-the-world); (4) human beings' inseparability from one another (*Dasein ist Mitsein*); and (5) appreciation that the questions of God and religiousness have "the highest practical

import in an age of religious crisis"; James Collins, *The Existentialists* (Chicago: Regnery, 1952), 244.

17 See his *The Phenomenological Movement: A Historical Introduction* (Berlin: Springer, 1960). Gary Gutting recalls that the venerable Walter Ong taught an influential course on existentialist literature, one that Gary had taken as a freshman. Ong was a polymath whom I remember attending my defence of a master's thesis on Scotus's doctrine of the predicables.

18 For excellent retrospectives on these currents, see John Caputo, "Confessions of a Postmodern Catholic: From St Thomas to Derrida," in *Faith and Intellectual Life*, ed. Curtiss Hancock and Robert Sweetman (Washington, D.C.: Catholic University of America Press, 2003), 64–92, and "Philosophy and Prophetic Postmodernism: Toward a Catholic Postmodernity," *American Catholic Philosophical Quarterly* 74, no. 4 (Autumn 2000), 549–68; my thanks to John Caputo for generously sharing not only these two articles with me, but also a copy of the paper he gave at SPEP for the anniversary year, entitled "Continental Philosophy of Religion: Then, Now and Tomorrow," later published in *Journal of Speculative Philosophy* 26, no. 2 (2012), 347–60, and included, in extended form, as chapter 3 of the present volume.

19 In 1967, for example, the Jesuit Walter Stohrer, who would go on to teach philosophy at Marquette for several decades, wrote a dissertation on "The Role of Martin Heidegger's Doctrine of 'Dasein' in Karl Rahner's Metaphysics of Man."

20 The title of the work by the SVD, Ralph Wiltgen, *The Rhine Flows into the Tiber: The Unknown Council* (New York: Hawthorn, 1967) has provided a telling image of this development. Though widely criticized for its unevenness and for not making its case sufficiently, John F. Kobler's *Vatican II and Phenomenology: Reflections on the Life-World of the Church* (Boston: Nijhoff, 1984) has also been roundly commended for exposing the considerable degree to which phenomenology contributed to the council's efforts to forge a new pastoral theology, doing so in a way that complemented rather than supplanted traditional Scholastic conceptions.

21 The leading political philosophies emerging from private and public universities at the time – for example, Rawls' *Theory of Justice* (1971) and Nozick's *Anarchy, State, and Utopia* (1974) – were largely apologists for the political status quo.

22 See John McCumber, *The Philosophy Scare: The Politics of Reason in the Early Cold War* (Chicago: University of Chicago Press, 2016), and *Time in the Ditch: American Philosophy in the McCarthy Era* (Evanston: Northwestern University Press, 2001).

23 Far from answering the question of the civic significance of P&E for Catholic philosophers, the past few paragraphs are an invitation to historians of this period of philosophy to provide some answers.

24 Herein lies yet another self-imposed limitation of this study. In addition to bracketing the influential work of Sartre and Merleau-Ponty, it also sets aside the work of such Catholic phenomenologists as Max Scheler, Edith Stein, Dietrich von Hildebrand, Gabriel Marcel, Eugen Fink, and Gustav Siewerth.

25 Husserl, *Ideen zu einer reinen Phänomenologie und phänomenologische Philosophie, Erstes Buch, Gesammelte Werke*, vol. 3/1, ed. Karl Schuhmann (Hague: Nijhoff, 1976), §58, S. 124f (hereafter "Ideen I"); but when asked by Roman Ingarden what he considered the fundamental problem of philosophy, he replied: "The problem of God, of course." See Louis Dupré, "Husserl's Thought on God and Faith," *Philosophy and Phenomenological Research* 29, no. 2 (December 1968), 201.

26 Husserl and Heidegger share a commitment to return to *die Sache selbst*, a commitment that entails rigorously excluding any appeal to something outside *die Sache selbst*, as explanation typically demands. Their shared commitment to describing *die Sache selbst* does not, of course, rule out ultimately different conceptions of the latter.

27 Leo XIII, Epistola encyclica *Aeterni Patris* (Librereia Editrice Vaticana online): "Vos omnes, Venerabiles Fratres, quam enixe hortamur, ut ad catholicae fidei tutelam et decus, ad societatis bonum, ad scientiarum omnium incrementum auream sancti Thomae sapientiam restituais, et quam latissime propagetis."

28 Pius X, Litterae encyclicae *Pascendi Dominici Gregis* (Librereia Editrice Vaticana online): "Primo igitur ad studia quod attinet, volumus probeque mandamus ut philosophia scholastica studiorum sacrorum fundamentum ponatur. Utique, *si quid a doctoribus scholasticis vel nimia subtilitate quaesitum, vel parum considerate traditum; si quidcum exploratis posterioris aevi doctrinis minus cohaerens vel denique quoquo modo non probabile; id nullo pacto in animo est aetati nostrae ad imitandum proponi* (Leo XIII., Enc. *Aeterni Patris*). Quod rei caput est, philosophiam scholasticam quum sequendam praescribimus, eam praecipue intelligimus, quae a sancto Thoma Aquinate est tradita …"

29 P&E were by no means the only alternatives toward which philosophers gravitated when they moved away from Thomism. In some departments (e.g., Notre Dame, St Louis), the history and philosophy of science represented an attractive direction; in others (e.g., R.C. Pollock, Vincent Potter, and Robert Johann at Fordham), American pragmatism exerted a strong pull, sometimes together with an interest in Lonergan (Boston College). See James Collins, "Thomism in the College" in *Three Paths in Philosophy* (Chicago: Regnery, 1962), 376–7.

30 Austria was an overwhelmingly Catholic country at the time that Husserl (who hailed from Moravia, part of today's Czech Republic) began his studies in Vienna with Brentano. Brentano was himself a student of Adolf Trendelenburg, a leading scholar of Aristotle and a critic of Hegel. Under the

direction of a prominent Catholic philosopher, Franz Jacob Clemens, Brentano wrote his dissertation *On the Manifold Meaning of Being according to Aristotle* in 1862; he was ordained in 1864; and, a few years later, completed his habilitation, *The Psychology of Aristotle, in particular his doctrine of Nous Poietikos* [*active intellect*]. Unable to accept the New Catholics' idea of papal infallibility, Brentano left the priesthood; this cost him his tenure at Vienna, which meant he could no longer direct graduate students, a turn of events that forced Husserl, then his student, to leave Austria and complete his doctoral studies in Germany with Carl Stumpf, one of Brentano's prize students.

31 Franz Brentano, *Psychologie vom empirischen Standpunkte*, vol. 1 (Leipzig: Duncker & Humblot, 1874), 115.

32 Roderick Chisholm brought home to mainstream American philosophers the importance of Brentano's conception of intentionality, though Quine made short work of it – or at least what he took to be the conception – in *Word and Object* (1960).

33 The latter use of "being," applicable across the categories, as well as Aristotle's three other senses of "being" (accidental, true, potential-and-actual), are transcendental. The fact that these divisions are not those of species falling under a common genus underscores the analogical character of being; it also corresponds to Husserl's differentiation of formalization and generalization, a differentiation crucial to Heidegger's initial attempts to develop a phenomenological method.

34 *Summa theologiae* I, q. 85, a. 2, ad 2. For Aquinas, the conception of Socrates as a human is a first intention, the conception of human (as the concept of how Socrates is conceived) is a second intention. The predicate "human" corresponds to the universal or, more precisely, a species, something predicable of many individuals. Yet whether the object of the conception is a thing or a concept, the act of conceiving itself is necessary but insufficient for the relevant conception (the first or second intention respectively). Just as "Socrates is a human being" is true because humanity is manifested in Socrates, so "humanity is a species" is true not simply because "human" is predicated truly of many individuals, but also because humanity manifests itself in them. Accordingly, logical concepts and forms that make up the objects of second intentions do so by virtue of the fact that they correspond to something in things. They are not to be confused with psychological contents, the objects of introspection, and the like (as Mill would have it). In this respect, Husserl's phenomenological investigations of such concepts, like many a Scholastic account, embed them within a larger account of reality and experience without sacrificing their objectivity. For an overview of these themes in Aquinas, see Gyula Klima, "The Semantic Principles underlying Saint Thomas Aquinas's Metaphysics of Being," *Medieval Philosophy and Theology* 5 (1996), 92–104.

35 Edmund Husserl, "Philosophie als strenge Wissenschaft," *Vorträge und Aufsätze (1911–1921)* in *Gesammelte Werke (Husserliana)*, vol. 25, ed. Thomas Nenon and Hans Rainer Sepp (Dordrecht: Kluwer, 1987), ss. 7–8; see also Daniel Dahlstrom, "Philosophy as an Opening for Faith," *Journal of Catholic Higher Education* 34, no. 1 (Winter 2015), 27–41.

36 Robert Sokolowski, "Husserl on First Philosophy," in *Philosophy, Phenomenology, Sciences: Essays in Commemoration of Edmund Husserl*, ed. Carlo Ierna, Hanne Jacobs, and Filip Mattens (Dordrecht: Springer, 2010), 4: "In his many efforts to define his transcendental phenomenology, Husserl has, in effect, been reconnecting with classical philosophy, which, in its Aristotelian formulation, theorizes being as being as it looks to the whole of things."

37 "Ideen I," § 57, S. 124.

38 Louis Dupré, "Phenomenology of Religion: Limits and Possibilities," *American Catholic Philosophical Quarterly* 66, no. 2 (Spring 1992): 175–88. Modifying Scheler's view, Dupré affirms the phenomenologist's need to move beyond a purely external description and enter into the religious act.

39 Debate has long raged over whether study of beings insofar as they exist (ontology) or study of the primary being (theology) is the centre of gravity of Aristotle's metaphysics. The opening question of Scotus's commentary on Aristotle's *Metaphysics* makes this abundantly clear: "Utrum subiectum metaphysicae sit ens inquantum ens, sicut posuit Avicenna, vel Deus et intelligentiae sicut posuit Commentator Averroes?" At the outset of *Sein und Zeit*, Heidegger contends that "all ontology [thus, a traditional part of metaphysics] … remains blind and a perversion of the objective most proper to it if it has not first sufficiently clarified the sense of being" (SZ 11). That clarification of the sense of being must start, he adds, with the entity that has an understanding of being or, more precisely, whose being matters to it. He designates this entity – equivalent but not identical to the human being – "being-here" (*Da-sein*). "Hence, the fundamental ontology, from which all others are first able to emerge, must be sound in the *existential analysis of being-here*" (SZ 13).

40 Catholic philosophers' appreciation of this insight does not entail acceptance of Heidegger's extension of this production model of being to Christianity itself. Thomas Prufer argues that Heidegger's assimilation of creation (*creatio ex nihilo*) to production, that is, making something real out of something possible (the idea) is a "misinterpretation," one of three such misinterpretations that Prufer finds in Heidegger; see Thomas Prufer, *Recapitulations: Essays in Philosophy* (Washington, D.C.: Catholic University of America Press, 1993), 74.

41 Martin Heidegger, *Beiträge zur Philosophie (vom Ereignis), Gesamtausgabe*, vol. 65, ed. Friedrich-Wilhelm von Herrmann (Frankfurt am Main: Klostermann, 1989), 423.

42 Nevertheless, a case can be made that Heidegger, influenced by Luther and Kierkegaard, was working toward developing categories for interpreting Aristotle that are at odds with Scholastic readings of the Stagirit.
43 In Leuven in the late 1930s Merleau-Ponty studied the manuscripts later published as the second volume of Husserl's "Ideas."
44 Martin Heidegger, *Sein und Zeit* (Tübingen: Niemeyer, 1972), 207.
45 Heidegger's insistence on the need for rooting ontology ontically echoes Husserl's demand that matters be returned to themselves; see SZ 13, 27.
46 Husserl, *Formale und Transzendentale Logik* (Halle: Niemeyer, 1929), §46, S. 113–16; Sokolowski, "Husserl on First Philosophy," 7, 16; Heidegger, SZ, §44.
47 SZ 38: *"Phänomenologische Wahrheit (Erschlossenheit von Sein) ist veritas transcendentalis."*

2 Philosophy between the Old World and the New: Neoscholasticism, Continental Philosophy, and the Historical Subject

GREGORY P. FLOYD

Vetera novis augere et perficere.

To tell the story of the North American reception of Continental philosophy, especially its reception by Catholic institutions of higher learning, we must begin not in the "New World," but in the Old World. We must begin not in the latter half of the twentieth century, but in the earlier half. And we must begin not with phenomenology and existentialism and hermeneutics, but with Neoscholasticism.

The need for new and expansive philosophical approaches, as well as an openness to such approaches in North America with its younger institutions and European-trained professors, was the result of seismic shifts on the continent across the sea. There are, to be sure, distinct characteristics, problems, and possibilities in the specifically North American reception of European philosophical thought. It is perhaps Gadamer who best articulates that *reception* is always *transformation* and that the momentum moves in both directions: we are transformed by our traditions even as we transform them. Nevertheless, these differences are most clearly seen and best appreciated against the background of the European context in relation to which they are both dependent and reactionary.

That context, for the purposes of this story, is defined by the emergence of Neoscholasticism in the late nineteenth century; by the largely reactionary position that Catholicism adopted toward modernism, which it conceived of primarily as a set of philosophical positions incompatible with traditional Christian commitments; and, finally, by the two world wars. The breaking apart of the Old World as the result of those wars led to new things (*rerum novarum*), among them new philosophies and, for the Catholic Church, a *nouvelle theologie*.

Because of its prior intransigence in the face of modernity and its questions as well as an older, more deep-seated philosophical negligence toward history and contingency, this transformation could not but be both fraught and painful. Fergus Kerr sums up well the situation from which our analysis begins: "The Roman Catholic church was so distant from Protestantism, the Enlightenment, 'progress,' 'liberalism,' 'modernism,' and so on, in the opening decades of the twentieth century that the engagement with 'modernity,' no doubt made inevitable by the two world wars, could not be other than traumatic. For decades, the pastors and most of the theologians sought to maintain the church in splendid isolation."[1] While such isolation was no longer feasible, it was far from clear what the way forward was to look like. The confusion was due not to a lack of answers but to a plurality of them. Yet there was also a freedom to examine figures and forms of philosophical thought. To ask what was useful or correct in them. And, perhaps as importantly, to ask what made them so compelling to modern women and men.

European – specifically continental European – thought was received in a particular way in the *New* World in part because the *Old* World had become a *different* world. This chapter will examine some of the main characters involved in the specifically Catholic strand of this story, first in Europe and then in North America. It argues that the new and different world that emerged was one whose philosophical and theological discourse had to contend with history in a new way and because of that with the philosophical and theological implications of human subjectivity. It argues that, while Thomism may not be incapable of engaging with these themes, nevertheless, as it was practised in mainstream Neoscholasticism, it did not engage those themes with sufficient philosophical rigour or generosity.

Neoscholasticism: Nineteenth-Century Ascent and Twentieth-Century Reactions

The Ascent of Neoscholasticism

Catholic theology in the first half of the twentieth century was conditioned by the second half of the century that preceded it. The nineteenth century saw the rapid rise and pervasive influence of Neoscholasticism and its formal promotion by Rome. Yet this occurred only in the last third of the century. As a whole, nineteenth-century Catholic theology was in fact more diverse and theologically rich than is sometimes thought.[2] Its animating question was the relationship between grace and nature. Implicated in that question were the *epistemic* question of the relation between faith and reason, the *philosophical* question of the relation between grace and freedom, and the *political* question of the relation between the church and the secular world. The religious historian Gerald McCool notes that "[t]he tension between the natural and supernatural orders was the single theme which ran through the diverse systems of Catholic theology and served as the focus of theological controversy from the early years of the century to its conclusion."[3] That debate was between the Tübingen school and Neoscholastics such as Matteo Liberatore and Joseph Kleutgen.[4] It was a debate about epistemic questions and their implications for how grace and nature stood in relationship to each other. For both schools, theology was to be scientific, but they differed on how one came to the first principles upon which theological deductions depended. Tübingen theologians posited that human knowledge of the first principles of metaphysics and ethics was the result of a primitive act of divine revelation, whereas the Neoscholastics worried, not without cause, that this primitive knowledge blurred the distinction between autonomous human reason and the gratuitous character of grace and divine revelation.

Neoscholasticism arose in the last third of the nineteenth century in response to the perceived inadequacies of both modern philosophy and the alternative responses offered by the theology of the day. It was greatly aided in its ascent by two papal pronouncements. On 22 April 1870, Pius IX promulgated his apostolic constitution *Dei Filius*, which stated that supernatural faith and natural reason constitute a "twofold order of knowledge, distinct not only in principle but also in object" and reaffirmed that "between faith and reason no true dissension can ever exist."[5] Almost a decade later, on 4 August 1879, Leo XIII promulgated his encyclical *Aeterni Patris*, which also treated the relationship between faith and reason but was by nature and intent more limited in scope, focusing as it did on the methods of philosophical instruction to be used in Catholic seminaries and faculties.[6] Taken together, the documents "amounted to a profoundly significant concrete decision by the highest authorities of the Catholic Church"[7] with respect to the nature, direction, and method of Catholic thought, theological as well as philosophical. They reaffirmed the importance of philosophy (as distinct from theology) for Catholic thought, but they also restricted its permissible forms. In essence and effect, these documents promoted Neoscholastic philosophy at the expense of its great nineteenth-century rivals, in particular, the Tübingen school.[8]

The Neoscholastics' reaction to Tübingen theology and its turn to the subject led them to overestimate the scope and authority of reason and to overlook important elements in the theology of their rival, especially its attentiveness to history. The Neoscholastics' dual emphasis on speculative truth and training evolved over time into a kind of rarified rationalism that was at once decadent and reductive: decadent in its playful removal from life and reductive in the forms under which it was actually taught to students of theology, who were not yet (and in many cases never would be) capable of breathing in such rarefied climes.[9]

In the early twentieth century the expansive and productive response to modernity envisioned by Leo XIII hardened into a reactionary position toward "modernism." This was brought about by a second set of papal pronouncements. In 1907, Pope Pius X issued his encyclical *Pascendi Domini Gregis*, which identified modernism as "the synthesis of all heresies" (§39) and provided a rather elaborate description of "the modernist" under the titles of philosopher, believer, theologian, historian, critic, apologist, and reformer. The document concluded with an unambiguous procedural admonition:

> All these prescriptions and those of Our Predecessor are to be borne in mind whenever there is question of choosing directors and professors for seminaries and Catholic Universities. Anybody who in any way is found to be imbued with Modernism is to be excluded without compunction from these offices, and those who already occupy them are to be withdrawn. The same policy is to be adopted towards those who favour Modernism either by extolling the Modernists or excusing their culpable conduct, by criticising scholasticism, the Holy Father, or by refusing obedience to ecclesiastical authority in any of its depositaries; and towards those who show a love of novelty in history, archaeology, biblical exegesis, and finally towards those who neglect the sacred sciences or appear to prefer to them the profane.[10]

A few years later, on 1 September 1910, Pius X issued the "Oath Against Modernism," which was "[t]o be sworn to by all clergy, pastors, confessors, preachers, religious superiors, and professors in philosophical-theological seminaries."[11] Together, these documents succeeded in focusing philosophical and theological instruction on the writings of Thomas and producing some of his most skilled readers, but they also created a climate of suspicion and fear on the continent and later in North America that often hampered productive theological work. As one American seminary instructor put it, the lesson of *Pascendi* was "Keep your mouth shut, your pen idle, and your mind at rest!"[12]

The Twentieth-Century Reaction to Neoscholasticism

The great shift in twentieth-century Catholic thought was from Neoscholasticism[13] to intellectual pluralism. Philosophically, this shift was signalled by a reorientation in interest and method away from systematic metaphysics toward philosophies of experience and history. Theologically, it was signalled – to take only the most dramatic contrast – by a reorientation away from debates about grace and nature toward the development of a nuptial mysticism.[14] The relatively rapid disintegration of the kind of Neoscholastic Thomism exemplified by figures such as Garrigou-Lagrange[15] can be explained by two related lines of pressure, one from outside Catholicism and one from within it.

The first challenge was that of history. For Liberatore, Kleutgen, and Garrigou-Lagrange, the success of Neoscholastic philosophy depended on its Aristotelian commitments, specifically its hylomorphism and account of science as knowledge of the universal and necessary causes of things. History and the historical subject, however, are beset on all sides by particularity and contingency and are therefore of at best secondary interest. Over the nineteenth century the "turn to the subject" that was the hallmark of post-Cartesian rationalism and post-Kantian idealism had come into contact with emergent historical consciousness.[16] This led to questions about the precise nature and different species of truth as communicated and apprehended by such a subject. This was more than a debate about mathematical truths and moral truths; it was also a more profound debate about language and meaning as the carrier of truths over time.

One consequence of the rise of historical consciousness was the recognition that propositions are made by and for individuals and that they are articulated in language and believed by persons who are part of distinct communities. Yet if faith is primarily a matter of the assent of the will to religious truth as articulated in the propositions of one's religious tradition, in what way do I believe what others of previous times and places believed?

The external challenge of historical consciousness and its critique of non-historical accounts of knowledge was aided by a second and related challenge from within Catholicism. This second challenge was that of a contextualist reading of Aquinas in light of his times and sources. This reading led to both interpretive and pedagogical critiques of the content and form of Neoscholastic scholarship and instruction. For the Neoscholastics, Thomas provided a philosophical and theological system – the only system, they claimed, that could reconcile faith and reason (against modernism) and validate the workings of natural knowledge (against Protestantism). For these reasons, a thorough study of his thought became mandatory academic training at all Catholic seminaries. This, in turn, required a distillation of that thought, which resulted, at one extreme, in the much-maligned "manualist tradition."[17] Manuals often reduced Thomas's thought to a set of twenty-four theses, which were subdivided into four content areas: ontology (being), cosmology (nature), psychology (soul), and theodicy (God). Such a reduction of a thinker of the magnitude of Aquinas would never serve any close reader. Gradually, careful students of Thomas began to read him in light of his own historical context, in particular, his patristic sources and his Dominican identity and spirituality.

The towering figure in this recovery of Aquinas was the French Dominican Marie-Dominique Chenu (1895–1990). He was a talented historian and theologian and focused his research on the sources used by Aquinas in his writings. Thomas's own attentiveness to and use of diverse religious and philosophical sources made Chenu and those who followed him critical of the purported "perennial philosophy"[18] of the Neoscholastics and its unfortunate pedagogical tool, the twenty-four theses. Chenu saw the manualist pedagogy to be of a piece with a reactionary apologetics against modernism *tout court*. He argued that reactionary thinking and the oversimplifications to which it was prone could not be further from the method of Thomas and his model of theological investigation: "[Manualists] oblige themselves thereby to summary condemnations of positions of which they are largely ignorant. This would certainly not be the path for disciples of Thomas Aquinas … [Others keep] for themselves a Thomism which is only a paragon of their own pseudo-religious integrist position."[19] Chenu and his successors did not contest that certain claims made by modernism posed challenging questions and in some cases consitituted real threats to Catholic orthodoxy; however, they maintained that these threats were not adequately met by the "exploitation of Thomas," nor by appeals to authority or by the rejection of rigorous argumentation.

Chenu became the founder for disciples and detractors alike of "ressourcement" Thomism, an approach to Thomas that sought to recover the sources and context of the theological *magister*. This was also the beginning of what came to be called *la nouvelle théologie*.[20] The standard-bearer of the *nouvelle théologie*, however, was fellow Frenchman Henri de Lubac. Although Chenu was never merely an historian,[21] it was de Lubac who made the broad and persuasive case not only for a rereading of Thomas, but also for nothing less than a rethinking of the entire practice of theology by means of a return to and retrieval of the tradition of Christian thought.

De Lubac was prolific and influential, and his arguments won the day, not only in bringing about a reconsideration of the nature, practice, and language of theology, but also in convincing people of the decidedly *non*-traditional nature of what he considered to be Neoscholastic rationalism. Chenu had argued (following Gilson) that the false conception of intelligibility besetting modern theology was native not to Thomas but rather to Christian Wolff (1679–1754). It was by means of Wolff that theology had become beholden to Enlightenment rationalism. The idea of truth as pure, extra-mental, and eternal was ultimately derivative of the very Enlightenment reasoning that undergirded much of the modernist thinking to which the Neoscholastics thought themselves the only response! How could such an account accommodate the historical and contingent character of the central Christian belief, the Incarnation?[22] Such a "hermeneutic of pure reason" led to a misreading of Thomas and the speculative reduction of his thought to the twenty-four theses, which, curiously, map exactly Wolff's fourfold distinction between ontology, cosmology, psychology, and theodicy. In accord with Gilson and Chenu, De Lubac argued that Neoscholasticism was a derivate of Enlightenment rationalism. Underlying this critique was the claim that if theology was to be a science, it could not be a uniquely speculative or abstract one because its foundation was a historical revelation. As Brian Daley observes, for De Lubac, "[t]he character of theological truth was always radically bound up in the historical limits of human language and culture, because God had revealed himself in the events and words of human history."[23] De Lubac's solution was a return to the fathers as well as "a classical form of Thomism."

Thus, the basic critique of Neoscholasticism – that as philosophy it was an inadequate foundation for theology and that as theology it was bad theology – was advanced historically by Chenu and theologically by de Lubac. It was then taken up by the main theologians of the next generation: Rahner, Lonergan, and Balthasar. Each of these thinkers claimed that he had been taught "Suarezianism,"[24] not Thomism, in seminary.[25] They, like de Lubac, sought to retrieve a more authentic Thomas by upending centuries of sedimented interpretations that (they claimed) distorted his true theological genius.

Thus, the dominant strands of mid- and late-twentieth-century theology were characterized by a rereading of Thomas and by a reading *behind* him to the patristic sources that had inspired much of this thought and language. However, while the critique becomes specifically *theological* by the time we arrive at de Lubac, we should not forget that its origins are *philosophical*. Neoscholasticism is proposed first and foremost as the *philosophy* most appropriate to Catholic theology, and its success or failure must be judged on philosophical grounds. It is the broader debate about history occasioned by European philosophy and the implications of that debate for philosophical accounts of subjectivity that underlie this theological debate. Therefore, it should not surprise us that, in addition to the Greek Fathers, the theologians who rose to prominence prior to Vatican II and in the post-conciliar period were also engaged with contemporary currents of European philosophy. Chenu and Charlier took the advancements in historical criticism and method seriously and integrated them into their work.[26] De Lubac engaged with Feuerbach, Kierkegaard, Nietzsche, and Dostoevsky in his *Drama of Atheist Humanism*. Rahner and Balthasar were both indebted to the thought and categories of Martin Heidegger – Rahner directly and Balthasar indirectly through the Erich Przywara and the Heideggerian Thomist Gustav Siewerth. Finally, Lonergan's monumental *Insight* is a rethinking of the Thomistic account of knowledge that enlists the aid while also critiquing the defects of the two great villains of the Neoscholastic polemic against modernism: Descartes and Kant. It is not coincidental that these last three – Rahner, Balthasar, and Lonergan – each felt the need to deconstruct the Neoscholastic epistemology they had been taught and to reconstitute Thomas's insights in the modern language of intentionality, subjectivity, and historicity.[27]

For the remainder of this chapter, we focus on the lone North American in the group and ask more precisely what the nature and influence of contemporary European thought was on the thinking of Bernard Lonergan, SJ.

Lonergan, Modernity, and Continental Philosophy

Bernard Lonergan is uniquely positioned to help us examine the confluence in twentieth-century Catholicism of Neoscholasticism, the *ressourcement* Thomism undertaken by the early figures of the *nouvelle théologie*, and the increasing influence on Catholic culture of postwar European philosophies, especially phenomenology, existentialism, and hermeneutics. He was the most significant English-language theologian at the time of Vatican II, though, while he attended as a *peritus*, he was not particularly influential in its proceedings or documents.[28] He was also a professor of Christology and Trinity at the Gregorian from 1953 to 1965, in which capacity he exercised considerable influence over generations of future North American priests and theologians. He was also professor of theology at Regis College (1940–53, 1965–75), Harvard University (1971–2), and Boston College (1975–83). His intellectual work and his life were tied more closely to the institutional life of Catholic seminaries and universities than could be said of some of his notable contemporaries (e.g., De Lubac, Balthasar).[29]

Echoing the programmatic motto of John XXIII at the start of Vatican II[30] and the Spanish existentialist Ortega y Gasset, Lonergan described himself as endeavouring to do philosophy "at the level of our time." In his case, this meant lecturing and writing in Latin in Rome in the final years of the manualist era, then living through the years of the Second Vatican Council and the tremendous shift it engendered in the institutional, intellectual, and liturgical life of the Catholic church, as well working well into the post-conciliar era until his death in 1984. His intellectual trajectory begins with early Latin writings on the relation between grace and freedom and the phenomena of *verbum* and *intelligere* in the work of Thomas Aquinas.[31] These works can be described best as textual: they are neither Neoscholastic system-building nor *ressourcement* historiography.[32] They constitute a theological and interpretive achievement that to this day stands in its own right.[33] Yet, after what he described as "eleven years reaching up to the mind of Thomas," Lonergan went on to write his great philosophical work *Insight* (1957), in which he develops a comprehensive response to modernity by rethinking epistemology and metaphysics on the basis of his cognitional theory. The work is expansive and generous in its dialogue with contemporary European philosophy. It engages with modern science and theories of evolution, with individual and communal fallibility and bias, and with ethics and religion. His second great work, published fifteen years later, was titled *Method in Theology* (1972). In it, he builds on *Insight*'s phenomenology of cognitional interiority to meet the challenges and the possibilities signalled by the rise of historical consciousness and the hermeneutic revolution it occasioned.

In 1980, a few years before his death and looking back on the development of his thought, Lonergan remarked: "All my work has been introducing history into Catholic theology."[34] He had come to see that "[t]he whole problem in modern theology, Protestant and Catholic, is the introduction of historical scholarship."[35] It is clear from reading Lonergan's work that by "history" he does not mean only the particular challenge posed by the modern biblical historian or form critic. The rise and development of historical criticism was due to the more pervasive phenomenon of *historical consciousness*, which not only situates texts in their originary *milieux* but also situates the people and traditions that interpret them. Thus, we are speaking not only of *history* but also of what Martin Heidegger called *historicality*:[36] the basic characteristic of all human beings as situated in history and conditioned by it to various degrees including, and especially, in their apprehension of truth. This point is important because it helps us grasp why a developing account of *history* necessitates a developing account of *subjectivity*. Lonergan's account of human subjectivity develops over the course of his work. While many of its basic features are articulated in *Insight*, there are further developments and essential additions that appear only later in *Method*, particularly those pertaining to the constitutive role of meaning in human lives and institutions. Ultimately, his full account of subjectivity recognizes two complementary vectors of development. In the first, a human being is conditioned by history in the forms of community and language, which secure for her the initial possibilities of her development. In the second, she takes increasing responsibility for the role she plays in the construction and development of history in ways that create and heal, rather than destroy and harm.[37] Thus, two of the broad themes that span the length of Lonergan's intellectual work are those of history and subjectivity. However, not far from either theme is always a discussion of truth: How is it that we as temporal, historical beings can know truth? Lonergan engages and incorporates these themes and questions theologically in a manner that is faithful to the insights of his tradition, above all to Thomas, but also honest about the difficult questions and real advances of modern science and contemporary philosophy.

Given the length of his career, Lonergan's engagement with modernity encompasses both modernism and postmodernism,[38] though these terms serve more as landmarks than as precise coordinates. In fact, Lonergan is as concerned with modern science as he is with the epistemic legacies of Descartes and Kant or the responses to them by Husserl and Heidegger. Yet across his varied engagements we can discern a basic disposition that is philosophically rooted. It can be summed up as both a presumption of and an openness to *development*. He does not repudiate or reverse the basic philosophical and theological positions outlined in his early Latin works on Thomas. On the contrary, he maintains that this early work was of lasting benefit to him.[39] Yet he also took the call to "aggiornamento"[40] seriously. The profundity of his engagement with contemporary thinkers in various disciplines is already on display in *Insight* (1957) and continues to grow in breadth and depth moving forward. While he had none of the inclination for polemic that characterized Daniélou and De Lubac, in his own more understated way he too worked to recover and preserve the authentic theological tradition by showing the insufficiency of certain prevalent forms under which it was supposed to be communicated and preserved. His critique of classicism and his careful "phenomenology" of bias and decline are the clearest examples of this.[41] Thus, Lonergan had to do in North

America what De Lubac and others did in France, Germany, and Belgium as well as in Europe more generally.

The history of modernism and Catholicism in North America is different in important ways. To begin with, it was less acrimonious and less personal. This was in part because in its early stages, the debate focused on institutions rather than on the thinkers within them. The first third of the twentieth century in America saw a renaissance in Catholic education. Much of that history revolves around the founding and early decades of the Catholic University of America. Founded in 1889, CUA "was a landmark in American Catholics' response to challenges of modernity on both the institutional and the ideological levels."[42] Ironically, perhaps, that response opened with a similar controversy. While American Catholics generally agreed that the university was the place to meet the challenge of modernity, they nonetheless disagreed about how best to go about it. This disagreement led to "liberal" and "conservative" factions within American Catholicism. The two lines of thought were predictable. Conservatives[43] emphasized the real threats that aspects of modernity posed to Catholic belief and practice, and they proposed to meet those threats by emphasizing the orthodox teachings that could correct them. Liberals felt that this account tended, in practice, to be monolithic, seeing only the negative aspects of modernity. Instead, they emphasized a "discriminating response" that would accept what was good and integrate it with traditional teaching. Moreover, they believed "that American culture most fully realized the possibilities for good in modern civilization."[44] Because of their emphasis on the distinct promise offered by America, they became known as "Americanists." Initially, CUA was founded and directed by these Americanists,[45] who advocated a discriminating but open posture toward modernity, but the tide turned against them when the apostolic delegate, Archbishop Francesco Satolli, formerly their promoter, switched his allegiances. Ultimately "Americanism" was condemned in 1889 by Leo XIII in his *Testem benevolentiaea*, which equated it with accomodationism. This moment in the institutional life of American Catholic universities is important for a few reasons.

First, it is a signal example of the American context in which religious institutions of higher learning occupy a central place in debates about religion and public life.[46] Second, the papal condemnation "exerted a broader negative influence by closing off self-conscious reflection on the relationship between the Catholic religion and the national culture for some years."[47] Third and finally, the Americanist controversy was still fresh in the minds of American Catholics when the largely European phenomenon of "modernism" moved across the pond a decade or so later. Americanists were at pains to distinguish their posture of openness toward what was authentic in modernity from the "theological liberalism" of some European modernists, which they rejected as heretical. The cumulative effect of *Testem benevolentiaea* (1899), *Pascendi Gregis* (1907), and the Integralist movement was negative to the extent that it confined Catholic intellectual life to safer channels of thought and prevented certain forms of productive self-reflection.[48] As on the continent, however, one effect of the narrowing of the Catholic engagement with the world was renewed attention to the sources of that tradition, which yielded lasting benefit: "[It] led to a great recovery [of] medieval history and culture and ... furnished the cognitive foundation of American Catholic intellectual and cultural life."[49]

Lonergan lived and worked in both these contexts, teaching in Roman, Canadian, and American universities amid these controversies, many of which focused on his Jesuit confrères. In his own work, he defined a "context" as an interrelated set of questions and answers, and his posture of critical openness to contemporary thought in its various forms is above all an openness to *questions*. As we turn to the texts themselves, we find a growing appreciation for the questions raised by key "continental" figures and their attempts to grapple with them.

From Insight *to* Method in Theology

Like his European counterparts, Lonergan grasped that history and subjectivity were the central issues to be integrated into Catholic philosophy and theology if they were to have any productive concourse with the modern world. As we noted earlier, his overarching goal was to introduce history into Catholic theology, where history encompassed the correct understanding and incorporation of historical critical exegesis into theological method as well as a deeper appropriation of the historicity of any knower and expression.[50] Summing up the changes some years later, Lonergan noted that for a century, "theologians have gradually been adapting their thought to the shift from the classicist culture, dominant up to the French revolution, to the empirical and historical mindedness that constitutes its modern successor."[51] This shift from a classicist model to a historical one implies a fundamental rethinking of the method of theology, though not of its primary nature. This fundamental rethinking requires the frank acknowledgment that theology has moved from a *deductive model* that began from indubitable premises of Scripture and tradition, and that deduced conclusions, to an *empirical model* in which "Scripture and Tradition now supply not premises, but data."[52] With this empirical model, there is a much longer road from data to interpretations to (probable) conclusions. While deductive theology sought universality and permanence, empirical theology is characterized, in contrast, by historical-mindedness. Here fixity has given way to *development*; it requires reference to time, context, and situation, and it also leads inevitably to specialization.[53]

For Lonergan, again like his European contemporaries, these concessions were not naive accommodations to a secular culture and academy, but rather philosophically necessitated conclusions about the human condition within which divine truth is revealed and appropriated. Yet he did not think these realizations, which constituted the "new context" of theology, fundamentally changed its directive, which remained to understand and communicate the God of revelation to contemporary men and women.[54] Finally, like many of them, he found in Aquinas a model of such an approach. For Aquinas, according to Lonergan, theology moulded and transformed culture. Therefore, the Thomistic theological approach provided a "paradigm of integration" by which culture and theology mutually influence each other: culture by raising problems and theology by thinking them in relationship to God, nature, sin, and grace. In short, "theology not only has to reflect on revelation, but also it has somehow to mediate God's meaning into the whole of human affairs."[55]

Such an *integral* approach was characteristic of Lonergan's engagement with contemporary culture over his lengthy career. That career was marked, on the one hand, by an unwavering commitment to his account of critical realism[56] – a realist epistemology rooted in the thought of Aristotle and Thomas – and of metaphysics, though the latter in a new sense, as we will see. Yet on the other hand, he considered these commitments compatible with a set of basic insights concerning subjectivity and history that constitute the foundation of much contemporary philosophical thought. This integrated position developed over the life of his thought and can be characterized as a gradual movement from dismissal to critical appropriation.[57]

In his work *Insight* (1957), which proposes a cognitional theory that he calls "intentionality analysis," the term "phenomenology" appears only a single time, in the context of a three-paragraph summary of the phenomenological method, after which it is roundly dismissed as the most "attenuated form of biological extroversion" (i.e., empiricism). In Lonergan's terms, Husserl's phenomenology is "counter-positional," which is to say that Husserl's account of consciousness disagrees with the "basic position" sketched by Lonergan and described as follows:

> [A philosophical position on cognition] will be a basic position (1) if the real is the concrete universe of being and not a subdivision of the "already

> out there now"; (2) if the subject becomes known when it affirms itself intelligently and reasonably and so is not known yet in a prior "existential" state; and (3) if objectivity is conceived as a consequence of intelligent inquiry and critical reflection, and not as a property of vital anticipation, extroversion, and satisfaction ... [A] basic counterposition ... contradicts one or more of the basic positions.[58]

In *Insight,* Lonergan takes phenomenology to be a form of "rarefied empiricism" that contradicts (1) and (3) by equating evidence with the "already out there now" and thereby limiting knowledge to what is known by a crude account of sense experience. This is a somewhat superficial and ultimately erroneous reading of Husserl, but Lonergan's critical interlocutors in *Insight* were not phenomenologists and existentialists, but the fathers of philosophical modernity: Descartes, Hume, Kant, and Hegel.

As Lonergan would learn, a commitment to engaging with contemporary philosophy involves a commitment to appropriating its language, at least provisionally, in an exercise of intellectual hospitality. For this reason, it can be tempting to see discontinuity and departure between Lonergan's early Thomistic studies and his later philosophical and theological work, which abandons, by and large, the idioms of Neoscholasticism; however, I think this would be a misrepresentation. Rather, like Chenu and Rahner, Lonergan's close study of Thomas led to his renewal of philosophy and theology: *Insight* and *Method in Theology* each are read more fruitfully as a reworking and development of those earlier works (*Verbum* [1946–9] and *Grace and Freedom* [1940], respectively) in light of the contemporary preoccupation with historicity and subjectivity. During his eleven years (1938–1949) "reaching up to the mind of Thomas," Lonergan recovered a more authentic Thomas and began to see how his insights could help one meet the challenges posed by modernity. Read in light of these early works, we ought to interpret those later works not as a departure from his early Thomistic studies but as an *aggiornamento* of them.

Already in *Verbum,* according to Fred Lawrence, Lonergan lays out a "hermeneutics of cognitional interiority." The work is an interpretation of the way in which, for Aquinas, acts of conceiving and judging depend on prepredicative acts of understanding. Lonergan notes perceptively that for Thomas the proof of this account is not a metaphysical deduction, but the advertence to one's own cognitional activity. In other words, Thomas invites his readers to verify the cognitional operations he describes in their own acts of experiencing, conceiving, and judging. In this sense, while no less a realist, Thomas invites a "turn to the subject," which is understood as a turning to oneself to understand and verify the set of cognitional activities that ultimately constitute epistemology and lead us to metaphysical knowledge. This turn inward has Augustine as its predecessor. "The heart of Lonergan's interpretation," according to Lawrence, "is the discovery that Thomas Aquinas learned from Augustine that one must understand the process in oneself by which understanding and conceiving, reflecting and judging actually occur in order to acquire the natural analogy for processions in God."[59] Thus, Aquinas's important principle – *secundum modum cognoscentis*[60] – must be read against the screen of Augustine's *interiore modo.* Lonergan integrates both insights when he states: "since we know by what we are, so also we know that we know by knowing what we are."[61]

In *Insight*, as in *Verbum*, we find a "phenomenology of the subject." The later work retains the insights of the earlier analysis, which are now in conversation with – and at times enriched by – the dominant currents of modern philosophy and modern science. *Insight* is a large and intimidating book burdened by the number and scope of the problems it engages and the depth of its responses. For this reason it is easy to forget the basic aim of the work as a whole; yet it too invites its reader to make the decisive turn inward: "More than all else the aim of the book is to issue an invitation to a personal, decisive act."[62] The "moving" or "developmental" viewpoint from which the work is written is a version of the scholastic *ordo inventionis* that endeavours to bring the reader to discover in herself the various operations and their relations and through them the world that comes into view. The result, in both cases, though more developed in *Insight*, is the discovery of a recurring and interrelated set of cognitional operations – experiencing, understanding, and judging – that underlie any form of knowing. This sets us on the path to greater clarity by identifying an order of questions internal to the order of our questioning. Once we have articulated what we do when we are knowing (cognitional theory), we can then articulate what knowledge is and why that is knowing (epistemology), and finally, what we can know actually and potentially when we know that (metaphysics).

Thus, Lonergan concedes the Kantian claim that epistemology is, *in one sense*, prior to metaphysics, but he claims that both are founded upon a still more basic phenomenology of consciousness, which he calls cognitional theory. This is, in its own way, a return to the priority of being, only in this case it is a return to the knowing human being who must affirm her own intelligent existence within being as a means of knowing what knowing is and thereby also knowing what she knows. This approach avoids restricting being pre-emptively to a prefabricated set of epistemic parameters (e.g., rationalism, empiricism, or idealism) or to a "naive" realism that lacks a sufficiently complex and differentiated account of meaning and that admits as real only what is "already out there now." We see then that Lonergan grants the subject as the unavoidable starting point from which to begin doing philosophy and consequently theology. This is to grant the Aristotelian dictum that we must begin with what is first for us (*quoad nos*), even if it may not be first in itself (*quoad se*). Yet in doing so we discover a set of operations that describe human intelligence *in se* and therefore provide the necessary conditions for collaboration between people and between disciplines. Lonergan seeks to do justice to the great cumulative and collaborative project of human knowing: to account for its past success and provide for its future continuation. Thus, in turning to the subject we need not turn away from metaphysics, as many of his contemporaries feared, although we must conceive of it differently.

To those who would claim that such an account reduces objectivity to subjectivity and therefore to relativism, Lonergan poses this rhetorical question: "Does philosophy begin from what is first for us, or from what is first in itself?" To claim to know what is first in itself is to claim to know in a manner that is inhuman; and that is to contravene Thomas's central principle that "what is known is known according to the mode of the knower." This, according to Lonergan, was precisely the mistake of the decadent Scholasticism of the sixteenth century and the Neoscholastic revival: "The scholastic tradition, by and large, was wont to consider 'being' first, though 'being' is not first for us but first in itself ... Does [philosophy] begin with 'being' or with the existential subject?"[63] To begin from the existential subject one must begin "from a phenomenology of coming to know."[64]

Precisely because *Insight* was an intervention in the modernist debate around the question of knowing, it was somewhat deaf toward the new questions being posed in Europe in the wake of the Second World War. Yet immediately after Lonergan published *Insight*, he began to revise his position on phenomenology and existentialism. In the summer of 1957 – the same year *Insight* was published – he gave a lecture series at Boston College titled "Phenomenology and Logic."[65] The second half of this series explored the broad lines and major figures of both phenomenology and existentialism. His engagement here with phenomenology was more extensive as well as more nuanced. He considered a wider range of thinkers working in the field of phenomenology,[66] and he conducted a related albeit distinct dialogue with existentialism. Moreover, the discussion was more nuanced, with a richer characterization of phenomenology in general and with greater attentiveness to differences in aim and approach between specific Continental thinkers. Suggestively, in the lectures, Lonergan referred to phenomenology not as a form of empiricism but rather as "a powerful instrument" for philosophers and psychologists.

Lonergan's change in attitude toward phenomenology, and toward Continental philosophy more broadly, can be characterized in two ways. First, *historically*, his context changed. By 1952 he had returned to Rome to teach, and it was his students, in particular his European seminarians, who led him to read again and more deeply the authors sweeping the continent.[67] This anecdotal evidence is corroborated by a number of playful asides throughout the lectures pointing to individual thinkers or tenets that were particularly attractive to European seminarians and for the same reason particularly inconvenient for their professor of dogmatic theology.[68] The lectures contained the results of his rereading of some Continental thinkers.[69] This new context constituted by new questions led Lonergan to reconsider phenomenology. *Conceptually*, he shifted from conceiving phenomenology as a *school* to conceiving it as a *tool*. As an *instrument* of philosophical investigation, phenomenology cannot be, strictly speaking, "counterpositional" in Lonergan's sense, although it can be extended beyond its proper field of application. The language of instrumentality allows for the possibility of a fruitful integration between phenomenology and Lonergan's method of metaphysics.[70]

In the lectures, Lonergan draws a number of favourable comparisons between phenomenology and his own critical realism, which I will summarize under three basic points of contact. The first is that both have as their intended goal being as such, and being is not preemptively limited to either the empirical or the ideal. To meet the criteria listed above, it is key that a "positional" philosophy admit both the "data of sense" and the "data of consciousness." Lonergan's insight into the equiprimordiality of these forms of evidence is his solution to the false problem of the Cartesian dualism of the *res cogitans* and the *res extensa*. The merit of phenomenology, in his view, is that in it too, "nothing is excluded from consideration."[71] Second, phenomenology recognizes the intelligibility of being. Husserl's account of *categorial intuition*[72] observes that in addition to simple perception we experience complex acts of consciousness that apprehend not just objects but also *relations*: states of affairs, objects *in combination with*, *separate from*, or otherwise *in relation to*. These acts of categorial intuition grasp that relations are necessary, non-sensible components of my experience and not imposed on sensible data by my understanding. Using his own terms, Lonergan describes this as "data as structured by insight."[73] In recognizing that preconceptual data are already structured by insight, the phenomenologist recognizes the identity of being and the intelligible and the organic complementarity of intending subject and intended object.[74] Thus, less than a year after the publication of *Insight*, in which Lonergan described phenomenology as a "refined empiricism," he describes it now more favourably as "an account, description, presentation of data structured by insight"[75] that grasps the way in which human understanding is constitutive of being.

Finally, Lonergan is persuaded by the way in which phenomenology's account of intentional consciousness allows us to make sense of the development, aberration, and conversion of subjectivity. He reserves his highest praise for Husserl's account of the way all thinking occurs within a *horizon*.[76] That account does justice both to the heuristic nature of human intelligence and to its conditionedness. A horizon[77] is a "known-unknown" that we come to understand incrementally. But it is also prone to change: to broaden or to contract. The language of horizons helps us grasp how conversion is integral to intelligence as well as the way our intelligence is conditioned by the role tradition plays in the formation of horizons as well as by our facticity.

The "Lectures on Phenomenology and Logic" give evidence of the degree to which Lonergan has moved beyond the particular questions and polemics of "modernism" (attended to with particular care, as I have suggested, in *Insight*) and is engaging with the early European figures in phenomenology and existentialism. The implications of this burgeoning historical consciousness for philosophy and theology and their accounts of subjectivity would occupy him for the next fourteen years. Thus, while the "Lectures on Phenomenology and Logic" represent something of a *Kehre* in Lonergan's thinking about Continental philosophy, we must wait until his second major work, *Method in Theology* (1971),[78] for a fuller account of what stance theology – and a philosophy hospitable to it – might take toward Continental philosophy. That fuller account requires Lonergan to engage not only with phenomenology and existentialism but also with philosophical and theological hermeneutics *tout court*.

Method in Theology *and Beyond*

Method in Theology approaches contemporary culture with what I have called elsewhere[79] a "hermeneutic of generosity." It begins from the premise that the function of theology is to "mediate between a cultural matrix and the significance of a religion in that matrix."[80] In its dialogue with Continental philosophy,[81] *Method* is not only a description but also an enactment of the method it propounds. Ultimately, these two impulses – the need for a method in theology and the need for an adequate response to contemporary culture – are of a piece. The purpose of this method is to enable an authentic and ongoing self-appropriation of one's knowing and living that can accommodate the peculiarly human temporality in which all knowledge, even if "objectively true," is also always "subjectively held" by concrete people in diverse circumstances and with varying degrees of insight and bias. In one sense, then, Lonergan's "Method in Theology" is a "Method in Hermeneutics" in the broad and undifferentiated sense employed by Heidegger. It is the means by which intelligent persons engage with history in such a way that insights become successive and cumulative without ceasing to be historically conditioned. *It is the means by which we come to know being in time*: the means by which we can come to an understanding of truth in the midst of development and also in view of future development.[82]

For Lonergan, the priority accorded to history implies a rethinking of subjectivity. While this was begun in *Insight*, *Method* takes a further step by recognizing what Ivo Coelho calls "the existential priority of the horizon of deliberation."[83] Lonergan supplements his earlier account with an additional operation of consciousness: experiencing, understanding, judging, *and deciding*. The deliberating and deciding subject is the starting point of theology for at least two reasons. First, any articulation of the meaning and implications of Revelation (i.e., any theology) is the product of a deliberating and deciding subject. Following Kierkegaard, Lonergan cautions us not to treat philosophy or theology as "so objective that it is independent of the mind that thinks it."[84] Second, for the theologian, these free and rational beings (herself included) are what is "first for us" in the order of knowing. Thus, there is an important sense in which the truths of Scripture and those of tradition are also "human truths" to the extent that they are "truths for humans," both in their manner of apprehension and in their intended terms. This is not a denial of metaphysics (what is first in itself), but it does relocate and relativize it: "The question of God may begin as a purely metaphysical question but it unavoidably becomes moral and religious, so that there can be no philosophy of God isolated from the cultural and personal background and expectations of the questioner."[85] Elsewhere, Lonergan explains that in this account, metaphysics is no longer first philosophy, but third philosophy:[86] we must know *who* we are and *how* we know in order to know *what* we know.

As we can see, increasingly, Lonergan comes to frame the achievements of *Insight* in light of the concerns and also the language of contemporary Continental philosophy, and phenomenology in particular.

He considers the clarification of the nature of human knowing to be central to many of the key disagreements in both philosophy and theology. However, in turning to theology specifically we encounter a second set of problems that are grouped not under the heading of *phenomenology*, but rather under that of *hermeneutics*.[87]

The broader engagement with modernity and postmodernity that characterized much of twentieth-century Catholic life was in many ways a recapitulation of the main issues faced by Protestant thinkers and theologians in the nineteenth century. The entrance of historical consciousness and the resulting methods of critical history called into question prevailing notions of truth as well as the nature of the human intelligence that grasps such truth. In the years between *Insight* (1957) and *Method* (1972), Lonergan came to see that "[t]he problem of hermeneutics coincides with the problems of Catholic Theology."[88] The early sections of this chapter sketched the initial reactionary model that proved inadequate as a response. Neoscholastic theology, Lonergan wrote years later, "replaced the inquiry of the *quaestio* by the pedagogy of the thesis" and "gave basic and central significance to the certitudes of the faith, their presuppositions and their consequences."[89] He, in contrast, sought a *via media* between such "ahistorical orthodoxy" on the one hand, and, on the other, a critical approach that evacuated religious texts and traditions of their meaning. His proposal was to develop a method that preserved continuity while also allowing for development. He summed up his intent in his 1970 essay "Philosophy and Theology" as follows: "Only a theology structured by method can assimilate the somewhat recently accepted hermeneutic and historical methods and it alone has room for developing doctrines and developing theologies."[90] Yet he maintained that these "new methods and conclusions do not imply a new revelation or a new faith."[91]

Lonergan's increased interest in hermeneutics was proportionate to his growing appreciation of the scope, complexity, and centrality of meaning in human life. The world of mature humans – lettered and unlettered, scientist, humanist, and soldier – that world is a world *mediated by meaning*. This insight required him to expand greatly his philosophy of meaning from the account of sign and signified in *Insight* in order to accommodate the entire complex of what he called "functional specialties"[92] in *Method*. Like *Insight*, *Method* was in some ways an *aggiornamento* or development of Lonergan's earlier Thomistic studies. A cluster of themes pertaining to the relationship between grace and freedom are taken up in *Method* – themes such as conversion, dialectic, and horizon, as well as meaning, morality, and the nature of God's relation to human persons. The work is a return in existential terms to the topics of his first Thomistic study, *Grace and Freedom*. It explores in greater breadth the ways in which humans use and misuse freedom and therefore of the ways in which grace enters history.[93]

Yet if *Method* is an "updating" of *Grace and Freedom*, it is also a further development of *Insight*. One could say, in fact, that it is its essential complement. Where *Insight* focuses on the nature of human consciousness, the formal unrestrictedness of its inquiry, and its development and aberrations, *Method* articulates the inverse direction of development wherein communities, cultures, and traditions make possible and condition that individual development. Lonergan calls these two movements the way from "below upward" and the way from "above downward." Lawrence observes – astutely, I think – that Lonergan's reaction to the harmful effects of intellectual communities displayed in the decadent forms of Neoscholasticism and the marginalization of the figures studied early in this chapter, initially led him to emphasize the way from below upwards, that is, that of individual inquiring intelligence. Yet these two vectors must be taken together if we are to have a clear picture of the development and performance of human intelligence. Indeed, they constitute the deep, existential structure of hermeneutics:

> These two developmental vectors (up and below) constitute the ontological structure of the hermeneutic circle ... By acknowledging the priority of the way from above downwards, Lonergan joined Gadamer's hermeneutics in stressing the aspect of the hermeneutic circle that had been relegated to oblivion by the Enlightenment's "prejudice against prejudice," namely, that intellectual development's rhythm of believing to understand and understanding to believe is both inevitable and reasonable because it describes just how reason works.[94]

The ultimate integration of these vectors with the publication of *Method* led to an "integral hermeneutics" that could acknowledge both the individual and her community; both the conditioned and the communal nature of truth; its historical situatedness yet the desire for transcendence propelled by our native impulse to inquiry. Lonergan's solution, according to Lawrence, was to "integrate Augustine's hermeneutics of love into his foundational methodology."[95] It is only in loving that we can come to understand fully because only love can dissolve the bias to which we all are prone – as individuals and as communities. Thus, Lonergan's integral hermeneutic circle is believing to understand and understanding to believe, where to believe is to love and also to believe on account of those who love us.

Conclusion

History is only a problem for we who are subjects of it and subject to it. Lonergan understood that more than scientific naturalism and atheism – two other great concerns of twentieth-century Christians – *history* was the greatest challenge facing Catholic philosophical and theological thought. Questions about the conditions of knowledge and non-belief are secondary to questions about who we are.

Lonergan's solution was to propose a comprehensive anthropology. In this, he resembles de Lubac and Balthasar and anticipates Wojtyla. He argued that an "updated" philosophical anthropology was needed because, while *abstractly*, human being may have an essential set of enduring properties, *concretely* human beings become in time. A fuller account of human subjectivity anticipated by Augustine but largely unknown to the medieval masters required adjustments, developments, and in some cases revisions.[96] It was not that human nature had changed, but rather that one had to distinguish between human being as *substance* and human being as *subject*.[97] Knowledge of oneself as a subject – as a being whose being is becoming – awakens historical consciousness and with it "the awareness that men [and women] individually are responsible for their lives and collectively are responsible for the world in which they live them."[98] Such an awareness constituted a new context in which philosophy and theology undertook their respective endeavours. That context was dominated by concrete questions of individual subjectivity, of history, and of the ineluctable but ambiguous power of institutions, traditions, and communities (political, religious, and scientific) in shaping human life. Contemporary culture, and Continental thinkers in particular, brought our attention back to the concrete world of human concern from which Neoscholasticism had become estranged.

Of course, diagnosis and treatment are two different activities. Lonergan could acknowledge the helpful developments in the empirical and human sciences as well as in much modern philosophy without conceding any number of problematic conclusions to which they often led people. For Lonergan, truth is not relative; however, our individual capacity to understand, to affirm, and to responsibly live in accord with truth *is*. What remains invariant and so "transcends" individual contexts are the recurrent and related operations of human consciousness and the drive to know that underpins their performance, as well as the gratuitous love of God "flooding our hearts" (Rom. 5:5) and calling us to deeper conversion in our intellectual, moral, and religious forms of life.

NOTES

1 Fergus Kerr, "Rebels with a Cause: Twentieth-Century Roman Catholic Theologians," *Theology Today* 62 (2005), 304.
2 As Gerald McCool has argued persuasively, at the beginning of the nineteenth century Thomism was studied only in small pockets. Its resurgence occurred only in the latter third of the century. The other and often overlooked major theological tradition was the Tübingen school, which was populated by careful scientific theologians who represented a serious orthodox alternative to nineteenth-century Thomism. See Gerald A. McCool, *Catholic Theology in the 19th Century* (New York: Seabury Press, 1977), 4.
3 Ibid., 17.
4 Liberatore (1810–1892) and Kleutgen (1811–1883) are considered the Jesuit founders of the Neo-Thomist movement (cf. ibid., 3). Liberatore was a professor of theology in Naples and founder and editor of the *Civilità Cattolica*, as well as the author of the widely influential *Institutions Philosophicae* (3 vols.). The *Civilità Cattolica* and *Der Katholik* were the two most influential organs of the Neoscholastic movement. See ibid., 30–2.
5 *Dei Filius*, §4. Joseph Kleutgen drafted the final version of *Dei Filius*.
6 See, for example: "Our first and most cherished idea is that you should all furnish to studious youth a generous and copious supply of those purest streams of wisdom flowing inexhaustibly from the precious fountainhead of the Angelic Doctor" (§26); and later, "We exhort you, venerable brethren, in all earnestness to restore the golden wisdom of St Thomas, and to spread it far and wide … Let carefully selected teachers endeavor to implant the doctrine of Thomas Aquinas in the minds of students, and set forth clearly his solidity and excellence over others" (§31). Visit http://w2.vatican.va/content/leo-xiii/en/encyclicals/documents/hf_l-xiii_enc_04081879_aeterni-patris.html.
7 McCool, *Catholic Theology*, 1.
8 This was in many ways a loss to Catholic thought and culture, one that was to be felt almost a century later in the fierce debates about modernism and *la nouvelle théologie*. These non-Scholastic theologies "manifested a sensitivity to the intelligibility of history, tradition and community to which the Aristotelian neo-Thomists were singularly blind" (Ibid., 13). Thus, their marginalization had two consequences: it sidelined a direction of inquiry that would become essential to twentieth-century thought in and outside the Church; and it heightened Neoscholastic suspicion of forms of philosophy or theology that made even attenuated appeals to subjectivity and history.
9 For a summary of the reasonable origin and unreasonable application of "manuals" in seminary education, see Fergus Kerr, "A Different World:

Neoscholasticism and Its Discontents," in *International Journal of Systematic Theology* 8, no. 2 (April 2006): 128–48.

10 *Pascendi Domini Gregis*, §§45, 48.

11 Full text here: http://www.papalencyclicals.net/Pius10/p10moath.htm.

12 Quoted in Philip Gleason's *Contending with Modernity* (New York: Oxford University Press, 1995), 16.

13 Neoscholasticism/Neo-Thomism is predictably hard to define. For our purposes we will use the definition offered by J. A. Weisheipl in his entry "Neoscholasticism and Neothomism": "Neo-Scholasticism was the attempt to solve the modern crisis of theology by picking up the thread of the high scholastic tradition of mediaeval times. The aim was to establish a timeless, unified, theology that would provide a norm for the universal church." In *New Catholic Encyclopedia* (Detroit: Gale, 2002), 244.

14 The retrieval of the epithalamic tradition originated with Deniélou's *Origene* (1984) and was followed by de Lubac's *Histoire et esprit: L'Intelligence de L'Écriture d'après Origène* (1950); Balthasar's edited anthology, *Origenes Geist und Feuer* (1956, rev.); and Dom Olivier Rousseau's translation, *Origène Homilies sur le cantique des Cantiques* (1953). Kerr notes that *Origen* is the source for the nuptial theology developed by Lubac and Balthasar and later by Wojtyla and Ratzinger.

15 Reginald Garrigou-Lagrange, OP, lectured at the Angelicum from 1909 to 1960. For him, according to Kerr, "Thomas Aquinas's work ... was an unsurpassed and unsurpassable speculative theological achievement. It might, and indeed should, be studied in light of the clarifications offered by a select band of 16th century commentators." *Rebels with a Cause*, 11.

16 Arguably this goes back as far as Spinoza's distinction between philosophical and experiential knowledge (*Theologico-Political Treatise*, 1670) with respect to biblical claims, which was developed by Lessing into the "broad ditch" between certain truth and history: "Accidental truths of history can never become the proof of necessary truths of reason" (*Lessing's Theological Writings*, 1956, trans. H. Chadwick). This emphasis on the contingent character of experience and history is then taken up in the nineteenth century by figures such as Schleiermacher and Dilthey, leading to the rise of biblical historical criticism as well as broader philosophical treatments of history, contingency, and truth.

17 For a discussion of the twenty-four Thomistic theses and the modernist oath in the context of Neoscholasticism and *ressourcement* Thomism, see Kerr, "A Different World." The theses are translated and listed on 132–4.

18 Chenu describes the perennial philosophy of Neoscholasticism as one in which no attention was paid to "the problems of existence, action, the individual, becoming, and time. [They preferred] a philosophy of essences, in which what counts is the non-contingent, the universal, ideal,

immutable relations – fine matters for definitions.'" Quoted in *Twentieth-Century Catholic Theologians* (Hoboken: Wiley-Blackwell, 2006), 23.

19 The Integralists or *Sodalitium Pianum* (Solidarity of Pius) were a group of unofficial censors brought together by Umberto Benigini to report those thought to be teaching modernism in some form. The quote is from Chenu's article, "Le sens et le lecons d'une crise religieuse" in *La vie intellectuelle* 13 (1931), 380. Translated in Thomas F. O'Meara OP, *Thomas Aquinas Theologian* (Notre Dame: University of Notre Dame Press, 1999), 182. Also quoted in *Twentieth-Century Catholic Theologians*, Kerr, 22.

20 See, for example, Mettepenningen and De Pril, who argue that "*la nouvelle théologie* is no less a thomistic *ressourcement*, a return to the original writings of St Thomas. This applies especially in its 'first phase' (1935–1942)." In "Thomism and the Renewal of Theology: Chenu, Charlier, and their Ressourcement," *Horizons* 39, no. 1 (2012), 51. The term *nouvelle théologie* was used first by Msgr. Parente in defence of the decision to place Chenu's *Une École de Théologie* on the Index of Forbidden Books. Parente's article, "Neuove tendenze teologische" (*Osservatre Romano*, 9–10 February 1942), although written in Italian, makes reference to "la nouvelle théologie" of Chenu and Charlier explicitly. For further discussion of this episode and the patristic revival more generally, see Brian Daley, "The Nouvelle Théologie and the Patristic Revival: Sources, Symbols, and the Science of Theology," *International Journal of Systematic Theology* 4 (October 2005), 362–82. The term *nouvelle théologie* was used again by Pope Pius X in his 1950 encyclical *Humani Generis.*

21 Indeed, his claim was that only in reading Thomas historically could one truly come to understand what the not merely historical nature of theology was for him: "Chenu was far too much a theologian to restrict himself to purely medievalist studies. His proper theological oeuvre consisted precisely in establishing an original synthesis between the speculative approach of Fardeil and the 'medievalism' of Lemonnyer and Mandonnet." Mettepenningen and De Pril ("Thomism and the Renewal of Theology" cited in the note above), 56.

22 This was a problem for Wolff in his own day – he was run out of his university position at Halle by the German pietists, who saw his notion of theology as a threat for precisely this reason.

23 Daley, "The Nouvelle Théologie," 381.

24 Francisco Suarez (1548–1617). The only substantial critique is that of Balthasar in *The Glory of the Lord: A Theological Aesthetics*, vol. 5: *The Realm of Metaphysics in the Modern Age* (Edinburgh: T&T Clark 1991), 21–9. Suarez, he writes, was "the father of Baroque- and Neoscholasticism" which focused on the univocity of being as "a neutral principle beyond God and world." Ibid., 21, 560.

25 As Kerr notes, "the 'Suarezianism which Balthasar denounces seems remarkably like the 'Wolffianism' which we found Chenu detecting in Garrigou-Lagrange's Thomism." *Twentieth-Century Catholic Theologians*, 126.

26 Mettepenningen and De Pril argue that Chenu not only integrated the historical method into theology, but also that the use of the historical method itself occasioned theological insights: "the integration of the historical method in theology is conceived by Chenu as an adaptation of Thomas's synthesis between faith and (Aristotelian) reason to the twentieth-century context ... The pure extrinsic use of the historical method ... resulted in the fundamental acknowledgement of historicity as an intrinsic dimension of Christianity." *Twentieth-Century Catholic Theologians*, 60.

27 Bernard Lonergan, *Insight* (1957 original edition), ed. Frederick E. Crowe and Robert M. Doran vol. 3, Toronto: University of Toronto Press (1992); Karl Rahner, *Spirit in the World* (1964, original German edition), New York, NY: Continuum (1994); Hans Urs von Balthasar, *The Truth of the World* (1985 original German edition), San Francisco, CA: Ignatius Press (2000).

28 Kerr, *Twentieth-Century Catholic Theologians*, 106.

29 Nor was he ever placed under censure or delated to authorities in the Vatican. He famously quipped that this was because "most of his writings were in a language unknown at the time in the wider RC [*sic*] theological community (English)." Reported in Kerr, "Rebels with a Cause," 299.

30 With his apostolic constitution, *Humanae salutis*, Pope John XXIII convoked the Second Vatican Ecumenical Council on 25 December 1961. In it he wrote, famously, "making our own Jesus's recommendation that we learn to discern 'the signs of the times' (Mt. 16:4)."

31 *Grace and Freedom*, in *Collected Works of Bernard Lonergan* (Toronto: University of Toronto Press) (hereafter CWL), vol. 1, ed. Frederick E. Crowe and Robert M. Doran (1988); *Verbum*, CWL, vol. 2 (1997). The volumes did not come out in order.

32 That is not to say they are *merely* textual. As the historian of twentieth-century Catholic theology Fergus Kerr writes: "[For Lonergan,] what was needed [in retrieving Aquinas] was not simply historical reconstruction of Aquinas' work but profound changes within the student." See Kerr, *Rebels with a Cause*, 115.

33 Speaking of Lonergan's early work on Thomas, Kerr continues, "*Grace and Freedom* ... [is] an as yet unsurpassed analysis of Aquinas' theory of divine transcendence and human liberty" (ibid., 115).

34 J. Martin O'Hara, ed., *Curiosity at the Center of One's Life: Statements and Questions of R. Eric O'Connor* (Montreal: Thomas More Institute, 1984), 427.

35 Elaine Cahn and Cathleen Going, eds., *The Question as Commitment* (Montreal: Thomas More Institute, 1977), 103. See also Frederick E. Crowe,

"'All my work has been introducing history into Catholic theology,'" *Lonergan Workshop: The Legacy of Lonergan*, vol. 10, ed. Frederick Lawrence (1994), 49–81.

36 For Heidegger's discussion of historicality (*Geschichtlichkeit*), historicity (*Historizität*), and historizing (*Geschehen*), see *Being and Time*, trans. John Macquarrie and Edward Robinson (Oxford: Blackwell, 2001), 41.

37 Fred Lawrence has made the important observation that "these two developmental vectors constitute the ontological structure of the hermeneutic circle" in Heidegger's classical formulation. See his "Lonergan's Search for a Hermeneutics of Authenticity" (unpublished typescript), 31. See also his set of articles "Hermeneutics, Postmodernism, Relativism," in *Divyadaan Journal of Philosophy and Education*, 19, nos. 1–2 (2008).

38 A note here on terminology. While *modernism* denotes a more or less identifiable set of philosophical commitments, the terms *modern* and *modernity* are more wide-ranging and often used as synonyms for *contemporary*. Given the length and particular time period of Lonergan's life, *contemporary* philosophy encompasses not only modernism but also the postmodern reaction to it. In promoting a frank dialogue with modernism that acknowledges some of the real gains in knowledge it has helped bring about, Lonergan is not advocating for a form of what is sometimes called "enlightenment reason" (monolithic, speculative, detached), but rather suggesting that the only way beyond the problems raised by modernism is *through* them. It is by providing a more adequate account of consciousness, truth, and being that we then can judge what is worthwhile in an opposing position and what is erroneous. As we have argued above, Lonergan's account is particularly attentive to the essential and constitutive role that historicity plays in all human endeavours. The implications of this are increasingly evident as we move from *Insight* to *Method in Theology*. It is historical consciousness, in so many ways, that leads to the postmodern suspicions of oversimplification and mischaracterization that often plague "grand narratives." These observations are not unrelated as it is Lonergan's training in openness and integration toward modernism that leads him to (re)consider the authors (and their questions) who are the precursors to postmodernity.

39 *Teaching* Thomas within the structures of the Gregorian, however, was another matter altogether, which Lonergan described as "laboring under impossible conditions."

40 In his essay "*Existenz* and *Aggiornamento*," Lonergan writes: "The word *aggiornamento*, minted by John XXIII and retained by Paul VI, is not entirely outside the range of the present reflections, for the problem set the church by the modern world is at once massive and profound." In CWL, vol. 4 (1988), 228.

41 See his "The Transition from a Classicist World-View to Historical-Mindedness," in Lonergan, *A Second Collection*, ed. William F.J. Ryan and Bernard J. Tyrell (Toronto: University of Toronto Press, 1996), 1–10. For his accounts of bias and decline see, Lonergan, *Insight*, chapters 6 and 7.
42 Gleason, *Contending with Modernity*, 6.
43 It is customary to note the inadequate use of the terms liberal and conservative to denote movements within early American Catholicism because they are generally read anachronistically in light of the political attitudes they would come to describe later in the century. At this point in time, both "liberals" and "conservatives" defended their distinct positions as unwaveringly "orthodox."
44 Ibid., 8. Gleason names, in particular, Bishops John J. Keane of Richmond, John Ireland of St Paul, and Denis O'Connell (Rector of the North American College in Rome).
45 Principally Keane, Ireland, and O'Connell.
46 Gleason suggests that the event "reveals the intimate connection that existed (and still exists) between higher education and the effort of American Catholics to accommodate themselves to the modern world in its intellectual and cultural dimensions." *Contending with Modernity*, 12.
47 Ibid., 13.
48 "The modernist crisis had seriously damaging long-range effects on the intellectual development of American Catholicism. Coming as they did on the heels of Americanism, *Pascendi* and the campaign of repression it sanctions … placed a premium on intellectual caution and discouraged American Catholic's form venturing out on new lines of thought." Ibid., 16.
49 Ibid., 17.
50 In his 1977 response to a "Questionnaire" on the role of philosophy for Jesuit seminarians, Lonergan suggests an addition to his four transcendental precepts (Be Attentive, Intelligent, Reasonable, Responsible) may be added a fifth: "acknowledge your historicity." In *Philosophical and Theological Papers: 1965–1980*, CWL, vol. 17 (2004), 378.
51 Quoted in David Tracey, *The Achievement of Bernard Lonergan* (New York: Herder and Herder, 1970), xi.
52 Lonergan, "Theology in Its New Context," in *A Second Collection*, 58.
53 See ibid., 58–60.
54 For example, he writes that "the novelty resides not in a new revelation or a new faith, but in a new cultural context. For a theology is a product not only of the religion it investigates and expounds but also of the cultural ideals and norms that set its problems and direct its solutions." Ibid., 58.
55 Ibid., 62.
56 Critical Realism is Lonergan's epistemological position, which holds that the real is the intelligible, and that it encompasses both the world of

immediacy and the world "mediated by meaning." The experiential data that ground any claim to knowledge include both the data of sense and the data of consciousness. He considers this a middle position between the "naïve realism" of empiricism and the inadequacies of critical (Kant) and absolute (Hegel) idealism. For more detail, see "The Origins of Christian Realism" in *A Second Collection.*

57 One of his most astute commentators describes the development this way: "Lonergan's approach to hermeneutics emerged gradually over the course of five decades of serious reading … His thought on hermeneutics culminated in *Method in Theology* (1972)." Fred Lawrence, "Lonergan's Hermeneutics," in *The Routledge Companion to Hermeneutics*, ed. Jeff Malpas and Hans-Helmuth Gander (New York, NY: Routledge (2015), 160.

58 Lonergan, *Insight*, 413.

59 Lawrence, "Lonergan's Search for a Hermeneutics of Authenticity" (unpublished typescript), 8.

60 The principle states that what is known is known according to the mode of the knower. See, for example, *Summa Theologica*. Ia, q.12, a.4; *ST*. Ia, q.14, a.1; *ST*. Ia, q.14, a.12.

61 *Verbum*, CWL, vol. 2 (1997), 86.

62 Lonergan, *Insight*, 59.

63 Lonergan, *Philosophical and Theological Papers: 1965–1980*, CWL, vol. 17 (2004), ed. Croken and Doran, 428.

64 Ibid., 429.

65 Bernard Lonergan, *Lectures on Phenomenology and Logic* (Hereafter, *Lectures*), CWL, vol. 18 (2004), ed. Philip J. McShane (2001).

66 For example, Husserl, Heidegger, Marcel, Jaspers, Sartre, and a number of phenomenological psychologists.

67 I offer many thanks to Msgr Liddy for ongoing and detailed conversations about the life and work of Lonergan. Liddy was in Rome and at the Gregorian during Lonergan's tenure there, and he corroborated what has been remarked elsewhere

68 This is particularly true for Marcel, for whom Lonergan has high praise (see *Lectures*, 230). As *attractive*, see page 223 on seminarians and Marcel; as a *problem*, see page 228: "[Marcel] is quite a problem for professors of dogmatic theology!"

69 I think it not insignificant that Lonergan, ever the teacher, was led to a reappraisal of dominant strands of European thought by the intellectual curiosity of his students and the new context in which he found himself as a teacher at a European university.

70 Here I do not think Lonergan's appraisal is far from part of Dominique Janicaud's assessment (1991), namely, that phenomenology need not be

(in Husserl at least) the *whole* of philosophy. For both thinkers, I believe there is room to see it as an essential moment in a larger philosophical method.

71 "Nothing is excluded from consideration ... It is concerned with everything that appears, everything that is given, everything that is manifest." Lonergan, *Lectures*, 266.

72 This is first worked out by Husserl in his *Logical Investigations* in the "Sixth Investigation." See *Logical Investigations,* vol. 2, trans. J.L. Findlay (New York: Routledge, 2001).

73 "Husserl and phenomenology are concerned with considering all data without any exclusion, as structured by insight, as given a form, an *eidos*, from the insight." Lonergan, *Lectures*, 267. In a manner similar to how Lonergan related sensing to understanding, for Husserl, categorial intuitions are *founded* upon sense perception, but not reducible to those perceptions.

74 This central insight is illustrated by the common phenomenological definition of the subject as the *dative of manifestation* – the person *to whom* being is manifest.

75 Lonergan, *Lectures*, 266.

76 "Husserl has done, with enormous labor, a fine analysis of psychological process. Including the two brilliant correlations of *Abschattung* and *Horizon*; and *Einstellung* and *Welt*." Ibid., 256.

77 Whether it is the internal horizon of an underdetermined object or the external horizon of Being.

78 To recount the story of the shifting intellectual preoccupations between the "Lectures" and *Method* I can do no better than to refer you to Ivo Coelho's very detailed and careful work, *Method in Hermeneutics* (Toronto: University of Toronto Press, 2012).

79 See Gregory P. Floyd, "Hermeneutic of Generosity: Lonergan's Rereadings of Phenomenology" in *The Lonergan Review* vol. 6, no. 1 (2015), 135–49.

80 Bernard Lonergan, *Method in Theology* [hereafter *Method*] (Toronto: University of Toronto Press, 1971), xi. He wrote later, "the concern of the theologian is not just a set of propositions but a concrete religion as it has been lived, as it is being lived, and as it is to be lived." In Lonergan, "Philosophy of God and Theology," in *Philosophical and Theological Papers: 1964–1980*, CWL, vol. 17 (2004), 159–220.

81 In *Method* this dialogue is both broader and deeper. In addition to Heidegger and Husserl – and Jaspers, Dilthey, and Bergson – Lonergan reaches back to the sources of that tradition – Pseudo-Dionysius, Luther, Pascal, Kierkegaard, Nietzsche, Brentano – as well as forward to a second generation of European thinkers – Foucault, Gadamer, Wittgenstein, Tillich, Ricoeur, and Voegelin. These engagements are both appropriative and critical.

82 Again, Lonergan interprets Pope St John XXIII's call for *aggiornamento* ("updating") as a call for development.

83 Ivo Coelho, *Hermeneutics and Method* (Toronto: University of Toronto Press, 2001), 7. He goes on to note, in relation to Lonergan's *Insight*, that in *Insight* there is a certain relation between *universal willingness* and the *universal viewpoint*; however, the level of decision is never asserted to form part of the *integral heuristic structure* at its base (Ibid., 88).

84 Lonergan, in *Philosophical and Theological Papers: 1964–1980*, CWL, vol. 17 (2004), 113.

85 Ibid., 117.

86 "I am quite willing to grant that in a philosophy primarily concerned with objects metaphysics must be the first science, for it is the objects of metaphysics that are both most basic and most universal. But in a philosophy that primarily is concerned not with objects, but with operations metaphysics cannot be the first science. What now is both most basic and most universal are the operations, and these are studied in cognitional theory. Secondly, comes the validity of the operations, and such is the concern of epistemology. Only in the third place do there arise the questions of objects which is the concern of a metaphysics … Metaphysics finds its proper place not on the primary, or even on the secondary, but only on a tertiary level." Lonergan, "The Religious Phenomenon," in CWL, vol. 17 (2004), 127.

87 Hermeneutics is not restricted to theology for Lonergan. As Lawrence notes: "On the basis of a methodically (read: phenomenologically or hermeneutically) grounded cognitional theory, epistemology, and metaphysics, Lonergan presented the basic semantics of whatever may be discovered by the classical, statistical, and genetic methods of explanatory natural science. This is grounded hermeneutically, because it is not confined to but transcends the logical scope of *apophansis*." Fred Lawrence. "Lonergan's Search for a Hermeneutics of Authenticity" (unpublished typescript), 20.

88 "Hermeneutics," in CWL, vol. 22, ed. Robert M. Doran and Robert C. Croken (2010), 210–11.

89 Lonergan, "Theology in Its New Context," 57.

90 Lonergan, "Philosophy and Theology," in *A Second Collection*, ed. William F.J. Ryan and Bernard J. Tyrell, 202.

91 Ibid., 196. Though he added, "but certainly they are not compatible with previous conceptions of theology."

92 Functional specialties are intrinsically related and interdependent moments or stages in the acquisition and cultivation of theological wisdom. They are either discrete functions distinguished by the questions they ask and the kind of meaning they pursue. See Lonergan, *Method in Theology*, chapter 5.

93 In his chapter on religion, Lonergan says that the word enters the world of human meaning, endowing it with "its deepest meaning and highest value," thereby taking part in the constitutive meaning brought about through the loving exercise of human freedom. *Method*, 112.

94 Lawrence, "Lonergan's Search for a Hermeneutics of Authenticity" (unpublished typescript), 32.

95 Ibid., 26.

96 Regarding the last of these, Lonergan saw the need to shift from faculty psychology to intentionality as a model for consciousness and also rethought the ancient and medieval notions of "habit" in terms of Jean Piaget's developmental psychology.

97 See Lonergan, "*Existenz* and *Aggiornamento*," in CWL, vol. 4 (1988).

98 Ibid., 229.

3 Continental Philosophy and American Catholics: Then, Now, and Tomorrow

JOHN D. CAPUTO

American Catholic philosophers played a central role in the emergence of "Continental philosophy" in the United States.[1] To be sure, there were internal philosophical reasons for the American interest in Continental philosophy, without which nothing would have been possible. These reasons are nicely summarized in what John Wild (1902–72) called as early as 1955 "the breakdown of modern philosophy":[2] the discontent with the epistemologies of the seventeenth and eighteenth centuries; the critique of metaphysics in the wake of Kant; the critique of Hegel launched by the Kierkegaardian pseudonyms; the intrinsic appeal of phenomenological ideas; and, in those days, even more so, the tremendous popularity of Existentialism, which the literary writings of Camus and Sartre helped make part of the general culture. Add to this the sociological factor that many European intellectuals, in flight from the Nazis, had come to teach in the United States. None of this need necessarily have anything to do with theology, Catholic or not. The point is that it did.

Why would that be the case? The basic reason, I think, is that the discontent with modernity described by Wild was acutely felt by philosophers with a religious sensibility, which is resistant to modernity's tendency to promote objectification and to deprivilege lived experience. This was particularly true of American Catholic philosophers in the middle of the twentieth century, whose philosophical sensibility proved to be uniquely attuned to the existential, phenomenological, and hermeneutical motifs in Continental thought. With the helpful hand supplied by hindsight, we can see that they would provide a perfect audience for a philosophical movement (1) at the head of which there stood Søren Kierkegaard's existential conception of truth (shades of Augustine's *Confessions*); (2) whose central figure, Heidegger, made a brilliant critique of modernist epistemology on the basis of a phenomenology that he moved away from Neo-Kantianism and toward Aristotelianism while raising the question of Being (shades of Aquinas and late medieval mysticism); and finally (3) that offered a hermeneutic theory set out by Ricoeur and Gadamer that effectively offered an explanation to a Catholic audience about how to understand "tradition" in the changing times of post–Vatican II. That is the story I want to sketch here, a story that is in no small part my own.

How It Started

Continental philosophy was first welcomed to America by theologically minded philosophers, Catholic, Protestant, and Jewish, and, just as interestingly, by philosophers who had been trained in theological seminaries but had in varying degrees given up their religious beliefs. The latter were looking for a successor form of thinking that would respect their (religious) passion for life without implicating them in supernatural beliefs. Their interest in Continental philosophy, we might say, was in a sense the becoming-philosophical of their earlier theological concerns. The significant thing is not so much that they gave up theology – some more than others – but that when they sought a successor form they turned to Continental philosophy. Some of them looked to Anglo-American sources for relief, not the then regnant Anglo-American analytic and positivistic philosophies, but classical American thought. Led by John Smith (Yale), they looked to pragmatists like William James, whose *Varieties of Religious Experience* remains today a standing classic in the philosophy of religion, and to Whitehead's process philosophy (theology), which was then quite influential in no small part because of the work of Charles Hartshorne. Very early on, an important philosophical and professional alliance was forged among Continental philosophy, American pragmatism, and the Whiteheadians in the Metaphysical Society of America, which later on blossomed into the "pluralist" group headed by Bruce Wilshire (Rutgers) and Charles Sherover (Hunter). The Pluralists practised pluralism up to a point. They meant anything-but-analytic, everybody and anybody except the analysts! This was a coalition of the discontent, a kind of resistance group to the systematic suppression of anything that was not analytic by the American Philosophical Association. They ran for offices in the APA, and did well enough, but without effecting any deep structural change. I myself was a part of this group, which met regularly in Sherover's apartment in Manhattan.

The biographies of the prominent people early in the Continentalist movement are instructive. James Edie, a central figure at Northwestern

University, had been a Benedictine priest, who studied at the Pontifical Athenaeum of St Anselm in Rome and did his doctoral dissertation at the Catholic University of Louvain on the work of Étienne Gilson.[3] Indeed, Calvin Schrag (Purdue), also a former theological student, reports that the first time he met him Edie was still wearing his Roman collar. Edie would also co-edit a volume titled *Christianity and Existentialism*.[4] Joseph Kockelmans (Pennsylvania State) had been a seminarian in Rome, although he was never ordained. Reiner Schürmann began his career in the United States (New School for Social Research) as a Dominican priest teaching at the Catholic University of America. For many years, the lay people teaching philosophy in Catholic universities were, like myself, former seminarians, priests, or members of religious orders. Some maintained their religious beliefs and some mutated into secular "phenomenologists" or "existentialists."

One dominant family trait of Continental philosophers is that for them philosophy is an "existential" matter, a matter of personal passion, a form of life not merely a profession, a way so to speak to be "saved," not by supernatural intervention but by the existential event. That is why Kierkegaard is arguably the central figure to the background of Continental philosophy. Kierkegaard fascinates everyone, Catholic or Protestant, theistic or atheistic. The similarity of his thought to the God-is-dead atheism of Nietzsche is uncanny. Even the analytically inclined could not resist dipping into this Danish well. But for my generation of pre–Vatican II Catholic philosophers, who had been raised on an austere bread-and-water diet of Neoscholastic textbooks, Kierkegaard was electrifying. James Collins, a Catholic layman at the Jesuit St Louis University, who had written a major history of modern philosophy, wrote two widely read books – one on Kierkegaard and the other on existentialism – that were staples of the early movement.[5] Even when Heidegger tried to brush off Kierkegaard as a (merely) "religious writer," that only betrayed a brand of "anxiety" known as the anxiety of influence. Heidegger was attempting to deflect our attention from how much he had lifted from Kierkegaard without citation or at least without a dismissive citation.

So it is no accident that Continental philosophy became an important component of the philosophical curricula of many American Catholic colleges and universities at just about the same time as the Second Vatican Council. Interestingly, the Second Vatican Council was convened on 11 October 1962 and the first meeting of the Society for Phenomenology and Existential Philosophy, the principal Continentalist organ in the United States, was held fifteen days later, on 26 October 1962 (which was my twenty-second birthday). Over the years, a good half of the doctoral programs in the United States that offer programs specializing in Continental philosophy have been found in Catholic institutions. Many prominent members of the early movement were either Catholic or at least had Catholic origins. *Philosophy Today*, one of the first and most popular American journals in the field, was founded and edited by Robert Lechner, a Catholic priest at DePaul University, and it is housed there to this day under the editorship of Heidegger scholar Peg Birmingham.

Catholics, to borrow a phrase from Bruno Latour, had never been modern,[6] and that was especially the case for Catholic European immigrants to a predominantly Protestant Anglo-Saxon country. They had survived by raising stable families in Catholic neighborhoods and attending Catholic schools in an effort to inoculate themselves against a Protestant culture, secularism, and in those days "atheistic Communism." As a grade-school child I was told by the nuns to watch Bishop Fulton J. Sheen's weekly television broadcasts and to be ready to answer questions about them the next morning in class. Before Vatican II, Catholic colleges were similarly insular institutions that served up a rigid regimen of Council of Trent theology and Neoscholastic philosophy. They enthusiastically embraced Leo XIII's call to return to St Thomas in *Aeterni Patris*, which mistook philosophy for a branch of Catholic apologetics. At the Catholic University of America, students were even asked to arm themselves with an oath against "modernism," which by no means should be understood as an oath to postmodernism.

That world, the Church of Pius XII, vanished in a surprisingly short time beginning in the turbulent mid-1960s, about the same time the religious orders in the United States began to experience what would prove to be a mass exodus from which they would never recover. Even before the Second Vatican Council, Catholic colleges and doctoral programs had begun to cultivate a historical sense. In an effort to show that Thomas Aquinas was the world-historical *telos* intended internally by the twin dynamics of Greek philosophy and the advent of Christianity, after which there was only decline, they always devoted time to Greek philosophy and the history of philosophy generally. The English Jesuit Frederick Copleston's multi-volume *History of Philosophy* was our trustworthy guide and has withstood the test of time quite remarkably ever since. Étienne Gilson had taught us all the need for a careful study of the neglected middle ages in order to understand that the medieval Christian world in which Aquinas lived was profoundly different from the Greek world of Aristotle, from whom he was separated by a millennium and a half, a pre-Christian culture, and the Latin translations of Aristotle he used. This was a point that the textbook talk of the "Aristotelico-Thomistic synthesis" failed to point out.

When the hegemony of Neo-Thomism was finally broken, Catholics literally put St Thomas in his place, converting him from a timeless ahistorical master to a historically situated thirteenth-century thinker, and then filled in the missing link of the middle ages in standard histories of philosophy. From this they went on to cultivate a strong historical consciousness (against which the oath against modernism had been directed), which also explains their interest in hermeneutics, my third point, which I will revisit below. Led by prominent figures at the Jesuit institutions, Catholics took up their Continental European heritage in a sustained way, in search of contemporary resources to think their way through this brave new post–Vatican II world.[7]

In the same way that American analytic philosophers shuttled back and forth to Cambridge and Oxford and invited "Oxbridge" philosophers to visit and teach in the United States, Catholics enjoyed easy commerce with the great Continental centres of learning in Belgium, France, and Germany. The religious orders could readily send leading European Catholic scholars to the American institutions conducted by their order. The Dutch Franciscans sent Andre Schuwer to Duquesne University in Pittsburgh to head up a major program in Continental thought there. Boston College brought in a steady stream of European Jesuits. Catholic laymen like Wilfrid Desan, a Belgian philosopher, who had taken a PhD at Harvard, began writing books about and teaching the work of Jean-Paul Sartre at Georgetown University, the Jesuit University in Washington, D.C.[8] Desan introduced Americans to what we used to call "atheistic existentialism," as opposed to the "Christian existentialism" of Gabriel Marcel, which we also greatly loved. Kenneth Schmidt, who had studied in Germany and attended Heidegger's "Zeit und Sein" seminar, was a central figure in the program at Marquette, where there was also interest in Gabriel Marcel. Schmidt later joined Thomas Langan at the University of Toronto, where they formed the core of a strong Continental element in a very large philosophy department. Langan, who had been trained at the Institut Catholique, wrote two of the first books in English on Merleau-Ponty and Heidegger.[9] Robert Sokolowski, a priest at the Catholic University who had been trained at Louvain, was an internationally recognized expert in Husserl.

Catholic philosophers came from a cultural and religious tradition with continental European roots, and they found no nourishment in positivism and analytic philosophy, which struck them as an Anglo-Saxon version of Neoscholasticism, as more dry and bloodless technical work. They readily turned to the philosophers of "concrete existence" and to the phenomenological movement that encouraged a return to the "Lebenswelt." Continental philosophy was the right thing at the right time for mid-century Catholic philosophers in America.

From Aristotle to Phenomenology

Next I want to point out that there is a kind of natural migration from the interest traditionally shown by Catholics in Aristotle to their new interest in phenomenology. This trajectory describes the path of thought (*Denkweg*) of Heidegger. Having made his way into phenomenology from an ultra-conservative German Catholic Neoscholastic world, which included a short time in a Jesuit seminary, Heidegger described Aristotle as the greatest phenomenologist of antiquity. Heidegger changed the game of phenomenology when he argued that its true background figure was not Descartes, whom the Husserlian tradition embraced, but Aristotle, whom Heidegger had been studying as a young Catholic. Heidegger's work in the 1920s was in no small way a reinvention of Aristotle (against a Scholastic Aristotle) by way of phenomenology and a reinvention of phenomenology (against the Husserlians) by way of Aristotle. This was also the path – and this bears emphasis – of the American John Wild, who made exactly the same migration and was widely read in those days by Catholics. Notice the title of chapter 7 of Wild's *The Challenge of Existentialism*: "Realistic Phenomenology and Metaphysics." Many Catholics had made their first contact with Wild in his realist guise, while they were being dutifully trained in Aristotelian realism through reading Wild and Francis Parker, with whom Wild collaborated. After Vatican II, many Catholics moved easily from the realism of Aristotle and Aquinas to phenomenology, just as Wild himself had done, and just as Heidegger himself had done before that. Husserl had adopted the medieval notion of *esse intentionale* from the ex-priest Franz Brentano, whose book on Aristotle influenced the young Heidegger. This proved to be an Aristotelian time bomb that was bound to burst open the Neo-Kantian philosophy of consciousness within which Husserl framed it. The explosion took place in Heidegger, who forged a phenomenology free from the transcendentalism and the egology that beset the pure Husserlian version.[10]

It is therefore no surprise that of all the Continental philosophers read by Catholics, Heidegger enjoyed pride of place. The wave of English translations[11] of Heidegger was accompanied by the appearance of William Richardson's landmark study, *Heidegger: Through Phenomenology to Thought*. Richardson was an American Jesuit philosopher who had been trained at Louvain and who attended the last lecture courses Heidegger gave at Freiburg. He taught at Fordham University and then moved on to Boston College in 1981, expanding his interests to include Lacan.[12] When Catholic philosophers read *Being and Time* it all made perfect sense to them. It was just what many of us had been waiting for. When Heidegger criticized Descartes's idea of a worldless subject and his reduction of the world to *res extensa*, when Heidegger said that the question of the existence of the world makes no sense when it is raised by a being whose being is being-in-the-world, this resonated with the Aristotelian and Neo-Thomistic sensibilities of Catholic philosophers. Having been raised as "realists," with an Aristotelian sense that the soul is the form of the body, that all knowledge begins in the senses, that human being is embedded in the order of natural being, and that the world is always and already given, Catholics were a perfect audience for the analytic of *Dasein*. When Heidegger said that as soon as *Dasein* comes to be it finds that it is already there, that made instant sense to Catholic realists in search of an alternative to Neoscholasticism.[13] They had been critical of modern Cartesian epistemology for decades,[14] and here was Heidegger – himself a one-time Catholic nurtured like them in Neoscholasticism – putting that argument on the map of contemporary philosophy in an original and magisterial way that allowed us to twist free of modernity for something postmodern without retreating into the pre-modern.

As Catholic writers like John Courtney Murray, SJ, showed, Catholics easily embraced the distinction between church and state – and the election of John F. Kennedy as president in 1960 dispelled any lingering doubt about *that*. But Catholic intellectuals could not embrace modernist epistemology, the whole idea that there were rigid territorial distinctions between a supposedly subjectifying faith and objectifying reason, between objective facts and subjective values. These were modern subject/object distinctions, modernist contrivances that had taken root in an Anglo-Saxon Protestant culture, which they distrusted in their bones. When the early Heidegger came along with his very Aristotelian critique of Cartesian epistemology, and when the later Heidegger came along with his *grand récit* about modernity and the age of the *Weltbild*, even enlisting the Dominican friar Meister Eckhart in his cause, Catholics thinkers were all ears and we understood it all perfectly. When Heidegger offered a critique of what he called "onto-theo-logic," when he said that an atheism about the God of metaphysics, about the *causa sui*, was closer to the truly divine God, Catholic philosophers knew from first-hand experience what he was talking about.[15] They had all been dragged through the pits of onto-theo-logic by the modernist Neoscholastic manuals; they had had enough of it and they wanted to "overcome" it. Catholics nurtured by a close reading of Aristotle and Thomas did not recognize themselves in any post-medieval philosophical movement until they encountered the concrete, intentionalist, and incarnational philosophies of the existential and hermeneutic phenomenologies.

Pure reason and its critiques, bloodless transcendental subjects, religion within the limits of reason alone – all of that looked like a Protestant church with no statues! Catholics had no taste for modernity's rigid divisions of labour, for its rigorous separation of science, ethics, art, and religion, a separation that confined knowledge to representations inside our own heads – flying directly in the face of what we knew about intentionality – and that turned ethics and religion into some sort of strictly private business. Philosophers who had been nourished by *pre*-modern sensibilities were ready to be romanced by any movement that offered the opportunity *not* to be modern without appearing reactionary, antediluvian, or *anti*-modern, that indeed was actually the latest word! That is what they found in existentialism and phenomenology. They had, of course, found this in Gabriel Marcel, but in Heidegger it had been set out authoritatively. The welcome extended to Continental philosophy in America by Catholic PhD programs at one time included St Louis, Marquette, Georgetown, Catholic University of America, and Notre Dame – all of which have, to varying degrees since, retreated from that commitment and adopted a kind of "analytic Thomism," especially in ethics. That is because, while they welcomed existentialism, phenomenology, and hermeneutics, they never really warmed up to the turn taken in French post-structuralism. Like many others, Continentalist and Anglo-American, they regarded post-structuralism as a form of relativism and scepticism. But that is another story.[16]

It Was Not Just the Catholics

It is important to add that while Catholic institutions played a crucial role in the early days, this was a *collaborative* undertaking evoking broadly religious interest and by no means an exclusively Catholic movement. Protestant and Jewish thinkers and secular institutions also played prominent roles in creating an American home for Continental thinking. John Wild, who taught at Harvard from 1927 to 1962, had spent 1931–2 in Freiburg attending the lectures of Heidegger and Husserl. Wild's study of Heidegger, which came to fruition for him only after he read Merleau-Ponty,[17] sent Wild back to the sources and led him to give courses on Heidegger at Harvard. This occasioned his own shift from realism to phenomenology and his departure from Harvard to Northwestern University, where he established one of the major programs in Continental philosophy at that time outside the Catholic institutions (the others were the New School of Social Research, soon joined by Vanderbilt University and the Pennsylvania State University). He stayed at Northwestern for only two years and then moved on to Yale, where a number of his students (and others') were to go on to distinguished careers in Continental philosophy. We should note, in addition to Wild's presence at Harvard, the arrival of Paul Tillich in the United States, first at Union Theological Seminary (1933–55), and then at Harvard (1955–62) (and finally at Chicago). Students at Harvard in the 1950s had the remarkable opportunity to study existentialism and phenomenology with Tillich and Wild.

Calvin Schrag was one such student. He was Paul Tillich's teaching assistant at Harvard, where he wrote a dissertation on Heidegger and Kierkegaard, directed by Tillich and Wild (and he also notes meeting a young French exchange student at Harvard named Jacques Derrida). Tillich promoted what was thought of as an existential theology. He spoke of religion as a matter of ultimate concern – let us say, as an ultimate *Sorge* – and of God as Being itself, or the "ground of Being" rather than a particular entity – which sounds a lot like the ontological difference between *Sein selbst* and *Seienden*. Tillich, who was articulating a radically new theology that drew deeply upon Schelling's critique of Hegel, which was taken up and extended by Kierkegaard, had come in contact with Heidegger, with whom he taught at Marburg (1924–5). After a year in Germany, where he studied with Karl Löwith and Hans-Georg Gadamer, Schrag returned to Harvard to complete his dissertation. In the preface to a book he would write many years later (during the "theological turn") titled *God as Otherwise than Being*, Schrag writes:[18]

> It should come as no surprise that it is difficult to write about Kierkegaard and Heidegger without having philosophical and religious topics and themes crisscross at rather crucial junctures. Thus in this very early work certain background interests that circumscribe the present project are already discernible.

Schrag's journey is a prism of the journey of many of the original American generation. Allow me to mention a similar recollection made by Don Ihde, who describes this scene very tellingly:[19]

> I got an M. Div from Andover Newton in 1959 before doing my philosophy Ph.D at BU, 1964. We had a consortium with all the local theological schools so I took most of my theology with Paul Tillich … Cal Schrag was his assistant then, too … I learned of Heidegger via Tillich. But even while

an undergrad I was reading Kierkegaard, Marcel, Sartre, Tillich. I did my M. Div with a thesis on Nicolas Berdyaev.

Along with Wild and Edie, Schrag was one of the five men who founded SPEP, making up the "executive committee" for its first meeting, held at Northwestern in October 1962. We have already noted that Edie had been a Catholic priest; also, that Wild was a man with theological interests and a background in Aristotle and Aquinas who had written a book on "Christian Philosophy." As a biographical point, I note that his daughter Mary married Tillich's son René. There were two other figures on that founding committee. William Earle kept a safe distance from anything resembling confessional religion, but he had taken a PhD at the University of Chicago under Charles Hartshorne, the leading process theologian of the day, and he had a mystical streak.[20] George Schrader (1917–98) first came to Yale in 1939 as a student in the Divinity School, where he earned his B.Div. in 1942. From there he went on to do graduate work in philosophy at Yale, earning his PhD in 1945. In all five cases, a theological project had turned philosophical.

The American movement also had deeply Jewish roots. Aaron Gurwitsch and the group of Jewish phenomenologists and thinkers who had assembled in exile at the New School had established the first beachhead of Continental philosophy in the United States emphasizing a pure Husserlian brand of phenomenology.[21] The first debate to break out in SPEP took place between pure Husserlian "phenomenologists" and the "existentialists" about which word would come first in the society's name. Still, the New School philosophers showed very little interest in Jewish theology or religion. So even here, we must go back again to John Wild, whose role in advancing the current interest in Emmanuel Levinas has been documented by Richard Sugarman, then a young Jewish student of Wild at Yale and Florida in the 1960s, who was first introduced to the work of Levinas by Wild.[22] Sugarman recounts the intense interest Wild showed in Levinas and the prescient grasp Wild had of the importance Levinas would eventually have. Wild also taught what was probably the first course in the United States on *Totality and Infinity* in 1971. According to Sugarman, Wild wrote a commentary on *Totality and Infinity* that "keenly anticipated" the changes Levinas would introduce in *Otherwise Than Being*.[23] Edith Wyschogrod reports that the first course she took in philosophy was one taught by Wild at the Harvard Summer School. With the mention of Edith Wyschogrod we come finally to the first woman I have mentioned, and to the first theologically minded philosophical Jewish presence in Continental philosophy in America. In her wake, a great deal of work has been done on Levinas,

Franz Rosenzweig, Walter Benjamin, and others,[24] and women now are at the forefront of the work being done in the Continental tradition.

The participation in the formation of Continental philosophy in America by Jewish philosophers was broad and deep. Maurice Natanson wrote a series of books on Husserl and phenomenology and the social sciences. Hubert Dreyfus was a student of Wild's at Harvard and collaborated with Wild on an early but unpublished translation of *Being and Time*. Herbert Spiegelberg wrote the authoritative history of the phenomenological movement. Natanson, Spiegelberg, and Dreyfus were founding members of the editorial board of the Northwestern University Press series, which was edited by James Edie and, of course, bore the same acronym "SPEP." Edith Wyschogrod's husband, Michael, an expert in the Jewish–Catholic dialogue, had like Calvin Schrag also written a book on Kierkegaard and Heidegger. Maurice Friedman was writing about Martin Buber, whose *I and Thou* was something of a classic in those days. Marjorie Grene did important work on Sartre. Marvin Farber established the journal *Philosophy and Phenomenological Research.* Hannah Arendt famously enlisted J. Glenn Gray to serve as editor of the first series of Heidegger translations from Harper and Row. But until the ascendency of Levinas later on, and the arrival of Edith Wyschogrod on the scene, SPEP did not directly engage the philosophical import of Jewish theology and the Jewish Scriptures.

In this connection we should also point out the arrival of Adriaan Peperzak, who had been a Dutch Franciscan priest, at Loyola University of Chicago in 1991. Peperzak, the pre-eminent Catholic expert on the philosophy of Levinas, offered a series of courses on Levinas at Loyola; along with Wyschogrod, he helped consolidate Levinas's importance for Catholic thinkers and for American Continentalists generally. If today it is unremarkable to hear even very secular elbow-patched philosophers discussing the "wholly other" – an expression borrowed from the darkest chambers of negative theology – that is almost single-handedly the doing of Levinas.

The Theological Turn in Continental Philosophy

It was inevitable – with the insight granted by hindsight – that with this much theological questioning running in the background, Continental philosophy would take a "theological turn." That turn was first made by French Catholic phenomenologists and has since found a warm reception among American philosophers of religion. To be sure, such a turn may be regarded as skidding off the road and ending up in a ditch, which was the view of Janicaud, who coined the phrase and for whom that turn represents one more attempt to make philosophy a handmaiden of a theological agenda, which is the most consistent argument made against it.[25] Or it may be regarded as a genuine renewal of what traditionally had been called the philosophy of religion, which is how it is embraced by those of us who involve themselves in it. Either way, a new subdiscipline has emerged that is usually referred to as "Continental philosophy of religion," an expression that positions it as a rival and alternative to the reigning Neoscholastic and Analytic approaches.[26]

The Continental approach to the philosophy of religion is vastly different from the business as usual of philosophy of religion, in that it replaces the standard debates about proofs for the existence of God, the immortality of the soul, and the problem of evil with a new project, one conceived in the spirit of what the later Heidegger called "overcoming metaphysics" and the critique of "onto-theo-logic." What theologians and philosophers of religion, Catholic and non-Catholic, sensed in Heidegger's meditations on God and the gods, the holy and the divinities, was an acute religious sensibility, an appreciation of the specific character of the religious, which in a letter addressed to the theologians Heidegger himself described as "non-objectifying thinking."[27] Whatever "God" means, God is not an object for a subject, nor is it the referent of a propositional assertion, nor is it the subject matter of a demonstration, all staples of "modernity," which is why the theological turn is sometimes called "postmodern theology." Heidegger is calling for a veritable paradigm shift in thinking about God, and the implications of this for the philosophy of religion, for theology, and for religion itself are considerable, indeed revolutionary.

Of course, as with anything new, it is also very ancient. Its antecedents may be found in mystical theology, and Heidegger himself was deeply interested in Meister Eckhart (a connection that served as my first "research project").[28] It is also found in Pascal's defence of the reasons of the heart, as well as in Luther's theology of the cross, his critique of the crust of Scholastic metaphysics that had been allowed to grow over the life of the New Testament, a crust that must be submitted, as Luther said, to a *destructio*. This was almost certainly the source of Heidegger's use of the word *Destruktion*,[29] and it served as a prototype for Heidegger of a project of a thinking bent on overcoming metaphysics in order to retrieve (*wiederholen*) the things themselves, the genuine substance (*Sache*) of the phenomena.[30] The entire project of the delimitation of metaphysics has a religious model, and philosophically it reminded us all not of Aquinas, but of Augustine, who today is getting a new hearing among Continental philosophers. If, as

Marx thought, the prototype and paradigm of criticism is the critique of religion, then the prototype and paradigm of non-metaphysical and meditative thinking is also religious, so it should not be surprising to see Continental philosophers taking a theological turn.

Heidegger set out to release the "truly divine God" from its captivity by the dominant figures of "Being" that hold sway in the history of metaphysics. While for the young Heidegger, immersed as he was in Augustine, Luther, Kierkegaard, and the letters of St Paul, this described a Christian project, the later Heidegger had in mind the Greek divinities, and by non-objectifying thinking he meant poetic thinking, not biblical. That was the basis for the critique of Heidegger, first by his contemporary Levinas, thinking from the Jewish tradition, and in the next generation by Jean-Luc Marion, working from the Catholic tradition; each proposed alternative ways of thinking God "otherwise than Being" or "without Being." Levinas and Marion were the central figures in the theological turn, and they are singled out for sharp criticism by Janicaud for just that reason. Marion was first introduced to Continental philosophers in a plenary address he gave at SPEP in 1993 (Chicago).[31] I was the co-director of SPEP at the time and had invited him to lecture on the "saturated phenomenon." Marion's work has since been the subject of numerous studies, inside and outside the society. As Ricoeur's successor at the University of Chicago, Marion has built up a very considerable American presence.

For Levinas, the liberation of God from Being was the definition of "ethics," which Levinas himself called "metaphysics" (if Heidegger said something, Levinas felt duty-bound, bound by ethics, to say the opposite). Levinas meant that ethics alone breaks the crust of Being, which he called the sphere of the "same." The ethical other breaches what we comprehend and pre-have in advance and exposes us to the "wholly other," by which he meant not God, but the "face" of the neighbour or the stranger, which is the "trace" God leaves behind in withdrawing from the world (Being). Levinas radicalized the ethics of neighbourly love and hospitality in the Jewish Scriptures; he thought that in this way "first philosophy" could be revitalized and ethics returned to centre stage in Continental thinking, a project in which he broadly succeeded. Marion's trope, "without Being," is structurally similar to Levinas's, but Marion really does mean God, the God of mystical theology, whom he approaches in an ingenious series of three "reductions" in the Husserlian sense: first of transcendental subjectivity (Kant and Husserl), then of existential agency (*Dasein*), and finally of Being itself. The upshot of reduction is to release the givenness (*Gegebenheit*) of what he calls the "saturated phenomenon." By this he means the phenomenon untethered from prior limiting conditions, which is free to be given in a flood of *donation* that overwhelms the conceptual resources of the one to whom it is given (the *adonné*). Reversing orthodox Husserlianism, the givenness of the saturated phenomenon exceeds the intentional act.

In my own work, I suggest that the most interesting expression of the religious turn in Continental philosophy is found in Derrida, because Derrida is by anyone's standards a secular thinker and even, by the standards of the local pastor or rabbi, an atheist. So it came as a shock for many secular deconstructors to read about Derrida's "religion" in his famous "Circonfession" (1989) – a deconstructive riff on Augustine's *Confessions* – in which Derrida restages the scene of the *Confessions*. Once again, we come upon a scene in which the speaker (Augustine/Jackie), an emigrant from North Africa to the Big Apple (Rome/Paris), has his back to us and is praying to someone (*te*, God/ *tu*), while his mother (Monica/Georgette) lays dying on the other side of the Mediterranean (Ostia/Nice). In this remarkable little book, Derrida tells us he is a man of prayer, and has been praying all his life, and that no one, not even his mother, has understood this, and that this has led to a misunderstanding of his work.[32] But to whom is Derrida praying, and how could he be praying at all? Does he not, by his own admission, "rightly pass for an atheist"? That is what they say about him, and they are right – "right," correct, as a propositional matter. But clearly (or not so clearly) there is a more obscure sense of religion "without religion" in Derrida, and a prayer to a God not only unknown but non-existent, that nonetheless constitutes a genuine prayer.

Indeed, if it is true to say, as does Jean-Louis Chrétien, one of the French religious phenomenologists, that prayer is a "wounded word,"[33] what word is more wounded than a word from one who does not know to whom he is praying (a lost letter, destination unknown), or whether anyone is there to hear his prayers, or whether he is praying at all, and who has to pray – to be able to pray at all – for something, he knows not what, something "coming," the coming or incoming (*invention*) of something unforeseeable, which we desire (Augustine) with a desire beyond desire? In this rich, allusive and haunting text, Derrida puts on a deconstructive performance (or per-ver-formance) that is suggestively religious. But this does not represent an Augustinian conversion. Derrida's atheism is crucially important to his religion because it allows him to isolate the very structure of prayer, and hence of the religious posture, with or without what we in the great monotheisms call "God," thereby putting into question the very binarity of theism and atheism. A whole body of work has sprung up in its wake, which takes its lead from the idea that deconstruction is structured like a religion (unless it is the opposite, that religion is structured like a deconstruction).[34]

A great deal of other work emerged in the transformed climate of Continental thought, in which it once again became respectable to raise the question of religion. There are of course other very good reasons to talk about religion inasmuch as the rise of fundamentalisms, Christian, Jewish, and Islamic, is at the heart of much of the current political turmoil in the Middle East, Western Europe, and the United States. There has been a renewal on several fronts of the theology of the "death of God," which links up with the work of the American radical theologian T.J.J. Altizer. The English translations of the work of Gianni Vattimo, once a daily Mass and Communion Italian Catholic, have also found a significant audience in the United States. Taking his cue from the history of nihilism in Heidegger and Nietzsche, Vattimo produced a series of essays under the umbrella of "weak thinking," by which he means non-metaphysical thinking. According to Vattimo, the histories of theology and metaphysics represent the withering away (weakening) of the supersensible being and transcendent God of metaphysical theology, finally mutating into the form of the world, of peace and justice, of a radically democratic order, according to which God's death represents God's greatest triumph, the arrival of the Kingdom of God in the world, the age of the Spirit first mentioned by Joachim of Fiore.[35]

More recently a series of atheistic and materialist interpretations of St Paul have arisen, beginning with Alain Badiou's *The Universalism of St Paul*, according to which Paul is an exemplar of the galvanized subjectivity that is required by a truth-process. Paul's letters are a journal of the transformation of the subject under the impact of the event, which produces an apostolic mission to establish the universality of the truth. The universality of the truth event is achieved through a process of subtracting ethnic particularity, resulting in a reign of truth where there is neither Greek nor Jew, male nor female, master nor slave. Of course, the content of Paul's letters, the resurrection of Jesus, is not the truth but a fantasy, but it is in the *form* of the truth. Slavoj Žižek contributes to this debate by way of an unorthodox version of Hegel read through Lacan, the watchword of which is Lacan's saying that the therapy is over when the patient realizes there is no Big Other. The final words of Jesus on the cross – my God, why have you forsaken me – bear witness to the final atheistic conversion of Jesus, when God himself ceases to believe in God. What remains after Jesus departs is the galvanization of the kingdom of the Spirit, the community of those who, having assumed responsibility for themselves, set out to produce a radical egalitarian socialist order. Just so a series of English translations of

Giorgio Agamben, which reveal a strain of thought drawing deeply from theological sources, has gained a large American audience.[36]

Hermeneutics: The Catholic Principle

The third and final theme in Continental philosophy that captured the interests of American Catholics is found in hermeneutics, which first took root in American soil in the 1970s, probably because Gadamer's *Truth and Method* (1960) was not translated into English until 1975. Richard Palmer, an American Quaker and pacifist, had published one of the first important introductions to Gadamer in English in 1969 in Northwestern's Continentalist series.[37] Hermeneutics proved to be central to the attraction Continental philosophy held for American Catholicism. If I may be permitted a personal recollection, I had the honour to serve as president of the American Catholic Philosophical Association in 1987–8. I used the occasion to urge the association to be more welcoming of the Continental work of its members. Even in this bastion of Thomism, serious work was being done in Continental philosophy. Sessions on the "Christian Existentialism" of Gabriel Marcel or on the problem of Being in Heidegger (especially in comparison with Aquinas on *ipsum esse*) were not at all uncommon. I formed a committee of former presidents to consider renaming the association's journal – it had been called *The New Scholasticism* – which resulted in the current name, *American Catholic Philosophical Quarterly*. This name had the twin virtues of virtually reproducing the association's own name and of opening the journal's windows to other Catholic (Continental) voices, which were already being heard quite regularly at the annual meetings. At the same time, Ralph McInerny, the longtime editor of *The New Scholasticism*, was stepping down as editor, and the Executive Committee wisely appointed Robert Wood, of the University of Dallas, as the new editor. Professor Wood had a lifelong interest in the interaction of the Catholic tradition with developments in Continental philosophy. I also nominated Wilfrid Desan, the great Sartre scholar at Georgetown, to give the "Aquinas Lecture," an invitation meant to honour a distinguished Catholic philosopher (even if he wrote books about a famous atheist!)

It was the office of the president to decide upon the topic of the annual meeting and to invite the plenary speakers. The topic I chose was "Hermeneutics and the Tradition," and I invited theologian David Tracy as one of the plenary speakers.[38] The choice of topic seemed obvious to me, but for many in this group, who showed up for the annual meeting all primed for arguments about prime matter and substantial form, it was a bit of a shock. I used to say in those days, only half in jest, that if the *Summa Theologiae* sat on the high altar at the Council of Trent, the conveners of Vatican II would have done well to have extended the same honour to Gadamer's *Truth and Method*. What else is hermeneutics if not *aggiornamento*, keeping the tradition alive, making sure we are animated by a living tradition not bound up by a moribund one?

To be sure, there is an irony in all this. Modern "hermeneutics" is of Lutheran-Protestant provenance. Luther put the Bible in the vernacular, which put it in the hands of the people, and he counselled them to take its ancient words (not Aristotle's) to heart. The result was that a great and productive conflict broke out, there being as many interpretations as there were hearts, and with the conflict came the need for some rules of interpretation. Enter hermeneutics. It is no accident that the first modern use of the word, and the first courses taught on hermeneutics, are to be found in the old European Protestant theological seminaries. It is also no accident that one of the first important discussions of hermeneutics on American soil took place at a series of conferences at Drew University in the early 1960s on Heidegger, hermeneutics, and Protestant theology.[39] But if hermeneutics starts out as a theory of reading a text, it soon became clear that a text has a context, and so that the text has a history. The meaning of the text is the history of its meaning, that is, its *tradition*. Enter Catholicism, if it dare!

It did. How so? When Paul Tillich spoke of the "Protestant Principle," the principle of *semper reformandum*, which extended beyond historical Protestantism and became a general principle of thinking – no conditioned form is ever the match for the unconditional matter which it is trying to express – he contrasted it with the "Catholic substance." For Tillich, the matter that is always to be re-formed is transmitted by the Church's Catholic past. But Tillich is mistaken on one point. The Catholic substance is the *history* of the Church, and this history is a self-correcting, self-reforming – Derrida would call it "autodeconstructing" – *process*, of which the Reformation itself is *a stage*. The old battle between "Scripture" and "Tradition" is settled before it starts. The Scriptures are the *effect* of the tradition, produced at a moment in the earliest *history* of the Church when it decided it had better write all this down, seeing that the return of Jesus was taking longer than the early church thought.

In short, *pace* Paul Tillich, the Catholic substance is also the Catholic Principle, and the Catholic Principle is *hermeneutics*.[40] After the long cold shower of an ahistorical Neoscholasticism, Catholic thinkers began to acquire historical consciousness. While Gilson as a medieval historian had long been pressing this point on the philosophers, the interesting thing is that this realization had dawned on American Catholic *theologians* before it hit a lot of Catholic philosophers. The theologians were deeply concerned with how theology was playing in the pews, with whether the ancient formulations were making sense in contemporary, pluralist, and increasingly hi-tech and secularist America. I remember being an amused observer at a debate in which a Thomistic philosopher (a layman), arguing that angels were immaterial substances, pure forms without matter, required by the perfection of the chain of being, was reduced to apoplexy by a Catholic biblical scholar (a priest), who maintained that they were a literary conceit, required by the sacred authors when God needed to pass on an "instant message." I well recall the first time I attended a meeting of the Catholic Theological Society of America and being struck there by how *little* I heard about Thomas Aquinas and how *much* I heard about Paul Ricoeur! I found myself much more comfortable at a meeting with the Catholic theologians than with the philosophers.

I also remember that, among the theologians at these meetings, David Tracy enjoyed pride of place. Tracy had written a book with the exquisite title *The Analogical Imagination* (at the sound of which every Thomistic heart should skip a beat), in which he argued that the *history* of theology is neither a univocal process of the unaltered repetition of the same, nor is it chaos and indiscriminate equivocity. It is instead an analogical process in which the theology of the Church is everywhere the same yet everywhere diversified, which is pretty much the (synchronic) Thomistic *analogia entis* put into (diachronic) historical motion. Tracy focused his analysis on what Gadamer called the "classic," meaning not a text of inerrant authority to which we must be literally loyal but one of inexhaustible depth that can be drawn upon again and again and that must be continually rethought, reinvented, and retranslated in the enduring history of its appropriation. The meaning of the classic is the history of its effects. The state of theology at any given moment is the fusion of the horizon of its ancient tradition (substance) with the horizon of the present (form). Tracy was very close to Tillich's method of correlation.

But this process, Tracy argued, is not a smooth and continuous glide. As an analogical process, it is faced at every turn by the challenge of the equivocal, of what Tracy called in another work "plurality and ambiguity," meaning the dissonance produced by the mobile, multicultural, plurivocal world we call "postmodern."[41] So interpretation, existential appropriation, had to cope with what Paul Ricoeur – Tracy's colleague at Chicago – called the "conflict of interpretations" and the "hermeneutics of suspicion." Like Henri de Lubac in the monumental *Drama of*

Atheistic Humanism, Tracy argued that theology has something to learn from these great atheistic critiques of religion, that we do not want a theology that oozes with *ressentiment* and offers an otherworldly off-ramp from this-worldly poverty and oppression. Ricoeur, too, enjoyed a very considerable following among Catholic philosophers and theologians at the end of the century, such as David Pellauer (DePaul), who had taken over the editorship of *Philosophy Today*, and Patrick Bourgeois (Loyola of New Orleans). Today, Ricoeur's work is alive and well in the figure of Richard Kearney, who came to Boston College from University College, Dublin, and whose "carnal hermeneutics" and "anatheism" are deeply marked by Ricoeur's movement from innocent faith through critique to a higher post-critical retrieval of faith.[42] By putting the hermeneutics of both Gadamer and Ricoeur to work under the venerable name of analogy, Tracy effectively showed that hermeneutics is cut to fit the Catholic imagination, and in so doing, he produced an impressive work of *aggiornamento* all his own.

What's Next?

I conclude with a worry – that I may be describing a movement that has had a good run but is now drawing to a close. Catholic philosophers and doctoral programs have become more seriously analytic (in the spirit of Aquinas's taste for a formal *disputatio*) and less Continental than in the past. Continental philosophy itself has been shocked from within by a new realist movement, variously described as the "new materialism"[43] or "object-oriented ontology" (OOO),[44] that is sharply critical of what it takes to be the "subjectivism" of the European tradition from Kant to postmodernism. Heidegger himself is under increasing fire as more and more information about the extent of his National Socialism continues to emerge. Furthermore, today, the hermeneutic scene in which American Catholic thinkers find themselves has changed. They face new and different challenges – the rising tide here and in Europe of an aggressive nationalism, of hostility to the immigrant and the stranger; the ominous prospect of relentless environmental degradation; the decline of church attendance, a phenomenon affecting all the mainstream congregations, but aggravated in Catholicism by the clerical sexual abuse scandal; the growing importance of information technologies; and the extraordinary developments in quantum physics and speculative cosmology. What we have been calling the "postmodern" condition is fast giving way to the "posthuman" one, about which Continental writers like Bruno Latour[45] and Catherine Malabou[46] have important things to say. We are all being forced to admit how deeply inscribed the human is in the non-human and the technical. Continental philosophy has been emphasizing that human being-in-the-world is historicized, gendered, and incarnate, but there are people working in the AI world who imagine *dis*incarnating it in varying degrees, up to and including eventually "freeing" it from its fragile corporeal basis and even evacuating it from its terrestrial home. Can it be of no interest to "philosophy," can there be nothing to "wonder" about, that matter and energy are interchangeable? We have yet to realize how deeply interwoven is the imagination of speculative physics with the wonder of the philosophers. In the first chapter of Stephen Hawking's *The Grand Design*, titled "The Mystery of Being," which sounds like something written by Marcel or Heidegger, Hawking says the big questions used to be addressed by philosophy but today philosophy is dead because it has lost touch with science.[47] If Continental philosophy is content to keep protecting its turf by repeating Heidegger's pronouncement that science does not think, it stands a good chance that the sciences will steal our thunder, that is, our wonder, right out from under us. Science does think and science wonders, because wonder is the piety of thought. Not only does the future of American Catholic philosophy and theology depend on meeting these challenges, but so also does the future of religion, and maybe of humanity itself, up to and including the challenge of whether it will have one.

NOTES

1 My thanks to Calvin Schrag, Don Ihde, Robert Scharff, and Richard Sugarman, who have taken the time to answer my questions about matters discussed in this paper of which they were witness. An earlier version of this paper appeared in "Continental Philosophy of Religion: Then, Now, and Tomorrow," *Journal of Speculative Philosophy* (Proceedings of the Society for Phenomenology and Existential Philosophy, 50th Anniversary Sessions) 26, no. 2 (2012), 347–60, parts of which are repeated here with permission of the *Journal*.

2 John Wild, *The Challenge of Existentialism* (Bloomington: Indiana University Press, 1955), 9ff.

3 Callistus James Edie, *The Philosophy of Étienne Gilson* (Louvain: Université Catholique de Louvain, 1958). See also Callistus James Edie, "The Writings of *Étienne Gilson* Chronologically Arranged," in *Mélanges offerts à Étienne Gilson de l'Académie française* (Toronto: Pontifical Institute of Mediaeval Studies; Paris: J. Vrin, 1959), 15–58. I am assuming that "Callistus" was a religious name, taken on the occasion of taking first vows.

4 James Edie, William Earle, and John Wild, eds., *Christianity and Existentialism* (Evanston: Northwestern University Press, 1963). See also

Edie, ed., *An Invitation to Phenomenology* (Chicago: Quadrangle, 1965); and Edie, ed., *Phenomenology in America* (Chicago: Quadrangle, 1967).

5 See three volumes by James D. Collins: *A History of Modern European Philosophy* (Milwaukee: Bruce Pub. Co. 1954); *The Mind of Kierkegaard* (Chicago: H. Regnery, 1953); and *The Existentialists: A Critical Study* (Chicago: H. Regnery, 1952).

6 Bruno Latour, *We Have Never Been Modern*, trans. Catherine Porter (Cambridge, MA: Harvard University Press, 1993).

7 See Floyd's chapter 2 in this volume for more on the development of American Neoscholasticism and its overcoming.

8 Wilfrid Desan, *The Marxism of Jean-Paul Sartre* (Garden City: Doubleday, 1965); Desan, *The Tragic Finale: An Essay on the Philosophy of Jean-Paul Sartre* (New York: Harper, 1960).

9 Thomas Langan, *The Meaning of Heidegger* (New York: Columbia University Press, 1959); Langan, *Merleau-Ponty's Critique of Reason* (New Haven: Yale University Press, 1966).

10 See also Dahlstrom's chapter 1 in this volume.

11 Harper & Row (New York City) had undertaken a series of translations of Heidegger's works into English under the editorship or J. Glenn Gray. Gray, a Hegel scholar, had been recruited for this job by Hannah Arendt through their mutual contact at the New School for Social Research, which was the first beachhead of Continental philosophy in the United States.

12 William J. Richardson, *Heidegger: Though Phenomenology to Thought*, with a preface by Martin Heidegger (The Hague: M. Nijhoff, 1974); John P. Muller and William J. Richardson, *Lacan and Language: A Reader's Guide to Ecrits* (New York : International Universities Press, 1982). The Heidegger book gave a generation of American readers their first serious encounter with Heidegger that pushed them past an "existentialist" reading of Heidegger and turned their attention to the later work.

13 Martin Heidegger, *Sein und Zeit*, 15th ed. (Tübingen: Niemeyer, 1979), §§29, 41; Eng. trans. *Being and Time*, trans. John Macquarrie and Edward Robinson (New York: Harper & Row, 1962), §§29, 41.

14 It is not an accident that both Gilson and Jean-Luc Marion started their careers and achieved international eminence as Descartes scholars.

15 Martin Heidegger, *Identität und Differenz* (Pfullingen: Neske, 1957). Eng. trans. *Identity and Difference*, trans. Joan Stambaugh (New York: Harper & Row, 1969).

16 See John D. Caputo, "Philosophy and Prophetic Postmodernism: Toward a Catholic Postmodernity," *American Catholic Philosophical Quarterly* 74, no. 4 (Autumn 2000), 549–68.

17 William McBride, "John Wild, Phenomenology in America, and the Origins of SPEP," *Continental Philosophy Review* 44, no. 3 (August 2011), 282. I have

found this entire special issue, "Remembering John Wild," dedicated to the memory of Alan Paskow, an invaluable resource.

18 Calvin Schrag, *God as Otherwise Than Being* (Evanston: Northwestern University Press, 2002), xi–xii.

19 Email correspondence.

20 Earle argued that "the transcendental ego is … in its essence, the essential intuition of God by God" and that the "passion for truth which men of good will manifest … always was and remains a passion for recognizing and honoring the divinity in oneself and the other." William Earle, *Mystical Reason* (Chicago: Regnery/Gateway, 1980), 106–7.

21 See Lester Embree and Michael D. Barber, eds., *The Golden Age of Phenomenology at the New School for Social Research, 1954–1973* (Athens: Ohio University Press, 2017).

22 Richard Sugarman, "Wild and Levinas: Legacy and Promise," *Continental Philosophical Review* 44, no. 3 (August 2011), 307–16.

23 Richard I. Sugarman and Roger Duncan, eds., *The Promise of Phenomenology: Posthumous Papers of John Wild* (Lexington: Lexington Books, 2006).

24 Today, SPEP numbers among its satellite groups both a "Society for Continental Philosophy in a Jewish Context" and a "Society for Continental Philosophy and Theology," the latter founded by Merold Westphal, Bruce Benson, Norman Wirzba, and me.

25 Dominique Janicaud, "The Theological Turn of French Phenomenology," in *Phenomenology and the Theological Turn: The French Debate*, ed. Dominique Janicaud et al. (New York: Fordham University Press, 2000), 3–103.

26 See Jim Kanaris, ed., *Reconfigurations of the Philosophy of Religion* (Albany: SUNY Press, 2018); Clayton Crockett, B. Keith Putt, and Jeffrey W. Robbins, eds., *The Future of Continental Philosophy of Religion* (Bloomington: Indiana University Press, 2014); and Philip Goodchild, ed., *Rethinking Philosophy of Religion: Approaches from Continental Philosophy* (New York: Fordham University Press, 2002). See also Gschwandtner's chapter 6 and Benson's chapter 9 in this volume.

27 See Heidegger's communication to the participants in a conference held at Drew University in 1964 in Martin Heidegger, *The Piety of Thinking*, ed. J.G. Hart, trans. J.C. Maraldo (Bloomington: Indiana University Press, 1977), 22–31.

28 See John D. Caputo, *The Mystical Element in Heidegger's Thought* (New York: Fordham University Press, 1986).

29 John E. Van Buren, *The Young Heidegger: Rumors of a Hidden King* (Bloomington: Indiana University Press, 1994), 167.

30 I have myself explored the implications of Luther's *theologia crucis* for a Continental philosophy of religion in *Cross and Cosmos: A Theology of Difficult Glory* (Bloomington: Indiana University Press, 2019).

31 Jean-Luc Marion, "The Saturated Phenomenon," *Philosophy Today* 40, no. 1 (SPEP Supplement; Spring 1994), 103–24. Marion gave this paper as a plenary at SPEP in 1993.
32 Jacques Derrida, "Circumfession: Fifty-Nine Periods and Periphrases," in Geoffrey Bennington and Jacques Derrida, *Jacques Derrida* (Chicago: University of Chicago Press: 1993), 154–5. See also John D. Caputo and Michael Scanlon, eds., *Augustine and Postmodernism: Confessions and Circumfession* (Bloomington: Indiana University Press, 2005).
33 Jean-Louis Chrétien, "The Wounded Word: Phenomenology of Prayer," in *Phenomenology and the Theological Turn: The French Debate*, ed. Dominique Janicaud et al. (New York: Fordham University Press, 2000), 147–75.
34 Mark Taylor's *Erring: An A/theology* (Chicago: University of Chicago Press, 1984) was the first major presentation of Derrida and theology to cause a stir at SPEP and elsewhere, but it was a "death of God" Derrida written before the quasi-Augustinian quasi-prayerful Derrida that became focal during the later so-called theological turn, which I had championed in John D. Caputo, *The Prayers and Tears of Jacques Derrida: Religion without Religion* (Bloomington: Indiana University Press, 1997).
35 See Gianni Vattimo, *Belief*, trans. Luca D'Isanto and David Webb (New York: Columbia University Press, 1999); and *After Christianity*, trans. Luca D'Isanto (New York: Columbia University Press, 2002).
36 Alain Badiou, *The Universalism of St Paul* (Stanford: Stanford University Press, 2003); Slavoj Žižek and John Milbank, ed. Creston Davis, *The Monstrosity of Christ: Paradox or Dialectic* (Cambridge, MA: MIT Press, 2009). For more on Žižek see O'Regan's chapter 12 in this volume. See also John D. Caputo and Linda Martin Alcoff, eds., *St Paul among the Philosophers* (Bloomington: Indiana University Press, 2009). See also, for example, Giorgio Agamben, *The Highest Poverty: Monastic Rules and Form-of-Life* (Stanford: Stanford University Press, 2013).
37 Richard E. Palmer, *Hermeneutics: Interpretation Theory in Schleiermacher, Dilthey, Heidegger, and Gadamer* (Evanston: Northwestern University Press, 1969).
38 See the *Proceedings of the American Catholic Philosophical Association* 61 (Washington, D.C.: Catholic University of America Press, 1988).
39 See James M. Robinson and John B. Cobb Jr, eds., *New Frontiers in Theology: The New Hermeneutic*, vol. 2 (New York: Harper & Row, 1964); see above, n24.
40 See John D. Caputo, "Tradition and Event: Radicalizing the Catholic Principle," in *The Challenge of God: Continental Philosophy and the Catholic Intellectual Tradition*, ed. Colby Dickinson, Hugh Miller, and Kathleen McNutt (London: Bloomsbury, 2019), 99–113.
41 See three volumes by David Tracy: *Blessed Rage for Order: The New Pluralism in Theology* (New York: Seabury Press, 1975); *The Analogical Imagination:*

Christian Theology and the Culture of Pluralism (New York: Crossroad Publishing, 1981); and *Plurality and Ambiguity* (San Francisco: Harper & Row, 1987).

42 Richard Kearney, *Anatheism: Returning to God After God* (New York: Columbia University Press); Richard Kearney and Brian Trainor, eds., *Carnal Hermeneutics* (New York: Fordham University Press, 2015).

43 Quentin Meillassoux, *After Finitude: An Essay on the Necessity of Contingency*, trans. Ray Brassier (London: Continuum, 2008), 28ff. For a robust rebuttal of Meillassoux, see Adrian Johnston, "Hume's Revenge: À Dieu, Meillassoux," in *The Speculative Turn: Continental Materialism and Realism*, ed. Levi Bryant, Nick Srnicek, and Graham Harman (Melbourne: re.press, 2011), pp. 92–113.

44 Graham Harman, *Object-Oriented Ontology: A New Theory of Everything* (London: Penguin, 2018). His work stems from an idiosyncratic interpretation of Heidegger's analysis of tools, which he forged in a dissertation at DePaul on Heidegger; he records his emigration from Continental philosophy in *Towards Speculative Realism: Essays and Lectures* (Winchester: Zero Books, 2009), a collection of papers whose rejection by SPEP and the Heidegger Conference he wears as something of a badge of honour. Harman also studied at Pennsylvania State University, with Alphonso Lingis, Levinas's first English translator, and took away from his work with Lingis the beginnings of OOO.

45 See Bruno Latour, *On the Modern Cult of the Factish Gods*, trans. Catherine Porter and Heather MacLean (Durham: Duke University Press, 2010), 93–4.

46 Catherine Malabou, *What Should We Do with Our Brain?*, trans. Sebastian Rand (New York: Fordham University Press, 2008).

47 Stephen Hawking and Leonard Mlodinow, *The Grand Design* (New York: Bantam Books, 2010), 5.

4 Meaning, Concreteness, and Subjectivity: American Phenomenology, Catholic Philosophy, and Lonergan from an Institutional Perspective

PATRICK H. BYRNE

In this chapter I hope to shed some light on the topic of phenomenology and Catholic philosophy, and the relationship of Lonergan's work to all this, by tracing developments at Boston College in the 1960s. I do not claim that the Boston College story is representative of how this trend developed elsewhere. But it is true that Boston College did become a significant player among Catholic philosophy departments, as well as Continental philosophy departments, and the issues that gave rise to the developments at BC certainly extended well beyond its own campus.

My thesis is that pivotal issues having to do with meaning, concreteness, and subjectivity favoured the rise of phenomenology, as well as the interest in Lonergan, at Catholic colleges and universities at the beginning of the 1960s. Although I believe these issues are still with us today, they were somewhat eclipsed by the end of the 1960s and the beginning of the 1970s, when the crises of race, poverty, the Vietnam War, and the nuclear arms race prompted a shift among Catholic students and professors toward social and political philosophy and its relation to the Catholic social justice tradition. But that is a story for a different volume.

I would like to begin with some anecdotes about the state of philosophy at Boston College in the early 1960s, because it can help us understand the enthusiastic reception (as well as strong resistance among some) that greeted the introduction of both phenomenology and Bernard Lonergan's philosophy into the curriculum. Around 1963, a large group of Boston College students assembled, threw their Scholastic philosophy textbooks into a big pile, set them on fire, and cheered. Was this perhaps inspired by Ignatius's exhortation to "Set the world aflame"? Well, the next year, the students' true intentions were made clear through a different symbolic expression, when they formed a procession to the edge of the reservoir that marks the eastern border of the BC campus and threw their Scholasticism books into the water.

That was also the first year that a budding Lonergan scholar, Joseph Flanagan, SJ, was a faculty member at BC. (He is the source for several of the ideas in this chapter.) Following the students' baptism of their Scholastic philosophy books, the president of Boston College, Michael Walsh, SJ, called Flanagan to his office and appointed him chairman of the Philosophy Department. He told Flanagan, "Joe, I don't care what you do. I just don't want to see the students burning or drowning their books anymore."

The student protests against their philosophy courses predated by a couple of years my matriculation at Boston College as a freshman in the fall of 1965. By the time I arrived, the undergraduate curriculum had been dramatically changed. For one thing, the philosophy requirements for graduation for all students, regardless of major, had been decreased from eight courses to four. For another, the four courses no longer followed the rigid Scholastic manuals. Those had been replaced by a greater emphasis on the history of philosophy, on philosophical anthropology, and on contemporary cultural issues and critiques. In addition, a wider choice of free electives was now offered in the senior year.

The older, eight-course regimen of Scholastic philosophy (which began with two courses in logic, followed by courses in epistemology, metaphysics, ethics, and natural theology) had been conceived as integral to the Jesuit educational model of *ratio studiorum*. That curriculum was intended to lift students to a sophisticated intellectual appropriation of their Catholic faith and especially foster their appreciation of the intellectual achievement of Thomas Aquinas as a model of faith seeking understanding. In his study of Catholic higher education in the twentieth century, Philip Gleason describes what was at least the vision of Neoscholasticism:

> [Its] God-centeredness, the emphasis on the supernatural dimension, the insistence on viewing all things *sub specie aeternitatis* [from an eternal perspective], which underlay the whole movement of the Catholic revival, and constituted its most important feature, involved much more than rationality, important as that was ... For God's *being* did more than illuminate the human intellect. Once understood, the divine plan for humankind required action, a commitment to its fulfillment on the part of every believer. And even more important, God's infinite perfection simultaneously awakened spiritual longings that could be satisfied only by personal union with God. To learn more of God and God's creation

> was not merely to be called to apostolic action; it was to be drawn more powerfully to God as the object of contemplation, of worship, of prayer, of devotion, of the soul's desire for spiritual fulfillment.[1]

Gleason further narrates how at the beginning of the twentieth century, this the Neoscholastic, integral vision, at its best, influenced the intellectual, literary, aesthetic, and mystical dimensions of the Catholic renaissance in the careers of such figures as Flannery O'Connor, Thomas Merton, Dorothy Day, Peter Maurin, and the Catholic Worker and Catholic Action movements of that period.[2] These developments were also inspired by the revival of reading the writings of Thomas Aquinas himself, rather than merely watered-down manuals and textbooks.

Unfortunately, the integral vision that Gleason describes so compellingly was seldom communicated effectively. The reasons for this were complicated. Some had to do with the intrinsic pedagogical challenges of such a course of study – the path from the early stages of preparation to the pay-off is very long indeed and demands an extraordinary degree of patience and deferred gratification from young people. Other reasons had to do with poor scholarly preparation: neither the teachers nor the textbooks reflected a proper understanding of the integral vision itself, and therefore communicated a distorted version of it.

But beyond these, I believe that one of the most significant difficulties was the epistemology that formed the very core of Neoscholasticsm. And the heart of that epistemology was its theory of abstraction and its naive realism, incorrectly thought to have been derived from Aristotle. The Neoscholastic theory of abstraction offered an answer to how human beings come to know universals as they really exist in things. But the universals, or forms, analysed by this theory turn out to be generalized sensory qualities. The concept of redness, abstracted from concrete sensations of redness, for example, was frequently offered as an example of a universal form. Other paradigms of universal forms – for example, the concepts of cup, table, dog, horse, humanity – really turn out to be shapes (or outlines) abstracted from the sensible shapes of particular entities. Abstract, rarefied sensible qualities had come to dominate scholastic teaching and thinking about universal forms. (Former BC philosophy professor Thomas Blakeley once pointed out to me that it is no coincidence that the Latin word *forma* is the mirror image of the Greek term for shape, *morphe*.)

According to this Scholastic theory of abstraction, after a person has had a sufficient number of sensory experiences of particular objects, the universal form of one of its qualities "unconsciously pops into the mind." That is to say, the individual instances of the form that resides in many real, concrete things produce an abstract, non-individuated version in the mind. Or in other words, the form that exists in a multiplicity of real things is abstracted out of those things and deposited in the mind (the "possible intellect").

There is a theory of meaning that follows from this way of thinking about knowledge of universals. This theory of abstraction tends to identify meaning with propositions. Propositions consist of subject terms and predicate terms. Subject terms denote concrete, particular objects residing in the external world. Predicate terms denote the abstract universals known through the process of abstraction. Propositions take their meaning from the application of universals to particulars. Just how this application happens is one of the more obscure and disputed aspects of Scholastic philosophy. But significantly, the universal predicates become the privileged elements in this Scholastic theory of meaning. Very little can be said about the particulars in their concreteness. There is in fact a slogan in Scholastic philosophy to the effect that "there can be no science [*scientia*, sometimes rendered just "knowledge"] of individuals as individual." (This, again, is a misinterpretation of Aristotle.) On this account, individual subject terms become meaningful only in virtue of the forms applied to them, and they do no more than instantiate forms. The individuals are merely minions, mere vessels for the realizations of abstract forms, which endow them with meaning. Concrete existing things are meaningless in themselves.

There is also a notion of subjectivity that goes along with this theory of abstraction – one that tends to make the human being abstract, impoverished, and impersonal. For example, one of the stock examples in Scholastic philosophy courses was "Socrates is a man." This tended to focus attention on the universal form, humanity, and to distract attention from the remarkable, concrete person that Socrates was.

In addition, the thinking subject in this process was not truly the agent of his or her own knowledge or acts of meaning. The abstract universals "pop unconsciously" into one's mind. Only after the concepts have been implanted does the human subject's consciousness enter the picture. The abstract universal forms already residing unconsciously in the possible intellect first become conscious when the faculty of understanding "looks" at the concepts that are "already in there now." But this eliminates the real creative work of human thinking and replaces it with an unconscious mechanism that operates without the agency of any human subject. Human conscious subjectivity provides no more than a mirroring act of understanding, one that merely acknowledges the presence of the universals that are "already in here now."

This dominance was a major cause of the alienation of Neoscholastic philosophy – at least as it was taught – from concreteness, human subjectivity, and meaning. The emphasis on abstraction of universal concepts (e.g., the concept of "man") tended to obliterate concrete differences – not the least of which were gender differences. In this system, the key to defining the concept of "man" was the further abstract concept of "rational soul." Every human being has a rational soul, be it awake or asleep. But human subjectivity entails consciousness, and one has to be awake to be conscious. Consciousness and all its special significances, complexities, and problems are obscured if the sole focus is on an undifferentiated human rational soul. The abstractness of the concept of rational soul also obscures differences that are profoundly meaningful when it comes to how people shape their own identities and live their lives. It abstracts from gender, race, ethnicity, religion, nationality, and all other historically situated cultural differences. The focus on abstraction and the neglect of meaningful differences tended to make Scholastic philosophy remote from and alien to the ways people actually live their lives. Almost no students found it helpful in answering the genuinely philosophical questions everyone asks about the meaning of life, reality, truth, freedom, God, and good and evil.

This style of Scholastic philosophy permeated the education of Bernard Lonergan, SJ, in the early decades of the twentieth century. Early in his training as a Jesuit, he grew very dissatisfied with the way Scholastic philosophy was being taught. To a large extent his own creative and original work was intended to overcome those limitations. According to Lonergan, this Scholastic theory of abstraction regards human knowledge as doing no more than producing "impoverished replicas" out of sensory experiences of concrete realities. Whether the realities in question are physical, chemical, botanical, animal, human, social, or religious, a philosophy based upon this theory of abstraction leads not only to impoverished replicas but also to an impoverished philosophy, an impoverished subjectivity, and an impoverished worldview. This, I believe, is why the Boston College students immolated and drowned their books. They were being taught a philosophy that had no relation to their concrete encounters with the world and other people. It also short-circuited their quest to find meaning and to find themselves.

In response to the student protests about their philosophy courses, BC's Philosophy Department, under the stewardship of Joseph Flanagan, SJ, inaugurated a reformed and reduced undergraduate curriculum for the 1965–66 academic year. It now emphasized primary texts from the history of philosophy in interactions with texts from literature, history, and contemporary social and natural sciences.

The following year, BC inaugurated its doctoral program in philosophy. The faculty involved in designing that program departed quite deliberately from the older Scholastic model. They also decided not to follow the prevailing model of Anglo-American (aka Analytic) philosophy. They chose instead to focus on existentialism and phenomenology and the antecedents of these in Descartes, Kant, Hegel, and Marx. They also chose to specialize in the philosophy of religion. Flanagan was a specialist in Lonergan; other faculty at that time were specialists in existentialism (John Rock, SJ, and Daniel Shine, SJ), Husserl, Kant, and Hume (Richard Murphy, SJ), Hegel, Marx, German idealism, and von Hildebrand (Joseph Navikas), phenomenology and Christian/Marxist dialogue (Frederick Adelmann, SJ), Soviet philosophy (Thomas Blakeley), Kierkegaard, Heidegger, and Scheler (Thomas Owens); and Blondel (Oliva Blanchette). The following year, two new faculty members were hired to strengthen BC's expertise in phenomenology: Jacques Taminiaux (secretary of the Husserl Archives in Leuven and an expert in phenomenology, German idealism, and Hegel) and David Rasmussen (who had studied with Riceour and Eliade). A few years later, Richard Cobb-Stevens, Hans-Georg Gadamer, William Richardson, SJ, Richard Kearney, and John Sallis would further enhance the faculty's strength in phenomenology.

I interviewed the three surviving members of the faculty from the year the doctoral program was inaugurated – Oliva Blanchette, Peter Kreeft, and Thomas Owens – to learn why the department chose this direction for the graduate program. Kreeft told me he did not recall anything in particular, but as 1966–7 was only his second year as a faculty member at Boston College, he may not have been involved in the discussions that had shaped the graduate program. Blanchette said there was not really a formal department vote or decision – that the emphasis on phenomenology just "took place over a few years." Finally, Owens told me that "after the Second World War, there was a great interest in European philosophy. Phenomenology had come into its prominence." He had written his dissertation on ethics at Fordham University under the direction of Dietrich von Hildebrand. He continued: "Phenomenology just seemed more substantive than Analytic philosophy, which seemed like desiccated algebra. Phenomenology had more blood in it." He said that he himself turned to study Heidegger because his work "seemed substantial, and not many people were working on his thought."

In addition to these reflections by my senior colleagues, I can add a few reflections of my own, concerning why phenomenology as well as Lonergan's thought received such an enthusiastic reception. Behind that enthusiasm, I think, was the recognition that both methodologies revealed much richer and more concrete worlds of meaning and subjectivity than late Scholasticism could offer.

From the beginning, of course, the phenomenological movement that followed in Husserl's wake was dedicated to the recovery of the richness of human experience and meaning in all its concreteness. The maiden voyage of phenomenology began with the publication of Husserl's *Logical Investigations.* Those investigations are overwhelmingly concerned with the problematic of the meaning of signs. Husserl showed how complex, rich, and concrete are the intentionalities – both empty and fulfilled – that constitute the meanings of even seemingly abstract realms of mathematical and logical expressions. In addition, his motto *zu den Sachen selbst* and the phenomenological *epoché* meant suspending assumptions about realities. In the natural attitude, we take for granted that the things we perceive consist of no more than the simple and obvious features we find useful in daily life. Even when the natural attitude imports scientific notions, the concrete richness of the *Sachen* as they are actually given in consciousness is reduced to the limited concepts and explanations that happen to be available in the present state of scientific theory. These assumptions obscure the concrete intricacies of perceptions, memories, beliefs, and judgments that are the actualities of human experience and thinking.

Over and again, Husserl's practice of the phenomenological method showed abundantly that all of our actual and concrete intentional acts of consciousness are composed of richly intertwined layers of *noetic* acts and *noematic* contents. This is true whether the intentional acts are perceptions, memories, imaginative fantasies, different grades of "*doxic*" intentionalities, or acts of valuing or willing. We only notice this rich and complex layering when we leave the natural attitude and adopt the phenomenological attitude, with its commitment to "absolutely faithful description," as Husserl puts it.[3]

Integral to phenomenology's turn away from abstraction toward the richness of the concrete is its overriding concern with meaning, especially meaning as the sense (*Sinn*) of something. In one of his most emphatic claims about intentionality in *Ideen I*, for example, Husserl writes: "In other words, to have a sense [*Sinn zu haben*] [of something] or 'to have something in mind' is the basic character of all consciousness that for that reason is not only any experience at all but a 'noetic' experience, one having a sense [*Sinn*]."[4] Sartre pushed Husserl's method further and delved into the meaning of emotions. Scheler followed a different route to explore the meanings of feelings and their complex consciousness of values. Merleau-Ponty's phenomenology of embodiment further concretized the meaningfulness of language. Heidegger radicalized Husserl's project by asking about the very meaning of being as such. His approach was to conduct an interpretive (a hermeneutical) phenomenology of the meaning of human existence, *Dasein*.

For phenomenology, revealing the meaning of *noematic* objects means opening up their intentional connections with the concrete, consciously constituting subject. Meaning means something to someone. Although there is probably no more hotly disputed topic among phenomenologists than subjectivity, I think all would agree that the Scholastic picture of subjectivity as the mere spectator of abstract concepts ignores the ineliminable role of the subject in the constitution of meanings and the world. In his recent book *Moral Emotions*, Anthony Steinbock underscores the constitutive role of human subjectivity, writing that Husserl's "unique phenomenological approach ... allowed him to describe the 'how' of giving [{the} sense, meaning] of 'what' something is ... in relation to the power and the limits of subjectivity."[5]

The enthusiasm my student peers and I shared in our encounters with the writings of phenomenologists had to do precisely with those writings' capacious openness to this broad world of meaning. Especially important for Catholic philosophers, this approach offered openness, respect, and the promise to enrich the concreteness of moral and religious experiences. While it was certainly true that many of my peers had cut their ties with their Catholic (or other religious) heritage, for those of us who were seeking to better understand the religious meanings of our heritage, phenomenology was refreshing and illuminating, and so was Lonergan's philosophy of self-appropriation.

Yet Lonergan himself initially dismissed Husserl's phenomenological method as "a highly rarified empiricism" and as an "abstract looking" that cut itself off from the particularities of things and subjects "as they really are."[6] Later, however, after reading *The Crisis of the European Sciences*, though he still found shortcomings in Husserl's approach, he arrived at a much more positive evaluation of him. In particular, he was appreciative of the much more concrete account of subjectivity he found in that late work.[7] At one point he even professed a great affinity between his own work and that of Husserl.

Lonergan of course argued emphatically that the Neoscholastic theory of abstraction was not a correct account of what human knowing or meaning actually is, nor was it an accurate interpretation of Thomas Aquinas's writings on these themes. As with phenomenology, Lonergan's method of "self-appropriation" seeks instead to ground philosophy in careful attention to the facticity of how human thinking actually does proceed. He draws attention to the abiding presence of questioning and inquiry that underpins all human endeavours to know correctly and live authentically. He lamented the neglect of the activity of insight that pervades all dimensions of human thinking and acting. Eschewing the Scholastic theory of abstraction, according to which universals arise unconsciously only to later be passively contemplated by understanding, Lonergan showed that the actual process of understanding in human consciousness is exactly the reverse of the Scholastic theory. Through his own phenomenological investigations, in interaction with his close reading of Aquinas's texts, Lonergan discovered that universal concepts actually come after and are produced by understanding. Understanding actively and creatively produces concepts, thereby expressing what it has come to understand prior to conceptualization. He identified understanding with insight. But insights do not arise unconsciously; they arise through the agency of intelligent, conscious subjects, as the subjects creatively construct flows of images in order to aid their quests to find answers to questions. Without conscious, imaginative, and intelligent effort and the collaboration between the subject and his or her questions, neither insights nor universal concepts will "unconsciously pop" into mind.

The same thing holds for the transition from understanding to true judgments. Lonergan famously decried those who "seem to have thought of truth as so objective as to get along without minds."[8] By way of contrast, he probed the "slow and laborious process"[9] of human self-transcendence. True judgments arise only when human subjects engage in authentic exercises of reflection, which is attentive to and actively pursues answers to all further pertinent questions. Truth about what is and what ought to be done comes to consciousness only in concrete human subjects committed to this deep form of authenticity.

In addition, Lonergan's attention to subjects in all their concreteness includes their self-constitution as social, cultural, linguistic, and embodied individuals. It especially regards the role that individuals' concrete experiences, questions, insights, reflections, and judgments of fact and value, and most importantly their *decisions*, play in the ways they take cultural, linguistic, and social norms into their own personal ways of being in the world. This also draws attention to the concreteness of individuals' acts of self-transcending and fleeing from the responsibilities of self-transcendence, as well as to the particular ways in which, theologically, grace makes possible conversions back toward self-transcendence that are always personal, never universalized.

Lonergan's method points not only to subjects in their authenticity but also to objects in all their concreteness. Self-appropriation reveals that our questioning is completely unrestricted. This means that we can, and sometimes almost actually do, ask everything about everything.

There is no aspect or detail or nuance of any concrete thing or concrete good, no matter how tiny or minute, that we do not desire to know, at least until the inhibitions of our culture squelch that native desire. Therefore, human knowing and ethical action are *not* caught up in abstractions. Rather, we are drawn toward understanding realities and goods in all their complex and fascinating concretenesses.

The theory of meaning that emerges from Lonergan's method of self-appropriation is what he called by the oxymoron, "enriching abstraction." By this he meant that the path of thought does not reduce the plethora of perceptual contents to an impoverished replica. Rather, inquiry prompts human intelligence to go beyond the richness of concrete sense experiences toward the still further richness of intelligibility and meaning. It does so by seeking, and frequently finding, insights into the meaning and intelligibility that enrich those experiences. The unrestricted self-transcendence of wonder is what underpins the quest for and the attainment of meaningfulness. Questions seek to know the meaning of experiences. Insights, when judged to be correct, reveal the meanings that unrestricted inquiry seeks so passionately. Insights and judgments do not replace but rather supplement and enrich experience.

Readers of Lonergan's major philosophical work, *Insight*, often find its first five chapters on science to be quite difficult. Those five chapters present one of greatest barriers to interest in Lonergan's work. But for me, Lonergan opened up science as a meaningful human activity in a way that no one else ever did, not even Husserl. He did this by placing inquiry and the creativity of insight at the core of science, rather than logic and abstract concepts.[10] According to Lonergan, science is a process of creative human activity where novel experiences elicit novel questions, creative insights respond intelligently to questions, further questions about the correctness and adequacy of the insights lead to new observations and experiments, still further questions and insights all headed toward correct and true understandings of the complex intelligibilities of the universe.

At the time of the publication of *Insight* in 1957, the creative act of insight and intelligibility formed the core of Lonergan's account of meaning. In the preface to that book he wrote: "Insight, then, includes the apprehension of meaning, and insight into insight includes the apprehension of the meaning of meaning."[11] But within a few years, Lonergan was already finding this account too limited. He announced his turn toward a deeper and more concrete exploration of meaning in his lecture "Dimensions of Meaning," delivered at Marquette University in 1965. Most notable in that lecture is the expansion of his view of meaning to include the "symbolic meaning" of affect-laden images,[12] in addition to the intelligibilities grasped through insights and authentic judgments. He went so far as to "proclaim that the human spirit expresses itself in symbols before it knows, if it ever knows, what the symbols literally mean."[13] This was also the point in his career where he turned from discourse *about* God and grace toward the much more concrete explorations of these traditional theological topics from the point of view of religious experiences and meanings as such.

By this time also he had abandoned his earlier *Insight* criticism of Husserl's phenomenology, acknowledging the contributions of phenomenologists who "have revealed to us our myriad of potentialities."[14] Still, he thought that something more was needed than phenomenology had yet provided. Moreover, he set forth his analysis of the crisis of our time as not only a crisis of meaning but also a crisis in our methods for *reflecting on* meaning. He saw that this crisis had profound consequences for Catholic faith. He offered his own work, and especially his method in theology, as a supplement for what he thought was missing from phenomenology.

It is something of a puzzle for me, therefore, that Lonergan has so fallen out of favour in Catholic philosophy departments. But one clue about this came to me at a recent conference on the work of French theologian Stanislaus Breton. One of the speakers, Professor Jérôme de Gramont from the Institut Catholique de Paris, identified two contrasting sources that lead people to philosophize. One of these, he said, is the wonder that Aristotle identifies as the beginning of philosophy in the opening lines of his *Metaphysics*. But, Gramont went on to say, "there are other, darker beginnings for philosophy, exclamations of terror rather than dazzlement."[15] I have to confess that it is wonder and dazzlement that led me into philosophy. It is wonder and dazzlement that are the foundations of Lonergan's philosophy and that made his work so attractive to me. Human meanings, lives, achievements, and individual expressions are responses to wonder and inquiry. But today the world of philosophy is more and more following the way of the world in general, and perhaps appropriately so. The twentieth and now the twenty-first centuries have witnessed some of the deepest terrors and darknesses in the history of humanity. Responsible philosophers cannot ignore this fact, and hence the great attention to suffering, loss, the negative, absence, uncertainty, brokenness, the abyss, difference, and especially otherness seems a much needed corrective for what has come to seem an irresponsible a lack of attentiveness to such phenomena. I think Lonergan's philosophy of wonder and dazzlement may also have come to seem not only irrelevant but culpably unresponsive. Still, the darkness of suffering and injustice was certainly not at all beyond the horizon of Lonergan's concern. In fact, his whole life's work was to develop a philosophy that could respond to what he called the social surd, the power of unintelligibility at work in the social world that has "landed the twentieth century in an earthly hell."[16] He wrote both *Insight* and *Method in Theology* in order to address the crisis of meaning and the longer cycle of decline in which we are currently mired. However, his approach was to turn toward the sources of creating and healing, rather than to delve more deeply into the phenomena of trauma and decline. I hope that in the future the work being done by philosophers motivated by dazzlement and those motivated by terror can be brought into productive dialogue. Cooperation between these two approaches now appears to me as a new challenge for Catholic philosophy in our time.

NOTES

1 Philip Gleason, *Contending with Modernity: Catholic Higher Education in the Twentieth Century* (Oxford: Oxford University Press, 1995), 121–2.
2 Ibid., 155–63.
3 Edmund Husserl, *Ideas I*, trans. Daniel O. Dahlstrom (Indianapolis: Hackett, 2014), 178.
4 Ibid.
5 Anthony J. Steinbock, *Moral Emotions: Reclaiming the Evidence of the Heart* (Evanston: Northwestern University Press, 2014), 7–8.
6 Bernard Lonergan, *Insight: A Study of Human Understanding*, in Collected Works of Bernard Lonergan, vol. 3, edited by Frederick E. Crowe and Robert M. Doran (Toronto: University of Toronto Press, 1992), 440.
7 See especially *Phenomenology and Logic: The Boston College Lectures on Mathematical Logic and Existentialism.* In *Collected Works of Lonergan* (Toronto: University of Toronto Press, 2001) (hereafter CWL), vol. 18, ed. Philip J. MacShane, 254–60, 264–5.
8 Lonergan, "The Subject," in *A Second Collection*, vol. 13 of *Collected Works of Bernard Lonergan*, edited by Robert M. Doran and John D. Dadosky (Toronto: University of Toronto Press, 2016), 221–34.
9 Ibid.
10 Anne Carpenter's chapter in this volume describes other ways in which Lonergan's account of science can be of value in this broader conversation, this time by distinguishing science from theology.
11 Lonergan, *Insight*, 5.
12 Lonergan, "Dimensions of Meaning," in *CWL*, vol. 4, ed. Frederick E. Crowe and Robert Doran, 264.
13 Ibid., 263.

14 Ibid., 264.

15 Jerôme de Gramont, "Breton: The Principle and Dissemination," unpublished paper, 1.

16 *Insight*, 255; *Macroeconomic Dynamics: An Essay in Circulation Analysis*, edited by Frederick G. Lawrence, Patrick H. Byrne, and Charles C. Hefting Jr., CWL, vol. 15, xxvii.

5 Catholicism and Continental Philosophy in French Canada: An Opening Followed by an Ungrateful Separation

JEAN GRONDIN

A Difficult and Sensitive Subject

A piece on Catholicism and Continental philosophy in French Canada might start with a little confession: there is no way that a short chapter like this one can hope to do justice to the theme alluded to by its main title. It could only be dealt with adequately in a book-length study or, ideally, by a multi-volume encyclopedia. I can offer here only a sketch, one with many omissions and shortcuts. I hope this will stimulate more extensive studies.

To begin with, "Catholicism," "Continental philosophy," and "French Canada" are for a host of reasons heavy-handed concepts that would strike many of those involved in the story as problematic:

1. What Catholicism *is* is itself far from obvious, and so is what it means to be a Catholic philosopher. It is certainly not here that the issue will be addressed, let alone resolved. In discussions of Continental philosophy, the issue of Catholicism is problematic – at least at this point in time – largely because the overwhelming majority of Continental philosophers in French Canada would not regard themselves as Catholic. French Canada or Quebec underwent a spectacularly quick process of secularization in the 1960s and 1970s, one with few parallels in the Western world, one result of which has been that Continental philosophy and Catholicism now have almost nothing in common. Indeed, most Continental philosophers would probably express a certain disdain for the "Catholic" label. Those Continental philosophers who do happen to be Catholic do not go out of their way to advertise it. When it is known that one or the other is a "catho," it is seldom viewed as a badge of honour for them – quite the contrary. This is true not only of Catholicism,

but also of most matters deemed religious or theological. Many Continental (and, needless to add, Analytic) philosophers would flee from them, and proudly. Furthermore, there is no real Catholic university in French Canada with a strong program in Continental philosophy, as one finds in the United States. Indeed, French Canadian universities have been thoroughly secularized. It is true that the most important ones – the Université Laval in Quebec City and the Université de Montréal – were founded and led by Catholics and served to promote the Catholic faith; however, all universities in French Canada are now independent and secular entities funded in part by the state.[1] Nowadays, one can hardly speak of Catholicism in the field of Continental philosophy.

2. "Continental" philosophy? Again, I do not want to dwell on the debatable nature of this concept in and of itself. In any case, the term is somewhat inappropriate in the French Canadian context, because until quite recently the label was seldom applied there to a form of philosophy. When I pursued undergraduate studies at a French Canadian university, the Université de Montréal, in the 1970s, I never seriously heard the term.[2] There *was* no Continental philosophy – there was only "philosophy," which one studied either through disciplines (logic, ethics, ontology, aesthetics, etc.) or through authors or periods (Plato, Descartes, Empiricism, etc.). This has perhaps something to do with the fact that Analytic philosophy was not deeply implanted in the university curriculum at the time. It was taught by a handful of teachers, but it was perceived as one current among many, a current that focused on epistemological matters and the clarification of language – matters that had been addressed by all philosophers since antiquity. In other words, all philosophy was basically "Continental" – it just didn't realize it. Things have changed. The American influence, which used to be modest in *French* Canada, has grown, and Analytic philosophy is now strongly present – in some cases even dominant – at many French Canadian universities, especially in the Université du Québec network, which was created in 1969. In turn, these Analytic philosophers have promoted the notion of "Continental philosophy," perhaps to distinguish themselves from what they view as an unpropitious form of philosophy. But for me, the notion of Continental philosophy as such has never been very relevant. I view it as an American import and as an imposition on the part of Analytic philosophers. Its use by "Continental" philosophers always strikes me as a kind of cop-out. But like the prose of Mr Jourdain, I guess it is the language I speak without knowing it.

3. "French Canada" is also a fraught concept. It used to be the natural way in which French-speaking people (who were overwhelmingly Catholic) living in Canada viewed themselves. Since the 1970s, it has been replaced in many places by another self-identity: "Québécois." There are reasons for this: most French speakers in Canada happen to live in the province of Quebec. This province, with a population of now around 8 million, is the only entity in North America where French speakers form the majority. Yet this notion of Québécois is not an obvious qualification for at least two reasons: (1) There are French-speakers in other parts of Canada, though in those places they will always form a minority. This is relevant for our topic because there are universities in those parts of Canada where French is spoken by a minority and where Continental philosophy is taught; I am thinking especially of the bilingual universities of Ottawa and Sudbury (in Ontario), and of the Dominican University College in Ottawa, all of which have a distinguished Continental tradition; as well as Moncton (in New Brunswick). Are these French speakers Québécois? No they are not (even if many Québécois teach at them). They are French Canadians, but many Québécois have ceased to understand themselves as such. (2) Quebec is not entirely French. There is a robust English-speaking minority with prominent universities, especially in Montreal (McGill, Concordia), and these too have a respectable Continental heritage. Are they Québécois? Many are not sure. They are Quebecers because they live in Quebec, but if their main language is English, are they really "Québécois"? Those who live here know that this venomous issue dominates our politics in multitudinous ways it would be too complicated to explain to an outsider. For the purposes of the sketch I am drawing here, "French Canada" will refer to all French-speaking philosophers as well as their universities and colleges, in the province of Quebec and in Canada.

A Little Historical Background on Catholicism in French Canada

After these necessary caveats, there are a few solid certainties that pertain to our topic. (1) Historically and until very recently, virtually all French Canadians were Catholic. The Catholic Church also used to be (again until the late 1960s and 1970s) overbearing in the life of French Canadians. It had a strong presence in nearly all of its schools (except, of course, in the schools of the Protestant anglophones or the Jewish minority) and hospitals, and even in its politics and its universities. Indeed, the oldest French Canadian university, the Université Laval, was originally conceived, when it was founded in 1663 by the first bishop of the French colony, François de Montmorency Laval, as a seminary for candidates to the priesthood. After the English conquest of New France in 1760, the university opened itself to the liberal professions.[3] In 1852 it became a full-fledged university through a decree signed by Queen Victoria. The Université Laval opened a branch in the city of Montreal (Canada's metropolis at the time) in 1880, which would become autonomous in 1919 and take on the name of Université de Montréal (hereafter UdM). Since the mid-twentieth century, Quebec's universities have expanded so as to encompass more disciplines; they also opened themselves to the outside world and thereby became thoroughly secular. When they were founded, the French-speaking universities, especially Laval and Montréal, were in the hands of the clergy. The first rector (or principal) of UdM not to be a member of the clergy was named in 1965, and the first at Laval not to be one was named in 1972. This Catholic vocation is evident in the motto of UdM: *Fide splendet et scientia* (it shines through faith and science).[4] This splendid motto is however often perceived, if it registers at all, as a relic from a bygone era. Some want to change it, and I doubt it will survive for long, because of the second certainty. (2) As already mentioned, French Canadian and Québécois society underwent a thorough secularization beginning in the 1960s, known as the "révolution tranquille" (Quiet Revolution). Over the course of this very rapid transition, the hold of the Catholic faith on Québécois minds and institutions unravelled completely. This has manifested itself in many ways of the sort one encounters in other Western societies: religious practice is way down; Catholic teachings are not followed and are viewed as out of touch with the times; the state has taken up most institutions; and religions are now often viewed in a very negative light. A pope might stir some interest in the media, but nowadays one mostly hears Catholicism spoken of in connection with past child abuse at a number of learning institutions, for instance the residential schools that were so tragically imposed on the Aboriginal population.

To make a long story short: a formerly strongly Catholic society has rapidly become secularized to the point that Catholicism is often strongly disparaged, even if most recognize that it is part of the cultural heritage of French Canadians and Québécois, as is evident in the incredible number of churches (many of which have been transformed into condominiums) and the religious names of the streets, cities, and various landmarks. The main streets of Montreal still carry names like rue St-Laurent, rue St-Denis, and rue Ste-Catherine. One must assume that this cultural heritage is being protected for historic reasons, not religious ones.

Incursions of Continental Philosophy through Thomism

In French Canada, philosophical culture is a relatively recent phenomenon.[5] Philosophy only started to emerge as an independent field of inquiry independent of religion around the middle of the twentieth century, with the expansion of the traditional universities in Quebec City (Laval), Montreal, and Ottawa and the founding of new ones throughout the province of Quebec (more on that later). Until that time, philosophy had largely been taught by clergymen at seminaries that educated candidates for the priesthood. There used to be plenty of these, because there was a strong demand for priests in such a profoundly Catholic community (French Canadians traditionally also had large families) and because the profession of the priesthood was itself highly regarded. For young (male) high school students, the most respected liberal professions were indeed medicine, law, and the priesthood. Many of those who had genuine philosophical interests would become priests.[6] When philosophy departments were established – the Faculté de philosophie de l'Université Laval was founded in 1935, that of UdM in 1921, that of the Université d'Ottawa in 1934 – almost all of the first professors to be hired were clergymen. No surprise, then, that the philosophy that was taught was essentially Catholic in inspiration and especially Thomist, as was the case, one can assume, at most American Catholic universities. In this tradition, medieval philosophy was held in high esteem, but there was also an interest in the Greeks, especially Aristotle, in light of his influence on Thomas. By comparison, modern and (non-Thomist) contemporary philosophy fared poorly. Indeed, these were ignored, or they were known only through textbooks that pointed out their glaring errors. The books of the most important modern philosophers (Descartes, Spinoza, Locke, Hume, Kant, etc.) were part of the infamous *Index librorum prohibitorum*, whose creation went back to the counter-reformatory Council of Trent.

During this era, which is often caricatured in our history books, there was some decent scholarship within the Thomistic tradition,[7] helped along by the fact (which would later serve the culture of Continental philosophy, I would argue) that many philosophy teachers knew foreign languages: most spoke and read French and English, and very often they knew Latin and perhaps even ancient Greek. Many today tend to look down on this tradition of Thomism and dismiss it as an age of ignorance and blind indoctrination, but it was probably more open to the outside world than it is usually given credit for. This showed itself in a variety of ways:

1. This tradition of Thomism was supported by prestigious guest lecturers from Europe, especially France and Belgium, who helped found lasting institutions in Canada and opened many minds to the wider world of philosophy outside the confines of Thomism. One thinks here of illustrious scholars such as Étienne Gilson (1884–1978), who encouraged the foundation of the Institute for Medieval Studies at the UdM and would later ground an English-speaking one at the University of Toronto; and Jacques Maritain (1882–1973), both of whom were regular visitors at French-speaking universities like Laval and UdM.[8] Gilson was mostly viewed as a medieval scholar; Maritain was praised as an intellectual beacon.[9] Naturally, they both stood in the tradition of Thomism, which was the official philosophy of the Catholic Church, but theirs was a "Neo-Thomism," as it became known, which engaged with modern currents, even if their outlook was, of course, resolutely "anti-modern."[10]
2. All of these "anti-modern" guest lecturers would thus often speak of the newly fashionable existentialism of Sartre, Camus, Marcel, Jaspers, and Heidegger, of the philosophy of life of Bergson, and of classical figures such as Kant, Hegel, Kierkegaard, Marx, Nietzsche, and Husserl, who together form the bulk of what is now known as Continental philosophy. They would also discuss the personalism of Emmanuel Mounier, who had a strong influence on a generation of Catholic philosophers, including Charles Taylor (born in Montreal in 1931), the son of an English-speaking father and a French Canadian mother. Taylor would study at Oxford with Isaiah Berlin and later teach at the English-speaking McGill University; he is perfectly bilingual and has had a lasting impact at French Canadian universities, where he has been a guest lecturer.[11] All of these foreign lecturers must have stirred the curiosity of their French Canadian students, many of whom were candidates for the priesthood or were already priests.
3. Quite a few of those French Canadian students were enticed to learn first-hand what this "European" philosophy – the alluring forbidden fruit, as it were – looked like, and some went abroad to study. Some went to the Sorbonne in Paris, but most went to the University of Louvain because it was *a priori* more Thomistic than the secular or "laïque" Sorbonne. Most of those who went there to study worked on Thomas or the Greeks (mainly Aristotle). It is thus that a breach started to open in the somewhat confined environment of Thomism in French Canada.

The Opening to Continental Philosophy at Laval University and UdM

This opening to Continental philosophy that occurred from within Thomism was promoted by open-minded professors at universities in Quebec City and at UdM. The most prominent figure at Laval was Charles De Koninck (1906–1965). Originally from Belgium, he came to Quebec City in the 1930s and founded the Faculté de philosophie of Laval University,[12] which he headed and dominated from 1939 to 1956. He was somewhat unique in that he was a lay professor at a time when most teachers, and most of the ones he hired, came from the clergy. One of his strengths was that he was well connected with European and American universities, especially Catholic ones. He also taught at the University of Notre Dame, whose press is now publishing a commendable English edition of *The Writings of Charles De Koninck*. He founded a philosophical journal in 1945, the *Laval théologique et philosophique*, which still exists and is French Canada's oldest continuous philosophical journal (half its content is obviously devoted to theology, which indicates the "neighbourhood" where philosophy used to be seen). In the annals of Canadian philosophy, De Koninck will often be depicted as the quintessential Thomist, but in fact he was noteworthy for his numerous and impressive publications (a rarity for French-speaking Canadian philosophy professors at the time), his influential teaching, and the fact that he was a European with many contacts in the wider philosophical world (which was seldom the case for his colleagues). He invited many great philosophers and authors to Laval. He died suddenly in 1965 while in Rome, where he was a prominent figure at the Second Vatican Council. His first son, Thomas De Koninck, would become an influential dean of the Faculté de philosophie at Laval. He would pursue the opening of Laval University by often inviting, from the 1970s to this day, prominent Catholic philosophers from the most recent generation, such as Jean-Luc Marion, Rémi Brague, and Jean-François Mattéi.

The opening of UdM to Continental philosophy and the wider world also happened through the prism of an open Thomism. Two of the most instrumental figures in this opening were the Dominicans Celas-Marie Forest (1885–1970), dean of the Faculté de philosophie of UdM from 1926 to 1952, and Louis-Marie Régis (1903–1988), his successor at that post from 1952 to 1960. Forest's tenure as dean was very long, for he was devoted to his institution, but he was not a prolific author. Indeed, as was not unusual at the time for clerics who taught philosophy, he refused to write.[13] He had studied at the University of Ottawa and for a time at the Dominican Angelicum University in Rome. Régis, a French Canadian who had studied at Le Saulchoir, the Dominican school in Belgium,[14] wrote for his part the short books *St Thomas and Epistemology* and *L'Odyssée de la métaphysique*.[15] Having studied abroad, both Forest and Régis had contacts with European Catholic thinkers, such as Chenu, Gilson, and Maritain. With the support of Forest, Chenu,[16] and Gilson, Régis founded the Institut d'études médiévales in Montréal in 1942 and was its director from its inception until 1952. Forest and Régis invited many European thinkers to teach at UdM, including Gilson, Louis-Bertrand Geiger, Henri-Irénée Marrou, Paul Vignaux, and Clémence Ramnoux, who were renowned specialists in ancient thought. In 1958, Régis also invited Paul Ricoeur to UdM.[17] Aware of his faculty's shortcomings in modern philosophy, he had asked Ricoeur to teach Kant, Husserl, Hegel, and Schelling![18] However, Ricoeur would only come in 1964 or 1965, when he taught a course on the demanding topic "Temps et liberté chez Kant," which dealt for the most part with the transcendental schematism of Kant's first *Critique*. The eyes of many students were thus suddenly opened to Kant and modern philosophy.

Ricoeur's host at that time, and for the years to come in which he would be a regular visitor, was another key figure for the opening of UdM to Continental and modern philosophy, Vianney Décarie (1919–2006). At the urging of Régis, Décarie had studied at Harvard, the Collège de France, and the Sorbonne, where he completed his doctorate, which was supervised by Gilson.[19] In 1946 he was one of the first non-clerics hired to teach philosophy (only Greek philosophy, of course) at UdM. In 1967, UdM's ecclesiastical Faculté de philosophie (ecclesiastical meaning here that its program corresponded, theoretically, to the teachings of Roman Catholicism, which in effect had not been the case for some time) became a secular "Département de philosophie," and Décarie was its first chair from 1967 to 1970. He was an open-minded Catholic, schooled in Thomism of course, but he felt, like many in the 1950s and early 1960s, that French Canadian universities and philosophy departments needed to open themselves to the realm of philosophy "out there," which was mostly Continental (and Analytic, as he would discover during his stays at Harvard and Oxford). He confessed to me that he was ashamed to have completed his degree in philosophy without having read a single page of Kant (which was not unusual). He thus set out to invite guest lecturers to teach modern philosophy at his department and to hire young scholars who had studied in Europe. Among the guests he invited were luminaries like Paul Ricoeur (his close personal friend),[20] the young Charles Taylor, and Pierre Aubenque. Ricoeur would impress and attract many pupils, many of whom travelled to Paris in the 1960s and 1970s to complete their PhD theses under his liberal supervision. I remember that when I was studying at UdM in the 1970s, no less than six of my teachers had been his direct pupils.[21]

Another towering hermeneutic thinker, Hans-Georg Gadamer, was also in the vicinity. After his retirement from the University of Heidelberg in 1969, Gadamer became a guest lecturer for many fall semesters at McMaster University in the early 1970s, and he would teach for many years after that at Boston College. From McMaster and Boston he would often visit the nearby universities of Montreal, Ottawa, and Laval, where he was happy to practise the French he had learned in school (he spoke it quite well). Thus, hermeneutics (Ricoeur first, later Gadamer) and with it the phenomenology of Husserl and Heidegger were introduced in French Canada by guest lecturers who were arguably some of its best representatives. The pupils they attracted and moulded would pursue their heritage. This hermeneutical and phenomenological thinking was able to take root in French Canada for a number of reasons: (1) its generous universal outlook, which took up the traditional issues of ontology and ethics, reaffirmed – in a modern way – the universality claim of more traditional philosophy, and professed to address its basic questions; (2) unlike the *tabula rasa* promoted by some of the more militant representatives of Analytic philosophy, it had an open and dialogical relation with the history of philosophy and especially ancient thought, which had been represented here through Thomism; (3) this hermeneutic, Continental tradition could also probably flourish here because of other conditions, such as the multilingual fabric of Quebec and Canadian society and the sense of debt toward Europe, which in many ways distinguishes the mindset of Canadians from that of many Americans, whose country is predicated on a revolution promising a new beginning. French Canadian students and scholars were all bilingual, many had learned Latin and Greek, and the strong French and English heritage made them aware of their indebtedness to history. In view of its proximity, most had a close familiarity with the United States, but many understood themselves as part of the European traditions – especially those of France, England and Belgium – with which they had historical contacts.[22]

Hermeneutics and phenomenology were by no means the only traditions to be introduced in the 1960s. Many students studied in France and Europe at that time, where they came into contact with the philosophical currents in vogue there, later to bring them back to a French Canadian society eager to overcome its self-imposed isolation. Marked as it was by the rise of structuralism, critical theory, and deconstruction, this was also an iconoclastic decade for philosophy in Europe. That iconoclastic thinking found fertile ground in French Canada.

The Break and Opening of the 1960s: An Ideological Rupture and New Institutions

Philosophically, the 1960s were characterized in French Canada by an ideological rupture and the founding of new institutions. The ideological fracture was that of the "révolution tranquille." One of its features was "emancipation" from the narrow-minded form of Catholicism that had held sway over French Canadian society until the early 1960s. The first philosophical casualty of this modernizing revolution was Thomism, which had long dominated the philosophical scene and had now suddenly become passé, if not the worst enemy of philosophy. The notion (in my view an often misunderstood one)[23] that philosophy was for Thomism nothing but an *ancilla theologiae* (a handmaiden of theology) amounted to its death knell. This modernization went hand in hand with the creation of new institutions of higher learning within just a few pivotal years at the end of the 1960s. In 1968, the Quebec government created the Université du Québec, a network of secular universities devoted to higher learning, in cities such as Montreal (Université du Québec à Montréal = UQAM) and Trois-Rivières (= UQTR), and later in Chicoutimi, Rimouski, Rouyn-Noranda, and Hull. (The secularization of UdM, the Université Laval, and the Université d'Ottawa occurred at about the same time.) In 1967, the Quebec government also created the colleges known here as CEGEPs (= Collège d'enseignement général et professionnel). Unique to Quebec, CEGEPs are a mandatory step between high school and university; they offer a curriculum of two to three years, corresponding roughly to the last year of high school and the first two years of college in the United States. As its name indicates, CEGEPs offer a path for those who want to pursue higher studies at the university and for those who want a more specialized and vocational education. They are crucial for philosophy and its presence in Quebec society because philosophy, owing perhaps to its traditional role in the older classical formation (provided by the "collèges classiques," which were abolished in 1967), was and remains an obligatory discipline in this formation (besides French). This is a unique (albeit often challenged) distinction for philosophy in French Canada and one that provides teaching opportunities for philosophy graduates.

At the end of the 1960s, many institutions of higher learning, all of the CEGEPs, the Université du Québec network, and the expanding older universities of Laval, UdM, and Ottawa were thus in need of philosophy professors. This need was filled in part by foreigners, especially from Europe; in part by young scholars who had just completed their studies in Canada or abroad or were in the process of doing so; and in part by the older philosophy professors already in place. Many of these latter were priests, but many of them rapidly defrocked, converting with often evangelical fervour to the new iconoclastic currents. The Thomist tradition, which in the words of Raymond Klibansky had long been "omnipresent and omnipotent,"[24] was suddenly viewed as oppressive and no longer defensible.[25] Its antimodern reputation certainly did not help in a society yearning for modernity in all its forms. Whether it was as anti-modern and as repressive as was then generally insisted is perhaps debatable.[26] Whatever the case, God-centred Thomism became a convenient philosophical scapegoat, the "dark ages" from which the new philosophical gods should free us.

It is predictable what kind of philosophy prospered in this new environment. Marx, Freud, and Nietzsche became all of a sudden prominent references, and one could now speak of the dominance of a certain Freudo-Marxism, especially in the new CEGEPs and the Université du Québec network.[27] Critical theorists such as Herbert Marcuse, who were influenced by Freud and Marx, were then very trendy, as were Althusser and Deleuze. Structuralism also attracted many, even the Thomist Louis-Marie Régis,[28] as did the post-structuralism that followed. Jacques Derrida would visit Montreal at the invitation of Claude Lévesque (1927–2012), who published in 1982 a book about and with Derrida.[29] Lévesque was an influential and emblematic figure during these transitional times:[30] an ordained priest, holder of an MA in Medieval Studies, a degree in theology, and a PhD in philosophy from UdM, he taught at the UdM from 1960 to 2002, and while there, he experienced and embodied the transition from an ecclesiastical Faculté de philosophie to a proudly secular Départment de philosophie. Like many in the 1960s, he left the priesthood and introduced many generations of students to the thinking of Freud, Blanchot, Bataille, Nietzsche, Lacan, and Derrida. He celebrated in all of them a liberation from "metaphysics" and especially its supposed repression of sexuality. Others would herald another form of liberation in the rigorous scientific approach promised by Analytical philosophy. After the dominant period of Marxism, which in many quarters went hand in hand with a Québécois nationalism, Analytical philosophy would become prominent at the Université du Québec in the 1980s,[31] and it would strengthen its presence at UdM and other institutions of higher learning.

We are of course primarily concerned here with the fate of Continental philosophy, which only started to become known under this (in my personal view not necessarily felicitous) name in the 1980s and later. As we have seen, many guest lecturers, most prominently Gadamer, Ricoeur, and Derrida, had made it familiar before that time. Newly hired teachers and scholars who came from or who had studied in Europe[32] as well as home-grown talent made it known at the leading universities, those of Montreal, Ottawa, and Laval. One can think here of an important figure such as Theodore Gearets, a professor of Dutch origin who taught at the University of Ottawa, where he introduced the thinking of Merleau-Ponty and Hegel.[33] In 1977, he organized in Ottawa a memorable conference on rationality to which he invited major thinkers such as Gadamer, Ricoeur, Habermas, Apel, and Henry, but also more analytically inclined philosophers such as Hempel, Vuillemin, and Granger.[34] The Université Laval remained under the influence of Thomism a bit longer than UdM and Ottawa, probably because it had mainly hired Thomist philosophers it had itself bred. I remember being hired at Laval in 1982 to teach Kant, Hegel, Heidegger, hermeneutics, and critical theory, currents that were viewed with suspicion by a few Thomist colleagues, most of whom, following an older Thomist tradition, published little. Things have changed dramatically in the last thirty-five years: Laval has opened itself spectacularly to new currents in Continental philosophy, just like the other French-speaking universities of Montreal and Ottawa. On the whole, the Université du Québec, after its love affair with Marxism, which still lingers here and there, widely favours Analytic philosophy.

It would be impossible, and unjust, in the space allotted here, to give an idea of the span of Continental philosophy that is nowadays taught at French Canadian universities. A glance at the websites of their philosophy departments would do a better job in this regard and can only be recommended. Let it suffice to indicate that there is a lively Canadian Society for Continental Philosophy (CSCP) – the Canadian equivalent of SPEP – that stages annual conferences and publishes a beautiful journal called *Symposium*. It grew out of the Canadian Society for Hermeneutics that was created by Gary B. Madison (1940–2016) with a few francophone colleagues in 1985.[35] Gary Madison, who taught at McMaster University in Hamilton, was a widely known figure in Continental philosophy who also published in French and had close relations with Gadamer and Ricoeur. The CSCP can thus be seen as a consequence of their influential presence in Canada.

But the main reason not to discuss the *present* state of Continental philosophy *as such* is that for the most part, this Continental philosophy has severed most ties to Catholicism and to the Catholic tradition that opened its arms to Continental philosophy in the 1960s. One can thus ask the question:

What Is Left of Catholicism in Continental Philosophy?

No one wishes a return to a Catholic form of philosophy that would be taught on the basis of textbooks bereft of the historical sense that so distinguishes Continental philosophy. The *révolution tranquille* of philosophy in French Canada that started in the 1960s was as inevitable as it was desirable. This *aggiornamento* led to a new flourishing of philosophy in French Canada, which is most eloquently documented for instance in the collection edited by Klibansky and Boulad-Ayoub titled *La pensée philosophique d'expression française au Canada. Le rayonnement du Québec* (Presses de l'Université Laval, 1998). At the beginning of this impetus, at the end of the 1960s, when many professors had to be recruited, the situation was far from ideal on a scholarly level: at the time, Thomism provided a convenient bugbear, but the philosophy that aimed to replace it was itself often very ideological. In this regard, it did not help that some of the professors who were hired at this time of upheaval were not always, as one can say in retrospect, what one could call first-rate scholars. The tradition of publication and scholarship at French-speaking universities took some time to take hold. A few generations later, things have changed remarkably. The philosophy and the Continental philosophy that is now taught at French Canadian universities is by and large up to the highest international standards, and the multilingual environment of French Canada, where French and English are spoken as a matter of course, makes it in my (biased!) eyes a stimulating place to study and pursue philosophical research (furthermore, tuition at Quebec universities is much more affordable than in the United States, at least for Canadians).

What has disappeared, however, in this *aggiornamento* is the link between philosophy, Continental or otherwise, and Christianity. I am probably one of the very few who would also deplore a certain loss in this. The hostility of Continental philosophers to Christianity is perhaps not as visceral as it used to be, but it is still present. If this situation is, in my (again biased!) eyes, somewhat unfortunate, it is because Christianity and its rich traditions have a few things to teach philosophers, namely that philosophy must also offer some guidance and direction in one's quest for the meaning of life. Moreover, since late antiquity most philosophers have developed their thinking out of their Christian or theological heritage, without which it is difficult to understand them adequately. Is it possible to study authors such as Kant, Hegel, Kierkegaard, and even Nietzsche, to say nothing of Heidegger, Derrida, Levinas, Marion, and Henry, without taking into account their religious origins and motives? A way of practising Continental philosophy that is oblivious of these Christian origins could be said to be short-sighted. What is also lacking in the current philosophical environment, if the reader can indulge in my ranting for a while longer, is the strong presence of disciplines traditionally associated with a Christian outlook, such as the philosophy of religion and metaphysics.[36] In this regard, Klibansky was right to observe in his overview of 1998 the near total eclipse of religion from the philosophical domain.[37] Is this only a gain for philosophy? I am not sure.

If I am not totally off the mark, a new breach has been opened in this anti- or "a-religiosity" of philosophy in the later work of Charles Taylor on *The Secular Age* (2007) and on issues such as a Catholic modernity.[38] They tend to suggest that it is possible and intellectually defensible to combine philosophy with a modern Catholic perspective. Of course, these works were written in English, and by an author of the "older" generation, for a worldwide audience, and thus they go beyond the scope of the present chapter, which has limited itself to Continental philosophy in French Canada. But Taylor is a thinker who has a lot of influence in French Canada and whose thinking has certainly been shaped by its Quebec environment.[39] At present, he is known in French Canada mostly for his valuable contributions to social theory and politics, but here's hoping that his philosophy of religion may also have a future in our philosophical community.

Will a Christian outlook survive in Continental philosophy? Will Continental philosophy itself survive? Will Catholicism? Only the future will tell. My only certainty is that philosophy itself will never die because *Homo sapiens* is a questioning being who will never cease to ask questions about the point of it all. As for Catholicism, it has often been banged up in its long, tortuous, yet continuous history. Against all odds and over the course of many crises, it has rebounded and transformed itself, perhaps because it views things in the long haul – indeed, it is one of the only institutions in our world to do so (it is also the oldest, by the way).[40] I harbour no illusions about its relevance for present-day Continental philosophers, but I can only wish that it will continue to be heard in philosophy and by philosophers, Continental or otherwise, because the current state of disrepute in which it stands is perhaps detrimental to philosophy itself. As far as the situation in French Canada and Quebec is concerned, one would hope that philosophers will learn to show toward Christianity the openness that Christian and Thomistic philosophers displayed toward non-Catholic philosophy when they opened themselves to the world in the 1960s.

NOTES

1 There are small, still confessional schools such as the bilingual Dominican University College in Ottawa, with a program in philosophy and theology. It publishes the excellent journal *Science et esprit* devoted to philosophy and theology.
2 According to Jean-Claude Simard, the divide between Continental and Analytic philosophy only became current at the beginning of the 1980s in French Canada, as a consequence of the globalization and thus Americanization of our cultural universe. See "La philosophie française des XIXe et XXe siècles," In *La pensée philosophique d'expression française au Canada. Le rayonnement du Québec*, ed. R. Klibansky and J. Boulab-Ayoub (Québec City, Presses de l'Université Laval, 1998), 55.
3 For a glance at the history of the Université Laval, visit https://www2.ulaval.ca/notre-universite/a-propos-de-lul/lorigine-et-lhistoire.html.
4 The motto of the Université Laval is "Deo favente haud pluribus impar" (With God's help, to no one equal). "Haud pluribus impar" was the motto of King Louis XIV.
5 On the history of philosophy in Canada from the francophone perspective, see G. Leroux and John T. Stevenson, "La philosophie au Canada," *Encyclopédie philosophique universelle*, vol. 4: *Le discours philosophique*, ed. J.-F. Mattéi (Paris: PUF, 2000); Jean Langlois, "La philosophie au Canada français," in *Sciences ecclésiastiques* 10, no. 1 (janvier 1958), 95–104; Vianney Décarie, "La recherche en philosophie au Canada français," in *La recherche au Canada français*, ed. Jean-Louis Baudoin, 243–8 (Montréal: Presses de l'Université de Montréal, 1968); Leslie Armour, "Religion et philosophie au Québec et au Canada anglais," *Philosophiques* 9 (1982), 307–16; G. Leroux, "La philosophie au Québec depuis 1968. Esquisse d'une trajectoire," in *Panorama de la littérature québécoise contemporaine*, series ed. Réginald Hamel (Montréal: Guérin, 1997); and Klibansky and Boulad-Ayoub, eds., *La pensée philosophique d'expression française au Canada. Le rayonnement du Québec* (Québec: Presses de l'Université Laval, collection Zètèsis, 1998). For a general bibliography on our subject, see: Bibliothèque et Archives nationales du Québec (BanQ), *L'aventure de la pensée philosophiqu e au Québec*, www.banq.qc.ca/collections/collections_patrimoniales/bibliographies/philosophie/apres1950_histoire.html.
6 See the moving testimony of Yvon Lafrance, whose interest in Greek philosophy led him to the priesthood: *La passion du savoir. L'itinéraire d'un intellectuel à l'ombre d'une Église triomphante. Autobiographie* (2009), https://uottawa.academia.edu/YvonLafrance.
7 See the studies of the historian Yvan Lamonde: *La philosophie et son enseignement; Historiographie de la philosophie au Québec (1665–1920)*

(Montréal: Hurtubise HMH, 1980); and "L'histoire de la philosophie au Canada français (de 1920 à nos jours): sources et thèmes de recherche," *Philosophiques* 6 (1979), 327–33. Out of this Thomist mould grew the work of the Jesuit philosopher Bernard Lonergan (1904–1984), who was born in Quebec, but who worked entirely in English. His major work, *Insight: A Study of Human Understanding* (1957), is a hermeneutic treatise of the first order and has been studied carefully by Continental philosophers such as Fred Lawrence ("Gadamer and Lonergan: A Dialectical Comparison," *International Philosophical Quarterly* 20 [1980], 25–47).

8 On the influence of those "thomistes réformistes," see Jean-Claude Simard, "La philosophie française des XIXe et XXe siècles," in *La pensée philosophique d'expression française au Canada. Le rayonnement du Québec*, ed. Raymond Klibansky et Josiane Boulad-Ayoub, 57ff. (Québec: Presses de l'Université Laval, collection Zètèsis, 1998). On the modernizing influence of Maritain's presence, see Y. Lamonde, "L'histoire de la philosophie au Canada français (de 1920 à nos jours): sources et thèmes de recherche," 334. On Gilson and Mounier, see ibid., 335.

9 Simard, "La philosophie française des XIXe et XXe siècles," 57.

10 Gilson defended Thomas against Descartes and Kant, whereas Maritain had himself published a book under the title *Antimoderne* (Paris: Édition de la Revue des jeunes, 1921). In 1925 he published an anti-modern pamphlet, *Trois réformateurs: Luther, Descartes, Rousseau* (Paris: Plon, 1925; *Three Reformers: Luther-Descartes-Rousseau* [New York: Charles Scribner's Sons: 1929]). The common thread of this antimodernism is that modern authors give too much importance to man and too little to God.

11 On Taylor's outstanding stature as a philosopher and a political persona in Canada, see G. Leroux and John T. Stevenson. "La philosophie au Canada," in *Encyclopédie philosophique universelle*, vol. 4: *Le discours philosophique*, ed. J.-F. Mattéi (Paris: PUF, 2000).

12 A *faculté de philosophie* was founded at the Université de Montréal in 1921 (see Y. Lamonde and E. A. Trott, "La philosophie avant 1950," *Encyclopédie Canadienne* (2012), www.encyclopediecanadienne.ca/fr/article/philosophie-avant-1950-la. See Lamonde and B. Lacroix, "Les débuts de la philosophie universitaire à Montréal. Les Mémoires du doyen Ceslas Forest, O.P. (1885–1970)," *Philosophiques* 3 (1976), 55–79.

13 See Lamonde et Lacroix, "Les débuts de la philosophie universitaire à Montréal," 59.

14 On Le Saulchoir, see M.-D. Chenu, *Le Saulchoir, une école de théologie* [1937]. (Paris: Cerf, 1985).

15 By L.-M. Régis: *St Thomas and Epistemology* (Milwaukee: Marquette University Press, 1946); *L'Odyssée de la métaphysique* (Montréal: Institut d'études médiévales; Paris: Vrin, 1949). A complete list of his publications

can be found in the Festschrift devoted to him in 1980: *Scolastique, certitude et recherche. En hommage à Louis-Marie Régis*, sous la direction d'Ernest Joós (Montréal: Bellarmin, 1980). One finds in it contributions by Étienne Gilson, Marie-Dominique Chenu, Dominique Dubarle, Louis-Bertrand Geiger, and Joseph Owens.

16 See Lamonde et Lacroix, "Les débuts de la philosophie universitaire à Montréal, " 73.

17 See S. Foisy, "L'œuvre de Ricœur en transit. Sur quelques contributions à l'étude de l'influence de Ricœur au Québec et au Canada," in *Fabula/Les colloques, L'héritage littéraire de Paul Ricœur*, www.fabula.org/colloques/document1878.php.

18 Ibid. On Ricoeur's presence in Montreal, see Yvan Lamonde, "L'espace et le temps: Paul Ricœur à Montréal," in *Fabula/Les colloques, L'héritage littéraire de Paul Ricœur*, www.fabula.org/colloques/document1914.php; and Jacques Poulain, "Communication et écriture: un différend phénoménologique entre Paul Ricœur et Jacques Derrida à Montréal en septembre 1971," in *Fabula/Les colloques, L'héritage littéraire de Paul Ricœur*, www.fabula.org/colloques/document1891.php.

19 V. Décarie, *L'objet de la métaphysique chez Aristote* (Paris: Vrin, 1961). See the obituary by P. Fine, "Trudeau-era philosopher helped liberate Quebec education from Church dogma," in *The Globe and Mail*, 29 September 2009; and G. Leroux, "Vianney Décarie (1917–2009) – Hommage à un grand humaniste," in *Le Devoir*, 28 September 2009.

20 Ricoeur dedicated the first study of *La métaphore vive* (Paris: Seuil, 1975) to him. On the context of Ricoeur's invitation to Montreal, see my "Une certaine manière herméneutique de faire de la philosophie. Petite reconnaissance de dette envers Paul Ricœur," in *Fabula/Les colloques, L'héritage littéraire de Paul Ricœur*, www.fabula.org/colloques/document1916.php.

21 See again my "Une certaine manière herméneutique de faire de la philosophie" and *À l'écoute du sens. Entretiens avec Marc-Antoine Vallée* (Montréal: Bellarmin, 2011), 16.

22 On the French influence see again Simard, "La philosophie française des XIXe et XXe siècles." On the links to the German tradition and their mediators, see my "Les débuts de la philosophie allemande," in *La pensée philosophique d'expression française au Canada. Le rayonnement du Québec*, ed. R. Klibansky and J. Boulab-Ayoub, 207–29.

23 I have always felt that the passage, at the beginning of the *Summa theologiae* (1a, q. 1, art. 5), where Thomas speaks of philosophy as a possible *ancilla* (servant) of theology (by way of a quote from *Proverbs* 9:3) has been widely misread. Thomas never says that philosophy has to serve (Christian) theology (which would be nonsensical for pre-Christian philosophers like the Greeks or for non-Christian ones like the Muslims or the Jews). Rather,

in a book dedicated to the Christian sacred doctrine (*sacra doctrina*), or theology, as the title of the *Summa* indicates, he asks whether this sacred doctrine can incorporate or make use of the philosophical disciplines (*dicendum quod haec scientia [sc. sacra scientia] accipere potest aliquid a philosophicis disciplinis, non quasi ex necessario eis indigeat, sed ad maiorem manifestationem eorum quae in hac scientia traduntur*) developed by human reason, independently of the Christian revelation, and which had been put forward by the Greeks and renewed by authors such as Maimonides, Averroes, and Avicenna on which Thomas draws so extensively. In this context, he munificently acknowledges that theology can indeed learn from the philosophical disciplines and thus use them as servants for its purpose, that is, to explain theological truths (*ad maiorem manifestationem eorum quae in hac scientia traduntur*; S.T., Ia, Q.1, art. 5). To speak of their ancillary nature *for* theology is thus not to call into question their autonomy, quite on the contrary. Classical texts are too little read!

24 Klibansky, "Introduction," in *La pensée philosophique d'expression française au Canada*, 11.

25 There were a few exceptions, such as my predecessor at the UdM, Bertrand Rioux (1929–2016), who had studied with Jean Wahl and Paul Ricœur in Paris at the end of the 1950s. A gifted teacher, he offered courses at the UdM on Thomas, Heidegger, and ontology from 1960 to 1991. He published a conciliatory book on *L'être et la vérité chez Heidegger et Thomas d'Aquin* (Presses de l'Université de Montréal; Paris: PUF, 1963), with a preface by Paul Ricœur.

26 Both Klibansky, "Introduction," 12, and Simard, "La philosophie française des XIXe et XXe siècles," 57, recognize that the Thomism of the 1940s and 1950s had indeed become more flexible.

27 On the strong Marxist orientation of philosophy at the time see Boulad-Ayoub, "Vingt ans de marxisme au Québec," and Simard, both in *La pensée philosophique d'expression française au Canada*; and Maurice Lagueux, *Le marxisme des années soixante. Une saison dans l'histoire de la pensée critique* (Montréal: Hurtubise HMH, 1982).

28 See Simard, " La philosophie française des XIXe et XXe siècles," 80.

29 See C. Lévesque, ed., *L'oreille de l'autre. Otobiographies, tranferts, traductions. Textes et débats avec Jacques Derrida* (Montréal: VLB éditeur. 1982). It was translated by C. McDonald, ed., as *The Ear of the Other: Texts and Discussions with Jacques Derrida* (Lincoln: University of Nebraska Press, 1988).

30 See the tribute by G. Leroux, "Claude Lévesque, 1927–2012. En mémoire d'un philosophe libre," *Le Devoir*, 3 avril 2012.

31 On its rise in French Canada, see M. Marion, "L'émergence de la philosophie analytique," in Klibansky and Boulad-Ayoub, eds., La *pensée philosophique*, 425–44.

32 On the introduction of German philosophy at French-speaking universities, see again my "Les débuts de la philosophie allemande."
33 See T. Geraets, *Vers une nouvelle philosophie transcendantale. La genèse de la philosophie de Maurice Merleau-Ponty jusqu'à la Phénoménologie de la perception* (The Hague: Nijhoff, 1971); Geraets, ed., *Hegel, l'esprit absolu* (Ottawa: Éditions de l'Université d'Ottawa, 1984).
34 See the outstanding volume edited by T. Geraets, *Rationality today / La rationalité aujourd'hui* (Ottawa: Éditions de l'Université d'Ottawa, 1979).
35 See the tributes to Gary B. Madison's work in *Symposium* 19, no. 2 (2015), a year before his passing. See also the tributes to Gadamer published by Madison and others in *Symposium* 6 (2004), 5–10.
36 Hence my ingenuous defence of both in *Introduction to Metaphysics: From Parmenides to Levinas* (New York: Columbia University Press, 2012); and in *La philosophie de la religion* 3rd ed. (Paris: PUF, 2009, 2015).
37 Klibansky, "Introduction," in *La pensée philosophique d'expression française au Canada*, 18.
38 I am thinking here of the essay "A Catholic Modernity?" and other texts related to *A Secular Age* (Cambridge: Belknap, 2007), in Charles Taylor, *Dilemmas and Connections: Selected Essays* (Cambridge: Belknap, 2011), 167–379.
39 Another exception in this regard, one who also belongs to the older generation, is the Catholic philosopher Thomas De Koninck at Laval. See for instance his most recent essays *La foi est-elle irrationnelle ?* (with Louis Roy, Montréal: Fides, 2013) and *À quoi sert la philosophie ?* (Québec: Presses de l'Université Laval, 2015). The recent work of Taylor and De Koninck seems to suggest that the themes of philosophy of religion are perhaps re-emerging in French Canada.
40 On the intellectual resiliency of Christianity, see P. Capelle-Dumont, *Dieu bien entendu* (Paris: Cerf, 2016), pp. 34, 161. (Indeed, the entire book is a reminder of the philosophical vitality of Christianity.)

6 Phenomenology and Catholic Thought: Unfolding the *logos* of the Logos

CHRISTINA M. GSCHWANDTNER

In memory of Helen Tartar and her labor of love to introduce French phenomenology into English.

Phenomenology[1] – at least in its more explicitly religious iterations – and Catholic thinking have an unusually close association. While most hermeneutic thinkers stand in the Protestant tradition,[2] phenomenologists with an interest in religion tend to be Roman Catholic. This is true of Jean-Luc Marion, probably at this point the best-known living Catholic philosopher; of Jean-Yves Lacoste, a Catholic priest, who is deeply informed by Martin Heidegger's philosophy and comments on it extensively; of Jean-Louis Chrétien, who wrote widely on various phenomenological topics and whose work is permeated with Catholic religious themes, terminology, and thinkers; of Michel Henry, who converted to Catholicism late in life but was influenced by Meister Eckhart early on; and of Emmanuel Falque, former dean of the faculty of philosophy at the Institut catholique de Paris, whose increasingly extensive work marries phenomenology with Catholic theology in a unique fashion. Richard Kearney, an Irish philosopher who wrote his PhD thesis in Paris under the direction of Paul Ricoeur and Emmanuel Lévinas, is similarly deeply influenced by the Catholic tradition in his phenomenological and hermeneutic work.[3] Indeed, several of these thinkers are associated with the Institut catholique de Paris, which, since the years when Stanislas Breton taught and worked there, has become a centre of Catholic thinking in France with many articulate phenomenologists – including Father Breton himself. Furthermore, the adoption of phenomenological approaches in the United States has occurred primarily at Roman Catholic institutions, often at Jesuit schools but also at Duquesne University, Villanova University, DePaul

University, and various smaller Catholic colleges. Why this affinity between Catholicism and phenomenology?[4]

Phenomenology and Catholicism: Background

Before getting to the more theoretical substance of the discussion, let me begin by providing some brief historical and cultural context.[5] As just indicated, most contemporary phenomenology – at least what has been appropriated by thought interested in religion – is French.[6] Yet in several respects the situation in France is quite different from the one in the Americas. One might thus ask why French phenomenology seems to attract so much attention today in the United States and Canada – and indeed in some Latin American countries, such as Brazil and Argentina – and how it is transformed as it enters the New World (usually in translation, which poses its own challenges). First, some words about the French context specifically before turning to the Americas.

French Philosophical Education

Philosophy has developed in a unique manner in France that is perhaps without parallel in any other academic system.[7] The most promising young scholars in philosophy, politics, the sciences, and other subjects are trained in special schools – the Grands Écoles – where they undergo intense and highly labour-intensive formation, leading up to major examinations. Acceptance to these schools is by examination, for which students often prepare through two years of intensive study, called the *khagne* and the *hypokhagne*, in special high schools. In philosophy, schools such as Condorcet – where Jean Beaufret taught for decades and where several of the thinkers mentioned above imbibed his brand of Heideggerianism[8] – prepare students for the École normale supérieure (ENS) on the rue d'Ulm. Almost all French philosophers have gone through the ENS. Until very recently it granted no degrees; it has always, however, provided rigorous training involving the close reading of philosophical texts and the development of an immense breadth of perspective.[9] Two years of training at the ENS prepare students for a crucial exam called the *agrégation*, which is passed by less than 10 per cent of those who attempt it in a given year. To pass that exam one must have acquired in-depth knowledge of the entire oeuvre of the several philosophers (usually four thinkers and two subject topics) who have been assigned in that particular year. The result of all this is that often the scholar's future work is deeply shaped by whatever philosopher(s) he or she had to study in so much depth for the *agrégation.*[10] Passing the *agrégation* – that is, becoming an *agrégé* – used to guarantee a job teaching philosophy (with the prestige of the *lycée* to which one was assigned corresponding to one's rank on the list of those who had passed the *agrégation*), and to this day, passing it guarantees higher pay, reduced course loads, and enormous prestige. It is almost unthinkable for someone who has not gone through this system to find a permanent teaching post in the university system, especially at the Sorbonne, the most prestigious French university as well as one of the oldest in Europe, besides being the most important university for philosophy (indeed, it was the only French university to grant degrees in philosophy before the university system was reformed in the wake of the student revolutions of May '68).[11]

This system has had several consequences. First, it means that French philosophers are trained in the close reading of texts and at the same time acquire a tremendous breadth of knowledge of the history of philosophy. Second, it enables much closer and more direct conversation because everyone has received essentially the same training under the same teachers in the same place.[12] Most students, teachers, and writers of philosophy know one other; besides, everyone who is anyone is in Paris (rather than the "provinces").[13] It also means that French philosophical texts often assume that readers will grasp any and all oblique references, which therefore require no explanation – something that can be extremely baffling for American readers on a variety of levels. Conversations are essentially conducted on the same playing field; even when there are strong disagreements, the participants share a common space of discourse. All of this injects a kind of overall coherence to French philosophical discussion, because all interlocutors are more or less familiar with the broad outlines of one another's texts and arguments and generally share roughly the same method of proceeding. This also implies that in order truly to distinguish oneself from one's mentor (or one's colleagues), one often practises a form of parricide; most French philosophers eventually criticize their teachers much more strongly than is the case in the United States, where the situation is more diverse and more scattered.

American Appropriation

How did French philosophical thought come to be introduced to the United States and Canada? The ground was obviously prepared by the appropriation of earlier phenomenology (especially that of Husserl and Heidegger), on which other chapters in this volume focus. One of the first French thinkers to teach extensively in the United States was Paul

Ricoeur, who taught in Chicago occasionally beginning in 1954 and regularly after 1967. He assumed Paul Tillich's chair at the University of Chicago in 1971, teaching there until his retirement in the 1990s. Jean-Luc Marion was first invited to Chicago through his contacts with Daniel Garber in the context of their work on Descartes at the Center of Cartesian Studies that Marion had founded in Paris. Thomas Carlson's early translation of Marion's *God without Being* (1991) also played an important role. For about a decade it was the only one of his works translated into English, and thus gave a rather distorted picture of his work. A youthful work – Marion was in his early thirties when he wrote it – and a heavily polemical one (it had been written for a particular debate in France concerning the "death of God"), it introduced Marion into English primarily as a theological rather philosophical thinker, and as a result, his rigorous studies of Descartes were ignored completely and even his more systematic phenomenological work found only slow acceptance.[14] It also significantly coloured his reception – that is to say, rejection – by some Catholic philosophers in the United States and Canada, because of its polemical engagement with Aquinas, which again was due to its situatedness in a French Catholicism that in the first part of the twentieth century had been shaped heavily by Étienne Gilson and Jacques Maritain. The entire rest of Marion's work is often ignored because of two paragraphs of rather facile critique of Aquinas in *God without Being*, although the real "target" of the book is Heidegger and, in particular, a specific group of Heideggerians in France (i.e., the circle around Beaufret). This outsized focus on *God without Being* in the United States is however also representative in some sense: interestingly, the explicitly religious work of these thinkers has generated a much larger echo in the United States than in France, and their religious work more than their more "secular" writings.

Another important element of the introduction of French thinkers to the United States is played by conferences hosted at Roman Catholic institutions, in particular, the series of "Religion and Postmodernism" conferences that John D. Caputo organized at Villanova University between 1997 and 2003; these were continued on a somewhat smaller scale by his colleague Michael Scanlon after Caputo moved to Syracuse University. It was Marion's discussion with Derrida at the 1997 conference on "God, the Gift, and Postmodernism" that most galvanized interest in his thought in this country. Caputo's teaching and that of others, such as Kevin Hart and Merold Westphal, increasingly exposed the next generation of students interested in religion from a philosophical perspective to French thought on this matter.[15] Hart, Westphal, Caputo, and Kearney have probably done more than anyone to introduce phenomenology, especially of the religious variety, into the American conversation. It is also not incidental that many translations of French writings have been published by Fordham University Press, although this should be credited at least as much to Helen Tartar's incomparable and indefatigable work as editor as to their Catholic "fit" at a Jesuit institution.

Laïcité and American "Possibilities"

In all these respects, the different situation in America opens possibilities. The conversation between philosophy and theology is highly restricted in the French context and indeed is not possible on the broader university scene. The French commitment to *laïcité*[16] since the French Revolution – it has been enshrined in the constitution since 1905[17] – means that theology cannot be taught in any form at French universities, which are almost all public institutions.[18] In France, theology departments – even departments of "religious studies," although that term is not generally employed – are always housed in private institutions, such as the Protestant faculty of theology in Paris and the Institut catholique, which was founded in response to the closing of the theology faculty at the Sorbonne in the 1880s. Indeed, an exception had to be made to allow Stanislas Breton to teach at the École normale because priests are explicitly barred from giving instruction at secular public institutions regardless of how highly their scholarship might be regarded by others. "Serious" academic work, especially in philosophy, by definition must be secular, and the more explicit theological work by such thinkers as Marion, Lacoste, Chrétien, and Falque would not "count" academically in France for appointments and other such matters.[19] Marion received his position at the Sorbonne based solely on his work on Descartes and his phenomenology; his theological work was irrelevant if not an actual obstacle.[20] The same is true of other thinkers.[21]

The American context opens possibilities for cross-disciplinary conversation that are simply impossible in France or that can only happen privately there. These thinkers' works can generally be read in the United States within philosophy classes or even in religious studies departments at entirely secular institutions without fear of academic repercussions.[22] And conversations across disciplines are possible and (sometimes) even encouraged, even if it is at times still difficult to find appropriate places to publish such interdisciplinary work or to have it taken seriously in tenure reviews.

Indeed, the situation of Catholicism in the "New World" is quite different from that in France, and this also has an impact on the shape that the reception of phenomenology has taken. On the one hand, whereas Catholicism's impact on French public discourse – be it political or academic – is quite restricted, the same is not the case in North America, or it is not the case in the same way. Although at least in the United States no explicit religious material can be taught in a secular school, the secular system does not have the same impact as in France because of the large network of private schools at every academic level from preschool to graduate school. On the other hand, while in France Catholicism is the predominant cultural tradition – one with centuries of cultural, architectural, and religious history – in the United States and Canada it is often the tradition of minorities from various backgrounds (Irish, Italian, Polish, French, Latin American, etc.). The immigrant situation has coloured the experience and expression of Catholicism in the New World in particular ways.[23] Furthermore, today every Catholic thinker must take into account the immense diversity of religious confessions and traditions in the Western Hemisphere. There is perhaps no other place on earth that has the same diversity of religious expressions and traditions, and in this respect Roman Catholicism is only one among many religious traditions and experiences itself as such. While religious pluralism presents its own set of difficulties, it also offers an opportunity for a broadening and deepening of perspective that otherwise might not be possible. When one must take the other into account, one's own account may well look quite different from how it would if that obligation were less pressing.[24] Thus, in America, a conversation with other Christians and, more broadly, other religious traditions imposes itself naturally and in ways that do not happen in France.[25]

In this respect, the French approach to "Catholic" phenomenology can seem somewhat insular. For example, Falque has developed what he calls a "phenomenology of marriage" in a very traditional Catholic vein without any acknowledgment of homosexuality and without taking into account any feminist thought. His analysis of the Eucharist explicitly follows the Roman rite of the Mass without any sense that eucharistic experience across Christian traditions is far more diverse. Richard Kearney, who broadly and consistently engages other Christian traditions, is one of the few thinkers to acknowledge the existence of Eastern Orthodoxy, and in marked contrast to French thinkers, he often engages other religious traditions, especially Judaism and Islam but increasingly also Eastern religions. The fact that Kearney is European and received his undergraduate degree in Dublin and his doctoral degree in Paris[26] shows the impact that years of teaching in the United States have made on his perspective, which combines French textual training with the broader and far more diverse American context. His

Anatheism, I would venture to say, is a very "American" book in that regard, not only in its consideration of other religious traditions and its openness to conversation with them, but also in its style of engagement. The same can be said of all of Caputo's work, which is certainly not narrowly "Catholic."[27] It constitutes a style of scholarship quite unlike what is published in Europe more generally, and especially unlike scholarly writing of the sort practised in France.[28]

This brings me to one final and perhaps minor point that is all the same worth noting, regarding the readability of the English-language work in this field. Some French thinkers have published more "popular" texts; that said, the particular style and specific rigour of French academia often restricts its exposure to a small group of elites – those who catch the references and are familiar with the conversation.[29] The work of Caputo, Westphal, and Kearney in particular (although others could be mentioned) is in comparison eminently more readable, and almost all of it much more "popular" and accessible. That means it can be read – and *is* read – by non-philosophers and even by non-academics. Conversation about phenomenology in America, at least in the United States, is not purely academic; it also takes places on any number of blogs and in other more popular venues.[30] It is also worth pointing out that many of the French phenomenological texts read by an American audience have been filtered through the teaching and writing of Hart, Westphal, Caputo, Kearney, and others.

Phenomenology and Catholicism: Practice

This section will focus more closely on the relationship between phenomenology and Catholicism, discussing three related aspects of the question. First, it will provide some theoretical context through a brief introduction to the sort of phenomenology adopted or proposed by French Catholic thinkers, which is not always explicitly "Catholic." Second, it will push further the connection to Catholicism by looking more closely at what these thinkers themselves say about the relationship of their work to theology specifically and to the Catholic tradition more broadly. Based on these brief analyses of phenomenological work by Catholic thinkers, several preliminary conclusions can be drawn about some of the possible dangers, challenges, and potential opportunities in the appropriation of phenomenology for Catholic philosophy or for a mutually enriching relationship, whether in Europe or the Americas.

One important caveat must be made up front, however. Most of these thinkers would *not* think of themselves as "Catholic philosophers" but simply as phenomenologists or philosophers *tout court*. Marion, for example, repeatedly contends that the expression "Catholic philosophy" is meaningless and makes no more sense than "Protestant mathematics." He adamantly refuses the title of "Catholic philosopher":

> There are Catholics who do philosophy just as there are butchers who are Catholic. The real question is whether they are good butchers, good metal workers, good firefighters or good philosophers. I assume that, if one has allowed me to have had a not entirely disgraceful career, it is not because I did Catholic philosophy, but because the philosophy wasn't too bad, and from that I get great satisfaction. And it so happens that moreover I try to be Catholic. I say that I try, because I make an effort, I apply myself to it; I hope to improve, but slowly.[31]

Similarly, Jean-Yves Lacoste always insists that his investigation is into the human being before God in the most general terms; it is *not* any particular confessional investigation.[32] In his first explicitly "religious" book, Richard Kearney heavily qualifies his Catholic allegiance:

> Religiously, I would say that if I hail from a Catholic tradition, it is with this proviso: where Catholicism offends love and justice, I prefer to call myself a Judeo-Christian theist; and where this tradition so offends, I prefer to call myself religious in the sense of seeking God in a way that neither excludes other religions nor purports to possess the final truth. And where the religious so offends, I would call myself a seeker of love and justice *tout court*.[33]

While Emmanuel Falque is slightly more open to the possibility of a distinctly "Catholic" contribution to phenomenology, the default presupposition for engaging the work of these thinkers should be that they "do phenomenology" and also happen to be Catholic. One should seek to understand and if possible articulate the relationship between these two traditions from that presupposition, rather than assuming *prima facie* that they are practising "Catholic philosophy" simply by virtue of the fact that their personal religious affiliation is to that tradition.

Catholic Thinkers and Phenomenology

What, then, is the content of this phenomenology proposed as relevant to religious but not necessarily specifically Roman Catholic questions and concerns? Jean-Luc Marion is probably the most well-known of these thinkers. Much of his phenomenological work[34] can be said to be directed toward providing phenomenological accounts, and hence strictly philosophical justification, for religious experience. Marion argues for a phenomenology of givenness, in which phenomena are understood via the way in which they give themselves or are given to us.[35] Experience hence is not first grounded in the subject that governs everything else as an object that is in its full control; rather, experience is characterized by the impact phenomena have on me, by the ways in which they come to the experiencing self, who is thus in a secondary position of receptivity, not of control. Marion especially depicts what he calls "saturated phenomena" – phenomena that are particularly intense and overwhelming and cannot be constructed, constituted, or even fully conceptualized by the one who experiences them.[36] Such phenomena are various: his examples include historical or cultural events, works of art, the immediacy of my flesh in experiences of pain, suffering, or pleasure, and the encounter with the other, especially the beloved other. The most saturated, most intense, most overwhelming experiences are phenomena of revelation: the experience of Christ, of prayer, of gift and sacrifice, and especially that of the Eucharist. Marion thus provides a way of describing and accounting for religious experience with phenomenological language and also explicates the kind of phenomenology that would allow us to do so.

Yet Marion is quite insistent that this is not only or even primarily about justifying religious phenomena. His phenomenology explores saturated phenomena in general, rich phenomena that are given to us in a mode other than that of objects. His philosophical project develops a phenomenological methodology that would allow heretofore unexamined phenomena to emerge and be subject to phenomenological analysis. While this includes "religious" phenomena or what he calls "phenomena of revelation" – that is, an experience of the divine – it is certainly not limited to them. Marion also stresses that he is uncovering basic structures of human experience, precisely our experiences of culture, art, history, and love, as well as a possible experience of the divine. It is the *type* of experience his phenomenology depicts, not the particular (epistemic) experiences of a concrete tradition or even of specific individuals. This is why he and others consistently reject the accusation that they are imposing a "theological turn" onto French thought. Marion sees himself as examining human experience in the broadest and most mundane (or "banal") possible sense – listening to an opera, enjoying a glass of wine, inhaling the fragrance of a perfume – not justifying the historical accuracy or even present occurrence of any particular religious event.[37]

He is joined by Jean-Yves Lacoste, who employs Heidegger in order to provide a phenomenological account of what he calls "liturgical being," human being-before-God, drawing on such religious experiences as the all-night vigil, the holy fool, the *peregrino pro deo*, and various other ascetic practices.[38] In a collection titled *La phénoménalité de Dieu*, he reflects on ways in which phenomenology can articulate an experience of the divine. The Eucharist and other "theological" topics also make an appearance in his most recent work critical of Heidegger, *Être en danger*, and even more fully in a collection of essays, *L'Intuition sacramentelle*, several of which are on the Eucharist.[39] Yet like Marion, Lacoste is quite clear that despite his choice of examples, he is depicting a human experience in the broadest possible terms. What does it mean to be oriented "coram deo," to face something or someone beyond ourselves, to go beyond just being-in-the-world? What might be the structures of such an experience? How can it be depicted in Heideggerian terms? While his description of these structures draws on language of kenosis and abnegation, he posits it consistently as an "additional" or "optional" experience rather than as one we must all necessarily undergo. Lacoste does not see himself as developing or advocating a "confessional" phenomenology, much less a theology, whether Catholic or not.[40]

Jean-Louis Chrétien similarly often meditates on religious experiences in a phenomenological tenor. One might say that while Marion is more interested in methodological questions – for example, in providing justifications or guidelines for how to employ phenomenology so that it has room for a description of religious experience – Chrétien simply exercises such description. He rarely explicitly addresses phenomenology as a topic; rather, he uses its tools to provide beautiful descriptions of the role of the voice and silence in prayer, the role of the body and the flesh in religious experience, how to read the Bible today, the religious dimensions of art and creativity, and so forth.[41] Chrétien draws extensively on the Christian tradition, its texts, figures, and experiences, but these are always intimately wedded to other cultural sources. For example, in a text on the topic of response and responsibility, he begins with some preliminary phenomenological reflections and then devotes a chapter each to examining the topic of response and responsibility in music, literature/tragedy, philosophy, and theology or the biblical tradition.[42] This sort of thematic approach is characteristic of Chrétien's work throughout – he alternates between literary, poetic, philosophical, and religious sources rather indiscriminately, weaving them all together into one highly varied tapestry.

Michel Henry absolutely refuses to think of any of his work as theological, but always presents it as strict phenomenology. Although after his conversion – at the age of seventy-two, as a result of reading the Gospel of John – he increasingly portrayed his phenomenology as best encapsulated by the "truth of Christianity" as explicated by the Gospels and began to speak of immediate and immanent life as God, conveyed to us as "sons of God" by the Arch-Son, Christ, he insisted on this as a purely phenomenological account of life. He contended that Christianity simply grasps its truth more fully than any other approach, but the account he gives of this truth of life as it is sensed in the experience of our self-affected flesh is basically identical to the account he gives of how it is manifested in the abstract art of Kandinsky or in other modes of aesthetic experience. Whether the invisible, material, immediate, immanent life of auto-affection is articulated via Kandinsky's paintings or through the words of Christ is ultimately irrelevant for his phenomenological analysis.[43]

Finally, Emmanuel Falque explicitly employs the Paschal Triduum and Christ's experience of human finitude, death, and resurrection in order to articulate phenomenological accounts of human suffering, death, life, resurrection, flesh, and corporeality, culminating in an analysis of the Eucharist and Christian marriage.[44] Yet the insistence on beginning with the human as such (*l'homme tout court*) is perhaps even stronger in Falque's work than in that of the others, whom he often criticizes for operating with too many religious presuppositions. Each of the three texts of his trilogy starts out with what he deems a purely philosophical section, reflecting on the phenomenology of finitude and death, birth and life, flesh and carnality, respectively, before moving on to more explicitly theological reflections. Falque argues that even to know God or to make sense of the sorts of theological insights we might gain from our tradition, we must begin with the human, must know our experience in its most intimate humanity, and of this a phenomenological account can and must be given: "To my eyes, the philosopher is not simply the one who uses philosophical tools, including phenomenological ones, but someone who respects and begins with the human per se – that is, from the horizon of the existence of the human pure and simple."[45]

Why do all these thinkers choose phenomenology? Is it inspired by their Catholicism? Despite the fact that they draw on religious themes or sources and make a contribution to the investigation of religious experience, their choice of methodology probably has more to do with their particular context: phenomenology is one of the most vigorous and vibrant philosophical methodologies available on the French philosophical scene, which has been heavily phenomenological for almost a century. And indeed most of that phenomenology – in Jean-Paul Sartre, Emmanuel Lévinas, Maurice Merleau-Ponty, and others – is not at all religious and certainly not Roman Catholic. The German sources, on which this tradition draws, those of Edmund Husserl and Martin Heidegger, similarly are not religious in any explicit sense.[46] Simultaneously, it is worth remembering that explicitly "Catholic" philosophy in France (but not only in France) is predominantly Thomist, associated with such thinkers as Étienne Gilson and Jacques Maritain. There is a long and strong tradition of explicating the thought of Aquinas in a philosophical manner as providing a distinctly "Catholic philosophy." It is really only this younger generation of Catholic thinkers who have turned to phenomenology and who use it in at least some recognizably "religious" ways (even when they insist on their own phenomenological "purity").[47] In what ways, then, is their work "Catholic" or "theological"?

Phenomenology as Catholic Philosophy?

As we have just seen, most of the phenomenologists who are committed to their Catholic faith see themselves as doing phenomenology proper rather than providing some sort of apologia for Catholicism. But do they make *any* contribution that might be recognizably Catholic or serve Catholic faith in more explicit fashion? Indeed, they all do at certain points make hesitant overtures in that direction. Let me provide a couple of examples.

Jean-Louis Chrétien engages in rich descriptions of religious practices in such a way that their meaning and character emerge much more fully and consciously. His poetic examinations of prayer, of responsibility, of beauty, of call and response, of speech, of vulnerability, and of any number of other experiences allow dimensions of meaning to emerge to which we might otherwise have been blind or deaf. While Chrétien does not seem to think of this as a specific contribution to "Catholic philosophy," his extensive use of the Catholic tradition as examples for his analyses of broader human experiences is itself telling. His descriptions and examples range from an analysis of the Song of Songs in the Christian tradition, the imagery of fire in mystical and patristic literature, meditations on breath and air in a wide variety of poetic and religious texts, the gaze of love as explicated by Augustine, Bernard of Clairvaux, Hopkins, von Balthasar, Angela of Foligno (and many others, including Protestant thinkers such as Luther and Kierkegaard), the joy of the heart in Augustine, Gregory the Great, Saint Teresa, and various poets, a meditation on interior space that draws on Augustine, Teresa of Avila, Origen, and Dante, to a detailed analysis of the various speech acts in Augustine's work (asking, hearing, translating, reading, ruminating, witnessing, confessing, chanting, etc.).[48] Here the Catholic tradition inspires and informs the phenomenological analysis in important fashion – indeed, provides the content for it – while the phenomenological methodology highlights aspects of the texts and experiences that might not have emerged otherwise. In the *Ark of Speech*, for example, a reflection on Adam and Noah enables Chrétien to develop a phenomenological notion of the voice that sees it as sheltering or as providing an ark and prepares his later analysis of the call and response pattern of speech in important ways. At the same time his phenomenological analysis of the fragility of the voice enables him to provide a richer account of the human role in listening to and sheltering the praise of creation in a more theological sense.

Jean-Yves Lacoste insists throughout his philosophical work that religious experience is "optional" and that we are always at first in the world "without God." Conversely, he claims that truly theological thinking should do without recourse to Heidegger (on whom his philosophy draws extensively).[49] Yet although he attempts to provide a purely phenomenological account of human being before the "Absolute" per se, his analysis is actually deeply informed by his Catholic tradition, and all the categories on which he draws in order to challenge or displace the Heideggerian ones are deeply Christian, if not explicitly Roman Catholic. World and earth are suspended by the *parousia*, a notion of labour is displaced by monastic non-labour, the encounter with the Absolute is that of a non-experience in the night deeply informed by the mysticism of John of the Cross, the vision of St Benedict challenges Heideggerian notions of care, and so forth. Throughout his analysis he draws on various aspects of the ascetic and sacramental Christian tradition in order to articulate our being-before-God and contends that these examples provide unique insight into the human condition.[50]

Marion repeatedly speaks of the potential of phenomenology for Catholic theology and philosophy. Occasionally he grows rather frustrated with what he sees as an exclusive obsession with hermeneutics on the part of theologians, contrasting it with a potentially more fruitful engagement with phenomenology.[51] And he has written many much more clearly theological pieces. He was a founding member of the francophone edition of *Communio* and co-edited it for years, and both he and his wife have frequently contributed to it – and indeed were closely associated with the luminaries of the French *ressourcement* movement, such as Jean Daniélou, Henri de Lubac, Louis Bouyer, as well as Hans Urs von Balthasar and Cardinal Jean-Marie Lustiger (whose former chair in the Académie française Marion now occupies). In his theological work Marion frequently draws on phenomenological terminology and descriptions in order to argue for correct understandings of the sacraments, of divine love, and of Catholic mission and identity.[52] His contributions to *Communio* include reflections on the role of the Catholic intellectual, on the relation between clergy and laity (where he argues for a rigorous recovery of the language of the baptized rather than that of the lay person), on miracles, on the Eucharist, and on various biblical passages. His recent Gifford Lectures work out a Trinitarian theology that draws on his phenomenology of givenness in order to unfold how God is revealed and manifested.[53] Marion's work as a whole *can also* be read as a contribution to theology, although this is certainly not the only, the primary, or necessarily the best way to read it.[54]

While I cannot review all of these texts here, let me highlight a couple of examples. In one context, Marion was explicitly asked to contribute to a conference on "Christian Philosophy."[55] He begins by rejecting or at least heavily qualifying that title, but then goes on to propose that the "Catholic philosopher" or "Christian philosopher" might contribute to philosophy by playing the role of phenomenological midwife: having access to religious phenomena through his or her faith, the Christian philosopher can formulate them rigorously with phenomenological tools and then "abandon" them in kenotic fashion to broader phenomenological investigation. Like the artist, the Christian philosopher has access to the realm of the "unseen," formulates and transfers the vision into phenomenality, and thus actually "produces" new phenomena, thereby increasing the phenomenality of the world. The philosopher hence draws on his or her experience of faith or the tradition in a way a non-Christian philosopher would not be able to do because of lack of experience, and in doing so contributes to a larger (and strictly philosophical) phenomenological investigation. A similar suggestion is implied in his occasional claim that one might have to "believe" in order to be able to "see": belief (or theology) provides phenomena that are actually experienced, whereas philosophy (or phenomenology) provides the tools for examining them. This is also why he repeatedly phrases the difference between philosophy and theology in terms of "possibility" and "actuality" (*effectivité*) respectively.[56] The philosopher investigates the forms, structures, and characteristics that an experience of revelation might take, but philosophy makes no claim whatsoever about whether such revelation actually *has* taken place – that is something left to theology.

Another important point is Marion's repeated methodological claim about givenness and love as alternate forms of rationality that allow us to investigate phenomena, which other tools miss altogether, misunderstand, or destroy by turning them into objects and examining them with inappropriate preconceptions and resources. Although Marion himself does not explicitly posit this as a "Christian" or Catholic contribution, but indeed insists on its wider applicability, especially in regard to love, it is undeniable that he is not only explicitly drawing on Pascal's notion of the third order of charity – one of the most common references in Marion's work overall, to which he always takes recourse when speaking of the relation between philosophy and theology or revelation and certainty – but that he thinks of this alternative rationality as particularly applicable to the excessive phenomena of revelation. The "logos" of the incarnation requires rationality of Christians today, and Marion expresses this kind of revelatory reason in terms of phenomenology: "The love revealed by the Word, hence by the Logos, is deployed as a logos, hence as a rationality. And a rationality in full right, because it allows us to reach the closest and most internal phenomena, those experienced by the flesh saturated by intuition … in Christ, love manifests itself as the final and first truth."[57] And he sees this as the particular task of the Catholic Christian, who is to proclaim this rationality of love to the world.

While Marion attempts to maintain some sort of division between the two disciplines, Emmanuel Falque merges them far more fully. One might say that he proceeds in the exactly reverse fashion from Marion. He always begins (or at least claims to begin) with the shared human condition and then informs it through confrontation with religious resources. Yet the relationship actually goes in both directions for him: he is quite emphatic in claiming that doing theology makes one a better philosopher and that doing phenomenology makes one a better theologian. For example, to read medieval texts phenomenologically opens us to dimensions of their work that were hitherto unrecognized, while providing philosophical insight that can challenge contemporary phenomenological assumptions and indeed provide solutions for some of its problems.[58] In his *Crossing the Rubicon*, he argues vigorously for a renewed conversation between philosophy and theology that crosses their boundaries more frequently and more fully. In that book he tries to bring together the hermeneutic and phenomenological traditions and provides a specifically "Roman Catholic" hermeneutics, namely one that would be concerned with the sacraments (in "body and voice") rather than solely with the biblical texts (like Protestant hermeneutics).[59] He goes on to articulate a phenomenology grounded in shared belief and sacramental participation. Ultimately, we must go beyond both hermeneutics and philosophy of religion to a traversal of the "Rubicon" between philosophy and theology.[60] While phenomenology precedes and grounds theology, theology transforms and recovers phenomenology. Both are always at work together and should not be separated too sharply. This conflation of philosophy and theology, grounded for Falque in the incarnational affirmation of the "God-man," leads to a conversion of the philosophical milieu into its theological consummation: "Far from some kind of serfdom or a petty service, phenomenology and theology respond to each other in a mutual way, similar to the incessant dialogue between God and man."[61] To have "traversed the Rubicon" is to have united phenomenology and (Catholic) theology permanently. Falque understands this as an "overlaying of philosophy by theology" and as a "liberation of theology by philosophy"; philosophy and theology hence work a mutual and reciprocal transformation on each other.[62]

Phenomenology and Catholicism – in America

Instead of "evaluating" to what extent the phenomenology of certain thinkers affiliated with Roman Catholicism might constitute "Catholic philosophy," let me turn in conclusion to a more deliberate reflection on how phenomenology and Catholicism might productively interact and how the uniquely American situation might contribute to such fruitful conversation. This question can obviously be posed in various directions: How might Catholic religious convictions or sources helpfully inform phenomenological practice? And conversely, how can phenomenology usefully be employed for Catholic faith and thought? I will highlight one example that might aid in giving a response to each question, while also pointing to some dangers and challenges in such a more explicit link, in each case concluding with some brief remarks about the particular opportunities in North America.

First, we might draw on examples from the tradition in order to push further a phenomenological analysis of human experience. Religious faith and practice is an almost universal element of human culture and society, not only in the past but also in the present political reality in our world – and obviously not solely in benign ways. If phenomenology really intends to grapple with the lived and experienced human condition in the widest sense, it has a responsibility also to confront and analyse human *religious* experience. Drawing on the extensive descriptions of such experience in the Catholic tradition and its documentary evidence may well prove eminently helpful here. Before providing a positive example, however, let me point to some dangers or at least articulate some qualifiers. In this particular use of religious experience for phenomenological purposes, the evidence would not be treated in either confessional or normative fashion, but rather be employed descriptively. If one is trying to understand what motivates people to engage in religious practices, what sort of lived experience they have in this engagement, and what these experiences mean for them, one must begin with careful description of all those aspects, rather than employing them normatively for *pre*scription of how religious experience "ought" to work.[63] That is to say, a phenomenological analysis of religious practices can provide insight into the meanings of such practices by examining, describing, and analysing them carefully, but it does not tell us what to do or even whether such practices are the "correct" ones to pursue. Here Marion's distinction between phenomenological possibility and theological actuality may well prove helpful: phenomenology has no business making historical judgments, investigating whether an event such as the resurrection actually occurred, whether the Bible is directly inspired by God, or even what the nature of God *is*.[64] Rather, it can describe and analyse religious practices and beliefs as they are actually experienced by people and examine their varied patterns of expression. Phenomenology can certainly help us gain insight into the *meaning* of these practices, inasmuch as it carefully examines the various iterations and forms they take, but that does not imply that it can judge whether these are the *best* practices and beliefs one should maintain or pursue.

I would also suggest that a *philosophical* investigation into religion is always an investigation into the *human* expressions of religion rather than into the nature of the divine. It is certainly possible that phenomenology can analyse how *people* experience God (or what they identify as God), but it does not seem particularly useful for speaking of *God's* experience or nature, something to which we do not have access apart from doctrinal claims. Phenomenology is eminently suitable for description and analysis of *human* faith and the meaning of human religious practices. But it is not best employed in order to make grand claims about the nature or experience of the divine. That is not to say, of course, that such experience could not be analysed closely for how believers claim to worship the divine and how they report experiencing what they identify as "God."

With these two caveats or dangers in mind, the Catholic tradition seems particularly well suited to provide "data" for a phenomenological analysis of human religious experience, because of its extensive textual tradition, its rich intellectual heritage, and the variety of its practices within a shared ecclesial affiliation. One often receives the impression from the contemporary analyses that religious experience for the phenomenologists is always of the excessive and entirely singular mode: Marion speaks of it as a saturated phenomenon that comes completely out of nowhere and blinds or bedazzles its recipient in a way that seems practically incommunicable. Lacoste constantly stresses the extraordinary and liminal nature of human experience before God, and excessive figures and experiences are his primary examples, such as the holy fool, the all-night vigil, or intense ascetic practices. Yet if the goal is to discover the structures and meaning of religious experience more broadly, presumably we should look not for utterly unique, extraordinary, and unprecedented events, but instead for repeatable experiences or ones that exhibit shared patterns.

The Catholic tradition is rich in such descriptions. For example, there are many and extensive depictions of spiritual or mystical experience in the high and late middle ages, often across a wide variety of traditions: Beguine, anchorite, and various monastic communities from all over Europe. Although these surely are "excessive" or "extraordinary" experiences in certain ways, there are sufficiently varied reports and descriptions that common patterns and shared structures can emerge in phenomenological analysis. The description of the spiritual life by the Beguine Dutch mystic Hadewijch of Antwerp, by the Benedictine German nuns Gertrude of Helfta and Mechthild of Magdeburg, by the English anchorite Julian of Norwich, by the Italian Dominican Catherine of Siena, or by the Spanish Carmelite reformer Teresa of Avila, have enough in common to detect general patterns of the spiritual life, while also being sufficiently diverse to discern and distinguish between essentials and incidentals. A thorough phenomenological analysis of these texts and the experiences they both report and recommend, including the suggestions they provide about how to test, discern, and evaluate the authenticity of religious experiences, provides a wealth of "evidence" for how the spiritual life was experienced and expected to be experienced (i.e., both intuitive data and clear intentionality are at work). In many cases we know enough about their particular contexts and communities to interpret their experiences in light of their horizons in responsible fashion. Religious experience, and especially mystical experience, is by definition elusive and difficult to analyse. What does it mean to have an experience of the "wholly other," and how might one verify that it is indeed an experience of the divine and not one of demonic possession, mental illness, or illusion? The breadth and depth of descriptions of mystical experience in the Catholic tradition across several centuries and various geographic locations makes it uniquely suited to provide at least very extensive data for reliable analysis, even if no normative claims about its source can be made philosophically. This, then, is one particularly rich way in which resources from the Catholic tradition could make a genuine contribution to the phenomenological study of lived human experience.[65]

The diversity of the American context can make a unique contribution here in several respects. On the one hand, even its experience of Catholicism is far from monolithic, often appropriating practices and styles from other religious traditions in quasi-syncretistic fashion and also drawing on a much wider range of traditions from various immigrant groups, whether European or South and Central American. Thus even the study of concrete contemporary Catholic religious practices provides a wide and diverse pool of "data" for phenomenological analysis. On the other hand, the diverse American situation makes a broader account of *human* religious experience, beyond narrow confessional lines, much more pressing. Similarities and differences among various religious approaches to the divine and different types of spirituality can be explored phenomenologically, enabling us to understand the fundamental human need for and inclination to religion more fully, but also showing us ways in which specific traditions express and manifest this aspect of human experience in their own particular ways. Such a more "pluralist" approach to the study of religious experience, especially with the rich resources already available on the American scene in terms of sociological and other studies, can both broaden our understanding of religion and justify it more fully philosophically as a valid dimension of human experience.

Conversely, how might phenomenology as a philosophical methodology be useful for or uniquely suited to Catholicism? Phenomenology has much potential for Catholic thinking. Unlike hermeneutics, which is more closely focused on interpretation of texts and hence has a natural affinity with Protestant insistence on the importance of the text, phenomenology allows for a description of religious *experience*: prayer, Eucharist, other sacraments, liturgy, mystical vision, bodily and sensory spirituality. All of these are important in Roman Catholicism and probably matter more there than in most forms of Protestantism. Catholicism hence shares with Eastern Orthodoxy (and with other religious traditions) an affinity for the sorts of aspects of human existence that phenomenology is particularly well suited to examine, namely lived experience. Phenomenology allows an engagement with Catholicism as a living tradition, expressed in the concrete liturgical and sacramental practices Catholic believers actually experience and pursue. It hence conveys a sense of authenticity and immediacy, which an examination of proofs for God's existence, for example, does not.

This aspect of Catholicism has often been neglected by philosophy, which in the past has tended to focus on more abstract arguments about the rationality of faith or the coherence of statements about the divine. Philosophy was far more occupied with discussing the sorts of things that might be said about God without contradiction or that might possibly even be open to proof or confirmation. How can we deduce insight about the divine from the realities of the world or the workings of the human mind? How might God's attributes be articulated intelligently in such a way that they are not in contradiction with one another – such as the reality of evil seems to imply? While such investigations are not entirely futile or uninteresting, they are often far removed from what is central to religious believers, namely the ways in which faith is actually practised and expressed. Religion is made meaningful in people's lives through prayer, participation in religious services, and belonging to religious communities. Phenomenology provides philosophical tools for describing and analysing these experiences and for articulating why and how they are meaningful. Phenomenology can provide much better justification for the reality of religion in the world precisely *because* it examines how this religious reality is manifested.[66] Instead of speculating about the unknown (be it the nature of God, the possibility of an afterlife, or compatibility and coherence of certain theological doctrines), it deals with the "given" of religious experience, what is there before us, the "thing in itself" as it is lived and experienced.

In this respect important work has already been done, by almost all of the thinkers mentioned, on the specific religious practice of the Eucharist. Marion, Lacoste, Chrétien, and Falque have all written about the Eucharist quite extensively.[67] Yet, again, many of these analyses tend to emphasize the personal and extraordinary nature of this phenomenon. For Marion it is an abundant gift that abandons itself entirely and that comes wholly without precedent. It is perhaps best encapsulated in individual contemplation of the blessed sacrament, which is an extremely important practice for Marion on personal and theological levels. For Lacoste it is always an indication of the radical nature of the *parousia*, "boring" *here* because we are precisely not yet *there*. For Falque, although a much more communal and even corporate exercise, Eucharist is still primarily about incorporation into Christ with fairly exorbitant – and not at all "testable" – claims about what that might mean. A more careful phenomenological description, one that focuses on how this important liturgical practice is actually experienced by most people who engage it – that is to say, closer attention to the life-world of the liturgy – would go a long way to providing a more sustained and genuinely phenomenological analysis of religious experience.

Again, the American situation might provide much more diverse data for such an analysis. Most phenomenological analyses of the Eucharist and even Marion's critique of Catholic "lay" movements refer to experiences shaped heavily by European or even specifically French situations and controversies. What might it look like to describe eucharistic experience as it is celebrated in South American or African communities? Would the ways in which these descriptions will differ from the European description taken as the standard provide insight into how Hispanic communities, for example, experience their Roman Catholic faith differently than Europeans? Might it even help explain when and why faith begins to fade and practices begin to whither? Or – to give one concrete example – why some Hispanic Catholics are increasingly turning to Protestant and more charismatic religious expressions? Phenomenology can provide deeper insight into specific religious experiences and penetrate further in explicating their meaning by helping us analyse and understand the diversity of practices within a tradition and the ways in which particular practices have been appropriated in radically different ways by different Catholic communities. This is not really suggested by any of the contemporary thinkers – except perhaps by implication in Richard Kearney's work – yet phenomenology might have the potential to provide an account of different cultural expressions of Catholic religious experiences and to explain some of the ways in which it "means" differently to or for different people (and perhaps also why it ceases to have meaning for many). I doubt that traditional philosophy of religion would have anything intelligent to say about these phenomena, but phenomenology may well provide useful tools for analysing such changes.

Conclusion

To do this successfully, however, I would wager – despite the earlier description of hermeneutics as more suited to Protestantism – that phenomenology always has to be hermeneutical. An analysis and description of religious practices always has a hermeneutic dimension, and any adequate interpretation must cycle back and forth between the interpreter and the practices as experienced by the believing community. At the same time, the interpretation must be closely connected to the experiences and practices themselves and their phenomenological explication. Phenomenology and hermeneutics check and balance each other. The interpretation or description is confronted with the reality as it is experienced, while the experience is prepared and interpreted by the hermeneutic exercise. Hermeneutics precedes or enables and follows upon or interprets experience, thus giving rise to further experience that can challenge and correct the interpretation. In this way phenomenology can provide genuine insight into what concerns religious believers most intimately and can become a useful tool for the philosopher who seeks to investigate and understand religious expression.

And it is precisely this recognition of a much closer connection between hermeneutics and phenomenology that is most characteristic of the appropriation of French phenomenology in a North American context. In the most prominent thinkers working on this thought in the United States – John D. Caputo, Merold Westphal, and Richard Kearney – hermeneutics and phenomenology are closely connected. Westphal has not only written an introduction to hermeneutics, but hermeneutic considerations pervade his phenomenological work, which is deeply influenced by Ricoeur and especially Gadamer.[68] John Caputo brings together hermeneutics, phenomenology, and deconstruction in what he calls a "radical hermeneutics" that would abandon any "romantic" pretensions to easy meaning and instead remain more fully in the liminal space of suspension of belief and certainty.[69] Considering Westphal is Protestant and Caputo identifies as "post-Christian," let me end with a few words about Richard Kearney's work instead.

Kearney has sought to work out a hermeneutic phenomenology or phenomenological hermeneutics from his earliest works, and this concern still profoundly motivates his work. This is particularly evident in his recent collection *Carnal Hermeneutics*, in which he comments on the unfortunate tension that has at times existed between hermeneutics and phenomenology and calls for a "return journey" that "might help us recover the body as text and the text as body: to restore hermeneutics to phenomenology and vice versa, making explicit what was implicit all along."[70] Indeed, several of the other essays in that volume explicitly draw on Kearney's explication of "diacritical hermeneutics" in order to work out their own hermeneutic–phenomenological approaches.[71] In that particular piece he explicates his methodology as an attempt to bring together a phenomenology of bodily "diacritical perception" inspired by Merleau-Ponty with the critical resources provided by hermeneutics for discerning between competing interpretations. Kearney has been particularly attentive not only to the human body and the senses, but also to the experiences of strangers and immigrants,[72] often drawing on film and other popular media to access human experience in its widest sense in ways that few other philosophers do. Diacritical hermeneutics ultimately involves "a caring for lived existence – a listening to the pulse of suffering and solicitation between one human being and another."[73] And these concerns, as important as they are in the broader culture on the social and political levels, are for him not disconnected from religion. Rather, he draws on the resources of various religious traditions for treating strangers with hospitality,[74] for sharing a cup of cold water with "the least of these,"[75] and for a sacramentality of the everyday.[76] Kearney brings together a deep grounding in Roman Catholic spirituality and sacramental practice at its best with a real commitment to address global issues of injustice and marginalization, hence engaging issues of deep concern for the human experience in a non-technical language open to a wide range of readers. He does so in a way that fosters genuine dialogue not only between various traditions and disciplinary perspectives, but also between people, bringing together friends, strangers, and enemies in open conversation. This unique phenomenological blend of hermeneutic, existential, religious, and ethical approaches, while informed and shaped by the French phenomenological sources, may well represent what is also most promising, most fruitful, and most distinctive in the dialogue between phenomenology and Catholicism in North America. We would do well to continue pursuing this kind of work.

NOTES

1 Phenomenology is obviously not a monolithic term and is practised differently by various thinkers. There is no complete agreement over what phenomenology means and how it should be exercised. Marion especially has been accused repeatedly of being "unfaithful" to a particular iteration of (Husserlian) phenomenology. I cannot engage in these controversies here and so employ phenomenology relatively loosely to speak of the sort of work contemporary French phenomenologists such as Marion, Henry, Lacoste, Chrétien, and Falque are doing.

2 Hans-Georg Gadamer and Paul Ricoeur are the most obvious examples of this. Jean Greisch comments on this affinity between Protestantism and hermeneutics, arguing that Ricoeur is not significantly influenced by Gadamer yet chooses to pursue hermeneutics and to focus on an interpretation of texts because of his Reformed background. Jean Greisch, *Le cogito herméneutique. L'herméneutique philosophique et l'héritage cartésien* (Paris: Vrin, 2000), 28, 54–73.

3 See several of the conversations in Richard Kearney and Jens Zimmermann, eds., *Reimaging the Sacred: Richard Kearney Debates God* (New York: Columbia University Press, 2016), where Kearney repeatedly speaks of the profound influence his Catholic upbringing had on him.

4 One could add a number of other thinkers to this list, both in the Americas and in Europe. It is perhaps also worth noting that John Paul II was trained as a phenomenologist and taught phenomenology in Poland for years.

5 I would like to note here that I am neither French nor American and intend no value judgment on either academic system in this description. I am merely trying to outline some of their differences to provide a context for the particular appropriation of French philosophy in the United States (and to a lesser extent in Canada, about which I know far less than the US situation – please see Jean Grondin's chapter in this volume, which considers the Canadian situation specifically). Even for the US situation my perspective is surely coloured by the situations in which I was trained or have taught – that is, almost all Catholic and predominantly Jesuit – though I am not Roman Catholic by affiliation or confession. There also my perspective is that of an "outsider" and hence implies a particular external perspective.

6 There are of course notable exceptions, but these serve to prove the rule. Some such exceptions are addressed by Jack Caputo in his contribution to this volume (chapter 3), where he notes a number of thinkers, including Protestant and Jewish thinkers, who are influenced more by Husserl than by Heidegger or post-Heideggerian French phenomenology.

7 For a much more detailed explication of this system and its impact on philosophical discussion in France, see Alan D. Schrift, *Twentieth-Century French Philosophy: Key Themes and Thinkers* (Oxford: Wiley-Blackwell, 2005). Schrift also argues (using the example of French work on Nietzsche) that the topics of the *agrégation* significantly influence the direction of French philosophy more broadly. Marion indirectly confirms this in *The Rigor of Things* when he admits that his focus on Nietzsche in *Idol and Distance* was a result of Nietzsche being assigned on the *agrégation* that year. Jean-Luc Marion, *The Rigor of Things: Conversations with Dan Arbib* (New York: Fordham University Press, 2017), 107. Conversation with several of the thinkers discussed here has confirmed to me the importance of this system, of the exam, and of its impact.

8 For the tremendous importance of Beaufret's teaching on the appropriation of Heidegger's thought in France, see Dominique Janicaud's *Heidegger in France* (Bloomington: Indiana University Press, 2015). Note that Beaufret was essentially a high school teacher all of his life yet significantly shaped the direction of French intellectual thought for a generation or more. See also Marion's comments on the impact of Beaufret's teaching in *Rigor*, 7–8.

9 It is worth noting that Jacques Derrida taught at the ENS for years, which means both that he influenced many students' view of the history of philosophy, but also that he never actually supervised doctoral work, as the *Écoles* function outside the "regular" university system.

10 The *agrégation* examinations began in the mid-seventeenth century in order to prepare a corps of teachers. They exist not only in philosophy, but also in several other subject areas, although some famous historians

and writers took the philosophy exam, which is one of the most prestigious ones. There is both an "internal" and an "external" version of the exam, the internal version for those students who pursue the traditional path from *lycée* to ENS to the exam, and the external version for others who try to take the exam later in their career. For the list of topics in recent years, visit the website www.philopsis.fr/spip.php?article1.

11 Lévinas is an important exception: coming from Lithuania, he did not go through the ENS or take the *agrégation*.

12 There is also an ease of conversation enabled by the fact that everyone pretty much lives in the same place or at least works there. One can easily meet for an afternoon colloquium of a couple of hours or a cup of coffee. Paris is a manageable city; it can be traversed on foot in an hour or so. Even the basic geographical situation in America is totally different. For academics to talk in person, often flights of several hours are required. One meets up at conferences – once a year if one is lucky and the funding sources allow for it – but the possibility for real conversation is quite different from the situation in France.

13 Michel Henry is a significant exception to this. Although repeatedly invited to posts in Paris, he remained in Montpellier all his life. In many ways the independence of his thought illustrates the same point.

14 Marion's first two works on Descartes – the second a key text for understanding the overall thrust and impetus of his work – are still not translated. While most of the other work has been translated, it is read much less, and the connection between it and the phenomenological work or the theological claims are for the most part simply disregarded.

15 Although Merold Westphal is Protestant, he taught for decades at Fordham University, a Jesuit institution. Kevin Hart taught for years at the University of Notre Dame, albeit in a department of literature. Richard Kearney holds the Charles B. Seelig Chair of Philosophy at Boston College, a Jesuit university.

16 The French government explains the term as follows on a French government website: "*Laïcité* relies on three principles: freedom of conscience and free ritual practice, separation between public institutions and religious organizations, and everyone's equality before the law regardless of belief or conviction. *Laïcité* guarantees believers and nonbelievers the same rights of freedom of expression of their convictions. It also ensures the right to change one's religion and to adhere to a religion. It guarantees the free exercise of ritual practices and the freedom of religion, but also the freedom from religion: no one can be constrained by the law to follow a certain dogma or religious prescription. *Laïcité* presupposes the separation of the state and of religious organizations. The political order is solely grounded on the sovereignty of the people as

citizens and the state, which does not recognize or finance any particular religious practice, does not interfere in the functioning of religious organizations. The neutrality of the state, of communities and public services, but not that of individual users, is based on these principles. The 'lay' nature of the Republic accordingly ensures the equality of citizens in regard to public service, regardless of their convictions or beliefs. *Laïcité* is not one opinion among others but grounds the very freedom of having opinion, subject to the respect of public order" (www.gouvernement.fr/qu-est-ce-que-la-laicite).

17 The law of 1905 officially proclaimed *laïcité* as a basic principle of the Republic. In 1924 the French government came to an agreement with the Catholic Church for the organization of Catholic life on the diocesan level that pacified some of the Catholic and Vatican resistance to the law of 1905.

18 This is different from the situation in other European countries. In Germany, for example, theology is considered a rigorous academic discipline taught at entirely secular (and publicly funded) universities. All prominent English universities (such as Oxford, Cambridge, and Durham) have important theology departments. The famous Gifford Lectures in Natural Theology are hosted by prominent Scottish universities, namely those in Edinburgh, Glasgow, St Andrews, and Aberdeen.

19 There is also a stigma attached to such work. Derrida refused to allow any translation of his discussion with Marion about God and the gift to appear in France during his lifetime. This text was only translated and published after his death in a collection of essays by Marion on other thinkers: *Figures de phénoménologie. Husserl, Heidegger, Levinas, Henry, Derrida* (Paris: Vrin, 2012), 189–214. (The "explanation" for this delay is based on conversation with Emmanuel Falque.)

20 The fact that his candidacy was twice turned down may have something to do with it, although that is pure conjecture.

21 Emmanuel Falque, who moves most smoothly from one field to the other, teaches at the Institut catholique, a private Catholic institution, as did Breton, Jean-Louis Chrétien, Jean Greisch, and many others. Jean-Luc Marion recently held the Dominique Dubarle Chair in Philosophy and Theology there.

22 The same is true to some extent also in the Canadian context, although perhaps slightly less so, as it is less heavily privatized and even more hostile to Continental philosophy than the United States.

23 According to the Pew Research Center, 20.8 per cent of the US population – roughly one fifth – identifies as Roman Catholic (www.pewforum.org/religious-landscape-study).

24 This is obviously not to discount the very real marginalization and at times explicit animosity and injustice still experienced by non-Christian religious

groups (especially Muslim). Yet although Protestant Christianity is still the predominant "face" of religion in the United States, it is a far from monolithic one. The varieties of Protestantism in America are staggering, especially in comparison with Europe, where all but the most mainstream versions of Christianity are miniscule and simply do not appear on the "radar screen" of most Europeans.

25 Despite the increasingly strong Muslim minorities, Islam never seems to be engaged intellectually by Catholic thinkers in France, with the exception of the French Catholic theologian Louis Massignon. (Derrida refers to his work in his writings on hospitality and also mentions the Islamic tradition in some of his texts on apophatic theology.) Marion has recently published a fairly polemic work arguing that Catholicism is not a threat to the French political vision and its institutions, while Islam is. *Brève apologie pour un moment catholique* (Paris: Grasset, 2017).

26 Indeed while a student there he was the co-organizer of the conference on Heidegger and the question of God, at which Marion first presented the nucleus of what became *God without Being*. Kearney also received an MA from McGill University in Montreal, Canada.

27 I suppose one could dispute that it is Catholic at all, but Caputo certainly does not hide the fact that he comes from a Roman Catholic background, had a particular experience of that tradition, and in many ways responds to it (often in a critical vein in regard to what he sees as its most serious aberrations). In that respect see especially his *What Would Jesus Deconstruct? The Good News of Postmodernism for the Church* (Grand Rapids: Baker Academic, 2007), which despite its heavy engagement of Derrida seems to me a quintessentially "American" book in flavour, including the allusion of the title to Charles Sheldon's popular *What Would Jesus Do?* (Caputo actually opens his own book with a discussion of this work and its "social gospel" message.)

28 Again, no value judgment is implied here in regard to either style of scholarship!

29 This also has something to do with the fact that French academic publishing is subsidized (and printed in much smaller numbers) and thus allows for much longer and more rigorous – but also far less readable – work to be published because it does not need to pay as much attention to economic considerations as American presses have to do. French books often go out of print and are then reprinted several months later. Some of Marion's books have already gone through four printings. One should say, however, that philosophy has a role in public discourse in France that is utterly unprecedented elsewhere. Rigorous academic work is valued (and read) by a broader intellectual public that one might imagine.

30 For a couple of examples, see: http://currentcatholics.blogspot.com; https://syndicatetheology.com; http://churchandpomo.typepad.com/conversation.
31 Marion, *The Rigor of Things: Conversations with Dan Arbib* (New York: Fordham University Press, 2017), 178.
32 See his reply to the essays discussing his thought in *Modern Theology* 31, no. 4 (2015), 676–83.
33 Richard Kearney, *The God Who May Be: A Hermeneutics of Religion* (Bloomington: Indiana University Press, 2001), 5–6.
34 As the topic of concern is phenomenology I here leave aside his work on Descartes, which constitutes about half of his published oeuvre and, as indicated above, is immensely important for understanding Marion's thought as a whole. While it is certainly not insignificant even for understanding his claims about the divine and religious phenomena, to set it out in any detail in this context would take us too far afield.
35 This is worked out the most fully in *Being Given: Toward a Phenomenology of Givenness*, trans. Jeffrey L. Kosky (Stanford: Stanford University Press, 2002); and *Negative Certainties*, trans. Stephen E. Lewis (Chicago: University of Chicago Press, 2015).
36 See especially *In Excess: Studies of Saturated Phenomena*, trans. Robyn Horner and Vincent Berraud (New York: Fordham University Press, 2002).
37 See his important essay "The Banality of Saturation" in *The Visible and the Revealed* (New York: Fordham University Press, 2008), 119–44.
38 Jean-Yves Lacoste, *Experience and the Absolute: Disputed Questions on the Humanity of Man*, trans. Mark Raftery-Skeban (New York: Fordham University Press, 2004).
39 Jean-Yves Lacoste, *La phénoménalité de Dieu. Neuf études* (Paris: Cerf, 2008); Lacoste, *Être en danger* (Paris: Cerf, 2011). Lacoste, *L'intuition sacramentelle* (Paris: Ad Solem, 2016). See also his *From Theology to Theological Thinking*, trans. W. Chris Hackett (Charlottesville: University of Virginia Press, 2014), where he provides an account of the shifting relationship between philosophy and theology from the beginnings of Christianity to the present.
40 Lacoste is editor of a major theological dictionary and has also written theological essays. He seems to try, however, to keep his phenomenological work rigidly separate from his theological investigations.
41 Translations of his works include *Under the Gaze of the Bible*, trans. John Marson Dunaway (New York: Fordham University Press, 2015); *The Ark of Speech*, trans. Andrew Brown (London and New York: Routledge, 2004); *The Call and the Response*, trans. Anne A. Davenport (New York: Fordham University Press, 2004); *Hand to Hand: Listening to the Work of Art*, trans. Stephen E. Lewis (New York: Fordham University Press, 2003);

The Unforgettable and the Unhoped For, trans. Jeffrey Bloechl (New York: Fordham University Press, 2002); *Spacious Joy*, trans. Anne A. Davenport (London: Rowman and Littlefield, 2019). Before his untimely death in the summer of 2019, he published more than twenty other works that are not yet translated (some listed in n49).

42 Jean-Louis Chrétien, *Répondre. Figures de la réponse et de la responsabilité* (Paris: PUF, 2007).

43 For a fuller exploration of these parallels, see my "The Truth of Christianity? Michel Henry's *Words of Christ*," *Journal of Scriptural Reasoning* 13 no. 1 (2014): n.p.

44 Emmanuel Falque, *The Guide to Gethesemane: Anxiety, Suffering, Death*, trans. George Hughes (New York: Fordham University Press, 2019); *The Metamorphosis of Finitude: An Essay on Birth and Resurrection*, trans. Georges Hughes (New York: Fordham University Press, 2012); *The Wedding Feast of the Lamb* (New York: Fordham University Press, 2016).

45 Emmanuel Falque, *Crossing the Rubicon: The Borderlands of Philosophy and Theology*, trans. Reuben Shank (New York: Fordham University Press, 2016), 122–3.

46 That does not deny that they can certainly be appropriated in religious fashion. There has also been some work showing the deep influence of Heidegger's reading of Luther on *Being and Time*, especially in light of its parallels to his lectures on *The Phenomenology of Religious Life*. Emmanuel Housset outlines Husserl's religious thought in his *Husserl et l'idée de Dieu* (Paris: Cerf, 2010). And phenomenological thinkers like Edith Stein, Hedwig Conrad-Martius, and Max Scheler do engage religious questions in their work, but at least Stein has had virtually no impact on French phenomenology, and Conrad-Martius and Scheler not on the thinkers discussed here.

47 One might point to Stanislas Breton as a transitional figure. His role in this conversation remains to be examined further.

48 By Jean-Louis Chrétien: *Lueur du secret* (Paris: Herne, 1985); *L'effroi du beau* (Paris: Cerf, 1987); *L'antiphonaire de la nuit* (Paris: Herne, 1989); *Traversée de l'imminence* (Paris: Herne, 1989); *La voix nue. Phénoménologie de la promesse* (Paris: Minuit, 1990); *Loin des premiers fleuves* (Paris: Différence, 1990); *Parmi les eaux violentes* (Paris: Mercure de France, 1993); *Effractions brèves* (Paris: Obsidiane, 1995); *De la Fatigue* (Paris: Minuit, 1996); *Entre flèche et cri* (Paris: Obsidiane, 1998); *Le regard de l'amour* (Paris: Brouwer, 2000); *Joies escarpées* (Paris: Obsidiane, 2001); *Marthe et Marie* (Paris: Brouwer, 2002); *Saint Augustine et les actes de parole* (Paris: PUF, 2002); *L'intelligence du feu* (Paris: Bayard, 2003); *Promesses furtives* (Paris: Minuit, 2004); *Symbolique du Corps. La traduction chrétiennes du Cantique des Cantiques* (Paris: PUF, 2005); *Répondre. Figures de la réponse et de la responsabilité* (Paris: PUF); *Pour*

reprendre et perdre haleine (Paris: Bayard, 2009); *Reconnaissance philosophiques* (Paris: Cerf, 2010); *L'espace intérieur* (Paris: Minuit, 2014); *Fragilité* (Paris: Minuit, 2019). None of these texts is translated. For Chrétien's works in English, see n42.

49 Jeffrey Bloechl rightly challenges this in his excellent introduction to Lacoste's *From Theology to Theological Thinking*, xvii–xviii.

50 This is a claim he makes repeatedly in *Experience and the Absolute*. For example, he concludes the book by saying: "we can now assert that man says who he is most precisely when he accepts an existence in the image of a God who has taken humiliation upon himself – when he accepts a *kenotic* existence" (194).

51 See for example, *In Excess*, 29.

52 See the essays collected in *The Visible and the Revealed* (New York: Fordham University Press, 2008) and *Believing in Order to See* (New York: Fordham University Press, 2017).

53 Published as *Givenness and Revelation*, trans. Stephen E. Lewis (Oxford: Blackwell, 2016).

54 I try to provide such a reading in my *Marion and Theology* (London: T&T Clark, 2016).

55 See the essay based on the conference in *The Visible and the Revealed*, 66–79. One should also note that Marion always speaks of "Christian philosophy" in this contribution, not of "Catholic philosophy," except for the initial lines where he is referring to a specific French debate on this question.

56 See the important explanatory note on this in *Being Given*, 234–5.

57 *The Visible and the Revealed*, 152.

58 See especially *God, the Flesh, and the Other: From Irenaeus to Duns Scotus*, trans. William Christian Hackett (Evanston: Northwestern University Press, 2015), xxi–xxii, 3–19, 279–83.

59 This is the main argument of chapter 2 (*Crossing the Rubicon*, 55–73).

60 Part III of the book.

61 *God, the Flesh, and the Other*, 282. He works this out more fully in *Crossing the Rubicon* and insists again: "In short, ever since God became man and showed himself as a man even in his Resurrection, we have access to Him via humanity and thus also through philosophy, albeit then to be transformed or 'metamorphed' into God within the crucible of theology." *Crossing the Rubicon*, 129.

62 *Crossing the Rubicon*, 128–36. He insists that this continues to "respect the boundaries" between them. Ibid., 138.

63 That is not to say that there may never be a normative element to phenomenology. Anthony Steinbock explores some of these possibilities in his work. But for this particular connection, that of understanding how religious experience functions (informed by how it has functioned in the

past in particular instances), I think phenomenology must be practised in descriptive rather than normative fashion.

64 Besides their unwarranted normative tendencies, the phenomenological descriptions are also often wedded to an uncritical use of Scripture, especially in Marion and Michel Henry (who is less explicitly Catholic). Marion often cites from Scripture as if every sentence were self-evidently literally true and all its reported events happened in exactly the way described. Context and the long tradition of biblical exegesis are basically entirely disregarded. This seems highly problematic and makes him (and others) appear more dogmatic than they probably are. See my critique of this in "Phenomenology, Hermeneutics, and Scripture: Marion, Henry, and Falque on the Person of Christ," in Special Issue: "Beyond Myth and Enlightenment: Phenomenology and Religion," ed. Michael Staudigl and Ludger Hagedorn, *Journal for Cultural and Religious Theory* 17.2 (2018): 281–97.

65 One could obviously provide any number of other examples, including examinations of present ritual practices.

66 This is also the case in regard to the way in which phenomenology thinks of truth. In general, phenomenology understands truth in a manner much more amenable to religion. Heidegger and others articulated truth as a kind of unveiling or manifestation, a *revelation* of reality or the phenomena, rather than a rationality dependent on logic or one-to-one correspondence. Truth is manifested, comes to us, is encountered; it is not primarily about a process of verification that would establish correspondence between claims and narrow states of affairs or reach complete objectivity. This opens the way to a much richer and experiential sense of truth, one that is also much closer to the ways in which religion in general and Christianity in particular speak about or experience truth. In fact, in some ways it locates truth and reason *in* revelation instead of in opposition to it and hence overcomes the traditional contrast between reason and revelation.

67 For a summary and critique, see my "Mystery Manifested: Toward a Phenomenology of the Eucharist in its Liturgical Context," Special Issue on "Sacramental Theology: Theory and Practice from Multiple Perspectives," ed. Bruce Morrill, *Religions* 10.5 (2019): 1–18.

68 See especially his *Whose Community? Which Interpretation? Philosophical Hermeneutics for the Church* (Grand Rapids: Baker Academic, 2009) and *God, Guilt, and Death: An Existential Phenomenology of Religion* (Bloomington: Indiana University Press, 1984). His *Overcoming Onto-Theology: Toward a Postmodern Christian Faith* (New York: Fordham University Press, 2001) also includes several essays on hermeneutics.

69 John D. Caputo, *Radical Hermeneutics: Repetition, Deconstruction, and the Hermeneutic Project* (Bloomington: Indiana University Press, 1987); *More*

Radical Hermeneutics: On Not Knowing Who We Are (Bloomington: Indiana University Press, 2000); *Hermeneutics: Facts and Interpretation in the Age of Information* (London: Pelican, 2018).

70 Richard Kearney and Brian Treanor, eds., *Carnal Hermeneutics* (New York: Fordham University Press, 2015), 17.

71 "What is Diacritical Hermeneutics?," *Journal of Applied Hermeneutics* (2011): 1–14. Ted Toadvine, for example, uses this piece heavily in his contribution to *Carnal Hermeneutics*. Some of the other contributions also mention it.

72 *On Stories* (New York and London: Routledge, 2001); *Strangers, Gods, and Monsters: Interpreting Otherness* (London and New York: Routledge, 2003); with Kasha Semonovitch, eds., *Phenomenologies of the Stranger: Between Hostility and Hospitality* (New York: Fordham University Press, 2011).

73 "Diacritical Hermeneutics," 14.

74 Richard Kearney and James Taylor, eds., *Hosting the Stranger: Between Religions* (London: Bloomsbury, 2011); with Eileen Rizo-Patron, eds., *Traversing the Heart: Journeys of the Inter-Religious Imagination* (Leiden: Brill, 2010).

75 A sentiment repeatedly expressed in his *The God Who May Be* but also worked out more fully in the central chapters of *Anatheism*.

76 Terminology he employs repeatedly in *Anatheism* and in *Reimagining the Sacred*, and works out in a different vein in his essay calling for an "open Eucharist." See his "Toward an Open Eucharist," in *Ritual Participation and Interreligious Dialogue: Boundaries, Transgressions, and Innovations*, ed. Marianne Moyaert and Joris Geldhof (New York: Bloomsbury, 2015), ch. 11.

7 The Use of Philosophy in Critical Catholic Theology

ANDREW PREVOT

Preliminary Remarks about Critical Catholic Theology

Critical theory arises in various forms and contexts, including in North American departments of philosophy and theology, and there is no consensus about who has the right to speak for or define it. But whatever its precise determinations may be, I submit that it can be understood generally as a way of thinking that exposes the contradictions, dialectical tensions, hidden injustices, or partial falsities in any given institution, practice, or cultural product that is unreflectively taken to be normative, beautiful, or true. The relation between critical theory and Continental philosophy is somewhat contested, but it may suffice for the moment to state that forms of Continental philosophy that perform such an exposure of negations may be counted as examples of critical theory but also that there are other examples of critical theory which, though dependent on some Continental philosophical sources, would not be classified as Continental philosophy because of their geographical contexts or broader methods.

Insofar as critical theory sometimes makes especially pointed critiques of religious traditions, including those associated with Catholic theology, one might suppose that critical theory and Catholic theology are fierce opponents caught in a zero-sum contest in which only one can prevail – as though it were possible to think in one of these ways, but never both. As though one really had to choose between the two. However, this presupposition of an essential antagonism fails to recognize that Catholic theology is not merely an object of critical theory but also an agent of it. There is such a thing as a "critical Catholic theology," that is, a way of exposing negations in concrete realities that is guided by Catholic faith in the God of infinite justice, freedom, and love. Like any critical theory worthy of the name (which implies *theoria*, a practice of contemplation), this critical Catholic theology is not merely confrontational; it is a work of disclosure and awareness. Through painstaking analyses, it unveils inconsistencies, harms, and other negations. It manifests the vitiated and vitiating realities of things as they are. Moreover, it is self-critical: it exposes negations not only in secular institutions, practices, and products but also in their religious, including Catholic, counterparts.

Although Catholic theology's critical and self-critical capacities may be increased through its interaction with modern secular traditions of critical theory, certain prophetic, apocalyptic, ascetical, and mystical features of the Catholic theological tradition also provide an intrinsic foundation for such critical activity[1] – a foundation on which not only Catholic political and liberation theologians but also many more nearly secular proponents of critical theory continue to rely.[2] The work of exposing negations was not invented in secular modernity, whether in Immanuel Kant's *Critiques* or in other instances of Enlightenment and counter-Enlightenment criticism, nor was it in the Reformation or Renaissance before that. It was invented in a theologically aspirated antiquity, both Jewish and Greek (to speak only of its so-called Western origins). It is as old as the biblical condemnation of idolatry and the earliest philosophical interrogations of Homeric myth. The questioning of culturally received wisdom is rabbinical and Socratic before it is ever secular. The most significant difference between our epoch and theirs is simply that, in modernity, we are confronted with new social realities and renewed obligations to think critically about the negations that permeate them.

These obligations to think critically are not obligations to be secular, or methodologically atheist, that is, to work and live in the world as if there were no God.[3] On the contrary, these obligations require one to question (among other things) the very taken-for-granted goodness of the secularity that reigns over much contemporary thought and culture, including some self-proclaimed forms of critical theory, precisely by exposing the negations that such secularity harbours and conceals.[4] The movement of "radical orthodoxy," championed by John Milbank, Catherine Pickstock, Graham Ward, and others may seem to be at the forefront of this theological critique of secularity,[5] but the apologetic work of certain Catholic *ressourcement* theologians such as Henri de Lubac and Hans Urs von Balthasar precedes it and arguably mitigates, to some degree, its at times too one-sided denunciations of the secular.[6] But the best Catholic political and liberation theologians have taken the possibility of a critical Catholic theology further by combining a theological analysis of the negative features of hegemonic secularity with an equally theological analysis of the negative features of the Church and society at large, revealing on all sides oppressions that masquerade as symbols of truth and freedom.

Critical Catholic theology has many faces and emphases. It is not limited to works of explicit political or liberation theology, though it finds much support there. It varies not only by the concrete issues it targets – poverty, racism, sexism, homophobia, ableism, ecological devastation, and so on – but also by the particular spiritual, theological, and philosophical sources it employs in such efforts. The most philosophically engaged critical theologians confront negations in philosophy itself, particularly surrounding the overcoming or loss of metaphysics (however this is conceived). Amid all these permutations, one finds a genuine critical theology wherever contradictions are exposed in service of the ever-greater glory of God (to invoke an Ignatian tradition on which many such critical theologians rely), and one finds a specifically Catholic form of critical theology wherever the Catholic tradition is prioritized as an agent of such critical and self-critical exposition.

A certain *de facto* nihilism that consists of the unacknowledged negations that pervade the status quo (the falsity, ignorance, barbarism, and injustice embedded in the seemingly normal order of things) is opposed with comparable forcefulness by the most serious efforts of critical theory and critical Catholic theology. But there is another sort of *de facto*, or at least incipient, nihilism which consists of critical theory's all-embracing and interminable practice of critical negativity: the grim eschatological horizon spread before us by negation after negation after negation, which allows no believable end to come into sight. Theodor Adorno's method of negative dialectics or *negatio negationis* is a good example.[7] This second sort of *de facto* nihilism (the totalized negativity of the critical theorist) is only opposed in a decisive way by a theological discourse that not only believes in the possibility of an unwavering affirmation but also reserves this affirmation for a divine other who escapes comprehension and exceeds the reach of institutional, practical, and cultural achievements – which all do in fact remain susceptible to a critical exposition of their internal negations. This critical exposition should continue without ceasing; I do not dispute this moral imperative. But this ethically necessary work can avoid implicitly absolutizing the critical negativity it employs only if it awaits a divine source more powerful and gracious than this negativity and than the many concrete contradictions it unveils. An imagined utopia of human construction, which is never really believed, is no substitute for sincere faith in a merciful divine victor over the evils of this world. The *negatio negationis* that seems to define the labour of critical theory *ad infinitum* is supplemented in critical theology by a doxological hope that recalls and anticipates the definitive advent of a God of life who is genuinely worthy of praise.

In Christian traditions of critical theology, this praiseworthy God is revealed in Christ. It is no mere indeterminate Derridean *khōra*, a paradoxical non-site of impossible possibility.[8] Nor is it interchangeable with Giorgio Agamben's "bare life," which is the threatened other of biopolitical power, though the cruciformity of this condition may have Christological overtones.[9] Rather, this is an agential, liberating God of justice and love. This is Jesus's Father, Jesus's Spirit, and the incarnate Word: Jesus himself (one God in three persons) all at work in history for the sake of historical and eschatological salvation. Although this revelation of the triune God in Christ makes doxological hope accessible in one sense, in another sense the excessive provocations and enigmas of Christ's eternal begetting, incarnation, teachings, healings, crucifixion, and resurrection make any attempted identification with his perfect embodiment of divine and human praise far from certain. As Dionysius recognized long ago, Christology and apophasis increase together.[10] To uphold doctrines and rituals centred on Christ, therefore, does not eliminate the need for critical questioning of their meaning and adequacy but rather should constantly reinvigorate such questioning. Even still, Christ makes praise believable. Christ gives hope that there is indeed a God, and that this God is no mere absolute abstraction but a source of infinite goodness that is really deserving of adoration. Christ shows concretely that there is an end worth fighting for, a divine righteousness that exists in more than name only. Christ gives Christians a life-changing confidence that eternity is not merely the endless unmasking of corruption but a communal entrance into a love that shatters all expectations – not mere judgment but peace.

Catholic critical theologians find this Christocentric, doxological hope embodied in the Catholic Church's sacramental, spiritual, and ethical practices but also warn that these are perilous contexts in which the claims to participate in Christological praise can be falsified just as much as verified. The exercise of what David Tracy calls "the analogical imagination," which reveals likenesses to Christ in Christian and non-Christian "classics," must be held in tension with an awareness of the dialectical (i.e., both positive and negative, or as the later Foucauldian Tracy would say, "ambiguous") composition of historical realities, including those of the Catholic tradition.[11]

To be very clear, any insufficiently critical theology, one that refuses to scrutinize the historical institutions, practices, and products that concretize, but may also badly distort, its doxological hope, cannot be affirmed just because it makes itself out to be theological. Such an affirmation would only further entrench the *de facto* nihilism of the presently corrupted order of things. In the final analysis, such an uncritical mode of consciousness, however religious or Christian it purports to be, ceases to be genuinely theological and becomes idolatrous or blasphemous. This is not an elitist point. Those not formally educated in theory or theology may nonetheless participate in exemplary ways in their various prophetic, apocalyptic, ascetical, and mystical modes of critical analysis, whereas highly credentialed scholars and Church leaders may remain lost in an ideological haze that prevents them from recognizing and resisting contradictions in the identity-forming traditions to which they belong or in their own interpretations of them.

Both critical theory and critical Catholic theology typically avoid any *de jure* or explicit nihilism, which would absurdly hold that nothingness is the meaning of everything. Adorno and other sophisticated negative dialecticians of a secular or post-secular variety cannot be accused of advancing this absurdist position. But their repudiation of it does not rule out a *de facto* complicity in another sort of nihilism, one that takes the form of a continual denial of any possibility of doxology. The rigorously anti-nihilistic (because uncompromisingly critical and divinely affirmative) power of doxology, especially as revealed in Christ, is something that Catholic theologians are still learning to think and embody, though some have already made impressive strides in this direction, which I can only begin to indicate below.

Different Ways to Use Philosophy

I have developed these thoughts about the structure and anti-nihilistic significance of critical Catholic theology in greater detail elsewhere.[12] The particular question I want to investigate further in this chapter is this: How is philosophy being treated and utilized in critical Catholic theology? The appropriation of philosophical themes by critical theologians was already under way in Christian antiquity (even though no strict distinction between philosophy and theology had yet emerged; it would be more precise in pre-modernity to draw a line between pagan and Christian philosophical theologies –that is, wisdom-loving discourses of God – even while recognizing their interconnections).[13] One might think especially of large-scale patristic borrowings from Stoic practices of *apatheia*, which encouraged detachment from worldly passions, and Neoplatonic models of henological ascent beyond sensible particulars and intelligible forms of being, which find expression in early Christian negative and mystical theology. However, what interests me more here is the question of how philosophy is being understood and employed in contemporary expressions of critical Catholic theology, that is, during a modern or postmodern era in which philosophy has emerged as a discipline distinct from theology. Philosophy is now defined more or less strictly by a commitment to secular reason, a methodological atheism, even when it treats religious phenomena; whereas theology presupposes faith in God. Nevertheless, the dynamic interchanges between them have not ceased.

In what follows, I make two central points. First, I argue that the use of philosophy in critical Catholic theology is irreducibly plural.[14] It would, therefore, be a mistake to try to cement it into a single pattern. Nevertheless, precisely by contemplating this plurality, we might begin to glimpse what an approximately plenary (which is to say expansive and multi-vocal, not exhaustive or homogenous) articulation of a critical Catholic theology could look like. Second, I argue that this use of philosophy need not, and often does not, lead to any unwarranted secularization of religious discourse. It would, therefore, also be a mistake to assume that the presence of a philosophically assisted mode of critical thinking necessarily diminishes the theological status of any particular critical Catholic theology. This diminishment is possible, as we shall see in some instances (e.g., the later works of Juan Luis Segundo and John Caputo), but it is not a given. Hence, the decisive questions before us are, first, whether some sort of philosophy has been employed critically, and second, whether it has been put in the service of a Christocentric doxology that incorporates it into a nihilism-resistant form of theological critique. The plurality in the use of philosophy (including differences in practice and sources) by critical Catholic theologians requires that one consider this question of an animating doxological hope afresh in each particular case, instead of positing a general rule about it. Although a critical theological use of Analytic philosophers is conceivable, I concentrate here on the critical theological use of Continental philosophers (mainly German, French, Spanish, and Italian). I focus on Catholic theologians who are being read and discussed in North America, even though many reside elsewhere.

The following analysis distinguishes three clusters of critical Catholic theologians. In the first subsection below, I discuss various Catholic theologians whose critical responses to modern political-economic conditions of impoverishment are indebted to Marxism of one kind or another. In the second subsection, I turn to Catholic theologians who, without forgetting poverty, are especially focused on critical issues of gender and race that require more than Marxist analysis to be understood. In the final subsection, I look at some Catholic theologians engaged in postmodern debates about metaphysics. The differences within and between these groups of critical Catholic theologians are important. These differences, however, do not amount to pure heterogeneity. Unifying contours of a philosophically conversant critical Catholic theology can be discerned through this (admittedly quick) overview of otherwise seemingly disparate theologians. Moreover, each of these cases shows Catholic theologians making critical use of philosophy while resisting its modern secularizing pull.

Does "Critical" Mean "Marxist," and If So in What Sense?

When one hears "critical," one might think this means "Marxist." However, as I aim to show here, it is not legitimate to assume that just because a form of Catholic theology aspires to be critical it will be overdetermined by the philosophy of Karl Marx or by the works of other philosophers who take Marx as an authority. To be sure, the Uruguayan Jesuit Juan Luis Segundo's later writings, especially after *Faith and Ideologies* (1982), do employ a Marxist philosophical method to determine what can and cannot be salvaged from Christianity, and the results are quite theologically meagre: only Jesus's humanity, not his divinity, and only certain aspects of this humanity that seem conducive to historical projects of liberation can be rescued on such Marxist grounds. Segundo styles his work as an "anti-christology." There is an unmistakable doxology-diminishing Marxist overdetermination here.[15]

But Segundo's secularizing approach is not predominant in Catholic liberation theology. Even the Argentinian Enrique Dussel, who writes not only as a liberation theologian but also as a Latin American Marxist philosopher in a somewhat strict sense, offers a robust interpretation of Christian liturgical practice and communal ethics that is significantly more theologically viable than Segundo's "liberation of theology." Dussel reads Marx through the lens of Emmanuel Levinas's theologically informed – that is, both biblical and Neoplatonic – phenomenology of the other. For Dussel, service to the poor – as other, as epiphany of the divine – is a doxological act, a communion of material and spiritual gifts that exposes the idolatry (or "fetishism") of profit-driven capitalist modes of exchange.[16]

Another variation in the use of Marx can be found in the French Catholic phenomenologist Michel Henry, who tends to be included in what Dominique Janicaud calls the "theological turn of French phenomenology."[17] Henry's work is not theologically problematic because of what he gleans from the early philosophical Marx – namely, an intuition of the reality of living labour, of the individual worker, as the real source of economic value, an intuition that allows Henry to develop his own sophisticated critique of late modern capitalism and Soviet-style communism as two forms of life-forgetting barbarism. Rather, Henry's work is theologically problematic because it is closely tied to a tradition of identity philosophy running from Meister Eckhart through German idealism, in which the "I" and God are insufficiently distinguished. Henry defines the life that is the essence of living labour simultaneously as auto-affective experience and as the divine nature itself.[18] One may reasonably question whether this univocal, or at least ambiguous, notion of life adequately preserves the traditional Catholic understanding, formalized by Erich Przywara, of an analogical relationship in which any given similarity between creature and Creator (such as their vitality) is always outstripped by an infinitely greater dissimilarity.[19]

For his part, the Peruvian theologian Gustavo Gutiérrez does not employ Marx primarily as a philosophical source but instead draws selectively on certain economic and social analyses of dependency that were cognizant of, but also significantly discontinuous with, Marx's later economic writings. When Gutiérrez defines theology as a "critical reflection," he does so in clear theological terms: "Theological reflection would then necessarily be a criticism of society and the Church insofar as they are called and addressed by the Word of God; it would be a critical theory, worked out in the light of the Word accepted in faith and inspired by a practical purpose." Although Marxist philosopher Antonio Gramsci's notion of an "organic intellectual" is in the background of Gutiérrez's methodological considerations, Gutiérrez's method is nonetheless unmistakably oriented toward praise of "that gratuitous God [who] strips me, leaves me naked, universalizes my love for others, and makes it gratuitous." He finds this God most fully in Christ, the divine and human liberator.[20]

If one considers Johann Baptist Metz's post-Auschwitz political theology (which represents a German tradition of political theology that has ties to but is distinct from Latin American liberation theology), then certainly the influence of the Western Marxist Frankfurt School, often seen as the standard-bearer of critical theory, is undeniable. But the most decisive philosophical source for Metz is arguably the apocalyptic (and, at least to some degree, genuinely Jewish and theological) figure of Walter Benjamin. With some assistance from Benjamin, Metz critiques the secular utopianism of Ernst Bloch, Max Horkheimer, and Theodor Adorno because it has no promise for the dead. More than that, he opposes the Hegelianism of fellow critically minded German political theologians, such as Jürgen Moltmann and Dorothee Soelle. In his judgment, they leave the God–world relation insufficiently differentiated by importing suffering into God. Clearly Metz is no left-wing Hegelian. Similarly, he resists Nietzschean conceptions of myth and time that have gained a certain currency in postmodernity. Although he defends early in his career the theological value of a certain sort of secularity, by which he primarily means active investment in the world as modelled in the incarnation of the Word, he ultimately demonstrates that most forms of secular philosophy, whether Marxist, Hegelian, or Nietzschean, that may be circulating in contemporary thought fail his critical test of expectant praise for the God of the living and the dead.[21]

These examples demonstrate that critical Catholic theology's use of Marx and Marxism (which are key sources of critical theory within and beyond Continental philosophy) is far from uniform. Moreover, these examples show that the mere inclusion of Marx or Marxist-inspired thinkers in the conversation does not necessarily undermine the doxological character of such formulations of a critical Catholic theology. Although significant secularization does occur in Segundo's case, there are other cases such as Dussel's and Henry's that are more promising in this regard (even if somewhat questionable for one reason or another), and there are other cases still such as Gutiérrez's and Metz's that are truly exemplary as far as the goal of a critical Catholic theology is concerned. It may be for this reason that, although Gutiérrez hails from Peru and Metz from Germany, they have both had an immense and lasting impact on North American Catholic theologians and students of the last several decades – much more so than the other Marx-related figures just considered. Often, in this context, Gutiérrez's and Metz's names have been treated as synonymous with liberation theology and political theology, respectively.[22] Although both convincingly represent the aims of a critical Catholic theology, their projects remain different and not interchangeable.

Critical Issues of Gender and Race

The range of philosophical usage only expands as one considers the diverse formulations of a critical Catholic theology that is committed to exposing not only the negative realities of economic injustice, which are destroying the lives of the poor, but also negations associated with gender, race, and a host of other concrete social factors. These contradictions of divine goodness have prompted critical Catholic theologians to engage with many other philosophical streams in addition to Marxism. US theologian Anne Carr, for instance, develops an influential approach to Catholic feminist theology by drawing on Karl Rahner's Thomistic and Heideggerian idea that the subject's experience of being-in-the-world mediates the subject's only possible openness to (divine) being. The path to God passes through the *conversio ad phantasma*; the transcendental arrives in the categorical; the eternal Word is communicated in the flesh of Christ. This Rahnerian framework supports the efforts of Carr and other Catholic feminist theologians to understand the grace and presence of God within women's experience. If concrete experience matters as much to theology as Rahner suggests it does, then women's experience ought to gain authority as an indispensable theological source, one that not only gives glory to God but also exposes androcentrism as a deadly form of idolatry in the Christian tradition.[23]

US Catholic biblical scholar Sandra Schneiders, for her part, finds a helpful critical resource for feminist theology and feminist biblical hermeneutics in the philosophy of Paul Ricoeur. She accepts as her own his recommended interpretive progression from a first naivety to a second naivety through a process of critical distanciation. She also embraces his insight that the meaning of a text, including any given biblical text, is determined not only by the historical world behind it or by the literary world represented in it but also by the possible world of the future that opens up in front of it and that depends on the critical hermeneutical activity of communities that read and receive this text in new historical contexts. These key features of Ricoeur's hermeneutical philosophy help Schneiders think about how women and men can continue to find life-giving meaning in the Bible, even while resisting the patriarchal power relations that distort its salvific purpose.[24]

British Catholic theologian Tina Beattie rethinks the question of difference in Catholic feminist theology by putting French feminist philosopher Luce Irigaray into critical dialogue with Hans Urs von Balthasar and Adrienne von Speyr. Beattie affirms Irigaray's effort to recover women's subjectivity from the fatal confines of a phallologocentric Western tradition and uses Irigaray's phenomenological and psycholinguistic philosophy of gender difference to critique the hierarchically subordinated definition of "woman" as man's "answer and face" that appears in Balthasar and Speyr. At the same time, Beattie embraces Balthasar's and Speyr's prayerful, Christian respect for divine distance and draws on their theological account of the God–creature difference to resist Irigaray's philosophical immanentism.[25]

In her attempts to combat racism, sexism, and homophobia from a theological perspective, black Catholic and womanist theologian M. Shawn Copeland has recourse to Bernard Lonergan's philosophy and theology of the human subject in its differentiated and contextually situated consciousness. Lonergan's anthropology and epistemology help Copeland develop a critical analysis of "bias" as a vitiating force of social myopia and misperception that keeps US citizens and institutions from fully recognizing the humanity of black individuals and communities. In recent works, her theological affirmation of the subject – particularly as enfleshed in poor women of colour and other despised human beings – has drawn on black existentialist and decolonial theorists such as Frantz Fanon, Lewis Gordon, Paul Gilroy, and Hortense Spillers. Her doxological hope takes the form of a Eucharistic solidarity in which all the diverse and wounded members of Christ's mystical body can find communion.[26]

Latina Catholic theologian Nancy Pineda-Madrid writes theology in response to the persistent horrors of feminicide along the US–Mexican border. To some extent, her approach depends on the work of American pragmatist philosopher Charles Sanders Peirce. She adopts certain crucial methodological points from Peirce about the historically contextual nature of knowing and about the need to prioritize practical criteria for the evaluation of truth claims. From these premises, she argues that salvation cannot be interpreted adequately through an abstract doctrine of atonement divorced from historical praxis. On the contrary, she contends that the concrete meaning of salvation becomes most manifest in practices of resistance to local experiences of violence and suffering. Pineda-Madrid's use of pragmatism does not diminish her sense that salvation is a real gift from the living God. Rather, it makes her hope in this gift more credible by situating it in the midst of real people's lives and deaths.[27]

These are just a few examples that illustrate a critical Catholic theology that is learning to become more responsive to contradictions associated with gender and race, which, intersecting with poverty, reveal the structural violence of our colonial modernity. The aforementioned theologians use various traditions of philosophy (transcendental, hermeneutical, phenomenological, psychoanalytic, existentialist, pragmatist, and so on) without thereby forsaking the doxological hope that makes their works genuinely theological. Other issues associated with marginalized sexualities, stigmatized disabilities, and ecological disasters are receiving more and more attention among critical Catholic theologians, who do not hesitate to borrow from philosophically informed streams of contemporary critical theory in each of these areas.[28] The test of these emerging – and, indeed, increasingly established – fields of critical Catholic theology is not whether they repeat precisely what has been said by theologians in the past or minimize their own interactions with secular philosophy and theory in the present but rather whether they perform a credible, doxologically oriented exposure of negations that inspires practical hope in a God of justice and love.

The Question of Metaphysics in Postmodernity

In the preceding discussion, I have attempted to give a sense of the highly variable uses of philosophy among liberation, political, feminist, black, and Latina representatives of critical Catholic theology (the phenomenologist Michel Henry perhaps being the one exception thus far: although he engages Marx and Catholic theological themes, he does not easily fit into the above-mentioned camps). Here I want to suggest that the rather flexible category of critical Catholic theology can also be extended to other thinkers whose work may not seem as overtly concerned with capitalism, patriarchy, white supremacy, or other pressing social issues. These historical realities contradict the goodness of God and must be exposed and resisted. I wholeheartedly support the foregoing efforts to do so, especially those (the majority) that in the process avoid secularization and its anti-doxological, *de facto* nihilistic tendencies. In addition to these real-world instances of negation – note: not *instead of* them, indeed preferably *in close connection* with them – critical Catholic theology also has the capacity and responsibility to expose negations of a more theoretical order. The use of philosophy in such efforts is often more extensive but also more contentious, at times seeming less like a use and more like a polemical confrontation, because the status of philosophy – or, more broadly, of thought – is precisely what is under consideration. If thought finds itself in a self-contradictory, aporetic, or deadening condition, then a critical Catholic theology has a stake in recognizing this negative condition and working to overcome it, precisely for the sake of a doxological mode of contemplation and hope that would permeate life and become concretely realized in action.

There is presently no consensus among Catholic theologians and philosophers, or indeed among others, about whether the *de facto* nihilism apparently endemic to modern thought – finite reason's variously characterized forgetting or denaturing; its estrangement from its supposedly original experience of wonder; its perversion into mere technocratic calculation or individualistic aestheticism; its uneasy oscillation between hubristic fantasy and self-destruction; the "deaths" of God, humanity, and the world that it seems continually to produce and reinforce – is more accurately associated with *metaphysics* or with its *loss*. But in any case the question of metaphysics seems to be at the centre of this postmodern debate. Voices of critical Catholic theologians and philosophers can be heard on both sides.

US philosophical theologian John Caputo does not hesitate to side first with Martin Heidegger's and then later with Jacques Derrida's still more unflinchingly critical suggestion that metaphysics, especially but not exclusively in its modern configurations, needs to be overcome. Although Caputo finds resources in Meister Eckhart, Augustine, and even Thomas Aquinas to support this effort, his work ultimately becomes problematic as an example of critical Catholic theology insofar as, following Derrida, he counts Christian doxology as one type of metaphysics among others. The hyperousiological praise that one finds in the Dionysian mystical tradition is, by Caputo's judgment, insufficiently apophatic – still too invested in a guaranteed "presence." Although Caputo does seek a place from which to say "yes," to affirm what will come, this place for him seems not to be Christ but rather the non-place of the *khōra*. What Caputo offers, then, is more nearly a post-secular form of critical theory than a fully realized critical Catholic theology.[29]

But the postmodern suspicion of metaphysics does not always move in this doxology-diminishing direction. Like Caputo, Jean-Luc Marion takes Heidegger's and Derrida's warnings to heart. However, unlike Caputo, Marion contends that the doxological hope expressed in figures such as Dionysius and Augustine does help us overcome metaphysics – and indeed, does so more rigorously than either Heidegger's poetic thinking of being-as-event or Derrida's deconstructive hermeneutics. Caputo elides metaphysics and doxology, Marion contrasts the two. Marion thereby leaves himself free to expose the conceptual idolatry of the Western ontological tradition (which, despite invoking being, culminates in nihilism) while simultaneously glorifying a God of pure charity, received and offered in the Eucharist. As much as he must be appreciated as a daringly innovative phenomenologist and an expert in Descartes – and in these respects as a genuine philosopher in the modern sense – we must also recognize that he offers us a striking example of critical Catholic theology in its more theoretical or philosophy-focused mode. To some extent, he is doing theology, and it is of a critical sort.[30]

The French Catholic sacramental theologian Louis-Marie Chauvet is similar to Marion in his critical turn from metaphysics to doxology. Although Chauvet draws on Heidegger, Derrida, and even Jacques Lacan to question the ways that Catholic sacramental theology has been adversely affected by an overly causal and ontological style of thinking, which he believes to be dangerously reifying, Chauvet does not merely adopt a posture of perpetual critique. On the contrary, he rethinks the church's sacramental practice through creative retrievals of its scriptural and traditional sources. He highlights the ways that bodily, communal, and linguistic rituals participate in a symbolic – but still very real, formative and transformative, indeed salvific – gift-exchange between God and humanity, which is made possible by the active, loving presence of Christ and the Holy Spirit. Chauvet's critical exposition of metaphysics-related shortcomings in Catholic sacramental theology is drawn forward by his hope in the possibility of a revitalized performance of thanksgiving and praise on the part of the Church, which can and must bear fruit in ethics.[31]

The US-residing Irish philosophical theologian Cyril O'Regan represents a somewhat more metaphysics-friendly approach. To be sure, he is not uncritical of metaphysics, especially in its modern forms. His first book, *The Heterodox Hegel*, and his multi-volume *Gnostic Return* project demonstrate that his level of critical awareness is on a par with Caputo's, Marion's, and Chauvet's, even more devastatingly detailed in certain respects. However, O'Regan seems largely convinced that Hans Urs von Balthasar – who, despite inspiring the post-metaphysical Marion, remains committed to a Christian retrieval of metaphysics – really does enough to overcome what is problematic about Hegel and related modern metaphysicians. Moreover, O'Regan argues that Balthasar avoids certain attenuations of Christian doxology that appear in various post-metaphysical thinkers, including not only Caputo but also Marion (who at least in early works seems reluctant to embrace Thomistic praise of God as subsistent *esse*). In more recent essays, including his chapter in this volume, O'Regan analyses and confronts the Lacanian Marxist philosopher Slavoj Žižek, an ever-provocative representative of post-secular (but not necessarily theological) critical theory. Although Hegel provides a substantive point of connection here, O'Regan's and Žižek's strategies for reading and responding to Hegel diverge significantly – and precisely on the question of whether there is a Christian doxological hope that can be salvaged and believed once rigorous negative dialectical thinking has begun. O'Regan ultimately suggests that the Irish philosopher William Desmond, who is an anti-Hegelian and simultaneously neo-Hegelian theorist of "the between," may have gotten the balance just about right. The question for Desmond is not whether we ought to think metaphysically but *how* we ought to do so. O'Regan appreciates this shift in emphasis, along with the phenomenological sensitivity of Desmond's metaxological proposal.[32]

Desmond's "Being True to Mystery and Metaxological Metaphysics," from the present collection, is a good example of his characteristic way of seeking to rescue metaphysics from Kantian and post-Kantian critiques, even while taking such critiques seriously. His argument rests on the claim that the term "metaphysics" ought to be taken not univocally but rather plurivocally. Rationalist approaches must be distinguished from more mystery-respecting alternatives, such as his own, that still belong to metaphysics in a broad sense. If we decide to pluralize our usage in this way, I only wish to add that, therefore, the term "post-metaphysical" must become plurivocal in its meaning too. Post-metaphysical figures such as Chauvet and Marion who preserve Christian doxological hope can be appreciated for their critical, Catholic theological overcoming of certain kinds of conceptually idolatrous metaphysics and need not be treated with the same trepidation that strict Derridean nominalism may justly occasion from theologians. However, a deeper question may lie here: in proposing "metaphysics" as a virtually inescapable umbrella category that includes both the rationalism he opposes and the agapic mindfulness he affirms, is Desmond seeking to situate the term itself beyond critique? Why not reserve such an exalted status only for the unknown God, which is perhaps the most doxological hope that a philosopher in the modern sense is permitted to hold – or, if one risks a theological voice, why not reserve such an exalted status only for the unknown God whom Christians believe has come in Christ and will appear again in glory? My contention is that *de facto* nihilism of whatever sort is more decisively counteracted by a critical theology for which only such a God is sacred than by any metaphysics, however repentant and metaxological. Nonetheless, I might be willing to concede that precisely this sort of metaxological metaphysics may, as O'Regan suggests, serve the needs of such a critical theology, especially in the face of certain doxology-negating forms of post-metaphysical thinking.

Caputo, Marion, Chauvet, O'Regan, and Desmond may all seem to be more closely associated with postmodernity than with critical theory per se. However, I include them in the discussion here because the dividing lines between such modes of philosophy, and philosophically informed theology, are not as clear-cut as they may at first appear. Notoriously difficult to define, postmodern thought nevertheless gains some consistent meaning insofar as it exposes the contradictions and negations inherent in modern philosophy, not least of all in Hegel. As we have seen especially in the cases of Marion, Chauvet, and O'Regan (less so in Caputo and Desmond, who remain more nearly philosophers), this postmodern work of critical exposition can be incorporated into a Christian doxological practice and open up new possibilities for it. Formally speaking, the structure of negative dialectics and doxological hope and the criteria of relative theological adequacy this structure imposes on theologians' use of philosophy are not radically different here from what we have seen in other forms of critical Catholic theology, such as political, liberation, black, feminist, Latina, and so on.

These postmodern theologians are part of the irreducible plurality of a Catholic theology that is resistant to both the deadening of thought and the destruction of life.

Conclusion

An obvious risk that comes with proposing such a general, flexible category – namely critical Catholic theology – is that it will, by striving to encompass so many diverse approaches to theology and to the theological use of philosophy, reduce them all to their lowest common denominators, de-emphasizing the particular struggles and achievements of each approach and disregarding the tensions or conflicts that may divide them. This danger can be significantly mitigated by continuing to read the sources themselves and by remembering that critical Catholic theology is an irreducibly plural web of possibilities and actualities, not a monologue or a monolith. The abstract category of critical Catholic theology is no substitute for the concrete determinations of these variously situated, motivated, and executed efforts, which are non-fungible. Moreover, the mere fact that any given project seems to qualify as a critical Catholic theology does not mean it is wholly beyond reproach. Evaluation of these sources must continue to happen with reference to the details of their arguments and not merely their most formal structure of a somehow-combined negative dialectics and doxological hope. It would be a painful irony if the very notion of a critical Catholic theology encouraged one to endorse uncritically any possible expression of it. That is certainly not my intention.

Yet whatever the risks may be, what we stand to gain from the idea of a critical Catholic theology is quite significant. First, there is the explicit recognition that critique – the exposition of negations – is not limited to secular representatives of critical theory or indeed even to post-secular representatives who have learned to question secularity but remain reluctant to commit themselves to thinking from within a particular religious tradition. There is a theological form of critique. There is a Christian form of it. There is even a Catholic form of it. The Catholic theological tradition can act as an agent of critical and self-critical exposition. The acknowledgment of this possibility is important, not merely because it may function as an *apologia* for Catholicism (which, if this defence has some truth to it, would be a good thing as far as it goes), but also and much more necessarily because it provides a critical means of exposing and resisting the incipient nihilism of a critical negativity that has begun to absolutize itself. The world needs critique. But more than that it needs a source of hope that radically transcends not only what needs to be critiqued but also the practice of critique itself. Critical Catholic theology and other comparable forms of critical theology provide just that gift of hope – or at least they provide a way of remembering and pointing to it.

A second crucial benefit of the idea of a critical Catholic theology is that it vigorously opposes uncritical and insufficiently critical claimants on the title of Catholic theology. It exhorts those who belong to the Catholic Church and especially the theologians who seek to develop its understanding of faith to think more discerningly about the many ways that their thoughts and practices may participate in this violent world's multifaceted negations of divine goodness as revealed in Christ. It urges Catholics not to overlook those prophetic, apocalyptic, ascetical, and mystical aspects of their tradition that would call them to higher forms of self-examination and critical social awareness. Indeed, it demands that they internalize these critical features of the Catholic tradition and let them spark and fuel their own vigilant struggles against self-serving idolatry. It asks Catholics to uncover and cast out the complacency in their hearts and to revise, as necessary, any institutional norms that derive from and support such complacency. In short, it insists that being Catholic and theological is not enough. Precisely on these grounds, and in order to do justice to them, one must also be critical. By this I mean minimally *no less* critical than the most critical secular theorist – though in fact, I believe that a doxological orientation requires one to be *more* critical than such a theorist.

A third benefit to the idea of a critical Catholic theology is that it allows those theologians who are already implicitly committed to it not only to recognize what they may have in common with others who are part of this effort, despite potentially major differences in context or approach, but also to learn from, challenge, and critique one another. Although some division of labour may be inevitable and useful, a greater sense of common purpose could also help critical Catholic theologians think more communally about how their particular attempts to overcome some specific contradiction in service of the God of life are interconnected with those of others. The idea of a critical Catholic theology opens up a space for mutually enriching conversation and accountability across diverse subfields of contemporary Catholic theology. Widely varying formulations of Catholic theology that are typically called political, liberation, black, feminist, Latino/a, queer, disability, ecological, postmodern, *ressourcement*, and more may all have something vital to contribute to this shared critical conversation.

Finally, to mention a benefit that is most directly relevant to the argument of this chapter and to the focus of this volume, the idea of a critical

Catholic theology helps clarify the contemporary state of the relationship between theology and philosophy by examining underexplored regions of it. First of all, this relationship is not limited to scholastic, transcendental, idealist, phenomenological, existential, and hermeneutical approaches to theology that are typically recognized as being philosophically informed; it also finds expression in political, liberation, feminist, black, Latino/a, and other approaches that less commonly receive this recognition. One conclusion that might be drawn here is simply that these latter approaches ought to receive such recognition too. The preceding analysis shows, moreover, that they deserve this recognition not only because of their interactions with the philosophical tradition of post-Marxist critical theory, which such theologians have engaged in significantly different ways and sometimes hardly at all, but also because of other philosophical traditions, including many of those mentioned above, that support their critical reflections. We have seen that the use of philosophy in critical Catholic theology is irreducibly plural. Commitments to combating capitalism, patriarchy, and white supremacy contribute to this plurality but do not, as a rule, make such approaches any less philosophical, provided there is a sufficiently critical and expansive understanding of philosophy.

A potential worry coming from the opposite direction is also addressed by this argument. Instead of being denied their philosophical credentials, political, liberation, feminist, black, Latino/a, and other socially engaged approaches to theology might be deemed "too philosophical," by which one would mean too indebted to secular concerns foreign to the Catholic theological tradition. We have seen, on the contrary, that the use of philosophy in such approaches is not necessarily secularizing. Although the Christocentric doxological hope at the centre of the Catholic theological tradition has been forfeited in some cases, the most influential representatives of these theological approaches have made no such forfeiture and, instead, have revealed the critical power of this sort of hope in concrete circumstances of economic, gender, and racial oppression. In general, they do not deviate from the traditional Catholic arrangement in which reason serves faith without usurping its place.

We have also seen that among postmodern critical Catholic theologians there is no agreement on the question of whether theology, insofar as it is philosophical, should be metaphysical. But there is an emerging consensus that the metaphysical tradition, particularly in modernity, cannot be embraced uncritically. A question that, in my opinion, warrants significantly more research concerns the relationship between postmodern critiques of metaphysics and socially engaged critiques of violence. Although philosophers may have their own reasons to investigate the possible interconnections between these two forms of *negatio negationis*, critical Catholic theologians who want to see a reintegration of contemplation and action, theology and sanctity, orthodoxy and orthopraxy, should be particularly eager to inquire into this relationship. Not every critical Catholic theologian needs to attempt to give voice to the whole of this ever-polyphonous sort of thought-and-action, but the worldwide community of such theologians ought to, as a group, bear witness to this whole and work together to make it known and effective in various micro- and macro-contexts of this aching world.

NOTES

1 These prophetic, apocalyptic, ascetical, and mystical bases of critical Catholic theology have been elucidated by Ignacio Ellacuría, "Utopia and Propheticism from Latin America," in *A Grammar of Justice: The Legacy of Ignacio Ellacuría*, ed. J. Matthew Ashley, Kevin F. Burke SJ, and Rodolfo Cardenal SJ (Maryknoll: Orbis, 2014), 7–55; Johann Baptist Metz, *Faith in History and Society: Toward a Practical Fundamental Theology*, trans. J. Matthew Ashley (New York: Crossroad, 2007); Leonardo Boff, *Francis of Assisi: A Model for Human Liberation*, trans. John Diercksmeier (Maryknoll: Orbis, 2006); and Maria Clara Bingemer, *The Mystery and the World: Passion for God in Times of Unbelief* (Eugene: Cascade, 2016).

2 See Ernst Bloch, *Atheism in Christianity* (Brooklyn: Verso, 2009); Georges Bataille, *Inner Experience*, trans. Leslie Anne Boldt (Albany: SUNY Press, 1988); Michel Foucault, *The History of Sexuality*, vol. 3: *The Care of the Self* (New York: Random House, 1986); Giorgio Agamben, *The Highest Poverty: Monastic Rules and Form-of-Life*, ed. Werner Harnacker, trans. Adam Kotsko (Stanford: Stanford University Press, 2013); and Amy Hollywood, *Acute Melancholia and Other Essays: Mysticism, History, and the Study of Religion* (New York: Columbia University Press, 2016).

3 Here I am not using "secular" in the broader way that Charles Taylor does, namely to name a condition of fragility brought about by the emergence of exclusive humanism as a widely available option in modern societies; I am using it in a more narrow sense to mean working and living as if there were no God. See Charles Taylor, *A Secular Age* (Cambridge, MA: Harvard University Press, 2007).

4 There is a "post-secular" questioning of secularity even in sources that have not become explicitly confessional or dogmatic. See Talal Asad, Wendy Brown, Judith Butler, and Saba Mahmoud, *Is Critique Secular? Blasphemy, Injury, and Free Speech* (New York: Fordham University Press, 2013); and Hent de Vries and Lawrence E. Sullivan, eds., *Political Theologies: Public Religions in a Post-Secular World* (New York: Fordham University Press, 2006).

5 See John Milbank, *Theology and Social Theory: Beyond Secular Reason*, 2nd ed. (Malden: Blackwell, 2006); Catherine Pickstock, *After Writing: On the Liturgical Consummation of Philosophy* (Malden: Blackwell, 1998); Graham Ward, *Contemporary Theology and Critical Theory*, 2nd ed. (New York: St Martin's Press, 2000); and Milbank, Pickstock, and Ward, eds., *Radical Orthodoxy: A New Theology* (New York: Routledge, 1999).

6 See Henri de Lubac, *The Drama of Atheist Humanism*, trans. Edith Riley, Anne Englund Nash, and Mark Sebanc (San Francisco: Ignatius, 1995); and Hans Urs von Balthasar, *The Glory of the Lord: A Theological Aesthetics*, vol. 5: *The Realm of Metaphysics in the Modern Age*, trans. Oliver Davies et al. (San Francisco: Ignatius, 1991).

7 See Theodor Adorno, *Negative Dialectics*, trans. E.B. Ashton (New York: Continuum, 1987).

8 See Jacques Derrida, "*Khōra*," in *On the Name*, ed. Thomas Dutoit (Stanford: Stanford University Press, 1995), 89–127.

9 See Giorgio Agamben, *Homo Sacer: Sovereign Power and Bare Life*, trans. Daniel Heller-Roazen (Stanford: Stanford University Press, 1998).

10 See Dionysius, letter 4, in *Pseudo-Dionysius: The Complete Works*, trans. Colm Luibheid (Mahwah: Paulist, 1987), 264–5.

11 See David Tracy, *The Analogical Imagination: Christian Theology and the Culture of Pluralism* (New York: Crossroad, 1981); and *Plurality and Ambiguity: Hermeneutics, Religion, Hope* (Chicago: University of Chicago Press, 1987).

12 See Andrew Prevot, "Negative Dialectics and Doxological Hope: Elements of a Critical Catholic Theology," in *Beyond Dogmatism and Innocence: Hermeneutics, Critique, and Catholic Theology*, ed. Anthony J. Godzieba and Bradford E. Hinze (Collegeville: Liturgical Press, 2017), 138–59.

13 See Jean-Yves Lacoste, *From Theology to Theological Thinking*, trans. W. Chris Hackett (Charlottesville: University of Virginia Press, 2014), 1–29.

14 My argument here echoes and updates Karl Rahner's "Philosophy and Philosophising in Theology," in *Theological Investigations*, vol. 9, trans. Graham Harrison (New York: Seabury, 1973), 46–63. In agreement with Rahner, I contend that philosophical activity (or what he calls "philosophizing") cannot be reduced to one paradigm and, moreover, that it cannot ever be eliminated from theology, as if this would make theology better. At the same time, and I think Rahner would concur, I argue that among all the possible theological uses of philosophy some are significantly better than others if one's aim is to formulate a critical Catholic theology.

15 See Juan-Luis Segundo, *Faith and Ideologies*, vol. 1 of *Jesus of Nazareth: Yesterday and Today*, trans. John Drury (Maryknoll: Orbis, 1987).

16 See these works by Enrique Dussel: *Philosophy of Liberation*, trans. Aquilina Martinez and Christine Morkovsky (Maryknoll: Orbis, 1995);

Ethics and Community, trans. Robert R. Barr (Eugene: Wipf and Stock, 1988); and "The Bread of the Eucharist Celebration as a Sign of Justice in the Community," in *Beyond Philosophy: Ethics, History, Marxism, and Liberation Theology*, ed. Eduardo Mendieta (Lanham: Rowman and Littlefield, 2003), 41–52.

17 See Dominique Janicaud, "The Theological Turn of French Phenomenology," trans. Bernard Prusak, in *Phenomenology and the "Theological Turn": The French Debate* (New York: Fordham University Press, 2000), 16–103.

18 See Michel Henry, *From Communism to Capitalism: Theory of a Catastrophe*, trans. Scott Davidson (New York: Bloomsbury, 2014); and *The Essence of Manifestation*, trans. Girard Etzkorn (The Hague: Matinus Nijhoff, 1973).

19 See Erich Przywara, *Analogia Entis: Metaphysics: Original Structure and Universal Rhythm*, trans. John R. Betz and David Bentley Hart (Grand Rapids: Eerdmans, 2014).

20 See Gustavo Gutiérrez, *A Theology of Liberation: History, Politics, and Salvation*, 15th[h] anniversary ed., trans. Sister Caridad Inda and John Eagleson (Maryknoll: Orbis, 2005), 9, 119.

21 See Metz, *Faith in History and Society*; *Theology of the World*, trans. William Glen-Doepel (New York: Herder and Herder, 1969); and *Memoria Passionis: Ein provizierendes Gedächtnis in pluralistischer Gesellschaft* (Freiburg im Breisgau: Verlag Herder, 2006).

22 See Gaspar Martinez, *Confronting the Mystery of God: Political, Liberation, and Public Theologies* (New York: Continuum, 2001).

23 See Anne E. Carr, *Transforming Grace: Christian Tradition and Women's Experience* (New York: Bloomsbury, 1996).

24 See Sandra M. Schneiders, *The Revelatory Text: Interpreting the New Testament as Sacred Scripture*, 2nd ed. (Collegeville: Liturgical Press, 1999).

25 See Tina Beattie, *New Catholic Feminism: Theology and Theory* (New York: Routledge, 2006).

26 See M. Shawn Copeland, *Enfleshing Freedom: Body, Race, and Being* (Minneapolis: Fortress, 2010).

27 See Nancy Pineda-Madrid, *Suffering and Salvation in Ciudad Juárez* (Minneapolis: Fortress, 2011).

28 See, among others, Mark D. Jordan, *The Silence of Sodom: Homosexuality in Modern Catholicism* (Chicago: University of Chicago Press, 2000); Mary Jo Iozzio, "Solidarity: Restoring Communion with Those Who are Disabled," *Journal of Religion, Disability, and Health* 15, no. 2 (May 2011), 139–52; and Denis Edwards, *Partaking of God: Trinity, Evolution, and Ecology* (Collegeville: Liturgical Press, 2014).

29 See John Caputo, *Heidegger and Aquinas: An Essay on Overcoming Metaphysics* (New York: Fordham University Press, 1982); and *The Prayers*

and Tears of Jacques Derrida: Religion without Religion (Bloomington: Indiana University Press, 1997).

30 See Jean-Luc Marion, *The Idol and Distance: Five Studies*, trans. Thomas A. Carlson (New York: Fordham University Press, 2001); *God without Being*, trans. Thomas A. Carlson (Chicago: University of Chicago Press, 1991); and *In the Self's Place: The Approach of Saint Augustine*, trans. Jeffrey L. Kosky (Stanford: Stanford University Press, 2008).

31 See Louis-Marie Chauvet, *Symbol and Sacrament: A Sacramental Reinterpretation of Christian Existence*, trans. Patrick Madigan SJ and Madeleine Beaumont (Collegeville: Liturgical Press, 1995).

32 See O'Regan, *The Heterodox Hegel* (Albany: SUNY Press, 1994); *The Anatomy of Misremembering: Von Balthasar's Response to Philosophical Modernity*, vol. 1: *Hegel* (New York: Crossroad, 2014); "Žižek and Milbank and the Hegelian Death of God," *Modern Theology* 26, no. 2 (April 2010), 278–86; and "What Theology Can Learn from a Philosophy Daring to Speak the Unspeakable," *Irish Theological Quarterly* 73 (2008): 243–62.

8 Continental Philosophy as a Source for Theology: The Case of the "Science–Religion" Debate

ANNE M. CARPENTER

Introduction

"God," writes the fourth-century Greek theologian Gregory of Nyssa, "is not dependent on anything for His beauty; His beauty is not limited to certain times or aspects; but He is beautiful by Himself, through Himself, and in Himself."[1] One of the essential difficulties for theology as a discipline is that its central object of inquiry, God, cannot be known directly. If God depends on nothing in order to "be," then it is hard to know or speak of God at all, let alone to speak sensibly of God in a universe filled with many other, more tangible things to know. As Gregory writes elsewhere, "Men have never discovered a faculty to comprehend the incomprehensible."[2] There is a way, then, that the modern conflict or crisis between science and theology strikes at the heart of a perennial problem in theology, which is that there are very many knowable things in the world, and God is not one of them. The more concrete and inescapable that science becomes, the less stable theology appears. Science makes the problem in theology particularly sharp and painful and has often come to symbolize fundamental doubt in the authority of theology. But it is not adequate to simply reinforce theology's legitimate reason and authority. We must also show how theology is able to engage with science and survive intact, and we must do so while at the same time learning from science. The purpose of my chapter in response to this problem is twofold: (1) to elucidate the essential contours of the relationship between science and theology, with particular attention to (2) how philosophy persists within or underneath both, performing the work of mediation. Phenomenology will prove itself to be especially helpful here, and we will come to see that *theology needs philosophy in order to mediate the discoveries of science to itself*. I will proceed through my argument by first reviewing some historical matters, then making key distinctions between types of knowledge, then clarifying aspects of theology's basic grasp of the world, and finally by explaining elements of philosophy's mediation using Continental philosophy. The work I do here exists at the border between philosophy and theology, seeking to establish possibilities for theology by reflecting philosophically.

Arranging the Pieces to a Problem: Theology and Science

It is not my goal to address every aspect of the problem of science and theology, or even to attempt a general reconciliation between them. In this section, I draw from only some of the dynamics peculiar to theological engagement with science and with the philosophies presumed by scientists, dynamics that are available to us both in the historical experience of America and in the discipline of Catholic theology as a whole. From there, I will stress a specific arena of difficulty that relates especially to the discourse of this volume: the relationships between theology, North America, and Continental philosophy.

One of the first elements that marks theology apart from philosophy is the particular role that authority plays in the theological conversation about science. There are unique American markers in this conversation, particularly around the authority of the Bible. Mark A. Noll argues that American evangelical Christianity underwent swift changes during the early republic, when Americans began to emphasize a "Christian republicanism" that focused on individual liberty and that "fundamentally distrusted authority handed down from on high."[3] The only unquestioned authorities in the early American republic were the Bible and science, which were not yet in conflict. Christianity and democracy were therefore understood together. Beginning in the mid-nineteenth century, the evangelical, republican emphasis on the literal interpretation of Scripture as grasped by the ordinary person came into conflict with the emergence of the modern university and more complex forms of scientific inquiry. Says Noll: "As they saw the practical and intellectual dangers of American life in the early twentieth century, most evangelicals turned with increasing fervor to traditional Christian confidence in the Bible, but also the Bible as it had functioned so powerfully in earlier American history."[4] That is to say, literal, individual interpretation of the Bible continued to be used as the essential hermeneutic for Christian self-understanding, a self-understanding that was not immediately separable from national identity. This hardened divisions between scientific inquiry and Christian faith.

Philosophy deals with authorities of its own, but theology concerns itself with the authority of revelation – that is, the authority of the God who speaks and acts in human history. Revelation is the totality of what God has said and done in the sacred history of the world, a totality that is ultimately understood to be at its final height in God's *self*-revelation in Christ.[5] Theology owes itself to this revelation and bears a certain deference to it. That deference extends variously to the authorities of Scripture, sacred tradition, the Church, and so forth. While these elements of authority can be mapped quite differently depending on things like denomination and historical location, still theology as a discipline emerges from distinct claims, which it strives to preserve. The conversation about science and theology is, at least in part, a crisis over what bears the authority of truth *in theology*, and in what way. I will not be addressing problems of authority directly, but we will see elements of it appear in the argument that follows.

Catholicism is marked by concerns of its own that have shaped its responses to science. Scholars speculate that the historical memory of Galileo influenced the Vatican's response to evolution, rendering the Magisterium hesitant to offer a single, universal response to a single theory.[6] At the same time, Catholicism is deeply characterized by analogical thinking that has continually emerged as trust and interest in the natural world as revelatory of God. Convictions such as the analogy of being render Catholicism unable to ultimately tolerate a division between faith and reason, with the consequence that one must choose between the Bible or science. This encourages Catholics to engage more positively with scientific theories or at least to work harder to reconcile those theories with faith.

It is also clear that, at least in America, much of the conversation about science and theology has been funnelled through problems between biblical creation and evolution.[7] This has had the somewhat problematic effect of narrowing the questions asked about just what is happening when science and theology interact with each other. A further and related constriction on the problem between science and theology is the emphasis on scriptural interpretation, a constriction that is important yet that threatens to leave out vital unasked questions. These unasked questions are of particular interest to me in this chapter.

We move now to those questions that underpin the problem of evolution and theology, and in doing so we move much more definitively into a Catholic theological mode of reflection, one focused on epistemological, methodological concerns. We need to ask how theology and science might both reasonably make sense of the created world, and how – before they interact with each other – they come to meaning on their own terms. This brings us into a confrontation with a familiar ghost of modernity: scientific reductionism, and its conflict with the possibility of metaphysics. It also demands that we ask questions about human knowing in general.

Science and Metaphysics

One of the great threats to theology has been the total identification of human knowledge with scientific knowledge. Such a collapse of reasoning entirely blocks the possibilities of theology and of philosophy, since neither employs exclusively scientifically verifiable data in its methods. In the reductionist account of human understanding, neither philosophy nor theology is "real." Only science, as empirically verifiable, is real. At best, theology and philosophy are word games, trading among empty meanings using empty language. Overcoming this kind of scientific reduction requires more than denying it, however. "The issue," Neil Ormerod explains in one of his essays on science, "is one of confusion between the nature of scientific explanation and that of metaphysical explanation."[8] Our definition of "metaphysics" here need only be minimal: metaphysics is non-material reality. Science explains what is material but not what is non-material. So another way of positing the confusion in at least some theories of scientific knowledge is this: scientific reduction presumes that science and metaphysics ask the same kinds of questions.

We can find a way to navigate these perplexities and the potential dangers for theology through Bernard Lonergan's careful reflection on the nature of scientific inquiry and its relationship to human knowing. In the work *Insight*, among others, Lonergan distinguishes between "classical" and "statistical" forms of investigation. These, he says, are complementary but nevertheless distinct horizons of questions – with different heuristic structures – focused on distinct types of events.[9] Classical investigations are those like Aristotle's reflections on nature, and they seek to understand what Lonergan calls *systematic processes*. In these processes, human understanding focuses on the wholeness of every event, a wholeness that forms a single intelligibility that corresponds to the event or events.[10] Aristotelian nature, to continue the example, considers an organized unity and the wholeness of its intelligibility: "human being," or "plant being," and so forth. Metaphysics is just one of several types of inquiry that seek to discover systematic processes. It asks questions of wholeness and of unified intelligibility. By contrast, statistical investigation seeks to understand *non-systematic processes*, where there is, according to Lonergan, "no single insight or set of unified insights, that masters at once the whole process and all its events."[11] As Patrick Byrne explains it, "the defining feature of a non-systematic process – whether ideally constructed or actually occurring – is that the concrete insights which enter into its explanation must lack unity."[12] Aristotelian categories do not apply here; or rather, Aristotelian categories are not what Lonergan would call "explanatory" in these cases. While these two types of inquiry (classical and statistical) are *not* unrelated, and their objects of study are *not* entirely separate, we can say that statistical investigation answers questions that classical investigation does not, and vice versa.[13]

We need to establish some further clarifications. First, there is not a strict separation between science as statistical and theology as classical, since the former can also be classical. Any abstract law, any idealized theory, is what Lonergan would call "classical." Classical laws, even in science, help explain systematic processes such as thermodynamics, but they do not predict or explain specific permutations or events. Byrne uses the example of an oxygen molecule travelling through a room: at the level of theory, every movement of the molecule could be explained by a classical law, but "a different concrete insight" is needed for each specific engagement or movement. "Hence the total path of the molecule – its nonsystematic process – will possess a complete, but not a unified, explanation."[14] In other words, there is no unified theory of the molecule's path through the room; there are theories about all the elements of that path.

Lonergan's distinction between classical and statistical forms of investigation allows us to attribute meaning both to intelligible laws and to the apparent randomness involved in many scientific processes, such as evolution.[15] Randomness, for Lonergan, is not ultimately intelligible to human reason.[16] We can grasp statistical, aggregate norms, but these are not the same as unified intelligibility. We cannot say exactly what evolution will do, for example; we cannot say which permutations will take place precisely *because* they are random and in that sense non-intelligible, at least to us.

There is one final insight from Lonergan that we need before we can move into the second half of this chapter, which will be the argument properly speaking. Neil Ormerod, relying on Lonergan's work, points out that we not only muddle classical and statistical inquiry but also tend to muddle the nature of inquiry itself. In scientific reductionism, Ormerod explains, "[t]he possibility that Aristotle identifies as the basis for making a distinction between physics and metaphysics – that not all reality is material – is not even considered a possibility. Physics becomes first philosophy."[17] Strict materialism cuts off any dream we might have of theology and philosophy serving a purpose at all, because there can be no non-material reality, and thus no metaphysics. There can certainly be no God. Yet, Ormerod points out, the scientific method is based not only on empiricism but also on a fundamental metaphysical (non-material) claim: that the things of the world are intelligible at all.[18]

Science's basic trust that the world is knowable is a metaphysical claim, and this not only implicitly affirms metaphysics but also implicitly affirms science's possible engagement with metaphysical questions such as those that occupy theology and philosophy. This does not mean that all of science's claims are identical with metaphysical ones. It simply means that science affirms and presupposes the basic reality of metaphysics and that it is open to a metaphysical universe. With this openness in mind, we move into metaphysics more properly speaking.

Transitioning to Continental Philosophy: Robert Sokolowski and the Christian Distinction

We have thus far spent our time establishing some of the contours of the dialogue – at times the conflict – between science and theology, especially as that conflict has taken shape in North America and as it takes shape in some of the philosophies that scientists sometimes presume. Lonergan, by allowing us access to key clarifications, helped make way for a more careful discussion of a fruitful relationship between science and theology. While those clarifications may at first seem to be negations – scientific understanding is not identical to metaphysical understanding – they in fact allow for scientific and non-scientific inquiries to have integrity proper to themselves. Each field asks questions in horizons unique to itself, and this allows for the possibility of engagement even while distinguishing those fields from each other.

I want to introduce a specifically *theological* concern at this point, or at least, a claim and an interest that persists at the ambiguous border between theology and philosophy. Robert Sokolowski, an American philosopher and theologian who has done considerable work in both phenomenology and metaphysics, has insisted that Christianity bears an absolutely unique metaphysical claim: the distinction between God and the world. Sokolowski calls this simply "the distinction," and I will spend some time with it before examining its relevance to Continental philosophy and, finally, to theology's relationship to Continental philosophy.

In *The God of Faith and Reason*, Sokolowski begins with the eleventh-century monk Anselm's understanding of God. For Anselm, Sokolowski explains, "[t]he God of Christian faith is such that reason cannot deny his existence."[19] This argument not only affirms the existence of God but also – indeed, primarily – establishes the relative freedom of reason with respect to faith.[20] Anselm's argument for God's existence famously involves his description of God as "that than which no greater can be thought" (*aliquid quo maius nihil cogitari potest*), the so-called ontological argument for God. This argument has been critiqued in subsequent generations, including by Thomas Aquinas.[21] What Sokolowski points out about the argument is that it is not only explicitly comparative – God is greater than all possible thought, and God is real – but also implicitly so: explicitly, it compares God with human thought; implicitly, it compares the world with God. Or rather, the argument suggests that the two are not separate items of comparison at all. In order to work, Anselm's logic presumes the following, in Sokolowski's words: "(God plus the world) cannot be conceived as greater than God alone; or: (God plus any creature) cannot be conceived as greater than God alone."[22] That is to say, God's greatness – or God's existence – is such that the existence of creation, and the existence of creatures, neither adds to nor subtracts from God. This presupposition is, for Sokolowski, what marks Christianity's understanding of God apart from others – most of all from the paganism that originally surrounded Christianity – and it is the presupposition that supports every other unique claim that Christianity makes about the divinity.

Christian thought begins with a distinction between God and the world, a distinction that clarifies both together while at the same time separating them. God is not an object in the world, and the world receives its existence from God. More radically, this distinction is such that God's goodness is neither furthered nor lessened whether or not the world exists. Whereas Plato and pagan philosophy considered distinction from the perspective of "the whole," Sokolowski explains that in Christianity "the world or whole itself is placed as one of the terms of a distinction."[23] Sokolowski then sets out this new thought-form's implication: "It is not just that things could have been very different from the way they are; we are now to speak of things, and of the whole, as possibly not having been at all."[24] Again, God and the world are not two objects of comparison. This distinction between God and the world is "most primary" yet also "capable of being obliterated," because the world does not *need* to exist at all.[25]

In other words, Christians imagine God such that his perfection, power, and goodness are complete and entire. It is as Gregory of Nyssa said at the beginning of this chapter: "God is not dependent on anything for His beauty." God does not need to create or to redeem in order to be God, nor to be "more" divine. This makes Christian discussion of God both radically analogical – Thomas says we can know *that* God is, but never *what* God is – [26]and it makes creation radically secondary, dependent. Perhaps paradoxically, this distinction also means that creation (as non-necessary, entirely secondary) receives its existence and integrity (that is, bearing laws of its own) out of the total freedom and goodness of God. Creation might not have been, and that it *does* exist renders it an immense gift.

For Sokolowski, the distinction is presupposed in the earliest decisions that Christians made in the midst of theological controversies.[27] "[I]t enters into their formulation and helps determine how they must be decided." For example, the distinction helps make sense of the Incarnation, since it describes how God is not in the world, and then helps us say how remarkable it is that God does enter his own creation as a part of it.[28]

The distinction persists at the ambiguous border between philosophy and theology as sensible to both. I follow Sokolowski in the conviction that, while its contours are deeply philosophical, it is in fact a theological claim, since it emerges with the advent of Christianity, is first formulated in theology, and explains Christian understanding particularly. It is nevertheless not necessary to follow either Sokolowski or myself in this insistence. The payout for these reflections may not be immediately clear to us at this point in the chapter, outside of making clear why theology would be invested in preserving the possibility of metaphysics from the grasp of reductive empiricism. That is to say, the Christian narrative of redemption in Christ relies heavily on the underpinning metaphysics of the distinction, and it cannot make (good) sense of itself without it. There is more here, more that will appear for us in the thought of Continental philosophers, but we have as yet only seen glimmers of it. For now, we hold the distinction in mind while we turn our attention to a specific scientific question and how it might be philosophically appropriated by theology.

Toward Continental Philosophy: Theology and Mediation

We can already see how philosophy, through both Sokolowski (who speaks in explicit theological terms) and Lonergan (who speaks implicitly so), *makes room for* theology in the modern scientific landscape. We still need to explore what it means for philosophy to "make room" for other thought-forms such as theology, but it is first important to notice the dynamic itself. Faced with an intolerable crisis between the authorities of reason and of faith – a decision between science and faith – philosophy appears on the stage with keen distinctions and deep awareness of the philosophy that rests "underneath" the scientific enterprise. This philosophical exploration or excavation allowed for us to discover the conditions of possibility for theology's continued legitimacy alongside science, without sacrificing the uniqueness of either. My central task through the rest of this chapter is to examine how it is that philosophy mediates the world to theology, especially how the tradition of phenomenology does so.

What we have so far, philosophically, are useful distinctions between theology and science. We have established a basic claim that theology cannot do without, namely, the distinction between God and the world. This leaves a lot of room for further reflection while still leaving open what it would mean for theology to seek and subsequently borrow scientific insights for its own, explicitly theological purposes. I want to claim that phenomenology in particular helps us by expanding the borders between philosophy and theology, as well as between science and what we might call "the real." That is to say, phenomenology enables a legitimate discussion of ambiguities between forms of knowledge and points to their potential transposition.

I will begin with a concrete example from science and its examination of human memory. Scientifically speaking, at this point in time individual memory is considered a highly unstable reality. While it is true that the human brain retains much in its complex neural pathways over time, it is also true that memories are "editable." In the process model of psychology, which uses the analogy of computer processes to describe the brain's functions, the "activation" of a memory as it is "retrieved" renders it malleable to change, and indeed the memory is *typically* changed based on present needs. Memory is not really retrieved by rote, as if it were stored whole somewhere like a digital recording, then filed away again. Other psychological models vary in the ways they describe the experience of memory, but all agree that memories can be changed. The effects can be far-reaching, even devastating, but they are ultimately a sign of psychological health. The brain is, somehow, "meant" to work this way. In trauma, memories lacking this element of flexibility or "edit-ability" become a *problem*: the trauma victim cannot grasp the difference between the "triggered" memory and the present. Theories vary greatly as they attempt to describe these phenomena, and this variation is often accompanied by disagreement and controversy.[29]

Another important element of memory that science has tried to name involves the active "reconstruction" of memories. Experimental data show that whenever we recall a memory, we also construct it. That memory does not exist as an independent set of images and sounds like an old film reel or a digital file. The brain re-creates the memory as it recalls it, and it does so effortlessly and immediately.[30] It is hard not to infer from the research that has been done that memory is entirely unreliable, especially when we speak at a popular level, but this is a reduction of the evidence to its lowest common denominator (that is, flexibility or change).[31]

Reducing memory to its neurological processes and calling it unreliable is problematic to theology for more than one reason. We are, first of all, observing a tendency we have already noticed thanks to Lonergan's work: an inability to differentiate between kinds of questions and kinds of claims. Neurological systems and their functioning are not identical with human consciousness. Second, the falsification of memory poses a threat to many of Christianity's deepest claims, particularly from a Catholic point of view. If memory is unreliable, then so is testimony; if testimony is unreliable, then so are the biblical and historical witnesses to the resurrection of Christ. The heart of Christian faith would be, on this view, either highly untenable or impossible to posit one way or the other. Tradition, which hands down the witness of faith from generation to generation (*tradere*, to hand over), would be rendered nothing but a large question mark, an untenable basic ground. Here we have the reduction of a scientific claim to "the real" that threatens some of the basic mechanisms of faith, much like evolution has done with regard to creation stories.

Memory is also an essential way that the other disciplines, including science, understand themselves. Science in conducted in the midst of narratives that emphasize the revolutionary power of scientific understanding and that – as schema – both allow for progress and require revision in order to make that progress. Such is Thomas Kuhn's argument in *The Structure of Scientific Revolutions*.[32] What is more, the scientific process relies on memory inasmuch as it needs to be able to recall past experiments in order to repeat and verify them. The problem of memory, then, constitutes more than a theological crisis. Science and theology face the same crisis, which further emphasizes the key role philosophy might play in mediating between the other two by considering the same underlying problem. I will focus on the theological element of the outcome. So now we must pause, and consider the human memory again, philosophically – especially phenomenologically.

Let us first ask what memory is. This requires us to ask questions about time, since memory takes place within – and is an experience of – time. Husserl's *The Phenomenology of Internal Time-Consciousness* is a key development here: for him, the passage of time is experienced by human consciousness in such a way that it "constitutes" time.[33]

Rather than imagining time as if it were an objective reality impervious to influence and external to the subject, Husserl imagines that time "constitutes" time in the experience of consciousness: within each present moment there is a retention of what has just past as well as an anticipation of the future. A present moment bears markers of where it comes from and where it is going, even if as yet inchoately. Pastness emerges in a direct, thematic way when the "now" of the conscious subject intends toward memory, and futurity emerges in this way when consciousness intends toward the future. In other words, for Husserl an experience contains dimensions of past, present, and future simultaneously, but only as experienced and thematized.[34] This profoundly affects our understanding of memory, since, within a phenomenological analysis, it means that memory is the intention of consciousness in the present, rather than a "calling up" of a static event in a pure chronology. Memory is the dynamic act of remembering, rather than the event alone. As Sokolowski reminds us in his own analysis, memory is "most" itself in the act of remembering, and the malleability of memory is an element of the depth of the phenomenon – which really *is* remembered – rather than a flaw of memory.[35]

It is possible at this point to turn our attention in a hermeneutical direction, particularly since theology is concerned not only with time or memory but also with tradition and interpretation. Ricoeur allows us to follow this link. His final book, *Memory, History, Forgetting*, is a summation of his philosophical career and at the same time a press into the unknown.[36] Or, as he puts it, into "incompletion."[37] He summarizes for us his era's major concerns about memory, and he suggests that philosophy's anxieties are much more ancient than they first appear. According to Ricoeur, our anxiety over the "faithfulness" of memory, and thus over our relationship to the past, reaches back as far as Plato, the Sophists, and the myth of *Phaedrus*. Our relationship to the past is troubled because we bear its "marks" (*sēmeia*), but we do not bear the past itself. We cannot bring back the past; at best, we can only mimic it – imitation, *mimēsis*, as in the arts.[38] In other words, the threat to memory, which is also a threat to our knowledge of the past, is not only that we can forget; it is also that we may not be able to (faithfully) remember at all. For Ricoeur, Augustine lives under the burden of this anxiety in his *Confessions*, and though he does not say so, so perhaps does the Western Christian tradition in general. Augustine's major achievement was to recognize that we have our own, inward sense of time; that is, he saw that "personal" time is not identical with "public" time.[39] What is more, Augustine realized that our relation to the past is first known inwardly, through memory, rather than merely externally.[40] (Husserl, it should be noted, radicalizes these insights.)[41] These claims very much follow Ricoeur's analysis of Augustine in *Time and Narrative*.[42] So, our relationship to "pastness" is first of all and primarily inward rather than "out there" or external to us.

In the modern era – that is, roughly beginning with the rise of historical consciousness in the eighteenth and nineteenth centuries – anxiety over memory widens into anxiety over history. Here Ricoeur recounts for us a worry that bears many analogous burdens to that of memory. History, after all, is also only known through its traces or marks, through artefacts and written records. Yet these must be interpreted by the historian. *This*, that is, this place where the historian arrives as a *reader*, is where history presents its own unique problems.[43] The historian comes to a text with questions and a hypothesis already, and, furthermore, the historian comes to a text that itself has already been shaped (pre-interpreted) by its having been archived in the first place.[44] All of this before the historian has even explained the text. Fundamentally, Ricoeur is showing us how history, often viewed as more concrete than memory, does not arrive to us as an unmediated, objective truth. Rather, it is an interpreting and interpreted reality. So, while memory and history are commonly opposed to each other, and while they are not the same, they nevertheless share troubles while also bearing troubles of their own. That is to say, the problem of memory and the problem of history are not problems of what does not work and what does; as Ricoeur points out, the problem for both is ultimately a problem of *temporality* itself. Here Ricoeur's perspective begins to broaden beyond the immediate puzzle of pastness.

Memory and history are each relations to the past, the present, and the future. Ricoeur's "ontological hermeneutics" of temporality is an attempt to show that there is a common reality (temporality, not just the past) that undergirds both memory and history. For him, this does not solve the problems of either so much as it reveals a larger horizon in which the dialectic between the two occurs. It also suggests that the dynamics living within the two are not merely sets of oppositions; this in turn means (for memory) that the *mimēsis* of an event need not be only the non-experience of it, and (for history) that the interpretive endeavour need not leave us without the marks of a real moment. All are, after all, embraced by time. Temporality itself gives way to what Ricoeur calls an eschatology of forgetting and of forgiving (which are not identical to each other). Forgetting, while possible to abuse, is in fact a sign that memory is more than the mere notation of events; Ricoeur points out that Jorge Luis Borges's man who can remember everything is "monstrous" rather than wondrous. Forgiveness, similarly, signals how our relationship to the past is more than merely rote or unchangeable. In other words, Ricoeur starts to use a "play of horizons" to try and indicate possibilities that negotiate our relationship with temporality itself.[45]

Ricoeur is willing to leave his eschatology open and somewhat vague, presenting it both as a possibility and as a necessity. Much more than forgetting, what forgiveness does is allow the real possibility that an agent might be "released from an action"; this release or "unbinding" is a wholly new relationship to the (immutable) past – a relationship to the past as *forgiven*. Ricoeur leaves us nothing more than this potency or incompletion, which closes *Memory, History, Forgetting*, and we might say that here he reaches the wild border between philosophy and theology, and can offer no more.

We can see in Ricoeur's understanding of memory the sketch of it we made in the preceding section: remembering is active, temporally rich, and a powerful symbol of the deep potency of our relationship to what is past. Memory is, even, an anticipation of (or perhaps open to) transcendent realities. Ricoeur shows us quite convincingly how our abilities to forget and forgive suggest that we are not related to temporality at a purely chronological, flat level. There is the potential for transcendence in our experience of time.

Ricoeur's ability to indicate what transcends philosophy without attempting to comprehend it – a skill that phenomenologists like Jean-Louis Chrétien share with him and even surpass him in[46] – can be interpreted simultaneously as a deference to "the difference" and as an affirmation that higher viewpoints are anticipated in lower ones. That Ricoeur is able to show us this latter affirmation reflects an ability held by philosophy most of all, since it is philosophical to indicate it even in the sciences, as Lonergan did. This is one reason why philosophy is both necessary and powerful when theology looks to mediate the truth of the world to itself. Ricoeur's acknowledgment of the difference between God and the world, and his ability to delicately trace the edges of that difference – which theology so precariously straddles – is essential for theology's self-mediation through philosophy. Here is our caution: if his philosophy were unable to defer to what it might be unable to say, or rather, if his philosophy were unable to allow for the possibility of something other than and higher than itself, then it would at best be a wounded and limping avenue for mediating truth to theology. The difference is something of a prerequisite for what theology brings to philosophy before it even begins the work of mediation, a litmus test for what in a philosophy may be useful and what may not be. It is not the totality of what theology approaches philosophy with, but it is a fundamental element. More vitally, "the difference" is what helps us (begin to) illuminate the distinction between theology and philosophy and – it follows – how they approach each other as much as how they part ways with each other. The difference is more than merely ancillary, and Ricoeur's reflections anticipate how this is so. Our hope, born from these insights, is that theology by using philosophy can appropriate scientific insights without conflating science and theology, and that phenomenology is especially attuned and fitting for this appropriation.

We are, in other words, allowed to make room for the depths of the memory of the resurrection of Christ. Deep calls to deep in a significantly more intensive, reverberating way if the phenomenon at hand is that of God. In this fashion, the handing on of tradition and the development of its insights – that "instability" observable in the development of doctrine – is a sign of the infinite richness of Christ, the Resurrected One, rather than a denial of memory's efficacy. As Chrétien says, "the truth given by God, even if given suddenly, needs an eternity to be received, for receiving is also an endless task, and receiving what does not cease is itself ceaseless."[47]

Regarding the Mediation of Meaning: Theology, Philosophy, Science, Memory

What is phenomenology enabling for us here? On the one hand, it clarifies the meaning of memory through its careful analysis of intention and its manifold qualities. New insights emerge from this analysis, allowing us a richer definition of what it means to remember. Phenomenology has often sought such expansions. As Dietrich von Hildebrand says of human feeling, so phenomenology continues to say of human experience generally: "It is high time that we free ourselves from the disastrous equating of objectivity and neutrality."[48] Memory is most itself in the midst of its active recollection, most itself amid the sharp demands of the past and the present. Rote memory, a neutral re-representation, is not the same as authentic remembering. Rote memory would in fact be a kind of *inauthentic* remembering. Phenomenology opens the door to this insight for us, allowing us to see that the popular idea of memory – the notion that it functions like a video reel – does not reflect how it lives in our experiences as human subjects. "The most important contribution phenomenology has made to culture and the intellectual life," writes Sokolowski, "is to have validated the truth of prephilosophical life, experience, and thinking."[49]

This dynamic between theology, philosophy, and science requires more attention. It is not simply that phenomenology has defanged science for the theologian, though that is part of its effect. Notice how the definition of memory has shifted. Phenomenology is able to encompass elements of the scientific understanding of memory's operation (as flexible and active); at the same time, it is able to expand that definition so that theology may employ elements of scientific memory without negating itself (to recall in new ways is not to deny the old). From here, a theologian would be able to introduce theological elements of memory such as tradition, witnesses to the resurrection, and so on, while attending to insights gained from science, such as the reconstruction of memory. These moves in theology, specifically those that begin to relate the active construction of memory to, say, authentic Christian tradition, would further adjust or expand the meaning of memory beyond phenomenology's direct commentary. So there is a certain shift or change effected through philosophy, such that the move from science to theology bears an attendant change in *what* theology is borrowing. I am not only borrowing from science; the meaning of the insight shifts as I do.

I do not wish to imply that the senses of "memory" used in science, phenomenology, and theology are entirely unrelated to one another, or empty in meaning, such that one can simply apply new meanings to anything for any reason. I want only to highlight that the transposition from one field onto another necessarily shifts what is understood, at least in part because the questions asked are shifting as well. We also need to notice how philosophy plays a key role in theology's ability to transpose insights for its own use. In this sense, philosophy is fundamentally mediatory; or rather, theology mediates fundamental meanings to itself through philosophy.

Lonergan understood something about the transposition of meaning between fields, or what he would have called (borrowing from Hegel and, later, Husserl) the move from one "horizon" or "viewpoint" to another.[50] First, he wants us to understand that certain insights rely on others in order for us to make sense of them, and these coalesce in various moving viewpoints that are increasingly integrative. An example is easiest before we can really understand what he means. His example is from mathematics:

> At each stage of the process [of learning mathematics] there exists a set of rules that govern operations which result in numbers. To each stage there corresponds a symbolic image of doing arithmetic, doing algebra, doing calculus. In each successive image there is the potentiality of grasping by insight a higher set of rules that will govern the operations and by them elicit the numbers or symbols of the next stage. Only insofar as a man makes his slow progress up that escalator does he become a technically competent mathematician.[51]

As I move from understanding arithmetic to understanding algebra to understanding calculus, I am learning new rules and operations, with accompanying symbols, each of which also means that I am learning a new set of insights. I am, in other words, understanding math in new ways. To understand the math, I need to know these insights as well as these symbols and processes. Memorizing the appropriate actions is not enough. As I learn, I am at the same time seeing how algebra and arithmetic are different from each other, how algebra employs insights from arithmetic, but in fact quite differently from arithmetic. Each has its own viewpoint, and, for Lonergan, algebra's is "higher" because it can integrate arithmetic's insights into its viewpoint.

Lonergan applies the concept of higher viewpoints outside the realms of mathematics, to other disciplines. So, for example, a higher viewpoint is necessary morally speaking in order for a society to make progress; otherwise, it would be restricting itself to lower viewpoints (and doing so increasingly, when it is experiencing decline). We cannot restrict ourselves to common sense, for example, when considering what we ought to do.[52] At each successive viewpoint, we need to grasp that the insights from what is "lower" anticipate what is "higher" and that *new* insights are required to actually reach a higher viewpoint. Arithmetic will never be algebra. This is why – and it is what Lonergan means when – he insists that higher viewpoints – even, say, within the sciences – are "essentially different" from what anticipated them: "it is because new insights intervene that the higher science is essentially different from the lower."[53]

For Lonergan, philosophy represents a viewpoint higher than that of science: science can anticipate it, as we saw in its implicit metaphysical affirmation, but philosophy is essentially different from it, and new insights are required to enter the discipline's perspective. Philosophy is able to integrate scientific insights, whereas science can only anticipate philosophy. More simply, the structure of questions shifts meanings as well as their consequent insights. Viewpoints are a way of trying to understand these shifts in meaning without rendering them arbitrary. My argument is, essentially, that when we transition from science to the higher viewpoint of theology, philosophy assists in the transposition of meaning. We do not leap from science to theology; rather, philosophy helps mediate our integration of a higher, theological viewpoint. This higher viewpoint is, at least in part, demarcated by Sokolowski's "distinction."

Conclusion

This chapter has spent its time considering the relationship between science and theology, not through a particular conflict between the two, but rather by trying to understand how each arrives at meaning and how those meanings might fruitfully interact. We reviewed a brief history of North America's experience of science and theology and from there considered distinctions important to each field. Lonergan introduced us to the difference between classical and statistical investigations, to science's implicit metaphysical affirmation, and to the differences between viewpoints. Robert Sokolowski helped us understand the difference between God and the world, that unique Christian theological conviction that undergirds much of its grasp of reality. We then saw how, in the distance between science and theology, philosophy not only opens the door for the possibility of theology but also helps theology mediate scientific insights to itself. Within this mediation, we observed that meaning shifts as our viewpoint becomes higher and more integrative. This means that, while dealing with overlapping problems, theology and science are not entirely determinative of each other. Each bears relative independence, and this has bearing on the networks of meanings important to each. Finally, we saw how phenomenology in particular is useful to the mediation between theology and science, and this is the case at least in part because of how adept Continental philosophy is at anticipating further meaning without overdetermining it. Theology itself is structured by a similar anticipation-without-circumscription: it always speaks analogously of the God who speaks and acts and who can never be entirely comprehended. Theology ever desires to speak of this God, and it is forced, in its poverty, to seek as many analogies as it is able. These analogies include those from science, which philosophy helps it mediate to itself. "[T]he true vision of God consists rather in this," writes Gregory of Nyssa, "that the soul that looks up to God never ceases to desire him."[54]

NOTES

1 Gregory of Nyssa, "On Virginity," in *From Glory to Glory: Texts from Gregory of Nyssa's Mystical Writings*, trans. Herbert Musurillo (New York: St Vladimir's Seminary Press, 1961), 111.
2 Gregory of Nyssa, "On the Beatitudes," in *From Glory to Glory*, 98.
3 Mark A. Noll, "Evangelicals, Creation, and Scripture: Legacies from a Long History." *Perspectives on Science and Christian Faith* 63, no. 3 (2011), 150.
4 Ibid., 155. See also 152–3.
5 "In His goodness and wisdom God chose to reveal Himself and to make known to us the hidden purpose of His will (see Eph. 1:9) by which through Christ, the Word made flesh, man might in the Holy Spirit have access to the Father and come to share in the divine nature (see Eph. 2:18;

2 Peter 1:4). Through this revelation, therefore, the invisible God (see Col. 1:15, 1 Tim. 1:17), out of the abundance of His love, speaks to men as friends (see Ex. 33:11; John 15:14–15) and lives among them (see Bar. 3:38), so that He may invite and take them into fellowship with Himself. This plan of revelation is realized by deeds and words having an inner unity: the deeds wrought by God in the history of salvation manifest and confirm the teaching and realities signified by the words, while the words proclaim the deeds and clarify the mystery contained in them." *Dei Verbum* 2.

6 Stefaan Blancke, "Catholic Responses to Evolution, 1859–2009: Local Influences and Mid-Scale Patterns," *Journal of Religious History* 37, no. 3 (2013), 355–6.

7 See, for example, George M. Marsden, *Everyone One's Own Interpreter: The Bible, Science, and Authority in Mid-Nineteenth-Century America* (New York: Oxford University Press, 1982); Karen K. Abrahamson, "Protestant Ecumenism, Religious Freedom, and Theology-and-Science Dialogue in Conservative American Thought: A Literature Review," *Andrews University Seminary Studies* 50, no. 2 (2012): 223–48; Bronslaw Szerszynski, "Understanding Creationism and Evolution in America and Europe," in *Science and Religion: New Historical Perspectives* (Cambridge: Cambridge University Press, 2010), 153–74. For American Catholics, see David Mislin, "'According to His Own Judgment': The American Catholic Encounter with Organic Evolution, 1875–1896," *Religion and American Culture* 22, no. 2 (2012), 134–5; and Alexander Pavuk, "Evolution and Voices of Progressive Catholicism in the Age of the Scopes Trial," *Religion and American Culture* 26, no. 1 (2016), 101–3.

8 Neil Ormerod, "Bernard Lonergan and the Recovery of a Metaphysical Frame," *Theological Studies* 74 (2013), 961.

9 Bernard Lonergan, *Collected Works of Bernard Lonergan* (Toronto: University of Toronto Press, 1992) (hereafter CWL), vol. 3: *Insight*, ed. Frederick E. Crowe and Robert M. Doran, 126–8.

10 Ibid., 71.

11 Ibid., 72.

12 Patrick H. Byrne, "God and the Statistical Universe," *Zygon* 16, no. 1 (1981), 351.

13 CWL, vol. 3, 72.

14 Byrne, "God and the Statistical Universe," 351.

15 See Patrick Byrne, "Evolution, Randomness, and Divine Purpose: A Reply To Cardinal Schönborn," *Theological Studies* 67 (2006), 654–65.

16 Ibid., 661.

17 Ormerod, "Recovery of a Metaphysical Frame," 967.

18 Ibid., 974.

19 Robert Sokolowski, *The God of Faith and Reason: Foundations of Christian Theology* (Notre Dame: University of Notre Dame Press, 1982), 5.

20 Ibid., 6–7.
21 Rather famously, Thomas implicitly does so in his *Summa.* See Thomas Aquinas, *Summa Theologica*, Prima Pars, Q. 2.
22 Sokolowski, *The God of Faith and Reason*, 8–9.
23 Ibid., 31.
24 Ibid., 32.
25 Ibid., 33.
26 Thomas Aquinas, *Summa,* Prima Pars, Q. 2, a. 1.
27 Sokolowski, *The God of Faith and Reason*, 33; see also 34–5.
28 Ibid., 37–8.
29 For the paragraph's information, see, for example, Lars Schwabe et al., "Reconsolidation of Human Memory: Brain Mechanisms and Clinical Relevance," *Biological Psychiatry* 76 (2014), 274–80; on trauma, see Grethe Johnsen, "Posttraumatisk stressforstyrrelse er forbundet med kognitive dysfunksjoner" (in translation), *Tidsskrift for Norsk Psykologforening* 50 (2013), 201–7.
30 A helpful summary of these various trends can be found in Oliver Hardt, Einar Örn Einarsson, and Karim Nader, "A Bridge Over Troubled Water: Reconsolidation as a Link between Cognitive and Neuroscientific Memory Research Traditions," *Annual Review of Psychology* 61 (2010), 141–67.
31 See, for example, the following essay from *The New Yorker*, which struggles with whether memory can be reliable at all: Maria Konnikova, "You Have No Idea What Happened" *The New Yorker*, 4 February 2015, www.newyorker.com/science/maria-konnikova/idea-happened-memory-recollection. The essay is not entirely reductive, but it does consign misattribution to inaccuracy. I suggest that the situation is more complex, and a charitable reading of this author suggests similar conclusions. There is a similar struggle in the psychologist Elizabeth Loftus's TED talk, "How Reliable Is Your Memory?," TED Conferences, June 2013; cf. Elizabeth Loftus, "Eavesdropping On Memory," *Annual Review of Psychology* 68 (2017), 1–18.
32 Thomas S. Kuhn, *The Structure of Scientific Revolutions*, 3rd. ed. (Chicago: University of Chicago Press, 1996).
33 Edmund Husserl, *The Phenomenology of Internal Time-Consciousness*, ed. Martin Heidegger, trans. James S. Churchill (Bloomington: Indiana University Press, 1964).
34 For a helpful explanation of this in Husserl, see Edward T. Oakes, "Christology and Time: Prolegomena to Any Future Apocalyptic" *Logos* 15, no. 1 (2012), 82–112, esp. 90–2.
35 See Robert Sokolowski, "Perception, Memory, and Imagination," in *Introduction to Phenomenology* (New York: Oxford University Press, 2000), 66–76.

36 Paul Ricoeur, *Memory, History, Forgetting*, trans. Kathleen Blamey and David Pellauer (Chicago: University of Chicago Press, 2004).
37 Cf. ibid., 506.
38 Ibid., 12–13.
39 Ibid., 101.
40 Ibid., 96–7.
41 For the comparison between Augustine and Husserl, see again, Oakes, "Christology and Time," 92.
42 See Paul Ricoeur, "The Time of the Soul and the Time of the World: The Dispute between Augustine and Aristotle," in *Time and Narrative*, vol. 3, trans. Kathleen Blamey and David Pellauer (Chicago: University of Chicago Press, 1988), 12–22.
43 Ricoeur, *Memory, History, Forgetting*, 166–76.
44 See ibid., 177ff.
45 Ibid., 413.
46 See the argument in Andrew Prevot, *Thinking Prayer: Theology and Spirituality amid the Crises of Modernity* (Notre Dame: University of Notre Dame Press, 2015), esp. 115.
47 Jean-Louis Chrétien, *The Unforgettable and the Unhoped For*, trans. Jeffrey Bloechl (New York: Fordham University Press, 2002), 113.
48 Dietrich von Hildebrand, *The Heart: An Analysis of Human and Divine Affectivity* (South Bend: St Augustine Press, 1965), 48. N.B.: *The Heart* was originally written in English.
49 Sokolowski, *Introduction to Phenomenology*, 63.
50 These are not purely identical terms in Lonergan, especially as his thought develops over time, but they do overlap and help convey his meaning.
51 Lonergan, *Insight*, 42.
52 CWL, vol. 3, 258–9.
53 Ibid., 282.
54 Gregory of Nyssa, "Life of Moses," in *From Glory to Glory*, 146.

9 How Continental Philosophy of Religion Came into Being and Where It Is Going

BRUCE ELLIS BENSON

Not all that long ago, the very idea of "Continental philosophy of religion" didn't really exist. To be sure, there were thinkers like Gabriel Marcel and Paul Ricoeur (one Catholic; one Protestant; both French) who were in effect *doing* Continental philosophy of religion. But they were in no sense part of a "movement" that could be called Continental philosophy of religion. On the other hand, they were both inheritors of the phenomenological tradition, in their respective ways. Marcel was known as a "Christian existentialist" (a category that for some seemed like an oxymoron), and existentialism, at least of the twentieth-century variety (for such a term has been applied to such figures as St Paul, Augustine, and Shakespeare), was deeply indebted to phenomenology. For Continental philosophy of religion to emerge, though, a new conception of phenomenology was required, one that built upon Edmund Husserl and Martin Heidegger but likewise went beyond and even contradicted them. Early key thinkers in this movement were Jacques Derrida, who effectively blazed a trail (with the help of his North American interpreter, John D. Caputo) and Emmanuel Levinas (who, though older than Derrida, wasn't introduced to the North American context until later). These thinkers helped usher in the era of the full flowering of Continental philosophy of religion.

In what follows, I intend to trace the development of Continental philosophy of religion from its phenomenological roots and then turn to where I think Continental philosophy of religion is likely headed. What we will see is that there are multiple important links that connect Continental philosophy of religion to phenomenology. Yet we will also see that Continental philosophy of religion has, in its own way, moved from the kind of phenomenology associated with Husserl to something that claims to be more Husserlian than Husserl – we might say more "orthodox." Furthermore, while much of Continental philosophy of religion is related to and grows out of phenomenology, not all thinkers working in Continental philosophy of religion arise directly from that tradition. In any case, Continental philosophy of religion is a movement that is very strongly wrapped up with the Catholic intellectual tradition and its institutions, though there are also complications with this assessment. I close this chapter by turning to the question of Continental philosophy of religion's future. Where exactly is Continental philosophy of religion going? What possibilities are there for its future?

The Introduction of Phenomenology to the Catholic Academy

It is not too much to say that the establishment of the Husserl Archives at the Catholic University of Louvain in Belgium was a key moment in changing Catholic thinking and education, in philosophy to be sure but also in other disciplines. Father Leo Van Breda, OFM, then a doctoral student at Leuven, visited Husserl's widow not long after his death and discovered 40,000 pages of unpublished manuscripts. Through a process that reads somewhat like a spy novel, he was able to smuggle those manuscripts out of Germany with diplomatic immunity.[1] This represented an important move because, at the time, Leuven was heavily Neoscholastic in terms of teaching and research interests. While Van Breda was not alone in his interest in Husserl, the climate of the Institute of Philosophy was hardly phenomenological. Despite this, the Neoscholastics found a kind of ally in Husserl, whose emphasis on "the things themselves" fit well with Thomist realism.[2]

Louvain was a strongly international university, and promising students went there from around the world to study philosophy and theology.[3] Of course, it would be too simple to trace phenomenology from Louvain to North America. Many of the early proponents of the movement in North America were at best distantly related to Louvain. For one thing, Husserl had a number of North Americans come to study with him in Göttingen and Freiburg, such as Marvin Farber, Dorion Cairns, and Charles Hartshorne. Furthermore, to escape the upheaval in Europe brought about by the Second World War, some phenomenologists immigrated to North America, such as Moritz Geiger, Aron Gurwitsch, and Alfred Schütz. In North America, centres for phenomenology early on included the New School for Social Research (NYC), SUNY Buffalo, Toronto, and McGill.

Yet there were many Roman Catholics who had studied with Husserl and found his work congenial to their faith; for others, it served as a kind of springboard to conversion. One was Dietrich von Hildebrand, who had studied with both Husserl and Max Scheler and who credited the influence of Scheler for his conversion to Catholicism. Another was Edith Stein, who served as one of Husserl's assistants and worked to bring about a kind of synthesis between Husserl and medieval thought. In Scheler, she found a Catholic who was nevertheless a highly respected philosopher. Given her then current identity as an atheist, this was a revelation. While she was particularly influenced by Thomas, her positions on various matters were not strictly Thomistic.[4] Although there are differing views regarding the success of her project, there is no question that the notion of intentionality – so central to phenomenology – was taken over from the Scholastics through Franz Brentano, with whom Husserl had studied. However, there were others less interested in Catholicism, including philosophers influenced by Husserl (though not his students per se), such as Martin Heidegger and Scheler, both of whom eventually left the Church. It is not incidental that Heidegger wrote his *Habilitationschrift* on Duns Scotus.[5] The early phenomenologist Roman Ingarden was a teacher of John Paul II, who himself was a phenomenologist and had been influenced by Husserl, Scheler, and von Hildebrand.

It comes as no surprise to discover that this trajectory is likewise true of Louvain, particularly in the 1960s. Two of the most influential thinkers in phenomenology and Continental philosophy of religion are Msgr Robert Sokolowski at the Catholic University of America, who finished his PhD in 1963 at Louvain, and Father William Richardson, SJ, who earned a PhD and *Maître agrégé* there and later taught at Fordham University and then Boston College. The former was a renowned Husserl scholar; the latter wrote a magisterial work on Heidegger that was supervised by Alphonse de Waelhens, who had published a very early work on Heidegger.[6] Numerous Catholic institutions are home to faculty who studied at Louvain and have spent time at the Husserl Archives. In recent decades, many Catholic institutions in North America have themselves become centres for Continental philosophy of religion. Those institutions include Boston College, Duquesne University, Fordham University, Gonzaga University, Loyola University Chicago, Loyola University Maryland, Loyola Marymount University, the University of Dallas, and Villanova University. Georgetown University and the University of Notre Dame, perhaps the most academically prestigious Catholic schools, are notable exceptions to this description. Why these schools have been less influenced by Continental philosophy is difficult to specify exactly. The most plausible reason is that the most distinguished universities in North America tend to emphasize (either in part or exclusively) Analytic philosophy, which is thought by some to be more "rigorous." There are, of course, quite a number of non-Catholic universities that have faculty working in Continental thought, though they generally do not work in Continental philosophy of religion.[7] In any case, Continental philosophy (and thus Continental philosophy of religion) has never been mainstream. It has always been on the fringe of the philosophical world, and it has been particularly prominent in Catholic institutions.

One explanation for the proliferation of Continental philosophy of religion in Catholic institutions is the genealogy I've offered above (which is hardly complete). That genealogy can be extended to include Paul Ricoeur, a Huguenot Protestant who taught at the Sorbonne and then Nanterre (now Paris X) before taking a post at Louvain for three years.[8] It is a significant part of our story that his assistant in the early 1960s was Jacques Derrida. While at Louvain, Ricoeur was offered the position of John Nuveen Professor of Philosophical Theology at the University of Chicago Divinity School, a chair that had been occupied by Paul Tillich. He served in that capacity until his retirement in 1992, though during this time he also taught at the Husserl Archives in Paris. His successor in that chair was Jean-Luc Marion, someone we will turn to later.[9]

Another explanation for the growth of Continental philosophy of religion is that Catholic universities in North America often found themselves in situations similar to that of Louvain. In short, they were largely Thomist in orientation and phenomenology provided a way of thinking that was different from yet also compatible with such an orientation. Furthermore, phenomenology provided something that was deeply satisfying *existentially*, something that touched the individual in a personal way. Consider what John D. Caputo says of his early years of study:

> Having come of age intellectually in the bosom of the Catholic Church, having had the good fortune to be educated by a handful of intelligent, progressive Catholic teachers in high school and professors in college, it was the intellectual culture of continental Europe, German and French, that most spoke to our hearts, addressing what we called in those days – and the word still has a use – the *existential* questions. Those questions show up pointedly in art, religion, and philosophy, and make up the passion of my life. They search for truth existentially conceived, which Søren Kierkegaard – a lifelong hero of mine – called a truth "to live and die" for. It was not an accident that so many Catholic graduate programs in philosophy – surrounded on all sides by an Anglo-Saxon Protestant culture and a philosophical climate that had abandoned American Pragmatism and adopted a more positivist, empiricist, and

> logicist approach to philosophy – went "Continental." After Vatican II, which was spearheaded by French and German theologians, Continental philosophy was the discourse of choice for most Catholic and recovering Catholic philosophers who were looking for an alternative to the austere scholasticism on which they were raised.[10]

Here I think Caputo lays out what would likely have been the two alternatives of the time and argues that neither seemed like a good choice. Regarding Scholasticism, his own take was that it was "austere," which I take to mean that (among other things) it was theoretical and detached from everyday life. Yet positivism, the alternative that had invaded most of the centres of higher learning – certainly the "Ivy League" – was not really an option. One can't forget that positivism had ruled out the possibility of either ethics or religion making truth-claims. In fact, as long as positivism reigned in North America (up until the 1980s), it really wasn't respectable to be a religious believer in philosophical circles such as the American Philosophical Association (APA). The proof for that claim is simple: once logical positivism had been thoroughly discredited, religious believers started to make significant inroads into such circles, and many of them cited this change, which led to the rise of the Society of Christian Philosophers in 1978. Officially, the SCP endorses no particular school of philosophy, though most of its members work in the Analytic tradition, doing what I will term here Analytic philosophy of religion. The SCP now has nearly 1,000 members, who are published by prestigious journals and university presses. Clearly, Analytic philosophy of religion has been a success.

A somewhat different take on being exposed to Continental philosophy is that of Adriaan Peperzak, who writes:

> While studying at the Institute for Philosophy at the University of Leuven in Belgium, I continued to discover the spiritual world of old and new philosophers. Kant, Hegel, Heidegger, Husserl, and French phenomenology were interpreted and admired by my professors, several of whom were priests; but, although the Institute had been founded as a school for Neo-Thomism, most of them refused to speak about the links between philosophy, faith, theology, and spirituality ... Although the climate of Leuven was Catholic, the theoretical assumptions on which most professors in philosophy based their teaching were hardly different from those that ruled the University of Paris, where I obtained my doctorate. There the only professor who thematized the links between philosophy and theology was Paul Ricoeur, whom I got to know and greatly admire while he was the director of my dissertation.[11]

What Peperzak is talking about here becomes clear when he says that his professors both in Louvain and in Paris had "accepted the modern postulate that separates autonomous reason, as displayed in philosophy and the sciences, from a theology that appeals not only to historical sciences and philosophical thought, but also, and principally, to the authority of Scripture and the Church." He rightly connects this view with modernity, though he claims that "'postmodern' is a word with so many meanings, including several vague and confused ones, that its utility has become minimal."[12] I agree that we are at the place where the word "postmodern" doesn't seem to do much work, though no one has come up with a better term to replace whatever it is that comes after modernity (itself a fraught term), assuming that modernity is really over (itself a fraught assumption).

However, what I find interesting about these two accounts is that they are so *similar*. This might not be apparent at first glance. Caputo speaks highly of the appearance of Continental philosophy because it spoke to him existentially. Similarly, Peperzak speaks of philosophy as being "a way of life." Peperzak's worry is that all too often, scholars both secular and Catholic disconnect their lives and traditions from their philosophizing. In so speaking, Peperzak is following Pierre Hadot's emphasis that ancient philosophy *was* a way of life. Hadot quotes Plutarch as saying: "Socrates did not set up a grandstand for his audience and did not sit upon a professorial chair; he had no fixed timetable for talking and walking with his friends ... He was the first to show that at all times and in every place, in everything that happens to us, daily life gives us the opportunity to do philosophy."[13] If philosophy truly is a way of life, then *everything* in our lives is connected to it. Peperzak speaks of "the existential elements of life" as conditioning our thinking.[14] This is one of the great faulty assumptions of modern thinking – that one's everyday life and one's scholarly work are two different things. If anything, it is exactly the opposite: *who* we are, *how* we live, and *what* circumstances we find ourselves in are all very much connected to our thinking and writing. In this respect, Caputo and Peperzak fundamentally agree, despite their differences on other matters.

This recognition that philosophy is a way of life may seem new – or, at least, *new to us*. As it turns out, it's a very ancient notion. Whereas modern thinking disconnects everyday life from thought, pre-modern thinking sees the two as deeply connected. Moreover, modern thinking puts forth the idea that we can know the world "objectively," which essentially is a claim that we can know in such a way that our subjectivity – that we are subjects – can be left behind. Yet we always see the world from a point of view, as both Husserl and Heidegger realized. Even this language is problematic, however, for it fails to take into account our existential being (which is not reducible to anything like a mental "view"). For philosophy to be a way of life it cannot simply be thought – it must be *lived*. Or, better, it can only be thought *by* being lived. This is, as it turns out, what both Søren Kierkegaard and Friedrich Nietzsche make very clear. And this is also what makes their writings so interesting and inspiring, whether one agrees with them or not. It's not hard to see why Caputo would name Kierkegaard his hero. Both Kierkegaard and Nietzsche play a prominent role in Continental philosophy of religion. It is hard to overstate their influence on thinking being done today.

I have discussed the importance of Husserl for Continental philosophy of religion. Now we need to turn to Heidegger. Among the important texts for the development of Continental philosophy of religion are the lecture courses Heidegger gave in the 1920–1 academic year, "Introduction to the Phenomenology of Religion" and "Augustine and Neoplatonism." In those lectures, he makes it clear that he is describing religious life, not "dogmatic or theological-exegetical concerns." Instead, he wants to provide "guidance for phenomenological understanding," for it is only with this that "a new way for theology is opened up."[15] What Heidegger provides are readings of Galatians and Thessalonians that attempt to return to what he terms "primordial Christian religiosity."[16] His goal is not to find something like the "essence" of religious experience but to describe that experience even while still acknowledging its historical and subjective features. It becomes clear in these courses that religious experience for Heidegger becomes paradigmatic for experience in general, though what he means is a kind of primordial Christianity that has not yet been covered over by Neoplatonic and Augustinian thought.

That paradigm of religious experience is clearly in evidence in Heidegger's *Being and Time*, a text that has proved highly influential in directing the course of Continental philosophy in general and Continental philosophy of religion in particular. Ostensibly, the text is about the question of the meaning of Being, yet Heidegger ends up studying the being of a particular being – *Dasein*. As such, *Being and Time* becomes a deep phenomenological investigation into how *Dasein* exists, in much the same way as one experiences religiosity. To be sure, the work is truly phenomenological in nature. Yet Heidegger himself, the former seminarian, reminds us that he never could have embarked on this path apart from his theological background.[17] In the years leading up to *Being and Time*, he spent time studying the medieval Scholastics and mystics, Luther, Hegel, Schleiermacher, Otto, and Dilthey. Yet a thinker very close to Heidegger – and to whom he would grow even closer over time – was Kierkegaard. Although Heidegger in *Being and Time* does not take up Kierkegaard's notion of "spirit," which he thinks entangles Kierkegaard in Hegelian metaphysics, he does take much over from Kierkegaard's ontology of the human being.[18] Like Kierkegaard, Heidegger believes that *Dasein* can only be understood by way of its relations both to the world and to others. The Kierkegaardian features of Heidegger's thought – some of which he acknowledges and others of which he hides – are many. Heidegger follows Kierkegaard in relating everyday historical life to thought. The existential themes that concerned Kierkegaard likewise concern Heidegger, though these are transformed into non-religious themes. Authenticity and fallenness are, for Kierkegaard, explicitly Christian notions, while for Heidegger they are simply descriptions of how *Dasein* exists. Regarding authenticity, Heidegger employs the Kierkegaardian themes of anxiety, repetition, and the moment. He likewise is influenced by Kierkegaard in speaking of "levelling down" and of such phenomena as idle talk, curiosity, and ambiguity.[19] Finally, Heidegger follows Kierkegaard in emphasizing death and anticipation as basic to human existence.

The Development of Continental Philosophy of Religion in North America

One of the key moments on the way to Continental philosophy of religion was the appearance in 1984 of Mark C. Taylor's text *Erring*, in which Derrida is presented as a thinker who has something significant to say about religion.[20] That this view seemed novel at the time is an understatement. For Derrida had been deemed by many as someone who promoted an agenda that was anti-realist, relativistic, and even simply nihilistic (though many who made these charges were often unclear as to what they really meant). Those who embraced such an agenda saw Derrida as an ally; those who eschewed it saw him as the enemy. Early on, Derrida was read in North America mainly in the English departments at Johns Hopkins, Yale, and Cornell, though he was also read in philosophy and theology departments to a lesser extent. For many in English departments, his notion of "deconstruction" provided a model of textual reading that was often more destructive than helpful. His "method" resulted in some interesting readings of texts, but those readings were often hard to take seriously, such as the "explication" I once heard at a prominent university that Thomas Paine's *Common Sense* showed that the American Revolution was about *food*.[21]

Another important milestone for Derrida's reception as someone who had theological interests and was not easily put into a neatly packed box marked "deconstruction" was Kevin Hart's book *The Trespass of the Sign*, which appeared in 1989.[22] Hart's book was particularly important because it displayed a deep theological knowledge combined with a sophisticated understanding of Derrida. Similarly, while Caputo's *Radical Hermeneutics* (1987) was more philosophical than theological, it likewise showed that Derrida's thinking was *not* nihilistic – that indeed, it lent itself to many religious themes.[23] However, before Caputo became explicitly Derridean, he had published various books that brought Heidegger together with Aquinas and that provided both an account and a critique of Heidegger's theological turnings, and that deconstructed standard ethical views by drawing on Kierkegaard, Nietzsche, and Derrida.[24]

The year 1997 was pivotal for the development of Continental philosophy of religion in North America. It was the first year of Caputo's postmodernism conferences at Villanova. The inaugural one, held in September, was titled "Religion and Postmodernism." It drew about four hundred participants. That conference included Jean-Luc Marion, Richard Kearney, Merold Westphal, David Tracy, Michael J. Scanlon, Mark C. Taylor, Edith Wyschogrod, Françoise Meltzer, and John Dominic Crosson. Many of these talks had responses by Derrida, who also participated in a round-table discussion with Marion on the nature of the gift. In October of that same year, at a meeting of the Society for Phenomenology and Existential Philosophy, Norman Wirzba and I announced the formation of the Society for Continental Philosophy and Theology. We had simply placed flyers at the registration table, not knowing if anyone would show up, but as it turned out, the room was packed. One couldn't say at this point that Continental philosophy of religion now existed, yet these conferences and society meetings brought together a critical mass of people interested in doing what would come to be known as Continental philosophy of religion. The society's first board included Caputo, Peperzak, David Tracy, Westphal, Wirzba, Wyschogrod, and myself. Yet another event that year was a publication in which Caputo truly baptized Derrida as a theological thinker: *The Prayers and Tears of Jacques Derrida: Religion without Religion*.[25] His text built upon his previous work on Kierkegaard, Heidegger, and Levinas, yet it also decisively demonstrated that Derrida was a theological thinker somewhere between his Jewish upbringing and Christianity. That same year, Caputo also published *Deconstruction in a Nutshell: A Conversation with Jacques Derrida*, a text that provides as clear an introduction to deconstruction as can be imagined.[26]

That Derrida can be read as quasi-religious thinker – or even as a religious person – can be explained by examining three texts in which religion figures prominently.[27] The first, "How to Avoid Speaking: Denials," connects to a long-standing criticism of Derrida's thinking, namely that it bears traces of negative theology. The second, *Circumfession*, is an autobiographical reflection in which Derrida has some telling things to say about himself. The third, *The Gift of Death*, is a meditation on the sacrificial nature of Christianity.

So let us turn to the first text. In "How to Avoid Speaking: Denials." Derrida begins with the notion of the trace, a notion that goes back to a much older text of Levinas. This immediately gets him to the question of negative theology (*apophasis*), which he links to the use of such ideas in his corpus as *differánce*, the supplement, and the *pharmakon*. Already in his essay titled "Differánce," he notes that difference resembles negative theology "occasionally to the point of being indistinguishable" from it. Yet he qualifies this by saying that the "aspects of *differánce* which [he delineates] are not theological."[28] For Derrida, theology and deconstruction are separated in that the former is concerned with God's hyperessentiality, which goes beyond predication and being. So he tells us that deconstruction is not simply the same as negative theology but that the two are not completely separable either, for both partake of the logic that says yet unsays precisely at the moment of saying.

Turning to Derrida's autobiographical reflections in "Circumfession," we see that it takes the pattern of Augustine's *Confessions* as its model. He speaks of "my religion about which nobody understands anything, any more than does my mother who asked other people a while ago, not daring to talk to me about it, if I still believed in God … but she must have known that the constancy of God in my life is called by other names, so that I quite rightly pass for an atheist."[29] What is Derrida's religion, and who is Derrida's God? He is unwilling or unable to delineate either, though they are "unorthodox" enough that he would seem to be an atheist. Yet, like Augustine, he asks: "Quid ergo amo, cum Deum meum amo? [What therefore do I love, when I love my God?]," something that Augustine asks in his *Confessions* but *after* his conversion. Derrida claims "not only do I pray, as I have never stopped doing all my life, and pray to him, but I take him here and take him as my witness."[30]

Finally, *The Gift of Death* contains a sustained reading of the story in which Abraham nearly kills Isaac. Derrida leads up to this story by discussing the logic of sacrifice. In French, the text is titled *Donner la mort*, a euphemism for committing suicide. But his reading is that the logic of sacrifice is that one gives up something of oneself – or even oneself – on behalf of someone else. Such a logic – which one finds in love, the gift, and other figures – is one that can never really explain itself. His reading of Christianity is that it revolves around this logic of sacrifice, which always involves a secret. Abraham cannot tell Sarah or Isaac what he is about to do. Furthermore, he cannot really explain his action. Following Kierkegaard, Derrida invokes the tension between the ethical duty of "giving reasons" for what one does and an absolute responsibility that cannot explain itself. To do so would be to revert to the ethical, which Kierkegaard insists Abraham must not do if he is going to be true to God and his responsibility. To give reasons for an action is not, thinks Kierkegaard, to take absolute responsibility for what one does. Derrida closes the text by invoking Matt. 6:14, which advises giving in secret (not letting the left hand know what the right one is doing). Is this, as Nietzsche would argue, just a ruse to get an even bigger reward, a calculation much more shrewd than giving in the open? Or can one truly give a gift without entering an economy of reward and return? Derrida leaves this question regarding Nietzsche open, though he calls gift-giving and love not impossible but *the impossible*. That gift giving – and love, hospitality, friendship – are in an important sense never fully pure is no reason not to pursue them.

There is an important figure in the development of Continental philosophy of religion whom I have so far left out. In terms of reception history in both France and North America, Derrida comes first and Emmanuel Levinas second. Levinas published *Totality and Infinity* in 1961, but it was some time before his thought became influential among French intellectuals. This was partly because the text appeared relatively late in Levinas's intellectual life, but also because of Levinas's positions in minor institutions (he received an appointment at the Sorbonne only a few years before his death). In contrast, Derrida became an established figure in North America early in his career, particularly in literature departments. Of course, already in an early, lengthy essay (1962), Derrida paid deep attention to Levinas.[31] He was critical of Levinas, but he also deeply appreciated his project. Indeed, as Derrida matured as a philosopher, his thought became progressively more Levinasian. In a 1986 interview, he said that "before a thought like that of Levinas, I never have any objection."[32] So what was this thought? One can read Levinas as responding (largely negatively) to Husserl and Heidegger, yet his critique is really of the entire Western philosophical tradition. In brief, his criticism is that Western metaphysics is all about mastering (one way or another) "otherness" so that there is "the rigorous coincidence between the thought" and the object "which this thought thinks."[33] That charge comes in a text about God, and the point is that Western metaphysicians have attempted to "reduce" the otherness of the other to coincidence with the sameness of the same.

How does one overcome this basic problem, or can it even *be* overcome? Levinas calls for a rethinking of the very structure of philosophy. In place of the freedom of the "autonomy" of the subject called for by Immanuel Kant, Levinas calls for a "heteronomy" in which the other curbs my freedom. In effect, one becomes free by serving the other. Yet the question arises as to just who this "other" is. If Levinas is correct, then the other can never be properly circumscribed, and to attempt such is deeply unethical, for the otherness of the other escapes our grasp. Given Levinas's religious perspective, the paradigmatic figures for the other are the powerless: "The Other who dominates me in his transcendence is thus the stranger, the widow, and the orphan, to whom I am obligated."[34] Given how Levinas draws upon Hebrew Scriptures for his philosophy, it should come as no surprise that his is not merely an ethics, but likewise a philosophy of religion. For Levinas, we encounter God *through* the other. "In the other, there is a real presence of God. In my relation to the other, I hear the Word of God. It is not a metaphor; it is not only extremely important, it is literally true. I'm not saying that the other is God, but that in his or her Face I hear the Word of God."[35] Of course, Levinas also makes clear that God is not merely another other but, instead, "other than the other, other otherwise, other with an alterity prior to the alterity of the other … to the point of his possible confusion with the agitation of the *there is* [*il y a*]."[36] Yet it is precisely regarding this point – the lack of identity of the other – that Derrida is critical of Levinas. If we cannot identify the other, then how do we distinguish between a human being and a stone? Furthermore, Derrida points out that it is precisely the tradition of Greek philosophy that Levinas criticizes that makes his own project even possible. The problem is that – and here Derrida is simply quoting Levinas – one cannot "arrest philosophical discourse without philosophizing."[37] Not surprisingly, Levinas resists this charge. He begins the essay "God and Philosophy" by quoting what Derrida says at the end of "Violence and Metaphysics" – "Not to philosophize is still to philosophize" – and then goes on to insist that he can escape from the Greek *logos* of philosophy. Whether such a project could succeed is a matter I cannot discuss here.

Continental philosophy of religion in North America has been decidedly – even if not completely positively – shaped by the worry of "ontotheology." Although neither Derrida nor Levinas takes up this concern explicitly, one can argue that it is implicit in much of their thought. The idea that the *logos* of philosophy has dominated theology is one that Heidegger took up in a late text, "The Onto-theo-logical Constitution of Metaphysics," which appeared in 1953. While the term "ontotheology" goes back to Kant, the concern for onto-theology, as articulated by Heidegger's text, has driven much of Continental philosophy of religion. Heidegger claims that "metaphysics is theology, a statement about God, because the deity enters into philosophy." In effect, God serves as the ground or ultimate foundation for philosophy by being the first or highest being and the first cause. *This* God is often termed "the god of the philosophers." As Heidegger points out, though, "the deity can come into philosophy only insofar as philosophy, of its own accord and by its own nature, requires and determines that and how the deity enters into it." The result is that "man can neither pray nor sacrifice" nor "fall to his knees in awe nor can he play music and dance before this god."[38] This is a thoroughly domesticized version of "God," one entirely within the domain of philosophy and there to do its bidding.

In 1991, the English translation of *God without Being* appeared. It propelled Marion almost immediately into the heart of the Continental philosophy of religion discourse in North America. One can argue that ever since, Continental philosophy of religion in North America has been shaped by his thought. Not surprisingly, he was given the John Nuveen Chair in Philosophy of Religion and Theology in 2004 (though he had been a visiting professor earlier).[39] For Marion, the death of God proclaimed by Nietzsche is long overdue, given that Marion reads Nietzsche as describing the death of the god of the philosophers. As such, it is merely an idol that "does not have any right to claim, even when it is alive, to be 'God.'"[40] In response to Heidegger's rhetorical question, "Will Christian theology one day resolve to take seriously the word of the apostle and thus also the conception of philosophy as foolishness?,"[41] Marion responds by saying that "to take seriously that philosophy is a folly means, for us, first (although not exclusively) taking seriously that the 'God' of onto-theology is rigorously equivalent to an idol."[42] Central to his text *God without Being* is the contrast between the idol, which is merely a reflection of us and so like a mirror, and the icon, which is like a window through which we gaze so that it "summons sight in letting the visible … be saturated little by little with the invisible."[43] Marion takes Paul's conception of Christ (as the "icon" of God, Col. 1:15) and claims that Christ is the model of all icons, which he terms "saturated phenomena." Whereas Husserl's "principle of all principles" states that the object of consciousness appears "within the limits" of consciousness, Marion argues that that some phenomena simply *exceed* those limits, which means that intuition is overwhelmed by that which is given. In such a case, the ego is no longer in control and is "mastered" by the object. In effect, Marion (following Levinas) is turning Husserlian phenomenology on its head. Marion is particularly concerned with the phenomenon of revelation, which is similar to the experience of going outside Plato's cave. He terms this experience "bedazzlement," in which the intuition of intentionality is simply overwhelmed by sheer excess. Much like Levinas's idea of thinking "otherwise," Marion attempts "to think God without any conditions, not even that of Being," a God who is *agápê*, who appears to us as gift. The result is that "predication must yield to praise" so that "faith neither speaks nor states."[44] Marion asserts that there is a "language" that goes beyond the true and false language of predication.

Given all that we have seen so far, it is no wonder that Dominique Janicaud wrote a text on the state of philosophy in France with the title *The Theological Turn of French Phenomenology*. In that text, he accuses Levinas and Marion (as well as Jean-Louis Chrétien and Michel Henry) of hijacking phenomenology for theological purposes. Although Levinas and Marion (like Ricoeur) make a point of publishing their "theological" works with one publisher and their "phenomenological" works with another, Janicaud's verdict is that the phenomenological texts are just as theological as the theological ones. As he puts it, "despite all the denials, phenomenological neutrality has been abandoned." Instead of providing "scientific" analysis, Janicaud accuses Marion and Chrétien of "theological veering" that "leads to analyses that verge on edification." Similarly, he accuses Levinas of "theological hostage-taking."[45] There are two obvious responses to Janicaud. First, these "new phenomenologists" are actually trying to be *more* true to the principles of phenomenology than were Husserl and Heidegger. In this they may not succeed, but that is what they are trying to do. Second, the question has to be asked: Why is some sort of scientific "neutrality" held up as the standard? Other than simply proclaiming it to be the standard, there is no *argument* that can be adduced that this is the way things must be. Of course, Janicaud is right that these religious thinkers – Levinas, a Jew; Henry, Marion, and Chrétien, Roman Catholics – have used phenomenology for causes that are at least partly religious, if not more so. But it's hard to see why focusing on religious phenomena – or even using religious phenomena as guiding principles – is somehow *bad* or unscholarly. (After all, we have seen that Heidegger takes primitive Christian experience as the model for experience in general.)

Once we realize there is no such thing as neutrality – which is what those who followed the logical positivists realized – then it becomes merely a matter of assumptions made that guide further analysis. To believe there is no God is hardly any more "neutral" than to believe God exists. Both are starting points. After all, one has to start *somewhere* – and that somewhere is never neutral. So one can never say "I am simply doing phenomenology" without any further qualification.

However, once one makes such a recognition, then it is possible for Continental philosophy of religion to bloom, as has been the case. It is no surprise that Continental philosophy of religion in North America has blossomed precisely because of the reception of these decidedly religious figures. One reason for this creative energy is that old assumptions regarding the relation between faith and reason have been strongly put into question. It is Derrida who reminds us that faith and reason always go together, that there is no reason that is without faith, be it scientific, philosophical, or theological.[46] But this, then, puts into question Kant's move of reason "making room for faith." Is it reason that is in control here, or does faith graciously make room for reason? It's not clear which has the upper hand. This is a central point in Levinas's "God and Philosophy," but it is likewise the theme of Marion's recent book, *Believing in Order to See*.[47]

As Continental philosophy of religion stands in North America, it seems to me there are two main strands of thought that are represented by Catholic thinkers. On the one hand, there is the work of Marion and other Catholics, as well as Protestants such as Westphal,[48] who see phenomenology as a way to approach theological concerns. Generally, they are not fazed by criticism from people like Janicaud regarding phenomenological neutrality, since they make no pretence to being "scientifically" neutral. That perspective has resulted in quite a significant amount of scholarship that is very much tied to explicitly religious concerns. On the other hand, one might be worried that such thinkers are still too close to onto-theology, even if they have formally renounced it. In such a case, one might be drawn toward what Derrida calls "religion without religion."[49] That is, a religion that is without the dogmatic and institutional factors of an actual religion. Elsewhere, Derrida distinguishes between religion and faith, saying that the former "can be deconstructed, and not only can be but should be deconstructed, sometimes in the name of faith. Kierkegaard is here a great example of some paradoxical way of contesting religious discourse in the name of a faith that cannot be simply mastered or domesticated or taught or logically understood, a faith that if paradoxical."[50]

Not surprisingly, given his work on Derrida, Caputo picks up on this idea of a religion without religion. He claims that he wants to move toward another "religious truth," one that is "beyond literalism, fundamentalism, and outright superstition without simply repeating an Enlightenment critique of religion whose presuppositions … have been widely discredited." This likewise means a move beyond claiming to be "*the* one true religion" or claiming to have "an *exclusive* possession of 'The Truth.'" Of course, he goes on to say that "a religion without religion cannot do without truth," but it is *"a truth without knowledge."*[51] His point is that believers do not truly understand what they believe (a point with which Marion would agree in principle, though not in degree). It is religion that does not exclude the tragic but fully recognizes it. And it is a religion that finds its basis in love of God, though a religion that is not sure what it means by the very word "God." This leads Caputo to think of God not in terms of strength (as traditional Christian theology would have it) but in terms of *weakness*. He finds inspiration in St Paul, particularly in what the apostle calls the "logos tou staurou" [logos of the cross], and in the "power of the powerlessness of Jesus." As he puts it, "the logos of the cross is a call to renounce violence." It puts God "on the side of vulnerability and unjust suffering" in order "to prophetically protest it."[52] Paul often appeals to weakness to oppose strength, a kind of reversal of the natural order. Yet Caputo points out that this is still a narrative of power, so that these reversals are only apparent. As it turns out, the weakness of God goes all the way back to the beginning of the Hebrew Scriptures, where it can be seen in the creation story, in which God creates not out of nothing (which would make him a truly strong force) but out of something that already exists. Moreover, if God is truly going to love, he must be vulnerable. It is Jesus on the cross, the same Jesus who grieves over the hardness of heart of the religious leaders of his day, who exemplifies this weak force. Caputo ends up giving us an alternative "otherwise," not that of Levinas or Marion, but a kind of "otherwise than power." This leads him to take up themes found in Derrida, such as hospitality and forgiveness. And he is able to refigure the kingdom of God as a community of everyone – since all are called by God – without sectarian differences. Clearly, Caputo is working hard to escape from any kind of onto-theology. As such, he represents a rather different, though clearly complementary, approach to that of Marion. They are both Catholics, but their theologies represent different strains of Catholic theology.

As should be clear at this point, Continental philosophy of religion tends toward apophatic thinking. An overriding worry (one might even say *the* overriding worry) is that of saying too much about God. If God is truly Wholly Other, than there must be significant limits to what can be said of God. In the next section, we turn, even if briefly, to considering the value of that emphasis and whether it might be complemented by the kataphatic tradition (one that assumes that we can say much more about God than the apophatic tradition).

The Future of Continental Philosophy of Religion

There are, then, two main alternatives in Continental philosophy of religion at this point, at least in Catholic theology. One can hold to a robust theological commitment, even if one is circumspect regarding just how far theological discourse can go. Such is the route of thinkers like Marion, Chrétien, and Westphal. *Or*, one can see that theology, as traditionally defined, is truly onto-theological at its core and so needs to be radically rethought. Such is the route of thinkers like Caputo. One might argue that Richard Kearney falls somewhere between these two poles.

Of course, there are many who work in Continental philosophy of religion who write with no explicit religious commitments – scholars such as Thomas Carlson, Jeffrey Kossky, Tyler Roberts, and Mary-Jane Rubenstein. Moreover, there is an entire group of scholars who are part of Continental philosophy of religion but who don't fit as neatly into the genealogy I've provided. French thinkers like Stanislas Breton, Emmanuel Falque, and Jean-Yves Lacoste follow in this trajectory. But things are less clear-cut when we think of Giles Deleuze or Alan Badiou. Similarly, among Italian thinkers like Giorgio Agamben and Gianni Vattimo who have played important roles in Continental philosophy of religion, the latter has written about his own take on religion and faith. In fact, if we consider the introduction to *The Future of Continental Philosophy of Religion* (a text containing papers from the last conference Caputo held at Syracuse), we might conclude there isn't any clear "future" because there is no homogenous past. Continental philosophy of religion has been influenced by far more figures than the ones we have been able to consider here. The editors of that text claim the following: "What we are suggesting, therefore, about the future of Continental philosophy of religion is that we have come to a time when it is more about its different futures."[53]

But let me close this chapter by suggesting two ways of thinking about the future of Continental philosophy of religion. One is how it is done. Over the years, I've come to see that Continental philosophy of religion in North America is largely *expository* in nature. Papers and books tend to be along the lines of "Heidegger on such and such" or "Levinas's view of X." In one very important sense, this is a key strength of Continental philosophy of religion. Those who work in it are generally well-grounded in tradition. They have a sense of the historical place of a thinker, how that thinker's ideas relate to the time period, and how that time period relates to the history of philosophy more broadly. There is much to commend here. Derrida speaks of the importance of a "doubling commentary" in which the reader attempts to provide a reading that is as close to the text as possible. Without this "guardrail," as he calls it, "critical production would risk developing in any direction at all and authorize itself to say almost anything."[54] Careful exposition, then, is crucial.

However, as you probably realized while I was formulating the previous point, there is a "but" coming. Derrida goes on to say that "this indispensable guardrail has always only *protected*, it has never *opened*, a reading."[55] Exactly what counts as a "doubling" commentary rather than a "constructive" one is somewhat difficult to parse out, except at the extremes. Clearly, there is a continuum between the two. The most remarkable doubling commentary I've ever read is one on Heidegger's *Origin of the Work of Art*. It tries to stay so close to the text that, at points, it literally simply repeats what Heidegger writes. What makes this commentary so strange is that it constantly shifts back and forth between quoting Heidegger (without any quotation marks) and commenting, with no separation of the two. Of course, most commentaries have a little bit more room between the text and the commentary. In fact, it's safe to say that even authors who are attempting something like a doubling commentary still end up adding their own point of view. It's like the classical music performer who simply wants to "get it right" and thinks that she's *merely* repeating the score when in reality there is no such thing as pure repetition. Those of us who are jazz musicians are much more aware that we are constantly improvising upon pieces and the tradition. In other words, we know that tradition is not static and that we cannot help but add to it. Put another way, to honour and carry on a tradition *is* to add to it.

Emerson says the following: "Our debt to tradition through reading and conversation is so massive, our protest or private addition so rare and insignificant – that, in a large sense, one would say, there is no pure originality. All minds quote."[56] To be sure, such a statement is somewhat hyperbolic, but the point is clear: none of us are saying something that is totally new. Still, the general tendency in Continental philosophy of religion is respectful commentary that hews rather close to the text. One may be critical at points, or even seriously disagree with the author, while still staying within the bounds of commentary. As I say, this is a *tendency*, not anything like an absolute generality. However, the result is that in Continental philosophy of religion, while there are important authors who move in constructive ways beyond the established boundaries and push the dialogue forward, most everyone else comments on these thinkers and that commentary often is about "getting it right." I spent significant time at the Hegel and Husserl archives and was often astounded how rarely anyone asked "But is Hegel or Husserl right?," as opposed to "What did they mean?"

What would it look like for Continental philosophy of religion to become truly constructive? Here's what I have in mind. A while back, I was speaking with a friend who works on Marion and revelation. My comment was: "This is all very interesting, but what's *your* view of revelation?" A way of getting at this – as well as a way of moving forward – is by considering Analytic philosophy of religion. Given my work, I am often asked to explain the difference between Continental philosophy of religion and Analytic philosophy of religion, or the difference between Continental and Analytic philosophy. We are familiar with the usual stereotypes. Continental philosophers write unclear prose (what the Brits call "woolly"); they don't make arguments; they use weird jargon. By contrast, Analytic philosophers tend to be clearer and to use arguments, but they often talk about wholly theoretical things that have nothing to do with real life – things that are more like some kind of logical puzzle. Although stereotypes often have some degree of truth to them, I think these stereotypes are largely unhelpful. For example, Analytic philosophy of religion has its own weird jargon and Continental philosophy of religion is hardly devoid of argument. Yet I think the real difference between Continental philosophy of religion and Analytic philosophy of religion is the latter's *tendency* is to be much more constructive in nature. There is much to praise about that. Having the courage to state one's own views, to actively put together a theory about some topic, to put something out there that is clear enough to be criticized, is commendable.

Yet I'm sure you can hear that there's a "but" coming here too. Practitioners of Analytic philosophy of religion all too often appear to be creating *ex nihilo*. They aren't, of course, but it often seems that way since they tend to write in a non-historical fashion. If practitioners of Continental philosophy of religion sometimes get lost in history, those of Analytic philosophy of religion tend to be disconnected from it or, at the very least, not aware of how much their work is indebted to tradition. Of course, one doesn't have to be aware of tradition to be influenced by it. Yet, since one is always embedded in a tradition – indeed, multiple ones at the same time – it is much better to be aware of what that tradition is, at least to the extent one *can* be aware. However, the challenge is also to have tradition serve us rather than to simply serve tradition. Nietzsche writes in his essay on history: "We want to serve history only to the extent that history serves life: for it is possible to value the study of history to such a degree that life becomes stunted and degenerate."[57] While I'm not suggesting that Continental philosophy of religion is filled with "stunted and degenerate" philosophers, it strikes me that it can easily become a ghetto in which one is preaching to the choir. That is *not* to say that Analytic philosophy of religion is not ghetto-like in its own way, but the ghetto of Analytic philosophy of religion happens to be considerably larger. Indeed, one need only think of the very category "philosophy of religion" to see that it almost always means *Analytic* philosophy of religion (as becomes clear when one scans the listings in PhilJobs or the catalogues of most university presses).

How, then, does tradition serve life? Nietzsche opens that same essay with a quotation from Goethe: "I have everything that merely instructs me without augmenting or directly invigorating my activity."[58] According to the OED, the term "construct" means "to make or form by fitting the parts together."[59] This is not *ex nihilo* construction, but one that is grounded in tradition. In her wonderful book, Catherine Keller reminds us that *ex nihilo* creation is a highly *masculine* way of thinking about creation and belongs to a discourse of power.[60] Thinking of construction in this way reminds us of our debt to tradition. Yet it also pushes us beyond mere tradition preservation, for construction is what enables us to keep tradition alive and growing. One can't help but think of the parable of the talents here, in which one person is given five talents and doubles these and another is given one talent but buries it in the ground out of fear (Matt. 25:14–30). Construction, then, takes us beyond mere exposition and doubling commentary, but still keeps us connected to tradition. To go back to a musical example, classical music tends to emphasize "originality" (or Bloom's anxiety of influence), but Baroque music and jazz are deeply connected to tradition. With this awareness, one may set out to be constructive by drawing on a wealth of resources, using historical texts to advance thought. This gives us a very different notion of "creativity," in the sense that it becomes about how one uses one's past. Instead of making the study of history an end in itself, one uses history as a springboard to the future.

Yet there is something further that Continental philosophy of religion can do, and I think therein lies great potential. As J. Aaron Simmons and I argue in *The New Phenomenology*, there are many ways in which Continental philosophy of religion and Analytic philosophy of religion relate. True, this is sometimes difficult to see, since jargon on both sides can obscure similarities. Furthermore, there are projects undertaken by Continental philosophy of religion that are of little interest to Analytic philosophy of religion and the other way around. However, as we have argued, these differences should not blind us to similarities, nor should we allow jargon to divide us. If one thinks about the current situation of Continental philosophy of religion and Analytic philosophy of religion, one sees that they are divided less by thought than by institutions. Earlier, I mentioned the phenomenon of respective ghettos or silos. So

Continental philosophy of religion has SCPT; Analytic philosophy of religion has SCP. Work in Continental philosophy of religion tends to be published with presses like Indiana and Fordham, which produce volumes that people in Analytic philosophy of religion generally don't read. Of course, Continental philosophy of religion returns the favour by neglecting publications by those in Analytic philosophy of religion. So why might now be a good time to change this? One thing that has begun to take shape in Analytic philosophy of religion is a move away from almost exclusive concern with questions of justification of belief to questions of practice. Continental philosophy of religion has always been less interested in questions of belief than in those of practice (or, better, how belief actually gets lived out). That Nicholas Wolterstorff has recently been publishing on liturgy is one indication of this move in Analytic philosophy of religion. Furthermore, I think we are at a time in which younger scholars, in particular, are less invested in the artificial distinction between Continental and Analytic. They don't see any reason to limit their projects to the boundaries of just one or the other. And these changes are likewise mirrored even in the APA, which now regularly accepts papers on figures in Continental philosophy (something that would have been unthinkable a couple of decades ago).

Yet the *rapprochement* of Continental philosophy of religion and Analytic philosophy of religion, while a huge step forward, may not be quite ambitious enough. For us to reach something like true interdisciplinarity, the way to proceed is to create a community of scholars who are not interested in preserving existing boundaries but are willing to create a new dialogue, albeit one that grows out of their respective traditions. Just to be clear, the goal is not to have folks in Continental philosophy of religion read Plantinga or people in Analytic philosophy of religion read Marion. I have no doubt that there will continue to be work done in Continental philosophy of religion that looks a great deal like what Continental philosophy of religion has been doing for a while. Yet I would insist that the long-term future for Continental philosophy of religion is one that becomes, to use a motif that is widespread in Continental philosophy of religion, *open to the other*. While Analytic philosophy of religion has long been viewed as "other," such a view promotes a lack of hospitality. Moreover, Continental philosophy of religion and Analytic philosophy of religion bring to the table great respective strengths. There is no reason why the two cannot learn from each other's strengths. If I am correct in that view, then the future of Continental philosophy of religion is not limited simply to one trajectory. It has multiple futures and possibilities that are waiting not only to be realized but to be invented.

NOTES

1 See Leo Van Breda, "The Rescue of Husserl's *Nachlass* and the Founding of the Husserl Archives," in *History of the Husserl-Archives* (Dordrecht: Springer, 2007), 39–69.
2 The great divide in Husserlian texts would seem to be *Ideas I*, in which Husserl seems to turn to an explicitly idealistic position. But this would be an oversimplification. My own view is that Husserl rejects the Realist–Idealist divide as commonly posited, though I can't argue for that here. For a brief but insightful discussion of this see Dan Zahavi, *Husserl's Phenomenology* (Stanford: Stanford University Press, 2003), 68–72.
3 See Dahlstrom's chapter in this volume for a detailed account of figures and institutions hospitable to the early waves of phenomenology and existentialism in North America.
4 See Sarah Borden Sharkey, "Edith Stein and Thomas Aquinas on Being and Essence," *American Catholic Philosophical Quarterly* 82 (2008), 87–103.
5 For more on these connections to Scholasticism, see Dermot Moran, *Introduction to Phenomenology* (New York: Routledge, 2000), particularly the chapters on Brentano and Heidegger. Heidegger's habilitation, *The Doctrine of Categories and Meaning in Duns Scotus*, was based on a text, *De modis significandi*, falsely attributed to Duns Scotus. It was actually written by Thomas of Erfurt.
6 These dissertations were, respectively, Robert Sokolowski, *The Formation of Husserl's Concept of Constitution* (The Hague: Martinus Nijhoff, 1964)l and William J. Richardson, SJ, *Heidegger: Through Phenomenology to Thought* (The Hague: Martinus Nijhoff, 1962). Both these texts were published in the *Phaenomenologica* series put out by the Husserl Archives. Also see Alphonse De Waelhens, *La philosophie de Martin Heidegger* (Louvain: Éditions de L'Institut Supérieur de Philosophie, 1942).
7 A listing of programs "interested in, supportive of, or specializing in Continental philosophy" can be found on the Society for Phenomenology and Existential Philosophy website. Visit www.spep.org/resources/graduate-programs.
8 When Ricoeur taught at Louvain, he would have taught on the French faculty there. At that time, there were Flemish and French faculties. In 1968, at the insistence of the Flemish students who wanted to have their own university, the university was officially split into the Flemish-speaking Katholieke Universiteit Leuven and the French-speaking Université catholique de Louvain, located in Louvain-la-Neuve. This division took place over a number of years. In keeping with the historic usage of the term Louvain in English, I follow that convention.
9 Marion currently holds the Andrew Thomas Greeley and Grace McNichols Greeley Professor of Catholic Studies, a position that had been held by David Tracy until his retirement.

10 John D. Caputo, *Hope against Hope: Confessions of a Postmodern Pilgrim* (Minneapolis: Fortress Press, 2015), 5.
11 Adriaan Theodoor Peperzak, *Philosophy between Faith and Theology: Addresses to Catholic Intellectuals* (Notre Dame: University of Notre Dame Press, 2005), 17.
12 Ibid., 195.
13 Plutarch, *Whether a Man Should Engage in Politics When He is Old*, quoted in Pierre Hadot, *What Is Ancient Philosophy?*, trans. Michael Chase (Cambridge, MA: Harvard University Press, 2004), 38. See also Pierre Hadot, *Philosophy as a Way of Life*, ed. Arnold Davidson (Oxford: Wiley-Blackwell, 1995), 38.
14 Peperzak also claims that even much "postmodern" philosophy can still be characterized as "autonomous, theoretical, thematic, and disengaged" (in *Philosophy between Faith and Theology* [Notre Dame: University of Notre Dame Press, 2005], 4), though he mentions no specific names.
15 Martin Heidegger, *The Phenomenology of Religious Life*, trans. Mattias Fricsch and Jennifer Anna Gosetti-Ferencei (Bloomington: Indiana University Press, 2004), 47.
16 Ibid., 57.
17 For a masterful treatment of Heidegger's relation to theology, see Theodore Kisiel, *The Genesis of Heidegger's* Being and Time (Berkeley: University of California Press, 1993), particularly the chapter titled "Theological Beginnings."
18 Martin Heidegger, *What Is Called Thinking*, trans. Fred D. Wieck and J. Glen Gray (New York: Harper & Row, 1968), 213.
19 These particular themes come from Søren Kierkegaard, *Two Ages*, trans. Howard V. Hong and Edna H. Hong (Princeton: Princeton University Press, 1978).
20 Mark C. Taylor, *Erring: A Postmodern A/theology* (Chicago: University of Chicago Press, 1984).
21 Derrida makes it clear that deconstruction is not a method but something that naturally occurs.
22 Kevin Hart, *The Trespass of the Sign: Deconstruction, Theology, and Philosophy* (Cambridge: Cambridge University Press, 1989).
23 John D. Caputo, *Radical Hermeneutics: Repetition, Deconstruction, and the Hermeneutic Project* (Bloomington: Indiana University Press, 1987).
24 Also by Caputo: *Heidegger and Aquinas: An Essay on Overcoming Metaphysics* (New York: Fordham University Press, 1982); *Demythologizing Heidegger* (Bloomington: Indiana University Press, 1993); and *Against Ethics Contributions to a Poetics of Obligation with Constant Reference to Deconstruction* (Bloomington: Indiana University Press, 1993).
25 John D. Caputo, *The Prayers and Tears of Jacques Derrida: Religion without Religion* (Bloomington: Indiana University Press, 1997).

26 John D. Caputo, *Deconstruction in a Nutshell: A Conversation with Jacques Derrida*, ed. and with a commentary by Caputo (New York: Fordham University Press, 1997).
27 One could add other texts here, but these three are sufficient to get an idea of Derrida's thinking regarding religion. Conversely, a reading of Derrida's texts vis-à-vis their relation to religion that very explicitly does *not* see them as quasi-religious but rather as strongly atheistic is Martin Hägglund, *Radical Atheism: Derrida and the Time of Life* (Stanford: Stanford University Press, 2008). I find this reading unconvincing on multiple levels, though I cannot make a sustained critique here. For Caputo's (highly critical) response, see John D. Caputo, "The Return of Anti-Religion: From Radical Atheism to Radical Theology," in *Journal for Cultural and Religious Theory* 11 (2011), 32–125.
28 Jacques Derrida, "Differánce," in *Margins of Philosophy*, trans. Alan Bass (Chicago: University of Chicago Press, 1982), 6
29 Jacques Derrida, "Circumfession," in Geoffrey Bennington and Jacques Derrida, *Jacques Derrida*, trans. Geoffrey Bennington (Chicago: University of Chicago Press, 1993), 154–5.
30 Ibid., 56–8.
31 Jacques Derrida, "Violence and Metaphysics: An Essay in the Thought of Emmanuel Levinas," in *Writing and Difference*, trans. Alan Bass (Chicago: University of Chicago Press, 1978).
32 Jacques Derrida and Pierre-Jean Labarrière, *Alterities* (Paris: Osiris, 1986), 74.
33 Emmanuel Levinas, "God and the Other," in *Of God Who Comes to Mind*, trans. Bettina Bergo (Stanford: Stanford University Press, 1998), 55.
34 Emmanuel Levinas, *Totality and Infinity: An Essay on Exteriority*, trans. Alphonso Lingis (Pittsburgh: Duquesne University Press, 1996), 88.
35 Emmanuel Levinas, *Entre Nous: On Thinking-of-the-Other*, trans. Michael B. Smith and Barbara Harshav (New York: Columbia University Press, 1998), 110.
36 Levinas, "God and Philosophy," in *Of God Who Comes to Mind*, 69.
37 Derrida, "Violence and Metaphysics," 152.
38 Martin Heidegger, "The Onto-theo-logical Constitution of Metaphysics," in *Identity and Difference*, trans. Joan Stambaugh (Chicago: University of Chicago Press, 2002), 55, 56, 72.
39 For more on Marion's place in Continental philosophy of religion, see the chapter by Gschwandtner in this volume.
40 Jean-Luc Marion, *The Idol and Distance*, trans. Thomas A. Carlson (New York: Fordham University Press, 2001), 1.
41 Martin Heidegger, "Introduction to 'What is Metaphysics?,'" trans. Walter Kaufmann, in *Pathmarks*, ed. William McNeill (Cambridge: Cambridge University Press, 1998), 288.

42 Marion, *The Idol and Distance*, 18.
43 Jean-Luc Marion, *God without Being: Hors-Texte*, trans. Thomas A. Carlson (Chicago: University of Chicago Press, 1991), 17.
44 Marion, *God without Being*, 106, 183.
45 Dominique Janicaud, "The Theological Turn in French Phenomenology," in *Phenomenology and the "Theological Turn": The French Debate*, trans. Bernard G. Prusak (New York: Fordham University Press, 2000), 68, 69, 43.
46 See Jacques Derrida, "Faith and Reason: The Two Sources of 'Religion' at the Limits of Reason Alone," in *Acts of Religion*, ed. Gil Anidjar (New York: Routledge, 2002), 42–101.
47 Jean-Luc Marion, *Believing in Order to See: On the Rationality of Revelation and the Irrationality of Some Believers*, trans. Christina Gschwandtner (New York: Fordham University Press, 2017).
48 See, for instance, Merold Westphal, *Suspicion and Faith: The Religious Uses of Modern Atheism* (New York: Fordham University Press, 1998); and Westphal, *Overcoming Onto-Theology: Toward a Postmodern Christian Faith* (New York: Fordham University Press, 2001).
49 Jacques Derrida, *The Gift of Death*, trans. David Wills (Chicago: University of Chicago Press, 1995), 49.
50 "The Villanova Roundtable," in *Deconstruction in a Nutshell*, 21–2.
51 John D. Caputo, *On Religion* (New York: Routledge, 2001), 109–11.
52 John D. Caputo, *The Weakness of God: A Theology of the Event* (Bloomington: Indiana University Press, 2006), 44–5.
53 Clayton Crockett, B. Keith Putt, and Jeffrey W. Robbins, eds., *The Future of Continental Philosophy of Religion* (Bloomington: Indiana University Press, 2014), 2–3.
54 Jacques Derrida, *Of Grammatology*, corrected ed. and trans. Gayatri Chakravorty Spivak (Baltimore: Johns Hopkins University Press, 1998), 158.
55 Ibid.
56 Ralph Waldo Emerson, "Quotation and Originality," in *The Collected Works of Ralph Waldo Emerson*, vol. 8: *Letters and Social Aims*, ed. Ronald A. Bosco, Glen M. Johnson, and Joel Myerson (Cambridge, MA: Belknap, 2010), 91.
57 Friedrich Nietzsche, "Forward," in *On the Uses and Disadvantages for Life*, in *Untimely Meditations*, trans. R.J. Hollingdale (Cambridge: Cambridge University Press, 1983).
58 Ibid.
59 *Oxford English Dictionary*, 2nd ed., s.v. "construct."
60 Catherine Keller, *The Face of the Deep: A Theology of Becoming* (New York: Routledge, 2003).

10 Phenomenology, Catholic Thought, and the University: Lessons from the French Discussion

JEFFREY BLOECHL

The encounter between Catholic thought and phenomenology cannot separate itself from the question of the necessary limits of rationality and thus cannot avoid the question of the university. It is a question of the metaphysical absolute, specifically as the horizon within which claims for truth and value would be grounded, and of arguments made against the intelligibility of that procedure. Catholic attempts to understand God variously as "it itself" (Augustine, *id ipsum*), "subsistent act of being itself" (Aquinas, *ipsum esse subsistens*), or simply "pure self-gift" (Balthasar) propose to uncover the distinctiveness of divine being as at once strictly unqualified yet sense relational. God, in short, already transcends the limitation that would be implied for a Creator that withdraws into itself as if alienated from creatures. But God also transcends the limitation that would be implied for a Creator that is comprehended by the creatures with whom it is in relation. This supreme being would alone be the principle by which there is order and unity in the manifest plurality of creation, and unless we have access to it our propositions are without ground, which is to say without coherence. To depart from this principle would thus be to depart from the very possibility of reason.

Yet phenomenology may seem to have done precisely this, and indeed in the declared interest of saving reason from pretence and illusion. When in a founding moment Husserl contends that philosophy, as phenomenology, is without valid access to the "transcendency pertaining to God [*die Transzendenz Gottes*],"[1] he has in view a being who cannot appear as itself among data given to consciousness, and he is guided by a concern to clarify the structure and dynamism of consciousness for a scientific rationality capable of truly understanding the world only to the degree that it first possesses a good understanding of the consciousness in which the world becomes available to us. But consciousness proves always to be consciousness of some *x*, and moreover an *x* that is given within the world according to the perspective and capacities of a subject. Would this be the necessary condition of consciousness of God? As everyone knows – including Husserl and Heidegger, to be sure – the God who becomes only such an *x* is not God at all, or at any rate certainly not the God whom the theologians understand as one and absolute.

For its part, phenomenology is intent simply on establishing its essential field of inquiry. At the decisive moment, which is to say *for Husserl*, the exclusion of the "transcendency" of God in fact goes hand in hand with committing phenomenological research to a study of finite modes of givenness such as are discernible in consciousness. In turn, this study alone will provide the sciences with a rigorous ground – one that proceeds without antecedent prejudice – for their own work. And in no case would God as God have a place even there, since according to the canons of phenomenology meaning is always and necessarily a matter of what is given as *x* in consciousness. To be clear, this would mean not only that the sciences can proceed without a theological reference but also that the theological reference to an absolute God cannot be rigorously affirmed.

It takes only a little effort to recognize the agreement between this kind of thinking, or at least its conclusions, and arguments proposing to shift religious thought from the centre of work at the university – including at some Catholic universities. In taking up the Catholic reception of phenomenology I call attention specifically to the matter of the Catholic university not simply to highlight a theatre of concerns that deserve more attention than they usually receive, but more so to suggest that an engagement whose merits seem evident when it is a matter only of improving our accounts of being, acting, and knowing might also have an impact on our manner of conceiving relations among the disciplines (chiefly between theology and the others), and indeed on what we are prepared to accept as a well-grounded rational proposition. If it seems far-fetched to suppose that the Catholic reception of phenomenology may be understood as one instance of the Catholic response to secularism – for that is what I have in mind – then one need only attend especially to the French experience for helpful instruction. To this may be added what is by now well known: the reception of phenomenology by Catholics in France has had considerable impact in other places.

I

The French reception of Husserl and Heidegger has been extraordinary even apart from its specifically Catholic variant. On the one hand,

and perhaps not unexpectedly, the texts themselves became known only slowly or partially and sometimes in questionable translation. To the best of my knowledge, we are still in need of a careful history of their reception that is truly attentive to the philosophical stakes, but for present purposes it will be enough to touch on only a few important features. Setting aside a handful of precursors,[2] phenomenology truly arrived with the lectures given in Paris by Husserl that became his *Cartesian Meditations*. Understandably then, Husserl was thus known first as having radicalized the Cartesian pursuit of apodicity with the achievement of a method capable of defining transcendental subjectivity. And this emphasis on the transcendental Husserl, as distinguished from an emphasis on his exploration of passivity, sensibility, and various modes of pre-predicative givenness, receives tacit reinforcement in Paul Ricoeur's introduction to his 1950 translation of the first book of Husserl's *Ideen*. Emphasizing a stated ideal against real possibilities, Ricoeur moves our understanding of phenomenology toward Eugen Fink's thesis that its success, which is essentially the success of the reduction, is ensured by a "third Ego," beyond the empirical ego of the natural attitude and the transcendental ego that reflects on it – one that alone would be truly capable of contemplating intentional acts without entanglement in them. It would be this phenomenologizing spectator that motivates the reduction and indeed carries it out, from outside the claims of the world.[3] Ultimately, Husserl will have wagered on this as the moment when the subject gains access to essences and in this way grounds the meaning of its own propositions. Whatever its legitimacy, it is specifically this subject, capable of assuring itself of its own place at the locus of meaning, and thus broadly Cartesian, that has attracted the particular interest of phenomenologists wishing to reinstate the phenomenality of religious existence and experience. Emmanuel Levinas characterizes such a subject by a power capable of forgetting a prior relation with the Other, and Jean-Luc Marion, somewhat in the same line, considers its every act to be predicated on a failure to recognize the givenness that is prior to the objective intentionality that Husserl would have us address first.[4] As for Heidegger, one notes only that it was not until 1965 that a complete translation of his *Sein und Zeit* was published, by which time much of the francophone academy had come to interpret his work through an uneven range of passages from the great books and a few subsequent essays, not all of which have stood the test of time.[5] Around the same time, those in the early generation who understood Heidegger well – one thinks especially of Levinas and Ricoeur – withdrew from extended commentary. In the resultant vacuum, the philosophy of Heidegger was understood until well after the Second World War as if its central intention was to develop a metaphysics grounded in the affirmation of human being as irreducibly singular and self-concerned.[6] Of course, Heidegger would have had his own reasons for arriving at this conclusion, but there is no mistaking its resemblance to that of his teacher. Phenomenology would be a philosophy that takes its bearings from the being of the human.

This is very briefly said, and one should not overstate the importance of what it indicates, but the developments it touches are highly suggestive of a readiness to understand the phenomenology of the founders as a theoretical affirmation of the possibility of being in the world without necessary reference to God. And by the end of the Second World War, French Catholicism had compelling reason to take that possibility seriously. This was the French Catholicism that had to face widespread and growing disaffection with the Church, and thus a disenfranchisement that, though not yet full-blown atheist secularism, was suddenly quite close to it. The history of this realization is no secret. In 1943, two young priests, Henri Godin and Yves Daniel, put the matter to paper,[7] and leading Catholic thinkers like Jean Daniélou, Henri de Lubac, and Hans Urs von Balthasar among the Jesuits in Lyon, and Dominique Chenu and Yves Congar among the Dominicans in Paris, set themselves the task of a responding plausibly to the culture depicted there. This was the birth of what soon became known as the *nouvelle théologie*, which was characterized by an attitude of *aggiornamento* – of the sort of openness to ongoing human experience that is willing to recognize that there is something legitimate about it, even when it seems to urge against faith – but also by a call for *ressourcement* that would go far beyond the study of classical texts in search of new inspiration, to seek new avenues into the fountainhead of a religious sensibility that the French theologians were convinced was present even in non-believers. From here, of course, it is only a short step, and perhaps an unavoidable one, to the thought that what is called for is nothing short of a positive interpretation of secular existence as an inner possibility of the religious relation to God. Our secularity will always have been a dimension of human being, and in recent developments one is to recognize its fuller emergence.

II

Phenomenology, especially as received from Heidegger, has helpful language for what all of this may imply for a conception of our humanity: we are in-the-world and in the presence of God (*coram Deo*), and what has to be faced is the evident possibility that the former will cover

over the latter.[8] We get further with this thesis if we develop it in terms of a fundamental distinction between the originary and the initial. The originary in no way denotes a temporal priority, but rather a constant anteriority with respect to the here and now. To seek the originary is to go looking for the principle on the basis of which we are what we are. It is to take note of the fact that our being has a movement and an orientation that are not determined by our own freedom and powers, but instead are always already in place as we conduct ourselves. In this sense, the originary appears constantly in what presupposes it but without appearing as such. As distinct from this, the initial is that from which we begin in the temporal sense. What we meet first in the order of experience is given in the mode of availability to sensation and intuition, whereby we engage things between anticipation of their meaning and some degree of fulfillment. Our initial condition thus includes finding ourselves among things. This is not rote subjectivism, since it is clear enough to rudimentary reflection that things call for our attention even while our attention also goes out toward them. In this much, there is not a hint of a givenness that would somehow remain unavailable. For what does "available" mean here, if not the agreement between things and what of them can appear in finite consciousness? And then under what conditions could the unavailable appear without ceasing to be itself, if not precisely in an interruption and refusal of availability? What is unavailable is not itself a thing, but precisely what cannot appear according to the same conditions by which things appear.

In their availability, things do not give themselves to us solely from out of themselves, but within a world. The philosophy of Heidegger gives particular emphasis to this fact by distinguishing *Dasein*'s relation to things, as tools, from its relation to its world, as the milieu in which tools receive their meaning from a relation to that which is to be worked. In this sense, the world is that by which things are available (whether or not one accepts Heidegger's specific understanding of things as tools). This means that the world transcends things and that our relation with the world is antecedent to our relation with things. But it does not mean that the world cannot appear as such – as one learns, for example, from the boredom that proceeds beyond disinterest in the concrete possibilities afforded by distinct things all the way to an indifference that refers negatively to the very world of their occurrence. In Heidegger's locution, this enables us to see "how things stand concerning us,"[9] which is to say how it truly is that we find ourselves engaged with available things in a world by which they are available. In the absence of interest in things, the world by which they are available comes into view, and in the absence of interest in the world, one is left alone with the interest itself, as the dynamism that sustains our being in the world among things.

This is very little. But it is enough for us to have recognized the peculiar status of the world. The world necessarily accompanies things in their availability but is not itself a thing among them. So, too, are we invested in a world in and through our investment in things, but without our investment in the world being only another instance of investment in things. Rather, our investment in the world is the primary condition of our investment in things and thus the horizon in which they appear. To attend to available things, to take an interest in them, is already to project the world of their meaning and relations. In this sense, we not only are *in* a world but also already *have* a world, and the having is expressed in our manner of engaging available things.

Now the world is a condition of the initial, but it is not the originary. The originary would be that by which we have a world and engage things in the manner that we do. In the philosophy of Heidegger, it is our relation to being that is originary, and this stands to reason inasmuch as being is evidently presupposed in being in a world. Moreover, being does not itself appear in the experiences that would enable thinking to catch sight of it. Anxiety at one's own death is the appearing not of being but of our *relation* with being. Anxious *Dasein* is deprived of speech and movement, and without world; these are the marks of separation and exposure, not of access to a ground or firmament. It is a teaching of fundamental ontology that we are, each of us, irreducibly and irremediably finite. And it is from our sense of that finitude that the meaning of the world and things is projected.

There is every reason for Catholic thought to take these proposals seriously. Whether one is provoked by a powerful new philosophy that proceeds without God, by the widening commitment to a secular mode of living (whether one considers this an essential possibility of our humanity or only a recent deviation), or by the perception of important correlation between the two, there can be no mistaking at least the occasion for some doubt about the premise, albeit long-held by many, that the originary condition of being human lies in a relation with God. The general form of the difficulty is striking. Either the originary can be known only via an analysis of predicates and effects – which, however, philosophy and culture seem no longer to recognize – or else it must reveal itself straightforwardly in experience. Phenomenology calls for the latter warrant – as does, we might note in passing, a more perennial desire in ordinary life.[10] We know where this will lead. God will have revealed himself from beyond the range of every human capacity to comprehend, which is to say from beyond the meaning that is given properly by a subject or *Dasein*. At first sight, the thought seems only to repeat a familiar theologeme: God does not depend on human cognizance in order to reveal himself any more than God requires worship in order to exist. But under present conditions, this requires nothing less than a redefinition of the finite conditions of experience and understanding as phenomenology has established them. If God does not enter experience, this will be due not to some constitutive indifference or inadequacy but only to a closure that is susceptible to being opened. But then the opening will have to come at God's initiative, since the act that is initiated by a finite being will itself have finite capacities. It will therefore be the accomplishment of this divine initiative to make God intelligible to finite creatures – to enter experience and become knowable – without submitting to their grasp. God, then, is mystery, which is neither riddle, if this word denotes the incomplete meaning of a hint, nor enigma, if this word suggests a meaning that is hidden or half-known. God is excess of meaning, and the excess surrounds and illumines discrete meaning, altering it without belonging to it, by causing it to appear in view of the immeasurable.

Phenomenology cannot accommodate this argument without violent revision: phenomenality is to admit theophany; the gaze of an ego that is otherwise encoded by its own natural interests cannot obscure the unencoded gaze that turns toward an absolute God, and intentionality should include instances of a "counter-intentionality" in which the relation is determined by the arrival of an object rather than the directedness of a subject.[11] As for the theology that comes into view, it exhibits only a refinement of certain concepts that are hardly new. To suggest that the proper meaning of finitude is closure is to rejoin the ancient problem of idolatry, but with the somewhat more modern discovery of its root in *auto*-idolatry: one falls short of the divine so long as one's own subjectivity remains at the origin of meaning.[12] Against this, it may be said that only God can correct our idolatry, by surpassing it in self-revelation. "God," Jean-Luc Marion has thus written, "can give himself to be thought without idolatry only starting from himself alone."[13] But this thought, he adds, can remain faithful to what is given to it – to the thing itself – only on the condition of denying itself the right to possess it. To repeat, the implication is robustly theological, even if it also claims the authority of phenomenology: when thought attends properly to God, it can only give back to God what God has already given, and indeed what God alone can give.

It is not difficult to understand the appeal of this argument for a good number of Catholic thinkers. The advance of secular life in modern culture is taken seriously both as a form of experience and as an intellectual position, but without abandoning a theocentric understanding of our humanity. Moreover, the argument leaves room for a specific response, if not indeed an apology: modern secular experience may be understood and addressed from within a basic affirmation of the one God, and if anything, a need to do so would only to call upon Catholic thought to recognize what is truly important and lasting in its tradition. More specifically, it appears possible for Catholic thought to engage some difficult elements of the modern ethos – precisely by maintaining the altitude that one might think has become most difficult to sustain.

III

Questions remain. We may begin by returning to the theme of the world, and ask for its status between the transcendence opened up by the icon and the immanence of life intent on idols. We have already taken notice of the fact that the world has its own transcendence, whether it is defined in Husserlian terms as the final context for the natural attitude, or in the Heideggerian terms used here, as the condition by which things are available to *Dasein*. The world has a transcendence that is consistent with the fact that it is specifically the world of *someone*, a world that exceeds the meaning of things encountered by this subject or this *Dasein*. It is therefore a transcendence that is necessarily limited, as opposed to the absolute transcendence of God. In its primordial sense, the world is always *my* world, projected as the horizon within which I take an interest in what is available. If, as Marion has contended, the relation with God is not a matter of my interest, it is not merely another, more encompassing horizon but must itself be without horizon. At this point, it is all but impossible not to wonder how what breaks into the horizon of meaningful relations without belonging there can nonetheless deliver a meaningful content. How can such an event be anything but sheer interruption, and what would license us to understand what interrupts as any more than the strict other of the world that is interrupted? There is no way around these difficulties that does not introduce a distinction into our understanding of world. Only if there is a way of being in the world that does not become having a world might the approach of God be intelligible without submitting to the rule of our finitude. But then what truly is the world between these distinct modalities (let us say, most generally, between secular and religious)?

There is of course a superficial distinction between modes of seeing to be carefully respected. We have already registered this in terms of the secular and the religious: one may look upon the world as if the world were the first and final condition of our being, and one may look upon the world in the light of faith in a Highest Being. The former receives conceptual support from an ontology of finitude; the latter appeals in the final instance to a theology of gift. Does the latter fully intervene in the claims of the former, or only contest it from the beginning, according to a different "logic of being"?[14] Nowhere in the remarkable phenomenology of vision that introduces Marion's engagement with Husserl and Heidegger is there an argument in favour of icon over idol that does not beg the question of formative experiences that are not available to all.[15] One instead passes between the definition of concepts and a characterization of experiences they would express, into a suggestion that the icon gives more, when in fact this is not at all evident to those who do not see it seeing them. Yet rather than rule out any further use for the word "idol," this only confirms that its meaning is embedded in a specific mode of being in the world. In establishing that mode as a distinctive and viable possibility – or better, in reinstating it after Husserl and Heidegger – Marion has also given phenomenology something of lasting importance to consider: our being in the world can take more than one form, and indeed the differences among forms may belie different originary conditions. But it follows from this – very much against the spirit of Marion's texts, if not their letter – that being in the world is irreducible to any one form it may take. In that case, philosophy is without the means to argue for a primary or supreme instance.

It is uncertain quite what this would mean for the self-understanding of rationality or its exercise among the disciplines, but we can at least dispel the appearance of simple relativism by attending to some features in common among the different forms of being in the world that are in play here. Let us note first that the existence *coram Deo* is not an existence without any interest in the world. It is rather that the interests – one's engagement with available things – receive their meaning from affirmations such as "God truly is," "God's being is love," "creation is gift," and so forth. Perhaps this is obvious, but it assures us that in no case can there be an unqualified claim *not* to have a world. It is rather a question of whether having a world occurs without some deeper (or higher) organizing principle. The pilgrim, for example, has a world as gift, and what is available is in use in view of an extramundane end. Naturally, it is different with the secular man or woman, for whom there is no ulterior ground or source for the world and for whom having is therefore in the final account uncanny. Yet none of this takes away the fact that the having of a world is in all cases substantially concrete and practical in its application; the taking up what is available is not speculative and not even primordially reflective. It is a matter of flesh on the things one engages, whatever desire animates it and whatever the goods one seeks. The having of a world emanates from the body, from the inner organization, tonality, and posture that inform our enactment of the initial. The body, it is sometimes said, is our insertion in a world. It is our opening and our access to things and to the world, the very condition of their appearance. But this does not occur in a generic manner. One's body is always one's own not merely as the vehicle of movement or surface for contact, but insofar as the movement itself results from an interplay of active and reactive impulses that is personal in each case, as is the sensitivity and porosity of the surface. These things result from a history and exhibit an orientation that neither repeats nor is repeated by any others, and they give our existence a distinctive style. And evidently enough, the contours of our world outline this style.[16] The way I am my body is inseparable from the way I have my world, and this is true equally of the plurality of human beings.

And so, between those who have a world according to an affirmation of God and those who have a world according to some other affirmation, the matters of body and style of being comprise a point of basic solidarity that nonetheless admits of their profound difference. The lived body of the believer is coded and her world is schematized in a manner apart from the lived body and the world of the non-believer. For the Christian believer, the body is already given by God and already ordered to God, which is to say inscribed in the order of the gift. The affirmation of God thus already sanctifies the body by conferring on it a transcendent meaning.[17] For those whose affirmation does not reach to the absolute God, the body is ordered to values that transcend otherwise, but without invoking an absolute end for its aspirations. The body of the Christian believer bears the mark of the absolute. Without this, the secular body instead bears the mark of original finitude.

IV

What would it mean for philosophy to commit itself to an articulation of this secular lived body and the world it entails? And what would it make of the Catholic thought that remains close to another experience of body and world? If we are not yet certain, this is in no small part because in the French discussion where these questions have been pursued with greatest urgency, a penetrating investigation of the secular experience has not been systematically present. Not that there was no opportunity. One finds the secular experience advocated most subtly, perhaps in any language, in the philosophy of Maurice Merleau-Ponty. The fact that its importance for the present concerns has long been overlooked is especially regrettable given that it includes not only a well-known commitment to thinking in strict accord with the implications of a phenomenology of body and flesh, but also a much less-known interrogation, for nearly two decades, of the relationship between Christianity and philosophy.[18] It is readily apparent that these two lines of thought are in agreement.

Let us briefly review each of them. Remarkably, Merleau-Ponty's interest in Christianity is in no small part provoked by concerns that are recognizably congruent with those motivating the theological response that dominated French Catholicism beginning in the middle of the twentieth century. But this was already in 1935, and Merleau-Ponty's orientation was political rather than essentially theological. Originally, his hope was to awaken the Church from a scandalous adaptation to the modern world, expressed in a spirituality that invested so much of its moral authority in the promotion of an invisible order that it had little to say about the injustices visited on the world by a bourgeois society and stood powerless before the rise of secular humanism. The call was plainly to renewal, but one that would take the distinctly leftist form of a radical commitment to charity and justice in this world.[19] The hope was soon enough disappointed; by 1946, just as French Catholic thinkers were truly facing a drift toward secularism, Merleau-Ponty was arguing that the Church could not be counted on to oppose injustice, not merely because of a correctable accommodation of modern culture, but also for deeply theological reasons. "Faith and Good Faith" is a complicated essay in part because the understanding of Christian theology is contestable, but more so because the manner in which Merleau-Ponty takes issue with it is genuinely difficult. On the one hand, he extends his early concern with a religion of the other-worldly into a critique of the interiority this implies: each of us finds God in his or her own heart, individually if also universally, and each of us thus feels answerable for his or her own life alone before God at the Last Judgment. The good life is reduced to submission of one's own will to that of the Father, to the detriment of a vital sense of community. On the other hand, there is the doctrine of the Son, whose death gives birth to a religion of Spirit in history (the proximity of Hegel is undisguised). The latter position has every chance of becoming more politically engaged but no longer has real need of God as Father. For Merleau-Ponty, in short, the religion of God the Father is a religion that was never capable of addressing human community, whereas the religion of Spirit, released by the Crucifixion, makes easy and evident the passage to anthropology. The Father becomes at best an anonymous force behind what human beings can and must do for themselves in history. Christianity would appear to contain an internal contradiction between the high theology of the

Father and the nascent anthropology that issues from the doctrine of Spirit. Can one truly serve these two masters equally? It seems undeniable to Merleau-Ponty that Christian women and men will serve best what they love most and that any attempt to save the contradiction will get in the way of doing so.[20] For the philosopher it is no different, so it is not long before Merleau-Ponty draws the necessary conclusions. In 1951, the same contradiction that in his view requires a decision between a conservative religion of Father and institution and the exercise of one's own freedom in service of justice is also intolerable to the philosopher. Whether or not Merleau-Ponty himself was ever personally an atheist, in "Man and Adversity" the idea that philosophy must be conducted on that principle is unmistakable: the contradiction itself is untenable, so one affirms either the distant transcendence of the Father or the immanent transcendence of human freedom. To be sure, at this point the choice for the latter is motivated largely by political concerns, but a close reading of the essay also discerns a willingness to follow the verdict of history. The earlier essays at least depict Christianity as the religion of the death of God the Father. In "Man and Adversity" there is more than a hint of the idea that this occurs by some necessity. That essay's final pages propose that from the death of such a transcendent assurance of universal order there comes a growing consciousness of contingency that announces the latest turn in the "metamorphoses of Fortune."[21]

Readers of Merleau-Ponty's phenomenological work know that "contingency" is an important concept that emerges in his interpretation of perception, body, and flesh. Interestingly, his relation to Christianity moderates two sets of concerns even as it migrates from one to the other. The concept emerges as his *Phenomenology of Perception* attends closely to the perceptual faith by which we accept as real what is presented to us in brute experience. This occurs prior to any critical awareness and without any question of reflective judgment. Strictly speaking, in perceptual faith "neither object nor subject is posited."[22] One originally lives through or perhaps lives *in* a "mosaic of qualities" whose relative values are determined according to the configuration of the whole (Merleau-Ponty's example is a sheet of paper that counts as white in accordance with its position in the shade). Perceptual faith is primordially corporeal, an occurrence at the living nexus of body and nature. The body itself is expressive, organized, and oriented ahead of itself, but it is also sedimented with a context from which that futurity has particular focus. It is in their appearance between past and future that objects have the particular meaning they do for a living subject. To perceive an object is for it to appear to an embodied subject against the background of a world within which it has its place among others, and indeed relative to the subject itself. We have spent considerable effort developing this in the terms of engaging available things and having a world according to the distinctive way of being one's body. Merleau-Ponty's notion of perceptual faith reminds us that whatever marvellous fit we may discover between perceiving and perceived, the act itself proceeds from conditions that are essentially finite and therefore without an ulterior ground (Heidegger might say that perception is conditioned by thrownness). This is what the philosopher must keep in view: perception, as our access to things and to the world, posits a world in contingency. Knowledge becomes possible with the achievement of critical awareness, but the latter does not guarantee it. And indeed, what passes for knowledge all too often forgets its own conditionedness by contingency, whereupon it stands in need of critique. Merleau-Ponty's later texts assign that work to philosophy. The philosopher is to remain as close as possible to contingency, pose questions for every claim that would be built upon it, and ceaselessly interrogate each new orthodoxy as it may appear.

This is no longer quite atheism. But it is an unflinching commitment to finitude. Moreover, the commitment entails its own form of ascesis. To hold as closely as possible to contingency is to deny oneself the rest provided by founding principles. This means more than refusing the dialectical struggles between theism and anti-theism and between belief and unbelief, both of which are maintained by a difference between fixed points of departure. The philosopher should instead situate his or her work in the space between things in their naked givenness and the concepts by which one or another theory would establish their meaning. And if this is to be the identity of true philosophy, then it must deny itself any propositions and perhaps even any enduring concepts of its own. Philosophy only interrogates non-philosophy, and Catholic thought must surely count among the latter. In his inaugural lecture at the Collège de France, Merleau-Ponty addresses himself as philosopher to the practice of theology: "Theology recognizes the contingency of human existence only to derive it from a necessary being, that is, to remove it. Theology makes use of philosophical wonder only for the purpose of motivating an affirmation which ends it. Philosophy, on the other hand, arouses us to what is problematic in our existence and in that of the world, to the point that we shall never be cured of searching for solution."[23]

We may leave aside the question of what this difference will imply for personal belief, since we already know enough to be sure that for Merleau-Ponty, the philosopher who wishes to offer a philosophical response will do well to interrogate the context from which the question of his own belief has been raised, and in turn the manner in which that context is articulated, in order to supply an answer to questions about the meaning of life and the world. Regarding Catholic thought and the philosophy that remains closest to the things themselves, in their nascent appearance, the difference, as it were, goes all the way down. Were this only a matter of opposed first principles such as "God truly exists" and "there is no God," one might imagine an apologetics capable of settling the matter. But interrogation is not contradiction and not even opposition. And its manner of affirming finitude does not issue from a refusal of the absolute so much as it is urged by a certain rigour. Philosophy considers itself incommensurable with Catholic thought at this level, where one form of thinking does not actively negate the other but only strives to awaken in it a critical sense of its own premises.

V

It is not impossible for Catholic universities to refuse active dialogue with secular experience and secular thought because it is not impossible to conclude that Catholic doctrine and the teaching authority of the Church prescribe only an apologetic response to modes of living and thinking they consider to have fallen into error. Other Catholic universities, adopting a different perspective, may instead take the view that there is something true and good even in what may seem in important respects inconsistent with the faith, and in this way come to the thought that it is best to invite secular experience and secular thought into the pursuit of their research and teaching goals. The former approach exhibits convictions that rationality is one, unified and universal, and that this is preserved within a Catholic vision. The latter approach has not abandoned the unity of reason so long is it remains firm in the conviction that people who think differently are nonetheless able to understand and argue intelligibly with one another. Indeed, nothing prevents such a university from projecting and pursuing the ideal of real consensus. But it is necessarily circumspect about the prospects, and if it sincerely recognizes truth and goodness in forms of thinking not alloyed to the faith then it knows that those prospects for consensus are to be pursued through on open and searching exploration of profound differences. Here one detects a somewhat different understanding of the word "catholic." If it is necessary to compare the two, let us say that the virtues of the former include clarity and consistency, whereas in the latter one finds a more capacious spirit.

Secular experience and secular thinking are considered an important presence in most Catholic institutions of higher education in North America. In the eyes of many, social reality and intellectual advances have made any other course of action unacceptable. It is an open question how much of this thinking went into the commitment that an unusual number of these institutions made to teaching and research in phenomenology. No doubt the excellence of the work will have spoken for itself. To a considerable degree, Catholic thinkers in North America owe it to the French for having made us better aware of the secular dimension and tendencies of our thinking. However, in many cases that awakening did not come without accompanying suggestions for how to respond. The specific decisions in favour of one or the other and the alliances that sometimes go with them are much less important than a clear vision of what is at stake. For Catholic thought to commit itself wholly to the idea that anything other than an affirmation of the absolute God represents a departure from coherent reasoning is to risk the suppression of certain kinds of questions that might not otherwise be posed. And vice versa. It is likewise an impoverishment for an institution or a department to commit itself to the principle that philosophy can and should have nothing to say about the positivity of God in our experience or the cogency of the idea of God in our thinking. The history of phenomenology records strong tendencies in both these directions, though the tendency has not been to prohibit questions outright so much as formulate answers within a single horizon. For a considerable period, this was a philosophy that with few exceptions saw itself as incapable of speaking to questions about faith and God, and often went as far as to reject the thinking that did so as incomplete or unreflective. The work of Levinas and Ricoeur, and not least among Catholics Marion, has succeeded in shifting that self-understanding from assumed to contested. But it is not clear that in all cases this new openness to religious phenomena has not come at the cost of plausibility in other areas. In that case, the active presence of other approaches remains essential.

The foregoing investigation responds directly to that thought and to a growing sense that even at Catholic institutions there is good cause for this admittedly contrarian concern. It is not that a renewed study of the classical phenomenology of the founders is newly urgent – those who criticize them from religious sympathies have long played an important role in motivating a great deal of this work – but rather that Catholic thought, including where it forges bonds with the so-called new phenomenology, stands in need of careful critique. It may be that someone who was as wary of Catholicism as was Merleau-Ponty, and as careful to hold philosophy clear of it, may nonetheless be exceptionally friendly to its highest aspirations. After all, one can profit greatly from a call to good critical self-awareness without necessarily accepting everything that comes with it. Who will interrogate Catholic thinkers wherever they appear ready to work on premises that are neither examined nor justified in the wider court of reason, if not their fellow citizens at the university? And who will ask best and acquiesce most slowly if not those who do not share their premises?

NOTES

1 E. Husserl, *Ideas Pertaining to a Pure Phenomenology and a Phenomenological Philosophy*, bk I (Dordrecht: Kluwer, 1982), §58, 134. Husserl's notion is clarified by the end of the section. The extra-worldly divine being, he reasons, would transcend not only the world but also consciousness. It is therefore absolute, but in a sense "totally different" than the sense in which phenomenology considers consciousness to be absolute (Ibid.).

2 In the francophone world, the importance of Husserl's philosophy was being promoted by 1925, albeit with only limited effect, by Léon Noël,Victor Delbos, Lev Shestov, and Jean Héring. See C. Dupont, *Phenomenology in French Philosophy: Early Encounters* (Dordrecht: Spring, 2014), 104–17.

3 This interpretation appears near the end of Ricoeur's introduction to his translation of E. Husserl, *Idées directrices pour une phénoménologie et une philosophie phénoménologique pures* (Paris: Gallimard, 1950). Ricoeur's introduction and extensive commentary have appeared in English as P. Ricoeur, *A Key to Husserl's Ideas I* (Milwaukee: Marquette University Press, 1996). Fink's influence is especially strong at pp. 48–50. I owe this reference to a conversation with Richard Cobb-Stevens.

4 For example, E. Levinas, *Totality and Infinity* (Pittsburgh: Duquesne University Press, 1998), 210; and J.-L. Marion, *Reduction and Givenness* (Evanston: Northwestern University Press, 1998), 24, 39.

5 The translation of Heidegger into French has been complicated by historical circumstance and fraught with disagreements that are not always philosophical. For a way into these difficulties, the interviews conducted by Dominique Janicaud are indispensable. See Janicaud, *Heidegger en France. II Entretiens* (Paris: Albin Michel, 2001). Regrettably, the English translation published as *Heidegger in France* (Bloomington: Indiana University Press, 2015) includes only seven of the eighteen interviews gathered in the French original.

6 This impression outlasts the association with existentialism promoted by Sartre and repudiated by Heidegger himself. As late as 1957, Gabriel Marcel recounts Heidegger's stated discomfort with the anthropological emphasis

of Alphone de Waelhens's influential study, *La philosophie de Martin Heidegger* (Louvain: Éditions de l'Institut supérieure de philosophie, 1942), only to argue that an interpretation of existence centred on the singularity of one's own death necessarily overlooks the possibility of "spiritual communion" and an impoverished conception of the sacred. G. Marcel, "Ma relation avec Heidegger," in G. Marcel, *Gabriel Marcel et la pensée allemande. Nietzsche, Heidegger, Bloch* (Paris: Aubier, 1979), 28, 35, 37–8.

7 H. Godin and Y. Daniel, *France, pays de la mission* (Lyon: Eds. de l'Abeille, 1943). For a brief account of this widely read book and its remarkable impact on twentieth-century French theology, see H. Boersma, *Nouvelle Theology and Sacramental Ontology: A Return to Mystery* (Oxford: Oxford University Press, 2009), 29–30.

8 The preceding few lines consciously invoke some terminology in J.-Y. Lacoste, *Experience and the Absolute* (New York: Fordham University Press, 2004), a remarkable work that both extends some of the essential impulses of the *nouvelle théologie* and enriches it with rigorous critical appeal to phenomenology.

9 M. Heidegger, *Fundamental Concepts of Metaphysics: World, Finitude, Solitude* (Bloomington: Indiana University Press, 1995), 136. The example of boredom is famously Heidegger's.

10 Before reducing this desire to a single expression of a distinctly modern empirical bent, one does well to consider the gospels. Luke and John depict Peter and John and running to the tomb of Christ upon hearing from Mary Magdalene that his body is no longer present there, as if the senses will confirm the meaning and perhaps the truth of the event (Lk 24:12, Jn 20:4). According to John, Thomas persists with this idea until the resurrected Jesus appears to him (Jn 20:24–9).

11 These are central themes in the philosophy of Jean-Luc Marion. "Theophany" is a synonym for what his early work calls "icon." My expression "unencoded gaze" characterizes what would be required of the subject who looks into what Marion himself calls the "counter-gaze" of the icon. "Counter-intentionality" is Marion's own later terminology for consciousness of icon. See J.-L. Marion, *God without Being: Hors-Texte* (Chicago: University of Chicago Press, 1991), 21–4; and *Being Given: Toward a Phenomenology of Givenness* (Stanford: Stanford University Press, 2002), 266–7.

12 One reads especially Feuerbach with this in mind. The claims of the *Essence of Christianity* are well known: what we worship as God is in fact a composite of predicates that are originally human. By the time of the *Lectures*, a later work, much effort is dedicated to showing that this objectification (*Vergegenständlichung*) is animated by a profound egoism (*Egoismus*) that seeks happiness in existential stability. This is evidently not the moral egoism that the *Essence of Christianity* sometimes opposes

to love, but one that is "necessary, indispensable," and "metaphysical," "inherent in the very organism, which appropriates those substances that are assimilable and excretes those that are not." L. Feuerbach, *Lectures on the Essence of Religion* (New York: Harper & Row, 1967), 50. The accomplishment is most remarkable, it seems to me, for making it clear just how far the projective impulse truly reaches, and in consequence just how far one will have to go in order to keep an understanding God free of it.

13 J.-L Marion, *God without Being*, 49.

14 My simple expression "logic of being" invokes Marion's slightly different "logic of Being/beings" (ibid., 100). Too little attention has been given to the alternative (though also quite traditional) metaphysics that accompanies his phenomenological proposals. The French title of the third and by far the longest chapter of *God without Being* is strongly indicative. But we do not have a vivid English translation for "La croisée de l'être," which has a sense of passing by one another along intersecting lines or routes.

15 See ibid., 9f.

16 This sense of a "style" of being in the world and having a world, and the thought that is rooted in the body, are inspired by some passages in the later work of Maurice Merleau-Ponty, to whom this chapter has begun to turn. However, since Merleau-Ponty's use of the term appears fluid from text to text, I stop short of ascribing my own conception to his work. His varied uses of "style" are submitted to careful study in L. Singer, "Merleau-Ponty on Style," in *Man and World* 14, no. 2 (1981), 153–63.

17 At this point it is necessary to take leave of Marion's phenomenological work, which one searches in vain for an account of the body specifically as sanctified. This is not to say with confidence that what he does put in black and white cannot be reconciled with such an account, but only to observe that the notions of body and world are underdeveloped in the methodological work where one would expect to find them, *Reduction and Givenness*. The reasons may be clear enough: this is a work intent on dislodging the figure of an ego that would be neither transcendental in Husserl's sense nor ontological in Heidegger's sense, and likewise intent on showing that such an ego is the recipient of a givenness anterior to intuition and perception or comprehension. This effort guides subsequent works – chapter 4 of *In Excess* (New York: Fordham University Press, 2004), and frequently the later passages of *Being Given* – that do take up flesh and body, but only as within the phenomenality of an ego already defined by its susceptibility to a "saturation" that awakens us to the situation of our finitude. As these works progress, Marion proposes to show the suitability of his donatology for philosophical reflection on theological matters such as the Passion and the Resurrection. Perhaps inevitably, this becomes a

case for a form of experience whose authentic meaning is religious yet is nonetheless available to any enfleshed ego – *from out of the experience itself,* without prior formation, commitments, or, as a matter specifically of the body, what I have called "sanctification." It may be that another position is taken in Marion's theological writings, but testing the phenomenological status of their claims would require a lengthy essay of its own. A good number of these writings are collected in J.-L. Marion, *Prolegomena to Charity* (New York: Fordham University Press, 2002) and *Believing in Order to See: On the Rationality of Revelation and the Irrationality of Some Believers* (New York: Fordham University Press, 2017).

18 Notable exceptions to which I am especially indebted are X. Tilliette, "Maurice Merleau-Ponty ou la mesure de l'homme," in *Philosophes contemporaines* (Paris: Desclée de Brouwer, 1962), 49–86; and G. Labelle, "Merleau-Ponty et le christianisme," in *Laval théologique et philosophique* 58, no. 2 (2002), 317–40. Tilliette's essay has the merit of situating Merleau-Ponty's response to Christianity in a synthetic reading of his philosophy as a whole. Labelle goes farther in distinguishing two distinct positions subsequent to Merleau-Ponty's early attempts to think within a Christian framework. It is the second of these that interests me here.

19 See M. Merleau-Ponty, "Christianisme et ressentiment," in *Parcours 1935–1957* (Paris: Verdier, 1997), 9–33.

20 M. Merleau-Ponty, "Faith and Good Faith," in *Sense and Non-Sense* (Evanston: Northwestern University Press, 1964), 178.

21 M. Merleau-Ponty, "Man and Adversity," in *Signs* (Evanston: Northwestern University Press, 1964), 242–3.

22 M. Merleau-Ponty, *Phenomenology of Perception* (New York: Routledge, 1999), 241. This is not the occasion to follow the notion of perceptual faith through Merleau-Ponty's works. But it cannot surprise us that it is never far from a thinking that is committed to contingency. Where there is experience and meaning, there is the faith by which the things are received in a manner that is already an ordering. And where there is philosophy, or truly interrogative thinking, this ordering does not pass without question.

23 M. Merleau-Ponty, "In Praise of Philosophy," in *In Praise of Philosophy and Other Essays* (Evanston: Northwestern University Press, 1988), 44–5.

11 Being True to Mystery and Metaxological Metaphysics

WILLIAM DESMOND

Opening[1]

The importance of metaphysics has never lacked for appreciation in the Catholic orientation to philosophy, yet the manners in which metaphysics has been diversely criticized since Kant have left it in a struggling condition. This legacy of criticism has had different aftereffects on both the Analytic and the Continental ways of doing philosophy. Analytic philosophy in its earlier incarnation was not hospitable to metaphysics, perhaps identifying this with overstated claims of idealistic speculation, against which were expressed the hostilities of positivism and the dismissiveness of more ordinary language philosophy cutting it down to commonsense size. Notable today is that within Analytic philosophy a practice of metaphysics is flourishing, though not always to the likes of everyone. With the Continental tradition one could not use the word "flourishing" in connection with metaphysics, though admirers of thinkers like Deleuze and Badiou do not share the more standard anti-metaphysical animus common in twentieth-century Continental philosophy. Yet here the influence of Heidegger and his admirers cannot be underestimated. How is this contested place of metaphysics to be approached in light of its important sources in modern thought? How is it to be approached with reference to the longer tradition in the relation of Catholic thought and the need of metaphysics? After the weakening of the hegemony of Thomistic practices of Scholastic philosophy, in America one of the attractions of Continental thought was the perception that it remained true to a larger vision of the human condition, as well as being attuned to a variety of important historical and cultural nuances in matters philosophical. Phenomenology, nevertheless, is one Continental approach that eschews "metaphysics." What this means is connected with certain practices of metaphysics, not least among these being a kind of rationalistic Scholasticism, not itself confined to Catholic traditions. Are there fruitful approaches to metaphysics that are not marked by such rationalistic practices? I want to defend a practice of metaphysics as metaxological, as I have tried to articulate in a number of different works such as *Being and the Between*, *God and the Between*, and most recently, *The Intimate Universal*.[2] I would also argue for the impossibility of avoiding metaphysics, even in the avoidance of metaphysics.

This approach to metaphysics might be contrasted with Jean-Luc Marion's eschewal of "metaphysics" in favour of phenomenology as first philosophy. Elsewhere I explore the contrast between his "saturated phenomenon" and what I call "the hyperboles of being," the latter having central bearing on the contested question of God.[3] In some respects, the practice of phenomenology without "metaphysics" reveals a kind of *Kantian flavour* to its understanding of things. But one of the most important sources of the contestation of metaphysics is the negative reaction to the speculative dialectic of *Hegel*. This has significance for the practice of philosophy in America in the twentieth century by Catholic thinkers. Interesting here is the willingness of some Catholic philosophers and departments in Catholic universities to engage in dialogue with Hegel, in sometimes sympathetic ways. The Hegelian approach was sympathetically greeted, in part, I hold, as a response to a loss of a sense of the whole, with the weakening of the prestige and centrality of Aristotelian Thomism in Catholic intellectual circles. Analytic philosophy offered nothing comparable, given its own roots in the rejection of Hegelian holism. The issue of the completion and end of metaphysics stems as much from a response to Hegel as it does from Heidegger, and if there is a continuing need for metaphysics, we have to come to terms with that. Metaxological metaphysics tries to address the question as much relative to Hegel as to Heidegger. Metaxological thinking is post-dialectical in a sense that does not give up on metaphysics, but develops it in directions capable of a generous hermeneutics of earlier metaphysicians in the Western tradition. Such a metaphysics contributes to being catholic as helping make sense of the intimate universal.

If a major attraction of Hegel for some Catholic thinkers was his philosophizing in light of the whole, a serious issue has always been the openness of Hegel's speculative dialectic to the irreducible difference and *mystery* of God. Hegelian thought seems adamant that there is no such thing as irreducible mystery. If we put the matter in terms of the classical formulation of analogy, there is for Hegel no *dissimilitude* of God to created being, dissimilitude always and ever greater than the similitude. The completion of metaphysics is not unconnected with the view that reason now finally has the full measure of mystery, and hence not only conceptually surpasses religious representation (to speak with Hegel), but also surpasses itself, especially in the form of contemplative *theoria*. A metaxological metaphysics in search of the true always remains porous to mystery in the sense relevant here. In what follows I want to address the relation of being true and mystery, a relation that will also help crystallize reflection on the contemporary unavoidability of metaphysics, even taking into account all the forms of critique it has endured since Kant.

Being True and Metaphysics

First I would like to offer some reflections on what I take to be a fruitful way to rethink the necessity of metaphysics. I am cognizant of the prevalence of contemporary claims about the overcoming (*Űberwindung*) of metaphysics (Heidegger), and the destruction (*Destruktion*) of the history of metaphysics (Heidegger again), and the scientistic repudiation of metaphysics (positivism, overt or covert), and the deconstruction of metaphysics (Derrida), and post-metaphysical thinking (Habermas, for instance). Aristotle offers to many an inaugural definition of the nature of metaphysics in terms of a threefold task, namely, as first philosophy (*protē philosophia*) treating of first causes (*aitiai*) or principles (*archai*); as the science of being *qua*; and as the science of the highest being, *ho theos*, the divine. The later, more Scholastic systematization of metaphysics reflects these tasks in terms of *metaphysica generalis* and *metaphysica specialis*, the first dealing with being as *ens commune*, the second dealing with God, the soul, and the world. This definition of Scholastic rationalism is at work in Kant's critique of metaphysics and also in Hegel's post-Kantian science of logic (his "objective logic," he claims, takes the place of *metaphysica generalis* or "ontology").[4]

These considerations help form the context of Heidegger's relation to "metaphysics" and also Marion's claim that phenomenology has now replaced metaphysics as first philosophy.[5] Perhaps it is true that the Aristotelian and Scholastic-rationalist practices of metaphysics are not the last word. Perhaps also they do not exhaust the possible plurality of practices of metaphysical thinking. I think a canonical saying of Aristotle that can still release us to this plurality is: being is said in many senses, *to on legetai pollachōs* (see, e.g. *Meta.*1003b5, 1028a10). Can there be an overcoming of metaphysics if there is no univocal essence of metaphysics to be overcome? What if metaphysics is plurivocal? What also if there are *many practices* of metaphysics: Platonic, Aristotelian,

Thomistic, rationalistic, transcendental, realistic, and so on? To address this plurality as if it were some univocal essence, would this not be too reductive? Is there a secret univocalization of metaphysics at work even in much of the rhetoric that attacks metaphysics as univocal and that proclaims itself as being "post-metaphysical"?

One might speak of metaphysics as first philosophy (*protē philosophia*) insofar as it involves mindful reflection on the plurivocity of meanings of the "to be." The different tasks assigned by Aristotle to metaphysics, tasks fundamental in their way, are secondary to the many senses of the "to be" and will be addressed differently if, for instance, a univocal sense is to the fore, or an equivocal. Nevertheless, all our efforts to be true, all our adventures toward intelligibility, are subtended by different senses of being, though mostly we are unmindful of these as such. We need to be awoken to these senses and their wide-ranging significance. Those who claim to be post-metaphysical are as much in their debt as are the metaphysicians they claim to overcome. From this point of view there is no overcoming of metaphysics – overcoming metaphysics is itself metaphysics.

The issue here is both historical and systematic, but the systematic point is crucial. Human beings can think and live intelligently and in openness to the intelligibility of things without an explicit metaphysics; however, to be a philosopher who engages with first philosophy, one must search for some more explicit mindfulness, attentive to the enabling sources of such intelligence and intelligibility. This means bringing a developed habit of mindfulness to bear on what is at play in being, first with regard to the many senses of the "to be," and then especially with regard to the basic presuppositions, sources, and orientations toward the "to be" that mark our being in the midst of things. Even when we claim to be post-metaphysicians we are the *animale metaphysicum* (as Schopenhauer put it). Post-metaphysicians may not be the best of metaphysicians, but willy-nilly some implicit metaphysics, or set of metaphysical presuppositions, is at work. This is not to say that metaphysics is everything, for we can understand things without reflection about the enabling sources of being and minding. But trying to be mindful of these sources is essential to the task of first philosophy. This does not make metaphysics a first grounding science on the foundation of which other sciences are then built. This is not a good way to put the point. In fact, metaphysics as first philosophy is always secondary, in the sense that it presupposes the enabling of these sources, in either an ontological or an epistemic sense. We wake up in the midst of things and this enabling is already effective, and it is only when our waking up turns in a certain direction to what is at play in the between that metaphysics as a more reflective mindfulness begins to take shape. This is not an *a priori* dictation to the between, but rather an awakening to a certain fidelity to it, to the *wording* of the between. Metaphysical presuppositions about the "to be" are at play mostly unacknowledged, in common sense, in politics, in ethics, in art, in science, in religion, in philosophy, indeed in "post-metaphysical" philosophy itself. We are called to ontological fidelity: to be true in mindfulness to what is thus at play in the wording of the between.[6]

The post-metaphysicians often present their point in epochal terms: ancient, medieval, modern, postmodern. And then, almost like postmodern Comtean priests, they announce the arrival of the new era of the post-metaphysical. But if the question is more crucially systematic than historical, then the issue is more elemental than epochal. The perplexities are ancient, yet not ancient: they are archaic in bearing on what originates all determinate questions, and so they abide with us and are as new as the day after tomorrow – always behind us, always before us, perhaps because always deeper than us and always above us too. Indeed in relation to the archaic perplexities – and Plato and Aristotle already gave admirable expression to them – there is never an absolutely final settlement. These perplexities are not determinate univocal problems that can be solved once and for all and so dissolved and put behind us. This point holds for the premodern, the modern, or the postmodern. "Post-metaphysical" thinking hinders rather than helps us if it blocks the living memory of these archaic perplexities. There is, for us, no univocal final settlement of the deepest metaphysical questions. They arise from primal astonishment, itself elemental rather than epochal. They give expression to perplexities beyond any one determinate settlement, perplexities that belong to no epoch but mark us as what we are: mindful beings astonishingly awoken to the intimate strangeness of being. These perplexities return to us again and again, and again and again we must turn to them. Post-metaphysicians turn away from the return, and miss the turn again and again.

What I call metaxological metaphysics has a kind of likeness to the "step back" (*der Schritt zurück*) out of metaphysics enjoined by Heidegger, though in a sense quite different from the one intended by him. The metaxological "step back" is from "metaphysics" understood as a determinate practice of metaphysical thinking, in this way or that. As with the many senses of being, there are many more or less determinate practices of metaphysics, and not all of them stay true to their own originating sources. Some practices of metaphysical thinking betray their enabling sources in the act of claiming to complete or realize them. An analogous point has relevance to ethics, and to the potencies of the ethical.[7] We need to "step back" out of different, determinate ethical systems in order to understand the ethos of being as hospitable, or not, to good as manifesting, or not, the good of the "to be." Understanding the different ethical potencies allows us to understand better the enabling powers of being ethical, different minglings of which, or particular dominances of which, go into the formation of determinate ethical outlooks, such as Platonism or Christianity, or Kantianism or Nietzscheanism, to name an important few. Analogously in metaphysics, there are ontological-metaphysical potencies that enable the practices of a determinate form of metaphysics and that can enter into a plurality of formations with one another but that are never exhausted by any particular practice. These ontological potencies enable us to configure the primal ethos of being, and we live in the reconfigured ethos, often forgetting the more primally given ethos of being. Part of the task of the metaxological "step back" is to come to some mindfulness of this primal ethos and to the already operative potencies of being that are at work there and that enable the different determinate formations of our thinking. This "step back" is not a step outside the between. We are determined out of the primal ethos and enabled to be relatively self-determining, but we participate in that ethos as more than all determinations and our self-determination. We cross through it, pass along it, we come to it again by passage in and through the determinate and the self-determining, and through the informing senses of the "to be," through univocity, equivocity, dialectic, and metaxology. The primal ethos and the enabling potencies cannot be deconstructed, for these are what enable both construction and deconstruction and are beyond both. They are at work even when we claim to be post-metaphysical, which is never post-metaphysical in fact, but always a condition more or less sleeping to what enables it as a determinate practice of anti-metaphysical thinking. And so even to be anti-metaphysical is again to be metaphysical.

Being True and Mystery

I turn to the question of metaphysics and mystery mentioned in my opening remarks. This seems to be an important consideration in thinkers considered Catholic, Marcel for instance. Below I will return to his distinction between mystery and problem in the context of different senses of being true. An adequate understanding of the relation between mystery and being true brings us closer to a practice of metaphysics consonant with its original vocation and with the contemporary metaxological metaphysics here proposed.

Mystery is often seen by philosophers as an *epistemic nullity*. We are said to invoke mystery when we do not understand, when we cannot understand, when we are unwilling to try to understand. Mystery stalls us on a limit, one on which nothing of epistemic note happens. To grant mystery is to surrender to obscurity, to abdicate the challenge of cognition, whether philosophic or scientific. Knowing and truth in the relevant regard here are often seen in the light of *determinacy* and *determinability*. If to know is to know something intelligibly, that is, to know it determinately, mystery must be seen negatively in this light of the indigence of knowing. To know the truth of something is to be related to it in a manner determinable in principle. As supposedly beyond determination and determinability, an appeal to mystery is symptomatic of epistemic emptiness, a concession to indeterminacy that conceals a sterile surrender to ignorance. Mystery perhaps *might* be invoked when a limit of knowing is reached, as a *provisional pause* in the otherwise endless quest for further and more adequate determination, but in itself mystery can claim no respect, much less reverence. I have worries here about Lonergan's approach to mystery when he speaks of it in terms of a "known unknown," as he puts it, relative to which "there always is the further question" to be asked.[8] But if the kind of further question is essentially oriented to determinability alone, it seems hard to avoid this negative sense of mystery.

This general view, I suggest, is not fully true to either truth or mystery. Interestingly, some of the same things so said about *determinability* could be turned in directions that yield quite different perspectives. Thus we might be referred to the "beyond" of determinability, where indeed there is a kind of poverty of knowing, but strangely this poverty is rich with promise – the promise of what I would call the *overdeterminacy* of being true, indeed the overdeterminacy of being. In this light, mystery could not be seen as the opposite of truth, except insofar as the latter is too rigidly tied to univocal articulation, tied to clear, precise, and fixed determinacy. The question is whether such a determination of being true is true to being true. Is it true to the overdeterminacy of being that, in the determinacy, communicates of what cannot be made completely determinate, and that exceeds the measure of our self-determination?

I speak of "being true," and deliberately so in that I want to invoke a condition *between* being and truth. One hesitates in speaking of truth with a big T, worrying about a potentially misleading substantializing of the true. One need not object to the intimation that there is truth in a superlative sense toward which we are orientated – indeed truth in a hyperbolic sense. But it is a fair question whether the superlatively true can be either simply objectified or simply subjectified. A certain articulation of "between-being" is manifested in the human participation in truth. This is something acknowledged, for instance, in Plato's recognition that we do not possess the complete knowing of the god nor are we marked by the absence of knowing we seem to find in the beast. In between, we know we do not know, otherwise we could not acknowledge our ignorance. But to be able to grant our ignorance is to *know* we do not know, and still this is to know. It is to know especially our desire for the true as an initially unwilled exigency to seek the true not yet known. This unbidden seeking is not something determinate simply, but opens and enables our attentive mindfulness to all determinate things, a mindfulness in promise that is not exhausted by any determinate limit. It emerges in and out of an original porosity of being, prior to and exceeding any determinate desire to know. Moreover, the unbidden seeking is not defined at the outset by our powers of self-determination. We wake up to ourselves as not-knowing before we know ourselves as desiring to know. There is the event of astonishment that carries into us the emphatic strike of an otherness that yet is intimately inward. The emphatic strike and the intimately inward pass into each other in the *dawning* mindfulness that we do not know and would know – what exactly it is we would know in a determinate sense, we do not know at the outset – yet we wake up to ourselves as in search.

We search, but yet again we could not search at all did not some secret intimation of what we seek companion our seeking. This companioning testifies to our between-being: we seek, but only because seeking carries a promise of being able to recognize the sought, if the sought is found, if perhaps indeed it finds us. Without the promise of this recognition, no knowing would be possible, no seeking would be enabled at all. We are seekers already in some enigmatic communication with what we seek, or it with us. Nor is the seeking only an indeterminate openness, for such an indeterminate openness would be just an opening and nothing more. There would be no seeking as such, no further determination, for any seeking and further determination are always governed by more than the purely indeterminate. Purely indeterminate seeking would not be able to acknowledge that we have found the truth we sought when we have found it. Through indeterminacy alone there will be no passage of seeking that genuinely passes as true seeking. It is not that we must reject the notion of an indeterminate openness; but there is more at play in the indeterminate than the indeterminate. We do not possess the absolute truth; we are not devoid of a relation to the true; we are *called* to be true, not only to ourselves but also to what as other to us calls us forth into the porous space of middle mindfulness between the seeking and the sought.

Being true: I would say this has to do with a condition of *being* – a condition of being mindful about being. In this there is the call of a certain fidelity – *fidelity* to what dawns in our waking up to mindfulness, fidelity to what strikes us into waking in its otherness to our self-determination. We do not construct any of this at the outset. It is prior to construction and deconstruction. For every construction and indeed deconstruction presupposes being true as enabling them to do their work. In this dawning, there is something intimate, indeed intimated – we might even speak of a *confiding*. There is a kind of *ontological confidentiality* in the happening of being true itself, and a call to a fidelity to, or with ("con"), what communicates itself in the confidence. An extreme sceptic might want to claim that this is all a "confidence trick" and in the end nothing trustworthy at all. But could we even talk at all of any "confidence trick" if there were not already given a space in which the *anterior confidence* was at work? To wake up to a "confidence trick" we must already be in a space of confidence relative to the trustworthiness of waking up at all. The betrayal in the "confidence trick" is derivative from the trustworthiness of an anterior confidence in waking up as an already given promise of being true. The "confidence trick" is a betrayal of the promise of the original confidence in being true.

Of course, we are using the language of *fides*, of faith here: fidelity, confidence, confidentiality. There is a kind of intimate loyalty, or claim of loyalty, in the dawning of the mindfulness that we are to be true. This ontological fidelity merits deeper consideration both from the side of we who seek to know, as well as from the side of that which we seek to know. What is true is what remains true, and remaining true signifies a constant "being with": our constancy in the light of what communicates itself as constant; the constancy of what communicates itself as most ultimately reliable, that is, what we can most trust, what is most trustworthy in the happening of being.

In some ways this is to state anew an old truth, namely, that with regard to truth we are dealing with a necessity we cannot entirely escape, though we can misunderstand or distort or betray it. In evading the call to be true we are unable to evade entirely the necessity of being true. At an extreme, the denial of truth is itself, by implication, a claim to be true, so the claim denying truth is untrue, in being itself marked by a certain embrace of truth. While we can here invoke the notion of performative contradiction, there is more at issue than a trick of logic. What we might call the cunning of logic reveals a necessity in being true that yet is also the enabling of the freedom to be true, or untrue. So we find a troubling doubleness: in the release of this freedom, fidelity to the promise of being true can also become betrayal of the promise. Our being true is placed between extremes of fidelity and betrayal, stressed between them, even torn. The fidelity of being true, or its betrayal, has both epistemic and ontological sides: it does entail an attentive mindfulness being true to itself, but it is a matter not of being true only to itself but rather to being as other to itself. One might say that the true is not simply for us, but it may be for us to transcend ourselves to what is true as it is for itself. There is a certain service of the true in our going toward its otherness, that is, in our openness to what is true in and for itself.

In the language of a certain form of love, and as I have put it elsewhere, being truthful may be an *agapeic service of the true*.[9] We do not have to know the absolute truth for this to be so. We can acknowledge the fact that often we are split creatures, torn between our doubt and our ardour for truth. Even when we know we are other to the truth, we are related to it in its otherness. Truth as other to us thus shows a certain intimacy to us in the very seeking by us of truth as not being in our possession. There may even be a *dispossession* in being true, intensifying as the intimate call of being true comes most deeply home to us. But even in dispossession the relation of "being between" holds. An extreme lack, when intimately minded – and we are as this intimate minding – cannot be called simply a lack and should be more truly named as a longing or a love. We are beyond ourselves in this intimate longing, but the other unknowingly loved cannot be simply beyond, or entirely beyond all knowing. There is a mysterious criss-crossing of the intimate and the beyond, an enigmatic interpenetration of the empty and the full, a marriage of dispossession and plenitude.

In a more sober way of putting it, one might say that the true sought in our being true cannot be just an indeterminate regulative ideal or only a determinate constituted reality. Yet it is both regulative and constitutive. It regulates our search yet it is not something we self-constitute. Our love of the true is regulative as an ideal to which we aspire, but it is also more than just an ideal, since even to be an ideal, hence regulative, there must be an actual bond with the true that is already constitutive and immanently at work. The service of truth we find in our being truthful is enacted in a between space of otherness that is also a sign on our part of an always finite knowing that knows it does not possess the true absolutely. Again, the language of possession may not be entirely the right way to speak of being true. Yet what is not attained by us is *with us* in our desiring of it.

Being True to Mystery: Between Determinability and the Overdeterminate

Being true, like being itself, is said in many senses. In analogy with Aristotle's *to on legetai pollachōs*, I would like to say *to alēthes legetai pollachōs*. The true is said in many senses correlative to the many senses of the "to be," and this has an important bearing on how we stand in relation to mystery. I summarize in broad terms four senses of being and then correlate them with different senses of being true.[10]

First, the *univocal* sense of being stresses the notion of sameness, or unity, indeed sometimes immediate sameness, of mind and being. Correlative to the univocal sense of being is the search for determinate solutions to determinate problems, impelled by specific curiosity. Second, the *equivocal* sense accentuates diversity, perhaps the unmediated difference of being and mind, sometimes to the point of setting them into oppositional otherness that can rouse restless perplexity in the face of troubling ambiguities. Third, the *dialectical* sense emphasizes the mediation of the different in terms of the reintegrating power of a more inclusive unity. In modern dialectic, we find a strong stress on the self-determination of thought and the primary mediation tends to become a complex form of self-mediation. Fourth, the *metaxological* sense gives a *logos* of the *metaxu*, putting the stress on the wording of the between, in light of the intermediated community of being, intermediation more than the self-mediation of the same. It gives articulation to pluralized intermediation(s), beyond the self-determination of the same. The *inter* is shaped plurally such that, in a way, the *logos* of the *metaxu* is closer to ancient practices of dialectic, for instance, Socratic-Platonic dialogue, than to modern ones, such as Hegel's. The spaces of otherness in the between remain open. In that between there may be disturbing ruptures that shake the self-satisfaction of self-determining thought, which again and again finds itself intruded on by the overdetermined givenness of being. The metaxological is not our construction (though we construct in the *metaxu*) but is at work before we articulate it reflectively in our categories. There is an immediacy to metaxological intermediacy: a pre-objective and pre-subjective community of being that is also trans-objective and trans-subjective. The *metaxu* enables the work of articulation in the univocal, equivocal, and dialectical formations, but if we absolutize any of these, we risk being untrue to the intermediacy of the given ethos of being in its overdeterminacy. A metaxological philosophy does not reject these other three senses, but seeks to bring them into true alignment with their own promise of overdeterminacy, be it in the form of determination, indetermination, or self-determination.

In light of this fourfold, there is a plurivocity of being true that itself could be correlated with the notions of the determinate, the indeterminate, the self-determining, and the overdeterminate. We will see how this has implications for how we remain true to mystery. Again in broad outlines, with the univocal sense given its head, truth tends to be defined in terms of determination and determinability; with the insinuation of the equivocal sense, the notion of a fixed truth is open to the flux of a more fluid indeterminacy; when dialectical considerations come to the fore, the search for the true as the immanently coherent emerges, and in the case of modern dialectic the inseparability of truth and self-determination; when metaxological mindfulness emerges, being true comes to be under fidelity to the overdetermination of being as given to be. The plurivocity of being true does not imply a relativism that claims "there is no truth." It does suggest a kind of relativism in the sense that "being in relation" is crucial to our being true. Nevertheless, "being in relation" is inflected in a plurality of ways, none of which are outside the space wherein the call of fidelity to the true is communicated to us as mindful beings. Different modes of being true reveal different, though related, modes of being in relation mindfully to the happening of being.

Univocity, Equivocity, Being True to Mystery

Where univocity is a dominant requirement, in practical common sense, for instance, or empirical science, the notion of truth as a form of *correctness* comes more to the fore, with a dominant stress on determination and determinability. A proposition is true if, given its univocal enunciation, it corresponds one to one to a state of affairs, itself conceived as there with a clear-cut, fixed, cut-and-dried status. There is an essential place for determinable truth obviously, without which we could not find our way around in the midst of things. Yet the terms of the relation of *adequatio* or correspondence are not themselves so easily fixed in a univocal sense, nor indeed is the relation between them, nor indeed is the milieu of being, the between, wherein these terms and their relation come to some determinacy. There is something more than the determinate at work on all these scores, and the hint of a certain indeterminacy is unavoidable, particularly with respect to what enables the dynamism of these terms and the relation between them. Finally, this needs the invocation of the overdeterminate, not just as the indeterminate, but as the too muchness of the given between of being.[11]

One might correlate determinability with a straightforward "either/or" between the true and the false: the true is what it is in virtue of not being untrue, and between the two there is a pure exclusion at work. But then: a prayer is neither true nor false, as Aristotle says (*On Interpretation*, part 4, 17a3–4). Yet, one might suggest, there is a being true in praying that seems impossible to fix with determinable univocity: am I, in praying, in communication with the ultimate, or do I communicate with nothing? Sometimes one cannot answer "yes" or "no," yet one prays, and there is something right in the praying and in the continuation without determinable certainty, and being before nothing is not entirely unlike being before God. Praying is hyperbolic to propositional univocity.

The equivocal has to be acknowledged, and this not merely in the sense of a problematic ambiguity that must be overcome with a further univocal truth. The equivocal testifies to a doubleness of showing and concealing, to be true to which requires a finesse for ambiguity over which a more imperial univocity is tempted to run roughshod. If we were to use Pascal's terms, being true in the univocal instance calls on the *esprit de géométrie*, whereas being true in relation to equivocal showing and concealing requires the *esprit de finesse*. Of course, there are challenges to the task of being true here. Equivocity may seem so all-pervasive that we are inclined to surrender to despair of ever attaining the true. The reign of the untrue can seem to be installed with an equivocity so dominant as to seem tyrannical, inducing a hopelessness about accession to a more constant truth. Some of the demands made on being true here are reflected in the stress on doubt, local or hyperbolic, even to scepticism about the possibility of attaining truth at all.

Interestingly, there are practices of sceptical thought that, while denying the adequacy of univocal approaches to the most important things, bring us through equivocity to the verge of a sense of mystery. I think of Pascal again. One might also recall Gabriel Marcel's important distinction between problem and mystery as reflecting the difference between a determinable univocity and an equivocity bordering on mystery.[12] A problem can be objectified; a mystery involves us such that it cannot be completely objectified. Because the problem can be objectifiably determined, in principle it admits of a determinate solution. Because mystery cannot be so objectified, we find ourselves implicated in what is at issue; in this same vein, mystery does not imply a necessarily correlated "solution." The language of the problem and univocal solubility is not appropriate to the mystery. I would stress that the mystery is of *being* – this is why it implicates us in a manner we cannot entirely objectify, or master through self-determining thought. But – and this is not a point really stressed by Marcel – it also implicates the ontological enigma of "objects": their being objects, both as objects and as being at all. One would not want to confine mystery solely to that wherein we find ourselves implicated. The mystery we are in passes beyond us, in more senses that one – perhaps even in an infinite sense. As I would put it, the overdeterminacy is of the being of both objects and subjects – and of what is more than can be captured in the language of objects and subjects.

Along the same lines one might suggest also: there is no problem of evil; there is the *mysterium iniquitatis*; there is a regard in which the problem of evil is insoluble. There is no problem of God; there is the mystery of the divine; the superlative mystery of God is insoluble. None of this means absurdity that puts an end to thought – quite the opposite. There is an intensification of mindfulness in the face of this problematic insolubility. There is the energizing of mindfulness in the dimension of the hyperbolic, an energizing that is paradoxically a recourse to an old and new poverty of philosophy. One must see mystery in terms of the original marvel of the middle – disclosed in astonishment. But this is not indeterminacy, tied to the teleology of cognition understood as driven forward from an indeterminate perplexity to a determinate solution. This latter is more a modality of curiosity that cognitively might be said to move from the initially more or less determinate articulation of a problem to the progressively determinate articulation and solution of it. Curiosity is driven beyond itself toward an account of the matter at issue as determinate as is possible. For curiosity, the goal is for there to be no marvel, no wonder, no mystery. Indeed this teleology of determinate cognition is inseparable from a secretly working project of self-determination. If we can prove ourselves cognitively on a par with, even superior to, the indeterminacy of the initial perplexity, we can prove ourselves to be the measure of all that is problematic, if only in principle – and hence the whole point is to further our own project of self-determination. Not that the determinate as such is the point of the project, but our determination of the determinate, and hence our powers of self-determination, as in excess of every determinacy so fixed by us. The teleology of intrusive curiosity is related to Descartes's ambition to become the "master and possessor of nature."

I see the situation here as double: scepticism may be unavoidable in relation to our failures to attain the true, but it may also be our *honest confession* that we do not know for sure. While the first outlook seems an all but negative outcome, the second is not so, since its very honesty is testimonial to the call to be true, immanently at work in our very failure to attain the true. We must be true to the failure not to attain the true, and in being thus true, we remain on the path of being true, and hence there is no complete failure here. In wrestling with the equivocal, there is an angel in the shadows. There is the possibility for the purgation of our porosity to the true. We are called into question by the failure, we call ourselves into question, but all of this means that the exigent call of being true is inextirpable in our seeking. Hence while we seem to be outside the truth, it is revealed immanently to us that the call to be true is intimate to what we are. What is at stake here is not a simple indeterminacy, though there *is* an indeterminacy. There is the intimate porosity to truth in our being true. And this intimate porosity, while all but nothing, is not nothing. It is the secret agapeics of the overdeterminate truth, that makes a way by making way – making way in a space of porosity where the spirit of being true springs up in us. Being truthful in not possessing the true – the (equivocal) conjunction of the opposites of our lacking and being full are there in that event of not knowing, and knowing we do not know.

When I speak of porosity to the true, it is appropriate to offer a remark or two on Heidegger's discussion of truth as *homoiosis* and as *alētheia*. With respect to the plurivocity of being true, the matter is not just the doublet of determinate truth and an otherwise indeterminate unhiding that is said to be more primordial than propositional truth. Heidegger is not wrong to call attention to a sense of being true that is more primordial than propositional truth, for we must presuppose our already being in a porosity to the true for us to be able to determine this way or that the truth-worthiness of this determinate proposition or that. His doublet of propositional truth (kataphatic?) and *alētheia* (apophatic?) is important, but there is more to be said and it is not evident to me that Heidegger always sees or acknowledges what more is at stake in the opening beyond determinable and determinate truths.

There is the fact that his sense of *alētheia* particularly stresses the privative nature of the unconcealing. *To alēthes* is the unhidden – *das Un-verborgene. Alētheia* is the privation of hiddenness – *Unverborgenheit.* Heidegger even uses the likeness of a robbery (*ein Raub*) when speaking of the uncovering of truth in *Being and Time* (§29). With respect to the primal porosity of our being true, it is not a matter of an oscillation between determinate and indeterminate. A privative unconcealing is not quite true enough to the overdeterminacy of the mystery as giving the porosity, and enabling our *passio essendi* as itself a *conatus* for the truth. One might venture that in the *conatus* is a kind of ontological "connaturality" between our being true and the true as other to us, and always as overdeterminate (not just indeterminate) in excess of our determination and self-determination. This is agapeic surplus rather than negation of a hiddenness and privative unhiding. Nature loves to hide, yes, Heraclitus is not wrong. But nature hides in being out in the open and being out in the open is more primordial than hiding. Being out in the open: the porosity as the between space of communication in which beings come plurivocally to passing.

In Heidegger, what seems like the equiprimordiality of hiding and revealing seems finally to tilt asymmetrically toward a more primal hiddenness. This might be true, in one sense (to speak theologically), for the hyperbolic God who dwells in light inaccessible, but not quite so, for nature naturing, or nature natured; though in another sense this hyperbolic God is nothing but self-revealing, even granting the asymmetrical transcendence of the divine. This God is not the Heideggerian origin. (An image comes to mind of a self-retracting source that is turned back in to itself in being turned out of itself.) I wonder if some residue of thinking as negativity is at work in our relation to this happening of unhiding, if it should turn out there is no unhiddenness at all, if we humans do not bring to express manifestation the work of unhiding. This seems to be the case to the extent that Heidegger suggests there is no truth without the human being. There seems to be a kind of violence in the pursuit of it – as in his interpretation of Plato's cave, especially with respect to the going up to the surface of the earth and into the light of the sun. Rather than the benign violence of the beautiful, as one might put it, rather than the sudden porosity and the *passio essendi* that comes to outing in erotic self-surpassing, this is more reminiscent of a willful *conatus essendi* forcing its way to the top, in a *polemos* that has too many traces of *eros turannos*. I do not doubt the equivocity of eros, but at times Heidegger seems relatively asleep to this matter. The affirmative sense of the being given of being, in its coming to be, is there in the porosity of being, and hence is not to be defined in terms of the privative or the negative. A pious question to (the later) Heidegger: How do you get from *Polemos* to *Gelassenheit*, from theft to gift, from robbery to a kind of grace? Answer: the silence of mystery?

Dialectic in Hegelian and post-Hegelian form is shaped by the dyad of determination and indeterminacy, and then by the transformation via negation of indeterminacy into self-determining thinking. Heidegger's sense of the unhidden is set against this last outcome, but there are dyadic elements of the syndrome as a whole at work in his thinking. Hence again my wonder about the dyad determination/determinability and the indeterminate, and a movement back and forth between the two, including a deconstruction of the determinate and the regress to the indeterminate. All of this is without dialectic, such that Heidegger can draw attention to a between space in the middle between these two. And while this between space cannot be univocally determined or dialectically self-determined, there is no pursuit of a wording of the between in the kind of metaxological terms I propose. In the end one wonders if there is more of a reiterated sense of the play of univocal determination and equivocal indetermination, with a repeated sense of the equivocity of the self-concealing origin, even in its partial determination out in the light of the unhidden. There is nothing of the paradoxical doubleness of the porosity of being which, if it is to be thought as indeterminate at all, must be given the more affirmative name of the overdeterminate: the always more that, when we try to determine or self-determine it, passes beyond us, before us, as if almost nothing, and not ourselves. Full and empty it manifests the kind of saturated equivocity relative to which the metaxological calls for finesse. One thinks again of Heraclitus (so beloved of Heidegger, as indeed of Hegel and Nietzsche) when he says that Zeus is both satiety and famine.

Dialectic and Being True to Mystery

To come back more directly to the fourfold sense of being: if the very notion of truth may be contested in light of the equivocal, the dialectical and metaxological orientations need not shirk the extreme challenge posed by this. The possible ways of developing the promise of truth are plural, and now to take the dialectical way, we are asked to nurture the seed of mediation that already is intimated in the equivocities of being true – intimated in the truthfulness to self and immanent exigency of honesty asked of us, even when we know we do not know the truth. Suppose the true is other to our comprehension, yet we can further this immanent exigency to be true, even while the true as *other* still solicits our attentive listening. The true as other in not incommunicably other, as we learn from dialogical exchange. In the communicative exchange between self and other, there is an interplay with a *being true more than self or other*, and that yet is immanent in the intermediation between them. The interplay of oneself and an other comes to be articulated along lines in which both sides are subject to the truth coming to manifestation in their communication. This is truth in one regard immanent, and in another regard transcendent, since though its eventuation happens between them, it either subtends or overarches the contributions of the partners in dialogue. Otherwise no true communication takes place, and no communication in the unfolding of being true.

One of the traditional theories of truth that stresses this immanence of the true is the *coherence theory* – not one side, not the other side, but all the sides of the matter, all the way to the whole of the matter, must be taken together, to get the best sense of the truth at issue. There is much to be said for this view. Still, the question for the coherence theory is whether it shortchanges what disrupts coherence, what resists inclusion in a whole marked by immanent relations only. Being true here finally seems to rest fully at home within a frame of things that is immanently inclusive, even all the way to the inclusiveness of the absolute whole. That is to say, the question of a more *heterogeneous truth*, in excess of an immanent holism, comes to trouble us here. An immanent holism may not be fully true to the mystery of the overdeterminacy of being. Perhaps indeed the fullness of the whole is not the surplus over-fullness of the overdeterminate. It is, of course, deeply perplexing to consider whether there is something more than the whole. What more could there possibly be? Is the question itself not enmeshed in self-contradictory equivocities? – not local equivocities here or there, but at the level of the whole, where, if anywhere, dialectical thinking holds that all equivocities are to be resolved. Yet the intimation that the overdeterminate is not exhausted by an immanent holism refuses to be put to sleep. If one were to put the point theologically, one would have to ask if there is a God beyond the whole, or whether all Gods are of the whole or within the whole.[13]

While dialectical interplay reveals plural possibilities, there can be the temptation to recur to a kind of inclusive univocity in the face of the multiplied equivocities. I find this not just in the coherence theory in general, but also see it carried to an extreme in the modern practice of self-mediating dialectic that reaches its consummation in Hegel's way of thinking. There is an interplay of self and other, but the other is a medial other and serves the dialectic as bringing thought through every opposition to being to a more ultimate mediation with itself. Hegel speaks of "pure self-recognition in absolute otherness,"[14] and contemporary pluralists, eager to make Hegel a more comfortable fellow-traveller with our *Zeitgeist*, pounce on the absolute *Anderssein* as evidence of his "openness to otherness." There is no question of this openness, but the issue is the form it takes and how the openness takes form in the relations *between* self and other. In fact, Hegel's *Anderssein* or "being other" is not really absolute otherness; rather, it is the *pure self-recognition* that governs the entire operation of the relation in-between. The absolute otherness is itself qualified by this and so is less absolute in its otherness as such than would appear to be the case at first glance. The true is the whole, in Hegel's famous phrase.[15] This is not untrue, but being true, as in the between, is more than the whole. The heterogeneity of the true over the immanent dialectic of being true is at stake in the metaxological understanding.

In this form of dialectic we witness the self-determination of being true, and the question is whether this form corrals the overdetermination of being. Certainly this self-determination could be seen as fulfilling a kind of teleology from indetermination through determination to thinking's desire to be true to itself and its own immanent exigency. Undoubtedly, this is something appealing in Hegel, but the question persists as to whether in all instances justice is done to the overdeterminacy. Not surprisingly, the mystery is dispelled. This form of dialectic is more linked to a teleology of knowing that proceeds from wonder to the dissolution of wonder – in terms not of a determinate truth but rather of a self-determining "being true," relative to which there is nothing finally other. Wonder at the mystery may, on this view, be granted at the beginning, but at the end this is entirely brought out of its hiddenness, and there is no more wonder, and no more mystery. This is explicitly so in Hegel's understanding of the teleology of art and religion, each privileged with membership of absolute spirit, but a membership that in the end is overtaken by the ultimacy of philosophy and its concept, for which there is no mystery, in principle and in the end. Interestingly, Hegel does speak of the mystical as passing beyond the understanding (*Verstand*), but the mystery does not pass beyond Reason (*Vernunft*), for on this truest level, it is perfectly manifest.

Metaxology and Being True to Mystery

In the metaxological orientation to truth, we are seeking to do justice to the overdeterminacy of being, beyond determination, indeterminacy, and self-determination. Moreover, the overdeterminacy is at issue with respect to both selving and othering, as well as to the between-relations in which and through which they are in communication. Both selving and othering have to be granted their truth and their asking of us that we be true to both. For there is an immanent otherness to selving that is the threshold of the overdeterminate in the intimacy of our singular being. Furthermore, there is the exceeding otherness of the milieu of being in its given thereness that communicates plurivocally the ontological potencies of the (primal) ethos. (In *God and the Between* I speak of these plurivocal communications in terms of the hyperboles of being, and they serve as thresholds of mystery.) A dialectical holism does not seem true enough to the overdeterminacy of selving and othering, and of both together. By contrast, a *logos* of the *metaxu* suggests a community of being true that is faithful to the pluralism of relations between self and other. The point could be put from the side of the universal *or* the particular. The point is evident even when the singular is in revolt against the community. The solicitation of this fidelity is at work even in the corrosion of scepticism or in self-congratulation about one's superior irony. There is always the call of truth – an *anankē* from which we cannot escape, since every escape is within this *anankē* we think we are escaping. This *anankē* witnesses to an already effective community of mind and truth, at work in the mindfulness that tries to be truthful. It would be difficult to make sense of our seeking this or that truth, were we not already in such a reserved community. We are what we are as truth-seekers by virtue of being in this metaxological community of truth. We are truthful by virtue of being able to cooperate faithfully in the work of its truth.

An interesting point is that the *pragmatic notion of truth* (in C.S. Peirce, for instance) in its appeal to the "the long run," vis-à-vis the community of inquiry, shares something with the more recent deconstruction of univocal truth, perhaps because both are in the end essentially "Kantian" positions.[16] We can see both as moving beyond a univocal fixation with the present, and what we now determine to be the case. We might fear that the present fixes us to what is, but there is an equivocity in all of this. I would ask: if we appeal to the long run, are we appealing just to the true as a regulative ideal, and if so, is it only a heuristic anticipation we cannot avoid, yet that never allows us now to say without demur: this is? Truth risks being an always deferred other, then, not entirely different from the indeterminate "to come" we find with deconstruction, or that place "somewhere over the rainbow" about which the song dreams. To cite the White Queen in *Alice Through the Looking Glass*: "The rule is, jam to-morrow, jam yesterday but never jam today … It's jam every other day: today isn't any other day, you know." Alice objects: "It MUST come sometimes to 'jam today.'" She truthfully answers the White Queen, "It's dreadfully confusing!" Alice is a wise child. We too must ask if there is any sense in which the true is constituted as actual. I think one has to say that if truth is only what will come to be determined "in the long run," then we risk evacuating it of its claim. In pointing beyond the univocal fixation of the present, and invoking a deferral that will never end, we offer in the latter case a voiding equivocation not only in relation to the true as such, but also in relation to our own being true. Suppose the true were only a regulative ideal toward which we move, or something to come on which we must await, perhaps in a painful process of infinite deferment – then can we even speak of the true as such an "ideal" at all, and can we make any intelligible sense of the character of our longing and waiting?

Put simply, can any ideal be regulative at all, if it is not in some respect *already at work* in our present circumstances, drawing on our seeking, or spurring our transcending, or communicating to us what we now lack, though we long for it? The true has to be already at play now; it cannot be deferred to what will eventually be established, for then it would never eventually be established. Our truthful longing moves us "toward" the true, and in this "toward" the true is already intimate, otherwise there would be no longing at all, and no being truthful, even when we know we do not know the truth. Being truthful points to a constitutive true, and this is there enigmatically, and overdeterminately at work in the between. Once again the overdetermination is not an indeterminacy, and while it may be beyond univocal determination, it is not exhausted by a self-determining process of thought. Put it this way: *One has to raise the doubleness of the equivocal to a higher level of finesse.* This is ingredient in what it means to be true to mystery. Thus one might suggest that the true is *both* a regulative ideal (for we never completely possess it, though we might always tend toward it) *and* constitutive actuality, especially with respect to its already effectively being at work intimately in our being truthful. The longing of being truthful is a belonging with and to the true as intimately communicating in and through our self-transcending. The true is constitutive in regard to our being truthful; it is regulative as the unconditional and ultimate, toward which we tend but of which we are never the masters. We are never on a par with truth's transcendence. The double nature of metaxological truth reflects this. This is a position that is neither Kantian nor Hegelian. Kant postulates a regulative ideal with a kind of transcendence – an always deferred completion that cannot explain the present work of the unconditioned. Hegel proposes a constitutive ideal entirely immanent – unconditionally immanent truth without proper reserve and without true transcendence.

In relation to being true metaxologically, it is not a question of pitting this against the other configurations of being true but more a matter of aligning them with the fuller reserves of the promise of truth diversely at work in each. We can recuperate something of the truth of correspondence in being true metaxologically. Correspondence is not univocal facticity, not idealistic generality, but *truthful responsibility*, a shared honesty of being inseparable from the communication of being true. Nor do we close ourselves off from the sting of scepticism or harden ourselves to all the seductive insinuations of equivocity, or turn our backs on the relative responsibility of self-determining thinking. These too awaken in the unconditional call to be truthful, awaken us to this call, and so partake of the community of being true. Our middle condition comes home to us in a shared metaphysical con-fidence of being. An intermediated condition of being truthful incarnates for human beings an elemental honesty and ultimate metaphysical con-fidence. We come to know ourselves in a community of truth already shared, and shaping us before we shape ourselves. (This is a very Catholic thought, especially too if one's sense of the catholic points toward the *intimate universal*.) Our share of truth, our sharing of truth in being truthful, partakes of what is always more. Once again we do not possess absolute truth, but in honesty we are not devoid of community with it. In the between-beings we are, these extremes of poverty and plenty touch and spark, in the night of mystery, an astonishing asking of us to be truthful. We cannot close back into ourselves out of relation to what is other and beyond us. Quite to the contrary, there can be no such closure, for as between-beings we are beyond ourselves in being ourselves.

In summary, then, there is a plurivocity to being true metaxologically. First, there is the unconditional demand of *truth to self*. This may entail a cruel purgation, since we are often vain, and love the untruth of the half-true. There is an agapeic generosity to self in being true to self – in the end a consent that is not at all cruel. The most intimate cruelty occurs in the way we are the untrue in fighting against the purgation of our clogged porosity of being, porosity to the true. There is something existential about this, and there can also be something confessional about this. It bears on a witness to self, a witness *of* self – and in community, because before others or another. If God is the ultimate other, sacred confession is the most intimate form of being true to self – in the sight of another. Augustine tried to enact this, finding that one cannot enact it completely, for one forgets, though one can witness to it, with purged porosity, with acknowledged forgetfulness, and with love for the other who attends. There is something merciless here and also something more deeply merciful. Practise the truth with love: this applies to our own self-knowledge also. If we hate ourselves, we are not being true. There is an agapeic consent in being true to self. We find ourselves in being affirmed before we find ourselves and affirm ourselves. Truthfulness to self is a kind of fullness after all, itself enfolded by the fuller fullness of the metaxological community of being. In a way, we are always talking about a love that lives in us – a love of truth alive in us. We may easily tell lies, but we hate to be told lies, as Augustine noted long ago. This testifies to that living love we are – and that we frequently betray – though we hate ourselves to be betrayed, and even this our hate reveals the more primordial love.

We are this living love not just in virtue of loving ourselves but in virtue of finding ourselves in being loved. There is *the other side* to being metaxologically true that is not and cannot be just our own truth. I do not see this as just an intersubjective acknowledgment of the truth of others, fellow others. That is part of it, to be sure, but more deeply the notion of the very otherness of the true is here at issue. One might even talk of the *transcendence* of truth. The immanently unconditional meets the hyperbolically unconditional. The intimate universal is what is here at stake. It is at stake in confession and witnessing. And there is nothing self-insistent here: there is a call that does not insist but invites; that makes way in making a way; that hollows out a space for spiritual freedom that will hallow truthfulness.

There is a kind of Augustinian suggestiveness to the paradoxical doubleness here: intimate interiorizing of truthfulness is coupled with emphatic accentuation of the transcendence of truth as other. We recollect truth in inwardness; truth thus recollected in being truthful recedes beyond recollection. We face the perplexing enigma of the true as excessive, both intimately and transcendently. It is always beyond us, we are always the quest of it, yet the quest shows that already we are intimate with it. A *metanoia* is required of us: reverse the reversal of defining the true as only for us. Rather it is for us to own that the true is not for us to own, and as so simply not for us, is it so for us. Otherness and interiority interface in the intimate universal.

In being true to mystery we remain true to our constitution as between-beings. The beast does not know it does not know, the god knows it knows, the human being knows it does not know, and thus knows, though it does not know. This last is a complicated double condition: between empty and full, and both empty and full, and neither empty nor full. It seems like something entirely equivocal, even duplicitous, but the question is whether this duplex being is just duplicitous or rather saturated with an equivocity that it must seek to intermediate. One might say: as dialectic raises univocity to a higher power, so metaxology raises equivocity to a higher power. Even then this may mean that the human being will never absolutely dissolve the equivocity through itself – to do so through itself alone would be to re-iterate the equivocity. The equivocity is not a duplicity to be replaced by univocity, but a mystery whose excess affirmatively constitutes the condition of between-being as such: a mystery whose intermediation yields an understanding that does not cause the mystery to evaporate but rather comes to know the mystery at depths of wonder that will never be dispelled.

NOTES

1 A version of this chapter has been published in my *The Voiding of Being: The Doing and Undoing of Metaphysics in Modernity* (Washington, D.C.: Catholic University of America Press, 2019).

2 *Being and the Between* (Albany: SUNY Press, 1995); *God and the Between* (Oxford: Blackwell-Wiley, 2008); *The Intimate Universal: The Hidden*

Porosity among Religion, Art, Philosophy. and Politics (New York: Columbia University Press, 2016).

3 "Saturated Phenomena and the Hyperboles of Being," in *Philosophies of Christianity: At the Crossroads of Contemporary Problems*, ed. Balázs M. Mezei and Matthew Z. Vale (New York: Springer, 2019), ch. 2.

4 See G.W.F. Hegel, *Science of Logic*, trans. by A.V. Miller (New York: Humanities Press), 63–4. Worth asking is whether one might look at both Continental and Analytic philosophy as two forms of a new Scholasticism; see my "Are We All Scholastics Now? On Analytic, Dialectical and Post-dialectical Thinking," in *Yearbook of the Irish Philosophical Society*, 2010–11, 1–24.

5 See "On Phenomenology of Givenness and First Philosophy," in *In Excess: Studies of Saturated Phenomena*, trans. R. Horner and V. Berraud (New York: Fordham University Press, 2002), ch. 1; see also "Metaphysics and Phenomenology: A Relief for Theology," in *The Visible and the Revealed*, trans. C.M. Gschwandtner et al. (New York: Fordham University Press, 2008), ch. 3. For a different take on metaphysics, in addition to *Being and the Between*, see *The Intimate Strangeness of Being: Metaphysics after Dialectic* (Washington, D.C.: Catholic University of America Press, 2012); see also the essay "The Metaphysics of Modernity," chapter 25 in *Oxford Handbook of Theology and Modern European Thought*, ed. Nicholas Adams, George Pattison, and Graham Ward (Oxford: Oxford University Press, 2013). The original and better title of this essay was "The Voiding of Being: The Doing/Undoing of Metaphysics in Modernity."

6 See my "Wording the Between," in *The William Desmond Reader*, ed. Christopher Simpson (Albany: SUNY Press, 2012), 195–227.

7 See "Introduction," in *Ethics and the Between* (Albany: SUNY Press, 2001); for a brief summary, see "The Potencies of the Ethical," in *An Ethics of/for the Future*, ed. Mary Shanahan (Cambridge: Cambridge Scholars Publishing, 2014), 62–75.

8 This is the language of Bernard Lonergan in his book *Insight* (Toronto: University of Toronto Press, 1992), 570.

9 See *Being and the Between*, 493ff.

10 For fuller elaboration see *Being and the Between*, chapter 12, "Being True."

11 In addition to classical notions of *adequatio*, see also in Analytic philosophy discussions such as those of Hilary Putnam in *Realism with a Human Face* (Cambridge, Mass,: Harvard University Press, 1992) concerning how propositions "hook on" to the world. Or Richard Rorty, say, in *Philosophy and the Mirror of Nature* (Princeton: Princeton University Press, 1981), and generally the questioning of foundationalism as claiming to provide us with univocal certainty the *fundamentum concussum* on which the epistemic warrant of all derivative determinations are to be based.

12 *The Mystery of Being*, 2 vols. (London: Harvill Press, 1951).
13 See *God and the Between*, chs. 11–12.
14 *Das reine Selbsterkennen im absoluten Anderssein*, *Phänomenologie des Geistes*, ed. J. Hoffmeister (Hamburg: Meiner, 1952), 24; *Phenomenology of Spirit*, trans. A.V. Miller (Oxford: Clarendon Press, 1969), 14 (§26).
15 *Das Wahre ist das Ganze*, *Phänomenologie des Geistes*, 21; *Phenomenology of Spirit* 11 (§20): I tend to see Hegel's famous saying as a post-Kantian displacement of the ancient view that the true and the one are convertible. Obviously, in a dialectical holism, the one is no simple univocal unity but an absolute self-mediating whole, short of which there is only conditional truth – unconditional truth is the one whole. Not a simple univocal unity, this whole is marked by a network of internal relations, and our relation to the true is itself always internal too. Outside of this immanent self-coherence nothing is true. Of course, there are limited, finite modes of knowing, but these too are true according to self-coherence, which, however, in the case of the finite, can never be absolute. As Hegel puts it, the finite does not coincide with its concept. Only in the absolute whole is the non-coincidence overcome. While finite wholes are not fully true, yet they are not fully untrue, since the play of the true and untrue evident in their becoming contributes to the dialectical articulation of the ultimate whole.
16 Aristotle said that the least number, properly speaking, is two (*Physics*, 220a27). To count to one you have to count to two. One thinks of Hegel's counting to three in order to be able to count to one truly. If one is univocity, if two is equivocity, if three is dialectic (becoming one again in self-mediating dialectic), then four is metaxology. Since four is beyond the self-mediating one, properly to count to two you have to count to four. Metaxology is not monadic, dyadic, triadic; metaxology is quadratic. One thinks of C.S. Peirce's firstness, secondness, thirdness, but a metaxological sense of secondness would require fourthness beyond dialectical thirdness.

12 Slavoj Žižek's Theory: The Christian Tradition and the Catholic Intellectual

CYRIL O'REGAN

While there are some constants prestige-wise in Continental philosophy, there is also considerable variability when it comes to estimates of value and importance. Few – even those who are suspicious of a philosophical canon – would deny the exemplary status of Kant, Hegel, Nietzsche, Husserl, Heidegger, and maybe Kierkegaard and Marx. It is likely, however, that there would be widely different estimates regarding the merits of Derrida and Foucault, Adorno and Habermas, Lyotard and Ricoeur, and latterly Agamben and Vattimo. Perhaps part of the reason for such variability is that widely different criteria would be adduced, some – but not all – of which would have to do with whether philosophy is taken to be descriptive or explanatory, saving the appearances or critical, apolitical or political, open to art or not, and open to religion or not. This brings one to the question whether an argument could be mounted that Slavoj Žižek might be put in the company of the second group of those Continental thinkers who are marked as possible members of an elite club even if not quite members of a very restricted canon.

Now whether this question is even pertinent depends both on prior interests and on prior estimates of intellectual performance. Should one's prior interests be critical, political, with an interest in culture and religion as well as philosophical legerdemain, then one might be disposed to give Žižek a hearing, even if the hearing did not guarantee a positive outcome. One could imagine, for example, that even *with* a hearing Žižek could be rejected as being too radical or not radical enough in his politics, and/or that his theory of culture could be found either wrong or incoherent, and/or that his critical apparatus might run aground when it comes to an analysis of religion, either because religion is not something he should be working on or because the very idea of working on it and presumably sanitizing and repurposing it is wrongheaded from the beginning. Žižek's public relevance and prodigious output might plausibly count in his favour or not depending on critical evaluations of whether or not there is a discernible theoretical core to an oeuvre best known for its pop culture analyses and interminable provocations of a Soviet-Leninist sort to a comfortably democratic West disinclined to criticize the capitalistic bases of the modern world. The paradox of Žižek is that he provides the reader with just about equal reasons to judge positively or dismiss with prejudice, in the latter case largely on grounds of verbal dissipation, chronic repetition and recycling, and inability to make distinctions between what is really important and what is really banal.

In this chapter, I offer the following response. First, that Žižek's main texts evince a synthesis of a heavily Hegelianized Marxism and Lacanian psychology, and that, moreover, the synthesis is such that it is difficult to decide whether the intellectual core of Žižek's thought is a kind of Lacanianism socially and politically repurposed or whether the intellectual core is provided by a form of Hegelianized Marxism with respect to which Lacanianism is a supplement to protect theory against making totalitarian claims. Although in principle, this labelling issue may be undecidable, for pragmatic purposes I will proceed as if the latter is the case, that is, that the theoretical core is constituted by an unusual – if not necessarily unique – form of Hegelian Marxism. In addition, while in his texts Žižek provides abundant evidence of theoretical sophistication, I draw attention not simply to its synthetic richness but also to the high level of complication involved not only in bringing together three discourses that can be conceived independently of one another, but also discourses that in each case have been submitted to serious emendation. Textually, I will focus on a small number of Žižek's more obviously theoretical texts: *Interrogating the Real*, *Tarrying with the Negative*, *The Indivisible Remainder*, and above all Žižek's self-professed magnum opus, *Less Than Nothing*.[1] Second, although Žižek's turn to religion in general and Christianity in particular is somewhat belated, I wish to highlight its function in his theoretical discourse, which is to challenge the dogmatic atheist, but also to essentially go beyond the conceptuality of the religious believer who does not know what Hegel and Žižek know. I intend to excavate Žižek's Hegelian commitments in his articulation of the essence and development of Christianity and its subsequent/consequent secularization in – or, better, *as* – the modern world. Or put otherwise, I explore Žižek's particular account of the "death of God," which can be put into conversation with other versions, especially those of Heidegger, Altizer, and Vattimo. Textually, I will tend to focus on *The Monstrosity of Christ: Paradox or Dialectic* (2009),[2] but I will not be shy of bringing other texts into a discussion of what I take to be nothing less than the thoroughgoing eclipse of Christianity in and through its total instrumentalization. Third, in the context of the emerging concern as to whether, counter-intuitively, the problem with Žižek's thought is not that it is insufficiently complex, but rather that is *hyper*-complex, I pose the question whether Žižek's profound disrespect not only for the Catholic Church as such, but also for the Catholic intellectual tradition, provides an additional disincentive for a self-ascribed Catholic intellectual to engage Žižek further, by turns to abide his many conceptual zigzags, to follow him into his numerous theoretical as well as cultural-studies cul-de-sacs, and to tolerate the persona who is a fool on the stage of world capitalism, bought but not enslaved, indicated by a merry and knowing wink and the ability to tell a joke, indeed, to string jokes together.

The Idiosyncratic Shape of Žižek's Hegelian Marxism: Theoretical Core

When it comes to Žižek, it is tempting to speak of the "return" of Marxism. If in one sense it is legitimate to speak in this way given that with the dissolution of the former Soviet Union and the dissipation of communist ideology in China and the country's complex ongoing negotiation with modern capitalism, the social-political and the economic bases have been lacking, in another sense, it is not at all clear that Marxist theory and philosophy have gone away. Influential French thinkers like Gilles Deleuze and Alain Badiou have proudly worn their Marxist credentials, even as they have theoretically brought Marxism into unfamiliar territory. And even Derrida has spoken to the "spectral" presence of Marxism in all contemporary discourse,[3] thereby challenging the view that Marxism is dead or at least raising the issue of whether the death of Marxism is not another and very peculiar form of life. In any event, if through Žižek Marxist theory once again enjoys a kind of intellectual currency, then the Slovenian continues a magisterial French line of interpretation. He does so less esoterically than Deleuze, the fundamentals of whose materialist philosophy do not explicitly recall Marx,[4] and, arguably, more exoterically than Badiou, who, if inclined to issue manifestos,[5] also writes books that articulate a complex and revisionist form of Marxism.[6] Žižek's very postmodern-looking prolixity and his penchant for cultural studies, in which at best his Marxist theory is performed rather than stated, tend to conceal the structural features of his Marxism.

Still, we can get to the identifying core of Žižek's form of Marxism by means of two strategies. The first involves determining Žižek's form of Marxism essentially by negation, in particular by comparing and contrasting it with Soviet-style Marxist orthodoxy on the one hand and with the non-doctrinaire Marxism of critical theory on the other. Notwithstanding his frequent apologetics on behalf of Soviet-style Marxism, there is nothing recognizably orthodox about Žižek's form of Marxism. There are a number of crucial features of heterodoxy. (1) Although he embraces the Marxist view of contradiction between forces and relations of production, refusing Fukuyama's view of the end of capitalism,[7] he acknowledges how capitalism has the ability to dampen tensions and thereby help immunize itself from immediate overthrow. (2) His work is characterized by a refusal of the topological model of infrastructure and superstructure, and his vast commentary on culture makes no sense unless he grants culture (both high and low) a relative autonomy. (3) He does not accept in any straightforward way the Scholastic Marxist view of the laws of historical development that are the putative object of Marxism as a science. Throughout his more theoretical work at least, Žižek is anxious to insist on the value of contingency in history. We will see later how and perhaps even why he has a complicated view of the relation between contingency and necessity. (4) In his work one finds little or no positing of utopia as constitutive of his particular version of Marxist discourse, any more than one will find millenarian projection as to when utopia will happen or apocalyptic fantasy concerning its constitution. Here Žižek is in line with revisions of Marxist orthodoxy of the sort enacted by the likes of Ernst Bloch,[8] where utopia can be played only in a heuristic and not a constitutive key – to avail of a distinction made by Kant in his famous theodicy essay.[9] (5) Although once again Žižek is committed to the value of praxis, his form of Marxism does not reduce to it. For him theory is intrinsically valuable. Here there is no need to reproduce the binary of theory and practice, since Žižek is obviously of the opinion that theory is a form of praxis. (6) He rejects the orthodox Marxist construction of the relation between Hegelian and Marxist philosophy/science, that is, a relation that if Marx is dependent upon Hegel for some features of his theoretical apparatus, nonetheless, the relationship is overall one of inversion from theory to praxis and a change in the focus of critique from "heaven" to "earth."

The above is not a complete inventory of Žižek's swerves from the standard model. More could easily be added. I think, however, each of the six swerves highlighted above is important and representative. Nonetheless, with respect to Žižekian swerves from standard Marxism, three qualifying points need to be made. The first makes explicit what is already implicit in my treatment of Žižek's swerves: with regard to each of the six, Žižek has precursors. For example, with respect to the relative autonomy of culture, as my *Doktorvater* Louis Dupré pointed out years ago,[10] we have the Russian example of Plekhanov, who believed that the realist novel might not be the only or best example of the relation of literary production to the world of real history. With regard to this point we might add the Hungarian example of Lukács. And if one is to provide a non-Western European precursor to a more nearly historicist rendition of Marxism, again we have the example of Lukács. This brings me to my second point. Whether out of intellectual conviction or for the perverse enjoyment to be gained defending the indefensible, Žižek defends Stalinist-style communism and makes an argument for the genius of Lenin, who modified Marx's own model of historical development, which insisted that revolution is possible only in and through the contradiction that emerges in late capitalism between the forces of production and the relations of production laid out by Marx. Lenin in fact had a more complex view of revolution, and his theory of the "weakest link" suggested there are plural possibilities of revolution and not just one that centrally involves economic factors and tensions.[11] Of course, Lenin is also a paragon for Žižek of intellectual praxis in advance of the revolution. My third point is, arguably, the most important point of all. Žižek is part of a quite definite French Marxist lineage in which Louis Althusser and Alain Badiou function as more or less constitutive. Both are Marxists who think that Lacanian psychoanalysis can be assimilated to Marxist theory and be reordered toward Marxist praxis.[12] Both are Marxists who break ranks with Marx with regard to the topological model of base and superstructure. Here the main bulk of the credit has to be given to Althusser – in particular, to his notion of "overdetermination," which suggested that transformation does not belong univocally to the economy but to the complex interactions among culture, social institutions, and the economy in which the economy is constitutive only in the last instance. Badiou is the single most crucial Marxist thinker for Žižek. Precisely because Žižek's Marxist Hegelian core is so dependent on him – and that will be treated shortly – we need not tarry with him other than to make the following crucial point. Whereas the work of Althusser is predicated on a "rupture" (*décalage*) between the thought of Marx and that of Hegel,[13] Badiou suggests not only that no such rupture occurs and that such a rupture would be invidious, but also, crucially, that Hegel is at the very least as materialistic as Marx, and that his phenomenological, historical, and especially his logical thought are all required to supplement the historical Marx.

Žižek's dependence on Althusser and Badiou also provides him with a Marxist profile very different from critical theory and much of

French-style Marxism.[14] Althusser and Badiou both affect a disdain for a more humanistic-style Marxism, which they judge to be infected by moralism as well as by reluctance to do the difficult work of revolution that requires violence. Žižek is ideologically in their wake – thus his often inflammatory and always provocative rhetoric. At the same time, on the level of theory, while Žižek overlaps with critical theory on a number of modifications wrought on Scholastic Marxism, in general he seems to be in competition with it and anxious to limit its intellectual authority with regard to a number of important conjugations and judgments: (a) in thinking through the relationship between Marxism and psychoanalysis in a way that involves a shift from Freud to Lacan; (b) in reading culture as a matrix of signs as symptoms, while embracing a more capacious view of culture as both low and high – thus, his reverse move from high to low culture, which is precisely in the opposite direction to Adorno, who tends to think of low culture as the subrevolutionary matrix of kitsch;[15] and (c) related to the latter, in his far greater openness to dialogue and debate with religions and with Christianity in particular.

Importantly, Žižek's negative strategy, which helps us distinguish his brand of Marxism from those of two different kinds of rivals, is complemented by a positive strategy in which he articulates a brand of Hegelian Marxism that also involves crucial emendations of the standard picture of Hegel to complement the emendations of the standard picture of Marx.[16] As already suggested, the Marxist thinker who is crucial for Žižek is Alain Badiou. This is true both in the sense that it is Badiou who is responsible for the conviction that theoretically Marxism is not fully coherent without the supplement of Hegelian theory, and in the sense that the Hegel rendered by Žižek throughout his voluminous writings displays the emendations exhibited in the thought of Badiou. In order to get at this Hegel, who is more theoretically sophisticated than Marx, and largely for this reason taken to be more "materialistic," I plan to avoid jumping from text to text and instead to burrow down into Žižek's magnum opus, *Less Than Nothing*.

As I see it, Žižek's construction of Hegel, which takes issue with the standard picture, consists of at least six significant emendations. I will deal with these emendations in two groups of three. The division is pragmatic rather than substantive. In addition, the relation between the two groups of emendations is complicated and thus should not be considered a *taxis* in the strict sense. The most that might be claimed is that the second group seems to illustrate marginally more dependence from the first group than the first group from the second. Risking the danger of being too cryptic, I want to speak briefly to the three more conspicuous emendations of the standard Hegelian model in *Less Than Nothing* and in the other texts of Žižek mentioned at the beginning, in which the theoretical can be taken to be dominant. (1) Žižek denies that the secret of Hegelian mediation is a closed system characterized by a reductive unity. Hegel's thought, he argues, is genuinely pluralistic (LN, 227). He declares that the true Hegelian totality consists of the Whole plus its symptoms, what he defines as "the excesses that do not fit into a system" (LN, 455). Challenging Derrida's excoriating critique of Hegelianism as upset by a contingency or remainder it fails to control,[17] Žižek insists that the Hegelian totality is not subverted by the remainder, but rather the remainder is created and/or mediated by the Hegelian totality. In general, this is one of the places where the influence of Lacan on both Žižek and Derrida is most conspicuous. Outside of *Less Than Nothing*, Žižek often has recourse to the language of "shit,"[18] which is chosen so as to provoke but which also plays a role in suggesting that read aright, Hegelian dialectic not only does not ignore or sanitize what cannot be reduced to system, but is also precisely the discourse that has the power to make it appear. (2) Žižek denies that the function of *Aufhebung* as the dialectical mechanism in and through which to negate and then negate the negation is to bring about narrative closure that preserves and elevates partial truths. In contrast to the standard model of narrative closure or return, in Hegel return is "purely performative, the movement of return creates what it is returning to" (LN, 460, also 465).[19] Another way of making this point is to say that, according to Žižek, Hegelian dialectic is more nearly epistemic-constructivist than speculative where the latter implies a kind of mirroring of reality, even if this mirroring is to a considerable extent productive.[20] (3) Žižek argues against the standard view that Hegel is committed to and articulates an infinite mode of knowing (LN, 61–3, 68–70). There is nothing absolute about the so-called absolute knowledge (*absolut Wissen*) about which Hegel commentators and major thinkers such as Heidegger and Derrida complain.[21] It denotes merely an epistemic or parallax shift in which defeat is seen as victory. Žižek has no more problem than Hegel himself in elevating the Christian pair of cross/resurrection as the paradigm for all would-be parallax shifts. Although once again with regard to this emendation of the standard model of Hegel Žižek finds himself in the company of Badiou, he is hardly eccentric to the main appropriation of Hegel in French beginning with the Lithuanian Alexandre Kojève, who enacted an interpretation of Hegel that fundamentally temporalized the Hegelian system.[22] Famously, Kojève's emendation, which fundamentally set the stage for French Hegel interpretation for much of the twentieth century, involved two main moves: (a) insisting that the *Phenomenology* (1807) rather than the *Encylopaedia* (1821) or *Science of Logic* (1812) is pivotal for the interpretation of Hegel, and further insisting that the fulcrum of the text is the discussion of the master/slave relation and the resolution of the crisis of recognition in work, which had the happy consequence of closely associating Hegel and Marx; and (b) internalizing Heidegger's critique of Hegel's infidelity to time and making it an essential part of the interpretation of Hegel's *Phenomenology* despite the embarrassment of Hegel's famous discussion of the overcoming of time in concept that concludes Hegel's astonishing text about the peregrination of individual and social consciousness. What is different about Žižek's particular emendation relative to Kojève, who more than occasionally seems to display a bad conscience with respect to both these moves and especially to the second, is that similar to Badiou there is no evidence that Žižek prefers the *Phenomenology* over the more "logical" texts of Hegel, and there is even evidence to suggest that the underscoring of the value of time is not only not prosecuted at the expense of the priority of the Hegelian concept, but is indeed a function of it. Žižek's view that temporality is provided sanction by Hegelian dialectical logic rather than working at cross-purposes is again heavily dependent on Badiou's articulating of a Hegelian logic that also provides the key to Marx's dialectical materialism.

This brings us to the second group of three emendations of the standard picture of Hegel. (4) Žižek rejects the triadic interpretation of Hegelian dialectic (LN, 473; also 305, 313–14). In line with his view of epistemological shift or parallax[23] – that is, looked at otherwise or more deeply – death discloses itself as resurrection, he reads Hegelian dialectic to be dyadic rather than triadic. Once again, this emendation of Hegelian dialectic is a conspicuous feature of Badiou's revisionist interpretation of Hegel. Nonetheless, arguably, this particular emendation is of somewhat less importance than the first three, since there have been any number of commentators and critics of Hegel who have upheld the standard model of Hegelian thought as illustrative of totalitarian closure who have not based their interpretation on the triadic interpretation of dialectic. Some Hegel commentators have argued that the triad functions generally rather than absolutely, since certain dialectical moves cannot be reduced to a formulaic triadic structure. Usually, however, this has involved the claim that sometimes dialectical movement is more rather than less than triadic.[24] (5) Badiou continues to be an influence in Žižek's rejection of the teleological construction of Hegel's view of Absolute Spirit. Žižek wishes to argue against the standard model of cause and effect in history, which, he believes, distorts the thought of both Marx and Hegel. The revolution in Hegelian thought is that it subverts the standard workings of cause and effect: instead of a cause preceding an effect, the cause is a retroactive production of the effect of the so-called cause (LN, 213; see also 205, 207, 227).[25] By far the better way of thinking about the relation between past and future is to deny that the past produces the future and affirm that the future retroactively produces or refigures the past. Now, if it is true that in one sense, Žižek's reflection here is influenced by the functional priority given to the future in the historical Hegel and greatly exacerbated in the thinking on time of both Kierkegaard and Heidegger, it is even more true that for Žižek and Badiou this is inbuilt into Hegelian logic, one of whose axioms is that what comes first comes first precisely because it is presupposed and thus in the final analysis answerable to what it produces. By constituting the presupposition precisely as presupposition, what is produced fundamentally shakes free of it. According to Žižek, this logic of reversal of priority is the logic of dialectical materialism and is regulative for Marx's account of history. (6) In his magisterial *Less Than Nothing*, Žižek scrupulously avoids speaking of history under the rubric of laws of necessity. Instead, patterning himself on Badiou, he elevates contingency. Hegel's articulation of categories is a contingently open process (LN, 227). While Žižek admits that these categories take on the form of necessity (LN, 468), even necessity itself is contingent: "the very process through which necessity arises out of necessity is a contingent process" (LN, 467). Once again, while one could make a case that this emendation is on the same level as the first three, overall it seems a little derivative in that, for the epistemic-constructivist, it depends somewhat on the fundamental option over the speculative option when it comes to interpreting Hegel's dialectic.

With regard to Žižek's Hegelianism or Hegelian-friendly style of Marxism, I have made it plain that while Žižek's forms of both are non-standard, they are not entirely without precedent. Although I have not provided a demonstrative argument, I have suggested with regard to the unusual determinative linking of Hegel and Marx and the associated emendations of Hegelianism required if Hegelianism is either to provide a theoretical basis for Marxist dialectical materialism or provide corrections for its not so materialist abstractions, that Alain Badiou is very much Žižek's precursor. Where there is one, there is two, and thus a referendum on the intellectual value of Žižek's theoretical elaborations is always at once a referendum on Badiou, who provides much of the structural armature. I have also said that Badiou provides a precedent for the linking of Marx and Lacan in general and perhaps the only precedent for linking Lacanian psychoanalysis to a thoroughgoing Hegelian form of Marxism avoided by Deleuze,[26] and judged impossible by Althusser, who thinks that the relation between Hegel and Marx is radically discontinuous. Still, even if Badiou supplies a precedent, what is without analogue in the thought of Žižek is the variety and level of deployment. In Žižek's variegated work, Lacan is to the fore in the Slovenian philosopher's voluminous excavations of the symptoms provided by the discourses of film, music, and literature, but is also a concerted presence in his theory such that at the very least Lacan can be thought to inflect Žižek's Hegelian Marxism in a non-trivial way. Given Žižek's own beginnings as a student of Lacan,[27] we can say, whether we are talking about *Less Than Nothing* or somewhat earlier texts such as *Interrogating the Real* and *Tarrying with the Negative*, that Lacan is a direct influence as well as one mediated in and though Badiou's prior synthesis of Lacan with Hegelian-Marxism. Granted that all six emendations of Hegelian dialectic can be found in Badiou, yet a number are anticipated by the historical Lacan, although the argument concerning the definition of the historical Lacan is an extraordinarily fractious affair. The denial of resolution of dialectic into the All or the All in One is axiomatic in Lacan, even if Žižek depends on Badiou and Althusser to carry the insight over into the philosophical sphere as such. The Not-All is the signifier of a block against triumphant reflexive self-knowledge. Moreover, the Lacanian triad of the Imaginary-Symbolic Order-the Real functions to block Hegelian or Hegelian–Marxist closure. The Symbolic Order is the system of signifiers that no individual or group can master: rather, individuals and groups suffer the symbolic order, which, like any form of signification in Hegel, is alienating – or "wounding," in the metaphor to which Hegel appeals in *Lectures on the Philosophy of Religion*.[28] But Žižek follows Lacan in denouncing as fantasy Hegel's view that "knowledge is the wound that heals itself."[29] The symbolic order is what makes impossible the acquisition of the real that is desired. If against Hegel Derrida has levied essentially the same Lacanian objection, the difference is conspicuous and is more than once drawn attention to by Žižek himself: on Žižek's view, the real is the other to the symbolic order that, nonetheless, is a function of the symbolic order and generated by it. To the degree to which Žižek, after Derrida, trades on the alimentary language that Hegel finds equivalent to the working of concept, excrement is not simply remains, what is left over after the labour of the negative. The production of excrement, of non-conceptual elements, is ingredient in the system itself.

Žižek's Hegelian Genealogy of Religion

Žižek is nowhere more eloquent about his "religious turn," which goes along with other postmodern "religious turns" in previously "atheistic" phenomenology and the equally "atheistic" postmodern semiosis of Derrida, than in *The Monstrosity of Christ*.[30] Equally, he is nowhere as baldly Hegelian in his genealogical sophistications concerning the realization of Christianity in Protestantism and consequent self-liquidation by the negation of any and all transcendence, which is now regarded as incompatible with the world to which we can be truly faithful only if we regard it as the domain of immanence. As I have argued elsewhere,[31] Žižek is all but Scholastic in his reprise of Hegel's narrative of the development of Christianity, even if he tends to lay the historical narrative of Christian history provided in *The Philosophy of History* over the schema Hegel provides of the development of Christian thought in *Lectures on the Philosophy of Religion*.[32] The latter text is obviously foundational in that it proposes a definition of the essence of Christianity as "incarnational," which means in practice a hallowing of the natural and the human. It provides a teleological account of the development of "authentic" Christianity toward its realization in Protestant Christianity. Hegel's teleological scheme represents an interesting emendation of the Protestant narrative itself. The Protestant narrative has it that the Reformation represents a return to apostolic Christianity, with Catholic Christianity functioning as the corrupt interregnum. In contrast, the narrative of *Lectures on the Philosophy of Religion*, articulated in 1821 and repeated in slightly different forms in 1824 and 1827 (anticipated in the *Phenomenology*),[33] constructs Protestantism not only as a correction of Catholicism as a negative form of Christianity – in some sense its obverse – but as the *telos* of Christianity, which requires time to be all that it can be.

As having come to completion in the Reformation, Protestant Christianity is far in excess of original Christianity, which suffered such major handicaps as having its origin in Judaism, being involved in an ancient world that emphasized asceticism, and above all suffering the disadvantage of having Jesus the founder of Christianity all too soon cease to be the messenger and become the message.[34] It is over this revised Protestant narrative that Žižek superimposes the somewhat different narrative of Christianity functioning as a basis of civilization. With regard to this purpose the origins of Christianity do not matter. Instead, Žižek recalls Hegel's discussion of the Byzantine Empire in *Philosophy of History*,[35] which is followed in turn by a discussion of the Catholic Church in the medieval period, and then by Protestant Christianity, which functions as the basis of the modern world. The superimposition achieves a number of things, some less, some more germane to the topic at hand. On the level of the interesting, albeit not necessarily important, is that this superimposition makes it easier for Žižek to launch a critique of current-day forms of Orthodox Christianity, which, as "primitive" rather than "primordial," function only as retardations of the optimal form of Christianity that both he and Hegel advocate. Given his East European connection and his ideological connection with Russia, Orthodox Christianity is relevant to Žižek in a way it is not for Hegel, who, much as with his judgment of Islam, thinks of it as having purely historical interest.[36]

Although Žižek's relation to Orthodox Christianity is not a sideshow in his work as a whole, it certainly is in *The Monstrosity of Christ*, in which the point of contention between Žižek and his interlocutor (John Milbank) concerns the value of Catholic Christianity, which insists on transcendence as definitional to Christianity, recommends the separation of the sacred from the profane, and constructs the Church as a participative reality that does not admit of being absorbed into either the state or the secular ethos. No less than Hegel of the *Lectures on the Philosophy of Religion* or for that matter the *Phenomenology*, Žižek thinks these are indeed features that identify the Catholic form of Christianity. Of course, he is no less open than Hegel in the *Phenomenology* and elsewhere to pointing out the self-interested and all-too-worldly features[37] – Žižek would say "perverse" features – of this particular form of Christianity. Following Hegel, Žižek thinks that those – non-perverse – features that would define Catholicism at its best in fact condemn it. The essence of Christianity is not to be found in otherworldy transcendence that alienates. This is a form of "unhappy consciousness" (*unglückliche Bewusstsein*) in which human beings on the individual and social levels evacuate their freedom and knowledge and compromise their integrity. Feuerbach quite literally thinks that God is the hypostatization of predicates into a distant and remote sovereign subject, a view that Marx later generalizes into the concept of "fetishization."[38] In addition, the screen set up between the sacred and the profane can be viewed as authoritarian power-play that fails to see the real value in the profane. Moreover, it contradicts the "incarnation principle" that both Hegel and Žižek extract from the once-and-once-only incarnation of Christ. And finally, the segregation of the Church from the world leaves the Church unmoored and irrelevant and the world and society untransformed. Hegel and Žižek execute, therefore, a logic of the reversal of sign: because Catholic Christianity is distorted Christianity or Christianity in its mirror image, what might be regarded as positives counting to the benefit of Catholicism are regarded as negatives.

The worst thing about Catholic Christianity, however, is that it has been made doubly obsolete – first by the Reformation and the construction of Protestant Christianity, and second by the emergence of the secular world in and through the full realization of Christianity, which, it turns out, is effectively its own overcoming. I will return to this point shortly when I consider Žižek's articulation of the "death of God." Yet what needs to be said here is that the ultimate strike against Catholicism is that it is "anachronistic." That is, it has been historically surpassed, despite which it continues to persist in existence, resisting both Protestantism as the authentic definition of Christianity and the modern secular world that has Protestantism as its abiding presupposition. Although Catholicism was useful in that it was dialectically necessary in order to generate the adequate form of Christianity that is Protestantism, its continued existence into and beyond modernity is in an almost literal sense "spectral" or "ghastly."[39] Indeed, reminding ourselves of the kinds of images routinely recurred to by Žižek in his role of popular culture commentator, it is not going too far to say that Catholicism provides an example of the "living dead" or zombie-like existence. Now, it is interesting that Žižek fails to note what Hegel himself notes time and again, that is, that Catholic Christianity represents something like a non-identical repetition of Judaism.[40] For Hegel, the repetition involves especially an emphasis on transcendence and alienation, as well as segregation from the world and broader society. But it also involves being a member of the league of "anachronism" that seems to shadow history: the anachronism of Catholicism both echoes and parallels the primal anachronism of Judaism, and this perpetually agitates and irritates Hegel's teleological reading of Christianity and of Christianity's relation to the other religions, as well as his overall view of religion. As anachronistic, Judaism is the prime example of the "living dead" that history cannot get rid of, but rather generates as the reality or non-reality impossible to accommodate within Hegel's archeo-teleological scheme.

Just one further observation on Hegel's and Žižek's construction of Catholicism. Stunningly, Žižek also avails of an interpretive tactic used by Hegel, on the one hand, to disclose the essence of Christianity by finding an exemplary instance of it in history, and, on the other, to subvert Catholic Christianity from within by presenting its heterodox, but in a sense far more veridical, alternative. The discovery of an exemplary instance and the embarrassment of medieval Catholicism go hand in hand. I am speaking here of their joint elevation of Meister Eckhart as bringing to light the truth of the knowing and free subject before the Reformation in principle made it available to all.[41] It should be pointed out that for both Hegel and Žižek, Eckhart the Dominican is anything but an example of a Catholic mystical theologian, who presents an extremely high form of Neoplatonic participatory metaphysics.

Rather, he is inside and outside his time and context, at once a reminder of the truth of Christianity versus Catholic untruth and an anticipatory appearance of the truth of Christianity represented by the Reformation and, through Protestant Christianity, of modernity as such.[42]

As indicated already, for both Žižek and Hegel Protestantism is the fulfilment of the "concept" of Christianity, which it also turns out was always the "concept" of religion as involving the relation of the human and the divine. It hardly requires saying that in neither case does this affirmation involve commitment to the Reformation principles of *sola scriptura* and *sola gratia* or to any specific doctrines such as predestination. In *Lectures on the Philosophy of Religion* and other texts Hegel shows himself to be convinced that the constitutive feature of Protestant Christianity, in addition to emphasizing human autonomy and knowledge, consists in its turn to the world, first, by focusing on Christ as representing the full disclosure of God, and, second, by the full appropriation of Christ in the spiritual community (*Gemeinde*), which, of course, is the concrete instantiation of the Holy Spirit. Now, for Hegel, this pneumatic appropriation of Christ involves an unequivocal valorization of humanity as capable of elevation (*Erhebung*) to the divine. Pneumatic appropriation also essentially implies a subversion of the distinction between the sacred and the profane: the sacred is always already profane, and conversely, the profane is always and already sacred. Žižek's construction of Protestantism repeats Hegel more or less exactly. The ever so slight differences between them concern a shift in vocabulary and what I might call a disambiguating of the status of the Holy Spirit. The shift in vocabulary concerns both the radical otherness that Christ, the divine-human or human-divine, is thought to overcome and how Christ is spoken of in terms of mediation. In the case of the former, instead of Hegel's "beyond" (*Jenseits*) marked by sovereignty and separation from the world, we have Lacan's "big other," where we can assume that an advantage of the locution, according to Žižek, is that it refers to transcendence as a function that can be satisfied in a number of ways that do not involve God as absolute reality, but might be satisfied by social reality or conscience. Instead of Hegel speaking of Christ as mediator, but also insisting that in order for Christ to mediate he necessarily has to cease to be an object of reference and concern, we have Žižek speaking of Christ as the quintessential "vanishing mediator."[43] With regard to disambiguating the status of the Holy Spirit, Žižek quite subtly performs a Feuerbachian anthropological reduction such that it becomes clear that the "Holy Spirit" is in no plausible sense a divine agent, but rather is without remainder the "Christian" community fully coming into its own in terms of emancipation from Christ, who provides the occasion and prompt for the community's avowal of freedom, truth, and unity.

In *The Monstrosity of Christ*, the truth of Protestant Christianity as the actualization of the "concept" of Christianity is the performance of its own liquidation of Christianity and its liquefying into – or better, *as* – the secular. Again, here as elsewhere, Žižek follows the Hegel of the *Lectures on the Philosophy of Religion* in speaking of Protestant Christianity in kenotic terms: Protestant Christianity, which is identified by the community that deconstructs and constructs its own conditions, has as its goal the fulfilment of divine-human immanence that cannot be fulfilled in terms of religion, that is subject to being haunted by the ghost of particularity that segregates the sacred from the profane as well as separates transcendence from immanence. Although neither Hegel nor Žižek quite put it this way, the emptying of Protestant Christianity in secularity or into the political and ethical realms (*Sittlichkeit*) of modernity continues an entire line of operation of emptying that reaches forward from the emptying of the transcendent beyond into Christ and of Christ as potentially fetishized object into Spirit and back to a hypothetical process of modulation of emptying in the Trinitarian divine that is a logical, but not a real subject of discourse.[44] Both Hegel and Žižek, however, trope kenosis. The crucial point is that a notion originally applied to the incarnation and the cross is now applied fairly promiscuously and especially regarding the generation of a modernity that is unthinkable apart from Christianity. This means that however antithetical the Enlightenment may appear to be regarding Christianity, both it and modernity as a whole – which includes but is not defined by the Enlightenment – are dependent upon Christianity in general and Protestant Christianity in particular. Here, clearly, Žižek proves himself far more Hegelian than most of critical theory, and ironically far closer to Benedict XVI on this particular point than to Jürgen Habermas.[45]

It is apposite to say a few words about Žižek's reflection on Saint Paul and how it aligns with his commitment to Hegelian-style Marxism in general and to an account of the generation of the secular from Protestant Christianity in particular.[46] Žižek does not have Nietzsche's problems regarding Saint Paul. Far from constituting a deformation of real Christianity centred around the actions and speech of its founder, Paul can be affirmed more straightforwardly than the figure of Christ, who is always subject to fetishization. The Pauline writings constitute nothing less than an "event," a definitive interruption of discourse with implications for practices and forms of life that demand a suspension of the grammar that maintains things as they are or have been. What is suspended is the particularity of forms of speech, practices, and forms of life and the elevation of universalism. Given the precise way that Žižek speaks of this universalism, it is clear not only that is it not derivative of the would-be universalism of philosophy, but also that it constitutes a different kind of universalism, one with far greater critical and transformative capacity. Indeed, Paul's universalism provides the type of the critical universalism of Hegelian Marxism. The view of Paul promoted by Žižek, which is authorized by connection with Hegelian Marxism and in turn authorized by it, is not especially original. Indeed, he follows with dot and tittle the thinking of Alain Badiou on this matter,[47] even to the point of specifying that the event of Paul lies more in how Paul is received than in the texts of Paul himself. This is in line with the general theory of event enunciated by Badiou:[48] an event is a contingent that has a history of effects. But in contradistinction to the reasoning of someone like Gadamer, though the history of effects is in one sense derivative, it is the history of effects that retroactively valorizes a phenomenon and thus constitutes it as event.

Undoubtedly, Žižek's reading of Paul as a universalist is not the fruit of a deep or exhaustive reading of the Pauline corpus; in fact it amounts to something like a primal intuition. Nor, strictly speaking, does Žižek's reading recall Reformation readings of Paul in terms of theological substance. If there is any continuity at all, it has to do with Paul providing the point of view from which to grasp what Christianity is about, which, of course, is Hegelian-Marxism with a Lacanian twist. But Paul can anticipate because his binary of law and gospel, which can be read formally rather than materially – that is, as a contrast between ethnic particularly and self-serving ideology and as a phenomenon that transcends particularity rather than a relation between two dispensations, with the gospel being very much the gospel of Jesus Christ, the one who saves, the *only* one who saves. As already indicated, Žižek is indebted to Badiou. But there is a much longer twentieth-century history of formalizing Paul's binary and of thinking of gospel solely in the purely negative terms of upsetting the law. Obviously, Giorgio Agamben's *The Time That Remains*, which is roughly contemporaneous with Badiou's reflections on Paul, provides one such example.[49] Perhaps it is worth pointing out that it is no accident that Agamben is a reader of Benjamin and that he appropriates Benjamin's notion of the messianic, which again is viewed negatively rather than positively. Before Agamben there is the work of Jacob Taubes, for whom Paul is both an apocalyptic and a political thinker,[50] that is, a thinker who thinks the rupture of the given and the prospect of an eschatological community whose structure cannot be specified.

Above, we gave an account of Žižek's Hegelian construction of Christianity, his elevation of Protestant Christianity, his negative rendering of Catholicism, and above all his contention that Protestant Christianity as Christianity at its most incarnational or immanent serves as the ground of modernity as the overcoming of transcendence and of the split between the sacred and the profane. Of course, a more concise way of rendering all of this is to put everything under the rubric of "the death of God." As stated already, the Žižekian form of the "death of God" is resolutely Hegelian. In fact, it corresponds exactly to Hegel's discussion of the theme extracted from a Lutheran hymn conducted in *Lectures on the Philosophy of Religion* and the *Phenomenology*.[51] In *The Monstrosity of Christ*, Žižek associates his view with Altizer's similarly Hegelian rendition of the death of God.[52] In *Less Than Nothing*, he essentially sanctifies Catherine Malabou's "plasticity" interpretation of Hegel and thus implicitly sanctions her reading of the "death of God" trope and her underscoring of its importance.[53] Of course, the Hegelian modulation of "the death of God" is not the only form of the "death of God" available. In modern and postmodern philosophy, the Hegelian version shares space with the more dramatic and considerably less sanguine Nietzschean form. And depending on how one adjudicates Heidegger's dependence on Nietzsche, the thought of the later Heidegger either recycles Nietzsche's recognition of the "twilight of the idols" or represents a new philosophical proposal about the eclipse of the disclosure of the holy that is inscribed in disclosure itself.[54] In this respect it is extremely interesting that the "death of God" thinker with whom Žižek associates most is Gianni Vattimo.[55] This is interesting because surprising: most of Vattimo's texts, for example, *After the Death of God* and *The End of Modernity* articulate a more Nietzsche–Heideggerian view of the "death of God,"[56] and in general Vattimo's constructive articulation of a "weak ontology" owes far more to these thinkers than to Hegel.

Arguably, however, *After Christianity* represents an attempt to link up the Hegelian view of the "death of God" with the Nietzschean–Heideggerian view. This can be seen in a number of ways. It is especially evident in chapter 2, in which, on the one hand, the trope of kenosis is central and also intrinsically linked with secularization and, on the other, support is given to Joachim de Fiore's recommendation of the pneumatic surpassing of Christ and institution, which a number of scholars have thought provided the template for Hegel's view of the relation between Spirit and Christ. In fact, even among the more Nietzsche- and Heidegger-heavy chapters, these two reminders of the Hegelian form of the "death of God" are woven in. So there is room for coupling, even if an alternative, more Nietzschean–Heideggerian, reading of the Christian grounding of modernity is in vogue. In any event, Žižek, who often has critical things to say about Nietzsche and harsh things to say about Heidegger, seems to take it for granted in *The Monstrosity of Christ* that Vattimo is sufficiently Hegelian to be regarded as a fellow-in-arms in the account of modernity. Of course, Vattimo, the Catholic, has little or nothing to say about Protestantism, and what little he says does not amount to sanctioning it above all species of Christianity in the way that both Hegel and Žižek do. While Christianity is the grammatical subject of his discourse, the real subject is Catholicism. In contrast with Žižek, then, he is thinking of Joachim's substitution of Spirit for institution as internal to Catholicism itself wherein it can become all that it can be by liquidating its oppressive institutions and repressive doctrines and moral precepts and liquefying itself into the secular. Formally similar to Žižek's theory of secularization, it seems different not only because Vattimo is equally – if not more – dependent on Nietzsche and Heidegger, but also because we are speaking of a single rather than double eclipse. If Catholicism stands proxy for Christianity in Vattimo's reflection, then Catholicism suffers a single rather than double eclipse, a single moment of emptying *into* the secular and *as* the secular. Catholicism only realizes itself in the secular, but it does not need to pass through its eclipse by Protestantism before liquidating itself, which is the same as its liquefying itself in the secular.

Žižek and the Catholic Intellectual

I have argued that Žižek is worthy of our contemporary philosophical and theological attention because he provides a sophisticated version of Hegelian Marxism with a Lacanian twist as well as a religious, indeed, specifically Christian account of the genesis of the modern secular world. The fact that with respect to both contributions Žižek is not original all the way down cannot be held against him. Very few modern thinkers are as genuinely Hegelian as Žižek and as knowledgeable about his major texts whether the register is historical, sociopolitical, phenomenological, or logical; very few Marxists have argued that a valid form of dialectical materialism depends more on Hegel than on Marx himself; very few Hegelians or Marxists have forged such a deep and comprehensive link with Lacan in and through which Lacan becomes at once a political and a religious thinker; and very few exhibit the kind of brave consistency of championing a Hegelian model of the genesis of modernity precisely as secularization in the broader context of genealogical construction in which the secularization hypothesis has become suspect[57] and the most that could be advanced is the highly modified and weaker form illustrated by Charles Taylor in *The Secular Age*.[58]

This is not to say, however, that there are not a number of structural weaknesses that pertain to the Slovenian thinker's theoretical apparatus and his genealogy of modernity, which centrally involves an account of the development of Christianity and its liquification into and as the modern world. The first problem has to do with the very integrity of Žižek's theoretical apparatus. Now, at first blush this does not seem to be a legitimate concern to raise, given my defence of the sophistication of Žižek's Hegelian Marxist theoretical model and my correlative denial of the common view of Žižek's thought as mere cultural commentary with appeals to theory being at best opportunistic, somewhat in the manner of Terry Eagleton, and at worst so much flotsam and jetsam indicative of the out-of-control nature of capitalist production. It should be remembered, however, that theoretical models can suffer integrity issues for quite different reasons. Theoretical models fail to be integral when the relations between the elements that constitute the model are underdeveloped from a conceptual point of view. Equally, however, theoretical models fail to be integral when they are overly complicated. If there is a general problem with Žižek's Hegelian Marxism, it has to do with the hypertrophy of theory rather than its absence. As already indicated, all three major constellations of thought, Hegelian, Marxist, and Lacanian, are subjected to serious emendation with a view to priming them for integration. While this might give testimony to the centrality of integration in Žižek's thought, it could equally – perhaps even more so – illustrate a kind of generation of "the night in which all cows are black," to evoke Hegel's famous put-down of Schelling's *Identität-Philosophie* in the Preface to the *Phenomenology* (# 6). There is an observable tendency in Žižek to think that Marx is always already Hegel, Hegel always already Marx, and Lacan always already both. The lack of differentiation of the always heavily primed elements has disastrous consequences regarding the synthetic power of the model, which repeats the same rather than integrating differences. This should give a Catholic *intellectual* some qualms. Moreover, while Žižek's heavy dependence at the level of theory on the work of Alain Badiou does not speak either positively or negatively to the question of the integrity of Žižek's apparatus, it cannot avoid raising questions concerning originality and whether in the last instance the Catholic *intellectual* who follows Žižek in and through the labyrinth of his mixed discourse might not be better off engaging the intellectually wide-ranging, conceptually rigorous, and discursively economic Badiou.

Žižek's model of secularization also should raise intellectual and more specifically *Catholic* concerns. In this instance the very fact that Žižek's model is so consistently – even univocally – Hegelian could be seen to be a problem. First, it is not clear that a model of secularization of the maximalist kind promoted by Hegel is even plausible, never mind true. It is one thing to say that the modern world, precisely as the modern world, is in some significant way dependent on a Christian prehistory, it is another thing entirely to claim that Christianity in general, and Protestant Christianity in particular, is the sole cause of modernity. Second, Žižek simply never considers whether Christianity has value in itself, or whether Christian self-consciousness has value otherwise than as the vehicle of the *saeculum*. In this respect Žižek and Benedict XVI, both of whom espouse this kind of dependence, are contraries. Benedict would want to say that as cause, Christianity exceeds its secular effects, and that as a whole the secular world both renders and distorts Christianity. Contrariwise, Žižek would want to say that secular modernity is more than the Christianity that produces it, and to the degree to which some version of Christianity can be licensed to exist, it would be precisely the kind of Protestant Christianity authorized by Hegel as a proximate signifier, and obviously rejected by the Catholic and Orthodox versions of Christianity that Protestant Christianity putatively surpasses. Both Benedict XVI and Žižek acknowledge Christianity as the original, but they depend on two very different logics. One could say that the logic in the case of Benedict is Neoplatonic: the distance from origin is tantamount to fall. By contrast, the logic in the case of Žižek is dialectical. One is obliged to say, after the model of Hegel's logic of essence,[59] in the case of Žižek that the result always exceeds origin. The modern world, therefore, is more than the Christianity that gives it birth and that essentially voids itself in the process. Indeed, this is the truth that an origin defined kenotically necessarily means. The process of emptying always pays dividends,[60] or in Žižek as in Hegel *kenosis* is always a form of *plerosis*.[61]

Third, an even more specifically Catholic concern: on Žižek's account what positive role can be accorded Catholicism in general and the Catholic intellectual tradition in particular either historically or in the present? As we have seen, there is nothing in Žižek's thought that would allow him to value Catholicism as institution and as a lived sociopolitical reality. As an institutional reality, Catholicism is totalitarian, and its official doctrines and moral precepts are fundamentally ideological in the pejorative sense. In addition, if Žižek's interpretation of Meister Eckhart is anything to go by, the only intellectual forms of Catholicism that are plausible candidates for validation are forms that explicitly subvert the standard world view of Catholicism and the doctrines and moral precepts that express and support it. For while there is a lively scholarly debate within the academy as to whether Eckhart is in the last instance orthodox or heterodox,[62] Eckhart is affirmed by Žižek precisely because he gives critical leverage against otherworldliness, hierarchy, and mystification, all of which are presumed to be defining characteristics of Catholicism.[63] Yet if Eckhart is deemed to be singular, he is not necessarily single. One finds an openness in Žižek to allow in that other favourite of Hegel-inspired philosophers such as Ernst Bloch and Vattimo to some extent, that is, the twelfth-century apocalypticist Joachim de Fiore. Of course, Žižek is not interested in the Dominican mystic as such, nor does he especially care about such intra-Catholic issues as to whether and how Eckhart's mysticism stretches Catholic doctrines and puts the virtues under pressure. Žižek is preoccupied with what he takes to be Eckhart's subversion of Catholic grammar in ways that anticipate both the Reformation and Hegelian epistemology and ontology.[64] For Žižek, Eckhart is a paradigmatic instance of a strategy of subversion, which necessarily can be replicated. I have already mentioned Joachim, who is deployed by the Hegelian Marxist Ernst Bloch, as an example. Given that the strategy of subversion is more important than particular figures, there is nothing stopping Žižek from adding Eckhart's contemporary, Marguerite Porete, who, influenced by the heresy of the Free Spirit, was burned at the stake in 1310 on the grounds that in her particular brand of mysticism the Trinity was surpassed as the objective correlative and that in ecstasy, prayer and the structure of addressor and addressee was at best penultimate.

There can be no doubt that Žižek's Hegelian framing of Catholicism as an anachronism puts a *Catholic* intellectual in something of a bind. By definition, then, Catholicism is a phenomenon that persists but ought not to. Its existence, therefore, is at best "unseemly" and maybe even "obscene." Žižek's delegitimation of Catholicism as anachronistic is straightforwardly Hegelian. Thus, he inherits Hegel's pattern of fully acknowledging historical realities – Judaism is another example – only then to shine a normative-evaluative light on that reality that compromises its historicality. If history is the actual, then the survival of Catholicism in modernity, as the survival of Judaism and the emergence of Islam,[65] has to be acknowledged without reservation: their reality explodes or defines the norm. *A fortiori* such acknowledgment should proceed from a version of Hegelian Marxism that underscores contingency far more than the historical Hegel. For Žižek the anachronistic character of Catholicism and the Catholic philosophical and theological tradition is not simply a matter of theory – however coherent this theory is, he enacts it. He ignores the bind he puts the Catholic intellectual in, even that kind of Catholic already experienced in intellectual self-abnegation in having abandoned metaphysics and wandering the labyrinth of signifiers, having given up all hope of contact with the transcendental signified. Of course, a Catholic intellectual can still engage Žižek's thought and even joust with it. But it is difficult to imagine that she will fare better than John Milbank, who in so-called debate with Žižek is completely ignored by the Žižekian intellectual machine that keeps on churning.

NOTES

1 Slavoj Žižek, *Less than Nothing: Hegel and the Shadow of Dialectical Materialism* (London: Verso, 2012); *Interrogating the Real*, ed. and trans. Rex Butler and Scott Stephens (New York: Continuum, 2005); *Tarrying with the Negative: Kant, Hegel, and the Critique of Ideology* (Durham: Duke University Press, 1993); *The Indivisible Remainder: On Schelling and Related Matters* (London: Verso, 1996). See also *The Parallax View* (Cambridge, MA: MIT Press, 2006); also *For They Know Not What They Do* (London: Verso, 2009). Lacan shares space with Hegel in all the above texts and is a presence in his own right, given that Žižek's dissertation (1982) was on Lacan. See the following: *Looking Awry: An Introduction to Jacques Lacan through Popular Culture* (Cambridge, MA: MIT Press, 1992); *Enjoy Your Symptoms: Jacques Lacan in Hollywood and Out* (New York: Routledge, 2007); also *The Sublime Object of Ideology* (London: Verso, 2009); foreword in *They Know Not What They Do*, x–cvii.

2 Slavoj Žižek (with John Milbank), *The Monstrosity of Christ: Paradox or Dialectic*, ed. Creston Davis (Cambridge, MA: MIT Press, 2009).

3 See Jacques Derrida, *Specters of Marx, the State of the Debt, the Work of Mourning & the New International*, trans. P. Kamuf (New York: Routledge, 2006).

4 Gilles Deleuze is a philosopher admired not only by Žižek but also by Alain Badiou, whose influence on the Slovenian philosopher is enormous. Deleuze is a philosophical talent with enormous range. He is expert in the history of philosophy and has written outstanding monographs on Nietzsche, Bergson, and Spinoza, while being an original philosopher in his own right who works out a dynamic pluralist ontology. The best example of this work is *Difference and Repetition*, trans. Paul Patton (New York: Columbia University Press, 1995). Deleuze is also expert on literature (Proust, Kafka), on painting (Francis Bacon), and on cinema. His political philosophy, which represents a conjunction of Marxism and Lacanianism, is best represented in *Anti-Oedipus* (1977) and *A Thousand Plateaus* (1987).

5 Alain Badiou, *The Communist Hypothesis*, trans. David Macey and Steve Corcoran (New York: Verso, 2010).

6 See in particular, *Being and Event*, trans. Oliver Feltham (New York: Continuum, 2005); and *Theory of the Subject*, trans. Bruno Bosteels (New York: Continuum, 2009).

7 Francis Fukuyama, *The End of History and the Last Man* (New York: Free Press, 1992).

8 This is exemplified in *Das Prinzip Hoffnung*, 3 vols. (1938–1947), in great detail.

9 For a convenient English translation of Kant's heralded 1791 essay on theodicy, see "On the Miscarriage of All Philosophical Trials in Theodicy," in *Religion within the Boundaries of Mere Reason and Other Writings*, ed. and trans. Allen Wood and George di Giovanni (Cambridge: Cambridge University Press, 1998), 17–30.

10 Louis Dupré, *Marx's Social Critique of Culture* (New Haven: Yale University Press, 1983), 156–63, 269–71. For a more detailed treatment, see Leszek Kołakowski, *Main Currents in Marxism*, trans. P.S. Falla (New York: W.W. Norton, 2005) (originally published OUP, 1978), 620–39.

11 Undoubtedly, here Žižek is indebted to Louis Althusser, the major antagonist of a humanistic reading of Karl Marx. The relevant text is *Ideology and Ideological State Apparatuses* (1971) (French text was published in 1968).

12 For Althusser on Lacan, see *Writings on Psycholanalysis*, ed. Olivier Corpet and François Matheron, trans. Jeffrey Mehlman (New York: Columbia University Press, 1999); and Alain Badiou (with Elizabeth Roudinesco), *Jacques Lacan: Past and Present: A Dialogue* (London: Polity, 2014). This is by no means to suggest in either case that the influence of Lacan is confined to texts dealing explicitly with the semiotic psychoanalyst. For example, in the case of Althusser the influence of Lacan can be seen (a) in his view of ideology as a function of any social system and not simply after the manner of *The German Ideology* (1845) as "false consciousness"; (b) more specifically in the notion of how the subject gets constructed or "interpellated" in and through family and education, both of which belong to the sphere of what Lacan calls the symbolic.

13 In texts such as *For Marx* (1969) (French, 1965) and (with Étienne Balibar) *Reading Capital* (1971) (French, 1968), Althusser argued against the univocal determination of the economy when it comes to revolution. Revolution can also come about in and through non-economic factors and through some combination of economic and non-economic factors. Thus the concept of "overdetermination," which relativizes the absolute primacy of tensions within the economy. In both of these texts, Althusser also argued for a "rupture" (*décalage*) in 1845 between an earlier humanist Marx indebted

to Hegel and a later, more scientific Marx who leaves Hegel behind to establish dialectical materialism. The science of dialectical materialism has its own logic and is not simply an inversion of Hegelian Idealism. Žižek does not accept the thesis of "rupture," and accordingly, for him, while he subscribes to Althusser's view of "overdetermination," he thinks it was discovered by Hegel and that Marx repeats it. See *Less Than Nothing*, 497–9.

14 This would include the humanistic Marxism articulated and promoted by Jean-Paul Sartre in the late 1950s and early 1960s in *Critique de la raison dialectique*.

15 As is well-known, Adorno's commentary and criticism on art is almost relentlessly highbrow, whether one is considering music (Mozart, Beethoven, Wagner, Stravinsky, Schoenberg, Berg) or literature (Goethe, Hölderlin, Baudelaire, Kafka, Beckett *inter alia*). Popular music and pulp fiction, for him, reinforce the status quo. This is not to say that Žižek never takes the high culture route. He does, but less often than he examines popular culture as a more reliable indicator of the fears and hopes of society. See, for example, Žižek's analyses of Wagner's *Parsifal* and Mozart's *The Magic Flute* in *Tarrying with the Negative*, ch. 5.

16 This is not to get to the issue of validity: deviance from the standard picture might not necessarily imply deviance from the historical Marx.

17 See Jacques Derrida, *Glas*, trans. J. Leavey, Jr, and Richard Rand (Lincoln: University of Nebraska Press, 1990). The original French text dates from 1974. For a critical reflection on *Glas*, see Cyril O'Regan, "Hegel, de Sade, and Gnostic Infinities," in *Radical Orthodoxy: Theology, Philosophy, Politics* 1, no. 3 (2013), 382–425.

18 For Žižek's excremental translation of what cannot be contained by concept or language, see *The Indivisible Remainder*, 33; see also *Interrogating the Real*, 49. In the latter text Žižek speaks of "shit" as "gift." For a more developed and more self-consciously anti-sacramental reading of Hegel, see "Hegel and Shitting: The Idea's Constipation," in *Hegel's Infinite: Religion, Politics, and Dialectic*, ed. Slavoj Žižek and Creston Davis (New York: Columbia University Press, 2011), 221–35. For a reading of "waste" that falls outside the process of signification, see Cyril O'Regan, "Hegel, Theodicy, and the Invisibility of Waste," in *The Providence of God*, ed. Francesca Aran Murphy and Philip Ziegler (Edinburgh: T&T Clark, 2009), 75–108.

19 See also *The Indivisible Remainder*, 125.

20 In *Glauben und Wissen* (1802) and the *Differnzschrift* (1802), Hegel decisively broke from the transcendentalism of Kant and Fichte, whose philosophies he characterized as belonging to the order of *Reflexion* and thus fated (a) not to come in contact with the real and (b) to be unable to form a system that requires closure. Both Kant and Fichte illustrate what Hegel later comes to call the "bad infinite" (*die schlechte Unendlichkeit*). The contrast

term to "reflection" is "speculation" (*Spekulation*), which in contrast is in contact with the real with respect to which it plays a role in construction and provides the epistemic means to form a Whole. For a good account of the distinction between "reflection" and "speculation," see Rodolphe Gasché, *The Tain of the Mirror: Derrida and the Philosophy of Reflection* (Cambridge, MA: Harvard University Press, 1986), 35–59.

21 The complaint that Hegel's absolute knowledge as "infinite" and "eternal" is systemic in Heidegger's engagement with Hegel. The status of the complaint is underscored by the prominence it has in *Sein und Zeit* (1927), where essentially it is the closing point of the text and something of an indication of a titanomachia between Heidegger and the great German Idealist. Heidegger continues to make the claim even after the so-called *Kehre* about the parousiac nature of Spirit. See *Hegel's Concept of Experience*, trans. Kenley Dove (New York: Harper & Row, 1970); and *Hegel's Phenomenology of Spirit*, trans. Parvis Mead and Kenneth Maly (Bloomington: Indiana University Press, 1988); see also "The Onto-Theological Nature of Metaphysics," in *Essays in Metaphysics: Identity and Difference*, trans. Kurt Leidecker (New York: Philosophical Library Inc., 1960). For Derrida, in addition to *Glas*, see "From Restricted to General Economy: A Hegelianism without Reserve," in *Writing and Difference*, trans. Alan Bass (Chicago: University of Chicago Press, 1978), 251–77; see also "White Mythology: Metaphor in the Text of Philosophy," in *Margins of Philosophy*, trans. Alan Bass (Chicago: University of Chicago Press, 1982), 207–71, esp. 225–6, 268–71.

22 I am speaking of Alexander Kojève's famous lectures on Hegel's *Phenomenology* in the 1930s, which were attended by a who's who of French intelligentsia. A partial English translation is available. See *Introduction to the Reading of Hegel*, ed. Allan Bloom, trans. James H. Nichols, Jr (Ithaca: Cornell University Press, 1980) (originally Basic Books, 1969).

23 Parallax is a concept frequently deployed by Žižek. It is also the name of one of one Žižek's best-known books. See *The Parallax View* (Cambridge, MA: MIT Press, 2006), esp. 68–122.

24 Gasché makes this point in *The Tain in the Mirror*, 47.

25 See also *Tarrying with the Negative*, 126; *Interrogating the Real*, 129–31; also *They Know Not What They Do*, ch. 5.

26 For a really good account of Deleuze's antipathy to Hegel, whom he judges to be incorrigibly an Idealist, see Henry Somers-Hall, *Hegel, Deleuze, and the Critique of Representation: Dialectics of Negation and Difference* (Albany: SUNY Press, 2012).

27 Žižek's first major text in English, *The Sublime Object of Ideology* (1989), argued for a relation between Hegel and Lacan and their fitness in

exposing ideology. A new edition of this text is available. See *The Sublime Object of Ideology* (London: Verso, 2009).

28 See Hegel, *Lectures on the Philosophy of Religion*, vol. 3: *The Consummate Religion*, ed. Peter C. Hodgson, trans. R.F. Brown, P.C. Hodgson, and J.M. Steward (Berkeley: University of California Press, 1985), 206. See also *Encyclopaedia*, #24 Zu, for a similar saying. In both cases the saying provides a teleological spin to the story of the fall.

29 As is typical of Žižek's use of irony, he will often displace and modify the original. See, for example, the chapter title for an analysis of Wagner in *Tarrying with the Negative*, that is, "The Wound Is Healed Only by the Spear That Smote You."

30 Slavoj Žižek (with John Milbank), *The Monstrosity of Christ: Paradox or Dialectic*, ed. Creston Davis (Cambridge, MA: MIT Press, 2009), 24–109, 254–306.

31 Cyril O'Regan, "A Critique of Žižek's Theological View of Secularity," in *Philosophies of Christianity*, ed. Balazs Mezei (New York: Bloomsbury, 2018).

32 With regard to Hegel's *Lectures on the Philosophy of Religion*, in addition to volume 3, which is on Christianity, one needs to keep in mind the other two volumes of the lectures, volume 1, on the concept of religion, and volume 2, which provides Hegel's account of the emergence of the religions, including Judaism. Interestingly, there is no treatment of Islam. Christianity is the absolute religion with respect to which any religion emerging later can only be a derogation. See also *The Philosophy of History*, trans. J. Sibree (New York: Dover, 1956).

33 This becomes especially so in section 7C of the *Phenomenology*, which goes under the title *Die Offenbare Religion*.

34 Of course, when Hegel makes this argument in his treatment of Christianity in the *Phenomenology*, as is well-known it has been preceded in earlier essays such as "The Positivity of Christianity" and "The Spirit of Christianity and Its Fate," which was published in 1907 by Herman Nohl as *Hegels theologische Jugendschriften*. For a convenient English translation see *Hegel: Early Theological Writings*, trans. T.M. Knox (Philadelphia: University of Pennyslavania Press, 1948).

35 Hegel, *Philosophy of History*, 336–40.

36 Despite the greater relevance Orthodox Christianity has for Žižek, his construction of it as a surpassed form of Christianity essentially repeats Hegel's position while also linking it with this view's subsequent rendition by Adolf von Harnack.

37 Famously in the section on "the unhappy consciousness" in the *Phenomenology*, in addition to speaking of the shift of the Jewish "beyond" (*Jenseits*) from the vertical to the horizontal (past), Hegel characterizes Catholicism not only as systemically "otherworldly" but also as having

a toxic mixture of unworldliness and worldliness. He essentially repeats the accusation in *Lectures on the Philosophy of Religion*, vol. 3, in which Catholicism is cast as inferior to Protestantism not only because of its unworldliness but also because of its confusion of the unworldly and the worldly.

38 The word Žižek uses in *Less than Nothing*, that is,"substantialization," can be regarded as equivalent to what Marx refers to as "fetishization."

39 Žižek co-opts for his own purposes in *Less than Nothing* (464) the concept of "spectrality" that has been given different elaborations in Althusser and Derrida. See Althusser (with François Matheron), *The Specter of Hegel: Early Writings*, trans. G.M. Goshgarian (London: Verso, 1997); and Derrida, *Specters of Marx: The State of the Debt, the Work of Mourning & the New International*, trans. P. Kamuf (New York: Routledge, 2006). Although Žižek's view of the "specter" is identical to neither, because of his commitment to retroactive constitution, it is somewhat closer to Derrida's view, which is more positive than that of Althusser.

40 Just as in his earlier and only posthumously published essays on Christianity, in the *Phenomenology* Hegel takes a negative view of Judaism. He does so in significant part because he thinks that Christian commitment to a mode of transcendence precisely as the transcendent is a Jewish legacy. This can be seen clearly in his implying in his section on "unhappy consciousness" that Christianity moves the beyond from God as such to Christ. By and large, with the exception of the lectures on religion in 1827, Hegel maintains his negative view of Judaism in *Lectures on the Philosophy of Religion*. For an account of Hegel's anti-Judaism and the relevant secondary material, see Cyril O'Regan, "Hegel and Anti-Judaism: Narrative and the Inner Circulation of the Kabbalah," *The Owl of Minerva* 28, no. 2 (1997), 141–82.

41 See *The Monstrosity of Christ*, 33–44, 249–51. Of course, given that the text is a presumed debate between Žižek and Milbank, the latter has a very different interpretation of Eckhart and essentially makes him a gold-star member of the Christian Neoplatonic tradition. See *The Monstrosity of Christ*, 111–17, 183–5.

42 Hegel invokes Meister Eckhart in defence of his speculative treatment of Christianity in *Lectures on the Philosophy of Religion*. In doing so, he at once exempts Eckhart from his castigation of Catholic Christianity and essentially casts him as throwing light on the Reformation discovery of intimacy with and certain knowledge of God. For a treatment of this point, see Cyril O'Regan, "Hegelian Philosophy of Religion and Eckhartian Mysticism," in David Kolb, ed., *New Perspectives in Hegel's Philosophy of Religion* (Albany: SUNY Press, 1992), 109–29.

43 Throughout his diverse work, Žižek speaks to numerous "vanishing mediators," but Christ is the archetypal vanishing mediator, the pure vehicle whose *raison d'être* is to disappear so that meaning, in this case the meaning of the incarnation, becomes transparent.

44 This has to do with Hegel's articulation of the speculative proposition in the *Phenomenology* (#63). As Hegel reasons in the proposition "God is Love," while "God" is the grammatical subject, the real subject is the predicate "Love." In the *Essence of Christianity*, Ludwig Feuerbach takes full advantage of this. The speculative proposition has been the subject of much discussion in the secondary literature on Hegel, particularly in France. Jean Hyppolite and Jean-Luc Nancy are just two of the more important commentators.

45 Benedict XVI argues for the Christian foundation of Europe. Without absolutely denying that Christianity gave birth to secular Europe, Žižek suggests it sacrificed itself to give birth to a more important reality. If, for Benedict, the secular world is less than its Christian origins, Žižek suggests that Christianity is less than the secular world it produces.

46 For Žižek's reflections on Paul, see "Thinking Backwards: Predestination and Apocalypse," in *Paul's New Moment*, ed. John Milbank, Slavoj Žižek, Creston Davis, and Catherine Pickstock (Grand Rapids: Brazos Press, 2010), 185–210; see also "The Necessity of a Dead Bird," in *Paul and the Philosophers*, ed. Ward Blanton and Hent de Vries (New York: Fordham University Press, 2013), 175–85.

47 Badiou, *Saint Paul: The Foundations of Universalism*, trans. Ray Brassier (Stanford: Stanford University Press, 2003). See also Paul de Boer, "Paul and Materialist Grace: Slavoj Žižek's Reformation," in *Paul and the Philosophers*, 186–209, for an excellent account of Žižek's dependence on Badiou for his articulation of the importance of Paul.

48 For Badiou an "event" is a happening that cannot be anticipated and thus cannot be inserted into a teleological scheme. Whereas usually such a construct is put in opposition to Hegelian dialectic, which supposedly is its teleological opposite, Badiou thinks not only that event and Hegelian dialectic properly understood are compatible, but also that event is best understood within Hegel's dialectical frame.

49 See Giorgio Agamben, *The Time That Remains: A Commentary on the Letter to Romans*, trans. Patricia Dailey (Stanford: Stanford University Press, 2005).

50 Jacob Taubes, *Occidental Eschatology*, trans. David Ratmoko (Stanford: Stanford University Press, 2009).

51 The "death of God" is central to Hegel's take on Christianity, since for him, as for Luther, incarnation is realized in the Cross. Hegel is quite self-conscious concerning the Lutheran backdrop of his catchy formula.

52 For the invocation of Thomas Altizer, see *The Monstrosity of Christ*, 260.

53 If there is a Hegel interpreter who is first among equals, it is Catherine Malabou, and especially her *L'Avenir de Hegel: Plasticité, temporalitá, dialectique* (Paris: Vrin, 1996). This has been translated as *The Future of Hegel: Placticity, Temporality, Dialectic*, trans. Lizbeth During (New York: Routledge, 2004). Žižek underscores her importance to his interpretation at the outset of *Less than Nothing* and depends on her for his view of the dynamic flexibility of Hegelian thought and more specifically for his articulation of the death of God. See *Less Than Nothing*, 232–3; see also *The Monstrosity of Christ*, 256–61.

54 Martin Heidegger, *Nietzsche*, vol. 4: *Nihilism*, trans. Frank A. Capuzzi, ed. David Farrell Krell (San Francisco: Harper, 1982).

55 For the relation between Žižek and Gianni Vattimo, see *The Monstrosity of Christ*, 256–9. The two texts that are most important for Žižek are *After Christianity*, trans. Luca D'Isanto (New York: Columbia University Press, 2002); and (with John D. Caputo) *After the Death of God*, ed. Jeffrey W. Robbin (New York: Columbia University Press, 2007).

56 Gianni Vattimo, *The End of Modernity: Nihilism and Hermeneutics in Post-Modern Culture*, trans. John R. Synder (New York: Polity Press, 1991).

57 Hans Blumenberg, *The Legitimacy of the Modern Age*, trans. Robert M. Wallace (Cambridge, MA: MIT Press, 1985).

58 Charles Taylor, *A Secular Age* (Cambridge, MA: Harvard University Press, 2007).

59 See *Tarrying with the Negative*, ch. 4.

60 This is Bataille's standard objection to the labour of Hegelian knowledge, to which he opposes his "non-knowledge." As already pointed out, this particular anti-Hegelian stance was taken over by Derrida in "From Restricted to General Economy: A Hegelianism without Reserve."

61 This was a constantly repeated point in my *The Heterodox Hegel* (Albany: SUNY Press, 1994).

62 The debate about Eckhart's heterodoxy and orthodoxy is current, with the yeas and nays just about equal.

63 This by way of contrast with John Milbank, who in his debate with Žižek in *The Monstrosity of Christ*, 183–5, 192–5, affirms Eckhart precisely because he is an exemplar of Neoplatonic metaphysics of participation and hierarchy.

64 To the extent that Žižek valorizes Eckhart's connection to Reformation and modernity, he replicates Hegel's deployment of the medieval German mystic.

65 Hegel creates no space in his account of the religions either in the *Phenomenology* or *Lectures on the Philosophy of Religion* for the emergence of religions after the emergence of Christianity. In terms of epistemic, metaphysical, and ethical value, Christianity does not tolerate a rival.

Grossly speaking, one can see that Islam is regarded by Hegel less as a replacement for Christianity than as the return of Judaism. Žižek's understanding of Islam is very much in continuity with what one finds in Hegel. See his "A Glance Into the Archive of Islam," in Slavoj Žižek and Boris Gunjević, *God in Pain: Inversions of the Apocalypse*, trans. Ellen Elias-Bursac (New York: Seven Stories Press, 2012), 103–26.

About the Authors

Bruce Ellis Benson is a reader in the Logos Institute at the University of St Andrews, where he is funded by the Templeton Religion Trust. He has taught and engaged in research at Loyola Marymount University, Wheaton College (IL), the Katholieke Universiteit Leuven, and Union Theological Seminary (NYC). He is the author or editor of thirteen books, including *Graven Ideologies: Nietzsche, Derrida and Marion on Modern Idolatry* (IVP, 2002); *The Improvisation of Musical Dialogue: A Phenomenology of Music* (Cambridge, 2003); the award-winning *Pious Nietzsche: Decadence and Dionysian Faith* (Indiana, 2007); *Liturgy as a Way of Life: Embodying the Arts in Christian Worship* (Baker Academic, 2013); and (with J. Aaron Simmons) *The New Phenomenology: A Philosophical Introduction* (Bloomsbury, 2013). He has published more than 100 book chapters, articles, and reviews. He serves as the executive director of the Society for Continental Philosophy and Theology and as philosophy of religion editor for *Syndicate*.

Jeffrey Bloechl is an associate professor of philosophy and director of the Joint MA program in philosophy and theology at Boston College, as well as honorary professor of philosophy at the Australian Catholic University. He is past founding editor of *Levinas Studies: An Annual Review* (2005–16) and founding co-editor of *Thresholds in Philosophy and Theology* (Notre Dame). His teaching and scholarship concentrate in contemporary European philosophy (phenomenology and psychoanalysis), philosophy of religion, and Christianity and philosophy. Recent publications include phenomenological studies of themes in the writings of St Paul, Francis of Assisi, and John of the Cross.

Patrick H. Byrne is a professor of philosophy and director of the Lonergan Institute at Boston College. His teaching and research interests include the relationships between science, evolution, and religion; ethics; the thought of Bernard Lonergan, Albert Einstein, and Aristotle; and the philosophy of service learning. His book publications include *The Ethics of Discernment: Lonergan's Foundations for Ethics* (Toronto, 2016) and *Analysis and Science in Aristotle* (SUNY, 1997). He was also co-editor of *Macroeconomic Dynamics: An Essay in Circulation Analysis* (Toronto, 1999; *Collected Works of Bernard Lonergan*, vol. 15). His recent publications include "The Integral Visions of Teilhard and Lonergan: Science, the Universe, Humanity, and God," in *From Teilhard to Omega: Co-creating an Unfinished Universe* (2014); "Neurociencia, consciencia, libertad y Lonergan (Neuroscience, Consciousness, Freedom and Lonergan)," *Revista de Filosofía* (2013); and "Lonergan's Philosophy of the Natural Sciences and Christian Faith in *Insight*," in *Going beyond Essentialism: Bernard J.F. Lonergan, an Atypical Neo-Scholastic* (Italian Institute for the Study of Philosophy, 2012).

John D. Caputo is the David R. Cook Professor of Philosophy Emeritus at Villanova University (1968–2004) and the Thomas J. Watson Professor of Religion at Syracuse University (retired in 2011). He is the author of some twenty books in hermeneutics, phenomenology, deconstruction, and radical theology, including most recently *The Insistence of God: A Theology of Perhaps* (Indiana, 2013); *Truth* [Philosophy in Transit] (Penguin, 2014); *Hoping against Hope: Confessions of a Postmodern Pilgrim* (Fortress Press, 2015); *The Folly of God: A Theology of the Unconditional* (Polebridge Press, 2015); *Hermeneutics: Facts and Interpretation in the Age of Information* (Penguin/Pelican, 2018); and *Cross and Cosmos: A Theology of Difficult Glory* (Indiana, 2019). He is a past president of the American Catholic Philosophical Association and past executive co-director of SPEP.

Anne M. Carpenter is an associate professor in the Department of Theology and Religious Studies at Saint Mary's College of California. She has published on theological aesthetics, monasticism, and Thomist metaphysics, and has published the monograph *Theo-Poetics: Hans Urs von Balthasar and the Risk of Art and Being*. Her recent work has focused on Maurice Blondel, Charles Péguy, and decolonial theory.

Daniel O. Dahlstrom, John R. Silber Professor of Philosophy at Boston University, is the author of several books, collections, and articles primarily on prominent themes and figures in German philosophy. He is also the translator of works by Mendelssohn, Schiller, Hegel, Feuerbach, Husserl, and Heidegger. His latest collected edition is *Kant and His Contemporaries* II (Cambridge, 2018).

William Desmond is the David Cook Chair in Philosophy at Villanova University; the Thomas A.F. Kelly Visiting Professor of Philosophy at Maynooth University, Ireland; and a professor of philosophy emeritus at the Institute of Philosophy, Katholieke Universiteit Leuven. His work is primarily in metaphysics, ethics, aesthetics, and the philosophy of religion. He has edited five books and published more than 100 articles and book chapters. He is also the author of many books, including the trilogy *Being and the Between* (Leabhar Breac, 1995); *Ethics and the Between* (SUNY, 2001); and *God and the Between* (Blackwell, 2008). *Being and the Between* was winner of both the prestigious Prix Cardinal Mercier and the J.N. Findlay Award for best book in metaphysics. In 2016, he authored *The Intimate Universal: The Hidden Porosity among Religion, Art, Philosophy, and Politics* (Columbia, 2016), which was also awarded the J.N. Findlay Prize for the Best Book in Metaphysics 2019. His most recent publications are *The Gift of Beauty and the Passion of Being: On the Threshold between the Aesthetic and the Religious* (Wipf and Stock, 2018) and *The Voiding of Being: The Doing and Undoing of Metaphysics in Modernity* (Catholic University of America Press, 2019). He has held numerous visiting chairs and is past president of the Hegel Society of America, the Metaphysical Society of America, and the American Catholic Philosophical Association.

Gregory P. Floyd is an assistant professor in the Department of the Core at Seton Hall University, director of the Lonergan Institute (SHU), and associate editor of the *Lonergan Review*. His teaching and scholarship focus on nineteenth- and twentieth-century European philosophy (phenomenology and hermeneutics) and the philosophy of religion. His recent publications include "Proclamation of the Words: Heidegger's Retrieval of the Pauline Language of Factical Life" (AD FONTES, 2018); and "Bursting the Bounds of Reason? Topologies of Immanence and Transcendence" (*Diakrisis Journal for Philosophy and Theology*, 2018).

Jean Grondin is a professor of philosophy at the Université de Montréal. Author of influential books in the fields of hermeneutics and metaphysics, he was a pupil and close collaborator of Hans-Georg Gadamer. His books include *Introduction to Philosophical Hermeneutics* (Yale, 1994);

Hans-Georg Gadamer: A Biography (Yale, 2003); *Introduction to Metaphysics* (Columbia, 2004); *La philosophie de la religion* (PUF, 2009); *Paul Ricoeur* (PUF, 2013); *Du sens des choses. L'idée de la métaphysique* (PUF, 2013); and *La beauté de la métaphysique* (Cerf, 2019). His work has earned him prestigious honours, among them the Killam, Molson, and Konrad-Adenauer Prizes. He is currently the president of the Academy of Arts and Humanities of Canada.

Christina M. Gschwandtner is a professor of philosophy at Fordham University. She is author of *Reading Jean-Luc Marion: Exceeding Metaphysics* (Indiana, 2007); *Postmodern Apologetics? Arguments about God in Contemporary Philosophy* (Fordham, 2012); *Degrees of Givenness: On Saturation in Jean-Luc Marion* (Indiana, 2014); *Marion and Theology* (T&T Clark, 2016); and *Welcoming Finitude: A Phenomenology of Orthodox Liturgy* (Fordham, 2019), besides many articles at the intersection of phenomenology and religion.

Cyril O'Regan is Catherine F. Huisking Professor of Theology at the University of Notre Dame, where he has been teaching since 1999. His work spans systematic theology, historical theology, and Continental philosophy, and he has published in topics ranging from nineteenth-century theology and philosophy, postmodern thought, mysticism, apocalyptic thinking, Gnosticism, religion, and literature, to major Catholic figures such as Newman, de Lubac, Hans Urs von Balthasar, and Benedict XVI, as well as on the doctrines of the Trinity and "last things." His publications include *The Heterodox Hegel* (SUNY, 1994); *Gnostic Return in Modernity* (SUNY 2001); *Gnostic Apocalypse: Jacob Boehme's Haunted Narrative* (SUNY, 2002); and *Anatomy of Misremembering: Von Balthasar's Response to Philosophical Modernity*, vol. 1: *Hegel* (Crossroad, 2014) and vol. 2: *Heidegger* (forthcoming).

Andrew Prevot is an associate professor of Theology at Boston College. His research spans the areas of spiritual and mystical theology; philosophical theology and Continental philosophy of religion; and various forms of political, liberation, black, and womanist theology. He is the author of two monographs, *Theology and Race: Black and Womanist Traditions in the United States* (Brill, 2018) and *Thinking Prayer: Theology and Spirituality amid the Crises of Modernity* (Notre Dame, 2015), and co-editor of a collection of essays, *Anti-Blackness and Christian Ethics* (Orbis, 2017). His articles include "Dialectic and Analogy in Balthasar's 'The Metaphysics of the Saints'" (*Pro Ecclesia: A Jour-*

nal of Catholic and Evangelical Theology, 2017); "Negative Dialectics and Doxological Hope: Elements of a Critical Catholic Theology" (*Beyond Dogmatism and Innocence: Hermeneutics, Critique, and Catholic Theology*, 2017); and "The Gift of Prayer: Toward a Theological Reading of Jean-Luc Marion" (*Horizons*, 2014).

Stephanie Rumpza is a visiting researcher in philosophy at the Sorbonne. Her current work explores the concept of mediation in the philosophy of language, aesthetics, and religion.

Index

www.ingramcontent.com/pod-product-compliance
Lightning Source LLC
Jackson TN
JSHW080758110325
80339JS00011B/54/J